JESUS

AND THE SUFFERING SERVANT

JESUS

AND THE SUFFERING SERVANT

Isaiah 53 and Christian Origins

◆

EDITED BY
WILLIAM H. BELLINGER, JR.
AND WILLIAM R. FARMER

TRINITY PRESS INTERNATIONAL
Harrisburg, Pennsylvania

Trinity Press International, P.O. Box 1321, Harrisburg, PA 17105
Trinity Press International is a division of the Morehouse Group

Cover art: SuperStock, *Christ the Man of Sorrows,* by Felipe Ramirez

Library of Congress Cataloging-in-Publication Data
Jesus and the suffering servant : Isaiah 53 and Christian origins /
    edited by William H. Bellinger and William R. Farmer.
        p. cm.
    A collection of essays presented at the Conference on Isaiah 53
and Christian Origins held at Baylor University in February 1996.
    ISBN 1-56338-230-X
    1. Bible. O.T. Isaiah LIII – Criticism, interpretation, etc. –
Congresses. 2. Servant of Jehovah – Congresses. 3. Jesus Christ –
Servanthood. I. Bellinger, W. H. II. Farmer, William Reuben.
III. Conference on Isaiah 53 and Christian Origins (1996 : Baylor
University)
BS1520.J47 1998
224'.1064 – DC21   97-49923

Printed in the United States of America

98   99   00   01   02   10   9   8   7   6   5   4   3   2   1

Contents

————◆————

v

Abbreviations

——————◆——————

ANRW   W. Haase and H. Temporini, eds., *Aufstieg und Niedergang der römischen Welt* (Berlin/New York: de Gruyter, 1972–)

ANTJ   Arbeiten zum Neuen Testament und Judentum

ArB   The Aramaic Bible

ATD   Das Alte Testament Deutsch

AThANT   Abhandlungen zur Theologie des Alten und Neuen Testaments

BAGD   W. Bauer, W. F. Arndt, F. W. Gingrich, and F. W. Danker, *Greek-English Lexicon of the New Testament* (Chicago: University of Chicago Press, 1979)

BDB   F. Brown, S. R. Driver, and C. A. Briggs, *Hebrew and English Lexicon of the Old Testament* (Peabody, Mass.: Hendrickson, 1979)

BDS   BIBAL Dissertation Series

BEvT   Beiträge zur evangelischen Theologie

BHS   *Biblia hebraica stuttgartensia*

Bib   *Biblica*

BibRes *Biblical Research*

BibS   Biblische Studien

BJRL   *Bulletin of the John Rylands University Library of Manchester*

BN   *Biblische Notizen*

BNTC   Black's New Testament Commentaries

BU   Biblische Untersuchungen

BWANT   Beiträge zur Wissenschaft vom Alten und Neuen Testament

BZ   *Biblische Zeitschrift*

BZAW   Beihefte zur *Zeitschrift für die alttestamentliche Wissenschaft*

CBQ   *Catholic Biblical Quarterly*

CGTC   Cambridge Greek Testament Commentaries

ConBOT	Coniectanea biblica, Old Testament Series
DSB	Daily Study Bible
ErFor	Erträge der Forschung
EtB	Études bibliques
ETL	*Ephemerides theologicae lovanienses*
FAT	Forschungen zum Alten Testament
FB	Forschung zur Bibel
FRLANT	Forschungen zur Religion und Literatur des Alten und Neuen Testaments
HAT	Handbuch zum Alten Testament
HDR	Harvard Dissertations on Religion
HUCM	Monographs of the Hebrew Union College
Int	*Interpretation*
IOSOT	International Organization for the Study of the Old Testament
JBL	*Journal of Biblical Literature*
JBTh	Jahrbuch für biblische Theologie
JJS	*Journal of Jewish Studies*
JSNTSup	Journal for the Study of the New Testament Supplement Series
JSOT	*Journal for the Study of the Old Testament*
JSOTSup	Journal for the Study of the Old Testament Supplement Series
JTS	*Journal of Theological Studies*
LUÅ	Lunds universitets årsskrift
MM	J. H. Moulton and G. Milligan, *The Vocabulary of the Greek Testament*
NICNT	New International Commentary on the New Testament
NTS	*New Testament Studies*
OTL	Old Testament Library
QD	Quaestiones disputatae
RB	*Revue biblique*
SBLSP	SBL Seminar Papers
SBS	Stuttgarter Bibelstudien
SBT	Studies in Biblical Theology

SJT	*Scottish Journal of Theology*
SNTSMS	Society for New Testament Studies Monograph Series
SNTU	Studien zum Neuen Testament und seiner Umwelt
SUNT	Studien zur Umwelt des Neuen Testaments
SVTP	Studia in Veteris Testamenti Pseudepigrapha
TBü	Theologische Bücherei
TDNT	G. Kittel and G. Friedrich, eds., *Theological Dictionary of the New Testament*
TDOT	G. J. Botterweck and H. Ringgren, eds., *Theological Dictionary of the Old Testament* (Grand Rapids: Eerdmans, 1974–)
THAT	E. Jenni and C. Westermann, eds., *Theologisches Handwörterbuch zum Alten Testament* (Munich: Kaiser Verlag, 1971–79)
TLZ	*Theologische Literaturzeitung*
TR	*Theologische Rundschau*
TRE	G. Krause and G. Müller, eds., *Theologisches Realenzyklopädie* (Berlin: de Gruyter, 1977–)
TWAT	G. J. Botterweck and H. Ringgren, eds., *Theologisches Wörterbuch zum Alten Testament*
TWNT	G. Kittel and G. Friedrich, eds., *Theologisches Wörterbuch zum Neuen Testament*
TynBul	*Tyndale Bulletin*
USQR	*Union Seminary Quarterly Review*
VT	*Vetus Testamentum*
VTSup	Vetus Testamentum Supplements
WA	M. Luther, *Kritische Gesamtausgabe* (= "Weimar" edition)
WBC	Word Biblical Commentary
WMANT	Wissenschaftliche Monographien zum Alten und Neuen Testament
WUNT	Wissenschaftliche Untersuchungen zum Neuen Testament
ZAW	*Zeitschrift für die alttestamentliche Wissenschaft*
ZNW	*Zeitschrift für die neutestamentliche Wissenschaft*
ZTK	*Zeitschrift für Theologie und Kirche*

Introduction

W. H. BELLINGER, JR., AND WILLIAM R. FARMER

What is the genesis of this book? What gave rise to its origin? This collection of essays was written in response to a historical question which has profound theological consequences for Christian faith. "Christians" go by different names. Some call themselves "Baptists" while others go by the name of "Roman Catholic" or "Orthodox." But all are united by their common acceptance of a canon of "scriptures" which includes all of the Christian writings known as the New Testament. The authors of these New Testament books in turn cite and allude to earlier scriptures of Israel. Jesus referred to these scriptures as "Moses and the prophets." Among the books of the prophets there was above all the book of the prophet Isaiah.

The historical question which has given rise to the essays in this book may be phrased this way: "Did the influence of Isaiah 52:13–53:12 upon Christian faith begin with Jesus?" We can phrase the question even more precisely: "Did Jesus interpret God's will for Israel, and therefore for himself and for his disciples, in terms of the suffering Servant of Isaiah 52:13–53:12?"

Before proceeding, the reader has a right to know what is at stake in how this question is answered. What is at stake is how members of the body of Christ understand the essence of their faith. The essence of Christian faith (without which Christianity is indistinguishable from the faith of those who worship the God of Abraham, Isaac, and Jacob yet do not know themselves to be Christians) is a ready assent to the affirmation that "Christ died for our sins" (Gal. 1:14). In the words of the Apostle Paul: "The life I now live in the flesh I live by faith in the Son of God, who loved me and gave himself for me" (Gal. 2:20b). This is to say that central and essential to a distinctively Christian faith is the belief that a particular person, namely, Jesus, died on behalf of others, including the belief that Jesus *freely accepted his death* out of love for others. We cite again the words of Paul: "I live by faith in the Son of God, *who loved me and gave himself for me*" (Gal. 2:20b).

It is natural for a mother to sacrifice her life for her children; a lioness will do this for her cubs. But what Christians claim Jesus did is clearly distinguishable from instinctive or biological self-sacrifice. The Apostle Paul put the point this way: "God showed his love for us in that while we were yet sinners [i.e., God's enemies] Christ died for us" (Rom. 5:8). So Jesus' love for us is in accord with his teaching on love of enemy (Matt. 5:43–48). We should be like God who loves his enemies and love our enemies. Jesus in dying for sinners is showing God's love for us even as we, enmeshed in selfishness and injustice, remain God's enemies. It simply is not natural for one to die for an unjust person. This goes against the grain of human instinct.

This raises the question whether it would have been possible for Jesus to have acted so unnaturally as to have died for the unjust without reference to Isaiah's teaching about the righteous Servant of the Lord, who poured out his soul to death and bore the sins of many (Isa. 53:11–12). The honest answer to this question, however difficult it may be for some Christians to grant the point, is "yes." At least it is possible in the sense that one can hardly assert the contrary — that it is *impossible*. On what grounds could one claim that it would be impossible for Jesus to do this? Such a denial would be going too far. It would presuppose knowledge about Jesus that is not available to us. We do not know all of the influences that may or may not have played upon him in his psychological development or his spiritual formation.

Therefore, in humility, granting the limits of our knowledge about Jesus' education and spiritual formation, New Testament historians should agree, for the sake of discussion, that so far as we know, we have to allow for the possibility that if Jesus Christ died for our sins, he may have done so without the teachings of Isaiah 52:13–53:12, or more precisely, without the teaching in that text, even if he knew it, having had any influence upon his psychological development, spiritual formation, or sense of mission.

But, since historians are concerned not only with what may be *possible*, but also, and in particular in cases like this, what is *probable*, can the historian say that it is *probable* that Jesus of Nazareth lived and died without the teaching embodied in this text having exerted any significant influence upon his ministry? More specifically, can it be said by the historian that it is probable that this text exerted no significant influence upon Jesus' understanding of the plan of God to save the nations laid out for the faithful by the prophet Isaiah? And can the historian say this about the purpose of his life and (in particular) his death in relationship to that plan? These are the kinds of historical questions which were in the minds of those who organized the conference on "Isaiah 53 and Christian Origins" held at Baylor University in February 1996.

On the surface it would appear that since Jesus was a Jew he would certainly have known about the book of the prophet Isaiah. And if he was a Jew who knew the scriptures of his people well, as evidence in the Gospels indicates he did, then it is reasonable to conclude that he probably was aware of the teaching of the prophet in Isaiah 52:13–53:12.

But even though it would be reasonable to conclude that Jesus had knowledge of this text, is there any evidence to indicate that this text was of special importance to him or significantly influenced his ministry?

It was Prof. E. E. Ellis, a member of the planning committee for the conference, "Isaiah 53 and Christian Origins," who nicely formulated the question which the committee put to both Profs. Morna Hooker and Otto Betz: "Did the use of Isaiah 53 to interpret his mission begin with Jesus?"

Professor Hooker actually adopted this formulation as the title of her article. She sums up her response in the opening paragraph: "To the question posed in the title of this lecture, I have to reply that I can find no convincing evidence to suggest that Isaiah 53 played any significant role in Jesus' own understanding of his ministry." Then in the closing paragraph she writes in a similar vein: "To the question that has been put to me, 'Did the use of Isaiah 53 to interpret his mission begin with Jesus?' I remain convinced that the answer is 'No.'" Then she adds: "To the question 'Where, then, *did* it begin?' I am far more ready than I was forty years ago to suggest that it may well have been with Paul." Forty years earlier Professor Hooker had concluded that such use of Isaiah 53 does not appear before the composition of First Peter, a generation after Paul.

The reader will do well to read carefully what Professor Hooker has now written about Romans 4:25 where she concludes: "In Romans 4:25, then, we have not only distinct echoes of the *language* of Isaiah 53:11f., but similarities in thought; this passage clearly meets the criteria I suggested should be applied to possible echoes of Old Testament texts." Professor Hooker is intrigued by the questions that arise for her out of her discovery that it may have been Paul himself who "first exploited the idea of atoning suffering" in Isaiah 53. She added that she was "particularly glad that this colloquium is concentrating on the writings of Paul."

This final comment takes us back to a conference held at Cambridge University in 1988. This conference on the Eucharistic texts focused on 1 Corinthians 11:23–26, with good results (see *One Loaf, One Cup: Ecumenical Studies of 1 Cor 11 and Other Eucharistic Texts*, ed. Ben F. Meyer [Macon, Ga.: Mercer University Press, 1993]). Both Professors Betz and Hooker took part in that conference and, while they disagreed fundamentally on the importance of Isaiah 53 for understanding Jesus, they agreed on the value of bringing Paul into the equation. Prof. Otfried Hofius was also present at that conference and presented what at the time appeared to be compelling evidence of the linguistic influence of Isaiah 53 on the text of 1 Corinthians 11:23–26 (see "The Lord's Supper and the Lord's Supper Tradition: Reflections on 1 Corinthians 11:23b–25," in *One Loaf, One Cup*, pp. 75–115).

The colloquy at Baylor University thus represents a methodological advance in the study of the question of Isaiah 53 and Christian origins, in that for the first time there was widespread agreement on the value of concentrating attention on the bearing of the writings of Paul on this topic.

A significant contribution to our understanding of how Paul used Isaiah to defend his mission to the Gentiles comes from J. Ross Wagner in his article, "The Heralds of Isaiah and the Mission of Paul: An Investigation of Paul's Use of Isaiah 51–55 in Romans." While not bearing directly on the specific questions that gave rise to the colloquy, Wagner's demonstration that Isaiah was crucial for Paul's defense of his mission serves to broaden our horizons and encourages us to look at the larger picture of the influence of this whole section of Isaiah on Paul, so that when we find suggestions of the influence of Isaiah 53 in pre-Pauline confessional statements like those in Galatians 1:4 and 2:20, and in 1 Corinthians 11:23–26, the historian is not surprised.[1]

In Daniel Bailey's contribution, "Concepts of *Stellvertretung* in the Interpretation of Isaiah 53," we have a unique introduction to one aspect of current exegetical work now underway at Tübingen University. Of particular interest is the citation by Bailey of a particular passage from the writings of Immanuel Kant to which German biblical scholars "always seem to return." This provides a suggestive insight into one of the current theological mysteries: Why is it that liberal theologians tend to shy away from dealing with the Christian doctrine of atonement? Bailey's suggestion that New Testament exegetes should probe more deeply into the "subcurrents" of their discipline needs to be heeded. Questions like the ones Kant raised should be addressed directly and not skirted. Exegetes need to be in a dialogue with their colleagues in theology — especially with those knowledgeable about the history of nineteenth-century theology.

In this connection Prof. Otto Betz has rendered the reader the service of identifying the first scholar who, in a powerful way, documented the decisive importance of Isaiah 53 for understanding Jesus, and thus for understanding Christians and the Christian faith. This scholar was H. W. Wolff, an Old Testament specialist. It is important to know that Prof. Rudolf Bultmann, whose work Wolff was criticizing, was not convinced by Wolff's arguments. Otto Betz and Peter Stuhlmacher have further strengthened the case first argued by Wolff. To date no student of Bultmann has effectively come to his defense on this decisive matter. While scholars at Tübingen, including Martin Hengel and others, continue to undergird the position of Wolff with more and more exegetical argumentation, their colleagues in the other German universities have generally abandoned the question and tend to concentrate on other matters.

In England, however, Professor Hooker, whose 1959 study independently reached the same negative results as did Bultmann, has by no

---

1. Wagner frequently refers to a paper prepared for the colloquy by Richard Hays, "Criteria for Identifying Allusions and Echoes of the Text of Isaiah in the Letters of Paul." These references served the purpose of illustrating how Hays's proposed criteria might be useful. Wagner's work itself, however, is not dependent upon the paper by Hays. Hays's paper and critical responses coming out of the conference can be expected to be published in journals whose pages are well-suited for the complex and detailed scholarly discussion of the question of criteria.

means abandoned an interest in the atonement. Daniel Bailey is a graduate student of Professor Hooker and carries on his work in Tübingen under Hooker's attentive supervision. Thus, in the work of Daniel Bailey the reader is in close touch with the minds of both the Tübingen scholars, whose work he follows assiduously, and their appreciative but unconvinced Cambridge colleague.

This volume would be worth its price if it had only the articles by Betz, Hooker, and Bailey. But it has much more.

The essays by Hanson, Reventlow, and Clements explore, from a variety of perspectives, the context of Isaiah 53 in the Hebrew scriptures. Hanson suggests that the Servant of the Lord arises as part of the thought world in Isaiah 40–55 and emphasizes new possibilities of divine action in the midst of the trauma of exile that overturned Israel's royal Zion theology. The Servant Songs are part of the polemic in Isaiah 40–55 against the Babylonian gods. The Servant brings new possibilities for leadership that is united with the divine purposes and can bring healing for the people.

Reventlow begins with German scholarship on the Servant Songs, especially the formative work of Duhm. He rejects the corporate interpretation of the Servant and searches for individuals who might have served as Old Testament antecedents for this vicarious sufferer: the righteous sufferer in laments, the king, Jeremiah, Ezekiel.

Clements takes the collective interpretation much more seriously and interprets the Servant Songs as more of an integral part of Isaiah 40–55. He also explores royal and prophetic figures as antecedents to the Servant. It is the Deuteronomistic portrait of Moses and Ezekiel's insistence that exiled Israel be purified that are most formative. In Isaiah 53, God provides a purification offering in Servant-Israel. Clements emphasizes the cultic dimension of the language in the fourth Song, but all three interpreters note that the Song's language is the open language of poetry.

Roy Melugin's article also attends to the open language of Isaiah 53 but moves in a different direction. Melugin presents a minority report on the historical-critical hermeneutic underlying most of the papers in this volume. He argues that we do not have the resources to resolve the historical issues and that a different approach is more beneficial for the church. He commends a hermeneutic which appropriates biblical texts to create a symbolic world which attends to the significance of the Servant for contemporary believers.

With the contribution from Prof. Adrian Leske we have the work of a New Testament scholar who has taken into account the major achievements of Old Testament scholarship on the exilic and postexilic periods of Jewish history — as this scholarship bears on the question of prophetic influence on Jesus. Leske's work goes on to illuminate the way the Gospels can be understood in light of modern Old Testament scholarship.

Perhaps the most unexpected scientific result that has emerged from the Baylor University colloquy is the work of David A. Sapp. The lengthy paper he presented for discussion at the conference was too long to be included in its entirety. However, one section was of special interest, and Sapp willingly expanded that section into an article that may go further than any other to date in offering an explanation for why, since Isaiah 53 seems to have been important for many New Testament writers, these authors tend to allude to it rather than citing it directly. Until now the standard answer to this question has been that Isaiah 53 was so well known that it was banal to cite it. But David Sapp offers another possible explanation. His explanation and the more usual explanation are not mutually exclusive.

There are indeed significant crosscurrents in the world of theological scholarship today. One of these is represented by the opposing positions of Prof. Morna Hooker and Prof. Otto Betz on a question of far-reaching import for Christian theology. But if this volume of essays is any indication of what is happening, we can say that there are also signs of scholarly convergence. The editors believe that what is called for in our day is more collegial dialogue like that which took place at the Baylor University colloquy and which in a developed form comes to expression in this volume of essays.[2]

---

2. Most of the discussions of the papers presented at the Baylor colloquy were audio-taped. These tapes are available in the Baylor University Library.

1

The World of the Servant of the Lord in Isaiah 40–55

Paul D. Hanson

$\blacklozenge$

The Value and Limitations of Historical-Critical Study

Lively debate persists over the relative merits of historical-critical study of biblical texts compared to reader-centered literary studies. While not dismissing the value of historical study outright, Roy F. Melugin in an article in this volume goes so far in stressing the contemporary theological value of "imaginative biblical interpretation" as to raise the question of whether the ancient text produced in a specific historical context in antiquity any longer is allowed to exercise any restraints on the creative imagination of the modern interpreter. In defense of his hermeneutics of personal involvement and of "use of scripture for personal transformation," he appeals to David J. A. Clines's argument that "when a literary work has been put forth into the public arena, the umbilical cord is cut between the text and its producer." This is a move in the direction of the "new criticism" that raises the specter of purely subjective exegesis.

I am not disagreeing with the well-established truths that interpretation includes a subjective dimension, that the presuppositions and questions we bring to the text contribute to the interpretive conclusions, and that the meaning of texts is enriched through the process of centuries of interpretation. Nor am I denying that interpretation is a creative hermeneutical exercise and that the history of interpretation is dynamic and ever changing in relation to the new situations within which communities of belief find themselves. The issue is rather this: Among the "vast variety of meanings" that can arise from one's encounter with a biblical text, does the text itself offer any assistance in sorting out fitting interpretations from unsuitable ones? Is David Koresh's understanding of messianic prophecy as legitimate as that of the author of Mark or Luke? Is Hal Lindsay's interpretation of the Book of Revelation as trustworthy in its time and setting as was Hans Lilje's in his? While denying neither the creative element in theological hermeneutics nor the complexity of the enterprise, I believe that all biblical interpretation must begin with a solid grounding in study of the historical setting(s) and meaning(s) of a text. Though just the first stage in theological interpretation, it is an important first stage, since it contributes a set of restraints on "creative imagination" and insists that a text cannot mean just anything to anyone.

Once the importance of historical-critical study is recognized, it is equally important to recognize that it by no means exhausts the interpretive process. To begin with, attention must turn to the study of instances in which a given text is interpreted in other parts of scripture. The history of interpretation that is such an important part of tradition in Judaism and Christianity preserves a special place of honor for interpretations already found within the Bible. This is consistent with the classical Christian view that the development of scripture is not arbitrary but in conformity with a divine purpose, which any group claiming to be descended from the Bible must respect in the course of its own efforts at interpretation. Beyond such inner-biblical interpretation the theological exegete faces the vast and fascinating world of centuries of interpretation finally leading to the living presence of the text within contemporary communities of faith.

These brief observations are intended to clarify the purpose of the kind of historical exploration undertaken in this article: It in no way replaces the creative engagement of the contemporary individual or community with the text, but rather provides one dimension in the multidimensional process of discernment that is at the heart of theological exegesis.

It is the goal of this essay then to see what light can be shed on the world from which arose the concept of the Servant of the Lord in Isaiah 40–55. It is presented as background to the further stages of theological interpretation that necessarily follow, stages engaging the larger biblical canon, the postbiblical history of interpretation, and contemporary theological engagement, all of which will be addressed at one time or another in the other essays of this volume. Even within the specific confines of our historical inquiry it must be conceded that access to the world of the Servant of the Lord imagery in Isaiah 40–55 is indirect and limited. Therefore, not all questions that are of interest will find answers. But some aspects of the text that a first reading leaves unclear can be clarified. This is true especially of those aspects that relate to the broad setting, such as: What political and historical conditions does the text reflect? Over against what ideological positions does it place itself? What is the understanding of sacrifice that it presupposes? Considerable evidence is available to scholarship both from the Bible and other ancient sources that sheds light on such general questions. Much less light can be shed on specific questions, such as: Who was the Servant? Who was Second Isaiah? But the literary character of the material in Isaiah 40–55 suggests that the latter specific questions are less important than the broader ones: We are dealing with poetic language conveying meaning through symbols and metaphors resisting unequivocal reference to specific objects and focusing attention instead on the complex and often mysterious dimensions of human existence.

We turn then to consider what we can know about the world of the Servant of the Lord, in the hope that this may shed light on the several texts revolving around this image that came to have such considerable importance in the subsequent history of Judaism and Christianity. Due to the specific theme of the conference in which this essay originated, focus will be primarily on the fourth Servant Song.

The Broad Setting of Isaiah 52:13–53:12

The Centrality of the Zion/David Theologumenon

We direct our attention first to the conceptual world that in the period leading up the exile represented the most comprehensive effort of the nation's intellectuals to explain reality. It was a theologumenon based on the dual theme of the divine election of Zion and David. The factors contributing to its widespread influence were many, but one of the most evident in relation to our topic arose during the reign of Hezekiah. The recent demise of the Northern Kingdom had enhanced the claims of the Southern Kingdom of Judah to entitlement to the Davidic promises and elevated the status of Zion/Jerusalem as the chosen city of Yahweh. Another boost to the Zion/David theologumenon came from the unusual alliance that was forged between the prophet Isaiah and the king Hezekiah. Right at the point when Sennacherib's offensive put the Zion/David ideology to the severest test it had yet encountered, king and prophet stood resolutely alongside each other. The alliance proved effective: In spite of the widespread devastation that fell upon the land (Isa. 1:4–9), Jerusalem withstood the attack. This, according to both the Deuteronomistic historians (2 Kings 18–19) and Isaiah (see especially the Ariel vision of Isa. 29:1–8), was no accident. God had intervened to save his city and his anointed one. The unique status of chosen city and anointed king thus received powerful confirmation.

After the troubling years of Manasseh's reign, Josiah elevated the Zion/David ideology to new heights, and it became a central theme in the history compiled by the Deuteronomistic historians during his reign. According to their account in 2 Kings, Josiah eliminated the countryside shrines that had detracted from the singularity and centrality of Jerusalem. In this king, they announced, the luster of the Davidic House reached an unprecedented plane: "Before him there was no king like him, who turned to the Lord with all his heart, with all his soul, and with all his might, according to all the law of Moses" (2 Kings 23:25).

The combination of religious enthusiasm with nationalistic fervor that characterized the proponents of the Zion/David theologumenon was not immune to criticism. Judging from the Book of Jeremiah it would seem that the prophet of Anathoth revived the skepticism earlier expressed by Hosea toward royal ideology. Jeremiah remained silent, it seems, during Josiah's reign, only to arise in stinging condemnation of the policies of Jehoiakim, the venerated king's son and successor (Jeremiah 22). As for the temple on Zion, Jeremiah, in his so-called temple sermon, refuted the notion of the inviolability of the temple mount, thereby calling into question the tradition of Zion's unassailability that rested on mythic motifs associated with the divine mountain, corroborated in the minds of many by the escape of the capital city from Sennacherib's offensive in 701. Jeremiah placed king and Zion alike under the same conditions of the Mosaic covenant that were binding on all humans and human institutions.

The Effects of the Babylonian Conquest
on the Zion/David Theologumenon

Alongside the Zion/David theologumenon, a historical event takes its place as the second important feature we must consider as part of the broad background of the Servant image. The Babylonian conquest that occurred in stages during the first two decades of the sixth century B.C.E., in sharp contrast to the escape of Jerusalem during the Assyrian invasion of 701, wielded a double blow to the two tenets of the David/Zion ideology: The humiliation of the Davidic kings that occurred in their capitulation to the superior might of the armies of Marduk undermined the notion of the eternally established divine election of the Davidic House that had been celebrated in hymns like Psalms 89, 110, and 132. The destruction of Jerusalem and temple similarly cast doubts on the notion of God's having chosen Zion as his earthly habitation (see Psalms 2 and 68). The literature of the time bears unequivocal testimony to the crisis precipitated by this crushing event, a crisis fitting the description of "chaos" given by Susan Langer: "Man can adapt himself somehow to anything his imagination can cope with; but he cannot deal with Chaos. Because his characteristic function and highest asset is conception, his greatest fright is to meet what he cannot construe, the 'uncanny,' as it is popularly called."[1]

This description at first may appear too modern to apply to ancient Israel. Its applicability becomes apparent, however, when one recalls that the myths and epics of ancient peoples, including Israel, served as maps of the cosmos guiding their adherents through the hazards of life so as to avoid chaos in its many forms. The *Enuma Elish*, for example, gave the Babylonians the conceptual means whereby they could understand all aspects of reality, from the changing seasons to the political and economic structures of their society. In the *Lament of Ur*, the inhabitants of that unhappy city gave expression not only to the bafflement they experienced when their city and temple were destroyed, but also to their struggle to understand the calamity within the terms of their myth.

According to the terms of the Jerusalem establishment's equivalent of the cosmogonic myth, namely, the Zion/David theologumenon, the events of 587 B.C.E. should not have occurred. The dismay expressed in

---

1. Susan Langer, *Philosophy in a New Key* (Cambridge: Harvard University Press, 1960), 287.

the Book of Lamentations bears resemblance to the *Lament of Ur.* Would the inhabitants of Jerusalem, as they grappled with the resurgence of chaos, draw a conclusion similar to that of the inhabitants of Ur, namely, that their god had fallen out of favor in the divine assembly? In Zephaniah 1:12, Jeremiah 44:16–18, and Ezekiel 8:12–14 we find references to people who had drawn that quite natural conclusion and who responded by switching allegiance to the deity who had proven himself superior in battle. Even within circles that clung to the traditional deity Yahweh, the struggle with bafflement was severe. For not only had the Babylonians under the talisman of their gods destroyed the place and accouterments of the Jewish cult, they had also called into question the efficacy of the elaborate sacrificial structure that had developed precisely to keep chaos at bay and to maintain the prosperity and security of the land. Even as the chosenness of the Davidic king was to assure the security of the land from foreign threats, so too the sanctity maintained within the temple cult through sacrifices providing purification from every conceivable defilement, and even the act of offering atonement on *yom kippur* for every overlooked sin, was to assure the abiding presence of God, upon whom the well-being of the land ultimately depended. And now, with the victory of the Babylonians, security and sanctity both had been violated. What could be said in defense of the God of Israel once the anointed king was banished in humiliation and the chosen temple lay in ruins?

The Struggle to Comprehend the Calamity of 587 within the Context of Yahwistic Faith

The exilic composition Isaiah 40–55 takes its place among a number of writings of the time that struggle with the question of how to make theological sense out of the devastating events that had led to banishment of much of the population from the Jewish homeland. Ezekiel, from a priestly perspective that upheld ritual sanctity as the key to restoration, reenvisioned a Jerusalem carefully ordered by its priestly elite so as to recreate the holy conditions within which God could again dwell (Ezek. 34:23–24). At the same time he did not overlook the necessity of individual responsibility vis-à-vis the moral stipulations of the covenant (Ezekiel 18) and the need for purification of the human heart achievable only by divine initiative (Ezek. 36:22–32). Jeremiah and his disciples, while battling against a magical view of the temple and its cult, envisioned a new *tora* pedagogy, in which obedience would arise from the heart (Jer. 31:31–34).

The attempts of Ezekiel and Jeremiah to explain the devastating events of 587 from the perspective of the faith of Israel shed light on the conditions within which the anonymous author of Isaiah 40–55 wrote his prophetic message and sketched his portrait of the Servant of the Lord. The viability of an official national worldview had been called into question by calamitous events. A spiritual struggle was underway to reformulate the conceptual underpinnings of the Jewish people. Second Isaiah, in addressing a wavering Jewish audience living in the shadow of pagan temples and under the din of Marduk festivals, mounts a counteroffensive. He is polite neither to pagan challengers nor to the stubborn defenders of national traditions. Boldly he speaks out in the name of the God who called him to service: "Do not remember the former things, nor consider the things of old. I am about to do a new thing; now it springs forth, do you not perceive it?" (Isa. 43:18–19).

Issues that cried out for explanation in his counteroffensive were kingship, temple, the remedies for the removal of the sins that had led to divine judgment on the nation, and the status of Israel's God among the rival gods, especially those who in the view of many had demonstrated their superior power in the Babylonian conquest and then in the meteoric rise of Cyrus. These issues stand in the background of Second Isaiah's ministry to the exiles and must be kept in mind if one is to understand the world of the Servant of the Lord.

Kingship and the role of God's anointed (*māšîaḥ*), comprising one of the twin pillars in the official theologumenon of Judah, could not be ignored by Second Isaiah. According to royal compositions like Psalms 2 and 89, Yahweh appointed and sustained and preserved forever the anointed one of the House of David, thus assuring victory over all enemies and safeguarding God's earthly habitation. Qualifying this promise was the provision for discipline of the descendants of David in the case of waywardness, but this did not nullify the promise of divine sponsorship and eternal steadfastness on God's part. Against the background of this lofty royal ideology, the so-called Cyrus Oracle in 44:24–45:7 takes a radical new turn. Yahweh addresses as his anointed one the Persian emperor Cyrus. Traditional responsibilities associated with God's anointed, the Davidic king, are assigned to the *new* anointed one, the responsibilities of restoring the exiled people to their homeland, restoring their devastated cities, and rebuilding their temple. In the divine plan disclosed by Second Isaiah, the role of the Davidic king has been assumed by a foreigner.

For a people accustomed to recognizing God's agency on their behalf in the person of their own leaders, from Moses to the Judges to the Davidic kings, this was a radical revision of the traditional view. And the revision, in relation to the election of David, went further. In 55:1–3, a messenger of the Lord proclaims an invitation to all to come to a banquet, where food and drink is free and where levels of social status are irrelevant. And then, astonishingly, they are invited to enter into the everlasting covenant that, in prophetic promises like 2 Samuel 7:8–16 and royal psalms like Psalm 89, was exclusively the privileged possession of the Davidic king: "I will make with you an everlasting covenant, my steadfast, sure love for David." After applying the official terms of the Davidic covenant (*bĕrît 'ôlām, ḥasdê dāwîd, ne'ĕmānîm*) to the people in general, the passage goes on to designate these ordinary folk as the ones the Lord will glorify, thereby attracting the attention of the nations much in the manner in which the royal house was to dazzle foreigners in more traditional visions of the future. Noteworthy in this connection is the reaction of "many nations" and "kings" to the Servant in the fourth Servant Song: They shall be startled and silenced before him, precisely because the phenomenon is so unexpected and novel (52:15).

The above passages caution us against restricting Second Isaiah's message in the fourth Song to narrowly conceived notions of spiritual healing and personal salvation. It must be seen as part of a larger proposal seeking to redefine the basis upon which the Jewish people were to reestablish themselves as a nation within the family of the nations of the world. In this proposal political deliverance is addressed, as is physical reconstruction of the land, as is restoration of the cult center, the temple. In the same breath it must be added, however, that the social-political-economic restoration is inseparably tied to spiritual health. Underlying the entire calamity suffered by the nation was a spiraling legacy of sin and an accumulation of guilt. Political health could not be regained until the problem of spiritual disease had been resolved.

God's New Way: The Servant of the Lord in 52:13–53:12

The fourth Servant Song (52:13–53:12) is a part of Second Isaiah's description of the new way God was opening up to Israel after the old way had failed to lead them to their divinely intended destiny as witnesses of God's will and salvation to the nations. The Servant is God's agent for opening up that new way in an era in which Davidic kings and temple priests had been discredited by failed programs. As was already the case in the first Servant Song in 42:1–4, in the opening verse of this Song descriptions are used of the Servant that remind one of language describing the kings of the previous era, indicating that Second Isaiah wants the audience to make connections between the old regime and the way of the future: The Servant shall be exalted, lifted up, shall be very high, and shall prosper (52:13). But again as in the case of the first Song, his appearance and modus operandi paint a startling contrast to Israel's kings. Suffering and despised, he pursues not the path to success guaranteed by special status, but accepts as his lot terrible anguish and pain. Nevertheless, as the framework in 52:13–15 and 53:11b–12 indicates, this unusual path leads to the positive results that Israel's exalted kings had failed utterly to achieve. The marks of radical revision of the standard theologumenon that we detected elsewhere are in even sharper relief here. In more specific detail, what is the nature of the revision?

I shall use 53:4 as a point of entry into this question: "Surely he has borne our infirmities and carried our diseases." Infirmities and diseases lie at the heart of the crisis, for they have accumulated without relief or cure to the point of dragging the nation to the brink of extinction. In this sentence the verbs are more important than the direct objects. It appears that they are intended to bring to mind the opening verses of chapter 46. There the verbs *nāsā'* ("bear") and *'āmas* ("carry") offer the basis for comparing the nature of the Babylonian gods Marduk and Nebo with the nature of Yahweh. The former are worse than useless; they are burdens on those who would implore them for help: "these things you carry [*něśu'ōtêkem*] are loaded [*'ămûsōt*] as burdens [*massā'*]" (46:1b). In contrast, Israel has "been borne [*'ămusîm*]" by Yahweh from birth, "carried [*něśu'îm*] from the womb" (46:3b). It is certainly comforting to know that the God one worships carries one rather than being in need of being carried.

This contrast provides the basis for the prophet to address the specific question weighing upon the defeated and humiliated community: What happens when a people is stumbling toward extinction under the burden of its sin-induced infirmities and diseases, and the traditional institutions of sacrifice and atonement have proven ineffectual to relieve them of their sin and guilt? What can be done about these infirmities and diseases? The surprising answer given in 53:4 is that they have already been lifted from the afflicted community by *the Servant:* "Surely he has borne our infirmities and carried our diseases." But when one is dealing with sin and guilt, that is, with matters bearing on the relationship between a people and its God, of what help is it for one human to assume the guilt-burden of another? In stages the next two verses answer this crucial question: "Upon him was the punishment that made us whole," and then follows the statement that points to the reason why one human's suffering can atone for the sin of other humans: "The Lord has laid on him the iniquity of us all." What the people witness in the sufferings of the Servant is *the Lord's doing.* This is certainly a daring new proposition.

A daring proposition to be sure, but what is to distinguish such sacrifice of a human being by God from sadism, or child abuse writ large? The clue to the answer to this difficult question is found in vv. 10 and 11: "through him the will of the Lord shall prosper... he shall find satisfaction through his knowledge. The righteous one, my servant, shall make many righteous." What is being described is not a scapegoat loaded with the iniquity of the people and then slaughtered capriciously as a substitute. Rather we encounter one who, having identified his human will with divine redemptive purpose, enters into solidarity with a people at their nadir point, in their guilt-ridden disease, and acts in partnership with God to break the bondage that is destroying them. The result is that they are shocked to their senses, accept the divine gift of healing, and thus are restored to the righteousness that enables them to carry on their vocation as God's people.

This recognition of the unity of purpose that characterizes the relationship between Servant and the Lord explains the significance of the author's use of the verbs *naśa'* and *sabal* in verse four. In the Servant who bears the people's infirmities and carries their diseases, these people can recognize the God by whom they are borne and carried, in other words, the merciful, living God contrasted with the useless idols of the Babylonians in chapter 46. It is obviously important to the prophet that this Servant is not just any guilt-ridden mortal, but one suited for this daunting task by uncommon qualities, summarized in the Lord's description in 53:11, "the righteous one, my servant." The Servant, faithful, obedient, and open daily to the Lord's instruction, becomes a living sign of the depths to which God's love goes in order to rescue a people yearning to return (see Hos. 6:1–2) but so hopelessly lost that all other means of redemption have failed. If, as seems likely, the enigmatic phrase in v. 10 that Yahweh made the Servant's life "a sin-offering" ('āšām) is intended to call to mind the offering by that name prescribed by levitical law as compensation for certain kinds of offenses (Leviticus 5, 6, 7, 14, 19), then we have here another instance of Second Isaiah's transformation of earlier tradition to produce a radical new message capable of addressing the postcalamity situation. Though intended to preserve the health of the nation, the old sacrificial structure of 'ašam had failed due to the unrelenting perversity of the people. Yet the conditions described by levitical law and repeated by Ezekiel as prerequisite for God's return to the people remained unaltered, namely, the conditions of righteousness and holiness. In the obedience and suffering of the Servant, God reentered the life of the people to establish righteousness in a new way, yet one in keeping with the earlier announcement: "Do not remember the former things, or consider the things of old. I am about to do a new thing; now it springs forth, do you not perceive it?" (43:18–19).

The title of one of Edmund Wilson's essay collections, *The Shock of Recognition*, describes the effect of God's new initiative in the Servant: Kings are caught short and put in their place as they witness the mystery of this most unlikely agent of divine purpose. The people who formerly ostracized the Servant as offensive and of no account are shocked into recognizing that they are made whole by his taking upon himself the suffering and punishment *they* deserve. The question in v. 8 captures their astonishment: "Who could have imagined his future?" What an unlikely place to encounter God's saving activity! But that is precisely the radical alternative offered in this Song to the more reasonable methods of restoration that had shipwrecked against the rocks of stubborn human perversity: "The righteous one, my servant, shall make many righteous, and he shall bear their iniquities" (53:11b).

It is of the very nature of the message of Second Isaiah that it does not lead us as far as Ezekiel's program toward grasping the exact contours of the community envisioned by the prophet for the returning exiles. What is clear is that it is an alternative vision. As an alternative to the militant ways of kingship it offers a patient, steadfast witness to God's will. In contrast to a definition of leadership that elevates an elite class and invests in it the prerogatives of discerning God's will and instructing the people, Second Isaiah's vision endows the entire community that accepts God's free gift of grace with the promises of the covenant. No longer are the qualifications for leadership to be pedigree and status, but obedience and righteousness. This is not to say that the human race is leveled until distinctions no longer exist. The image of the Servant of the Lord stands out as a reminder that the way of righteousness is so unique among the options available to humans that only the individual and the community that submits completely to the will of God, in effect identifying the human will with divine will, will be enabled to overcome the snare of sin that entraps and entombs humanity, and thereby "make many righteous."

Rather than offering a blueprint for reconstruction to the exiles upon their return, the message of Second Isaiah and its image of the Servant of the Lord must have functioned as an inspiration to envision new possibilities, to dream new dreams, to try new possibilities. If the concluding section of the Book of Isaiah, chapters 56–66, is any indication, it seems that the vision went unfulfilled. The old regime reasserted itself. Power politics repressed the alternative way of patient, loving witness to God's righteousness. Yet, in the manner of inspired visions, the vision of Second Isaiah was to have a future that extended far beyond the more pragmatic programs of his contemporaries. The alternative way of the Servant of the Lord could not be obliterated from the consciousness of a people whose birth in slavery instilled in them the sense of being on the earth for purposes other than to be lords over others. The history of the Servant of the Lord was to be long and enduring. It continues still.

Conclusion

The exilic period was a time of testing for the Jewish community. As is often the case, testing was the mother of deep searching and new insights into the faith that gave this people its unique identity. These insights related both to what was essential to the faith and what could be discarded as outworn and superseded. At times propositional language proved inadequate to express the inspired vision of God's future plans for this people, and words were enabled to take flight on another plane, borne upon the wings of poetry in the form of metaphors and images. Among the several inspired glimpses into the future that arose during the exile, Second Isaiah's is the most poetic of all, and his poetic creativity perhaps reaches its apex in the image of the Servant of the Lord.

Ezekiel, by way of contrast, himself endowed with a rich imagination, put forth plans for the return of the people that are replete with detail pertaining both to physical rebuilding and community organization. For this reason, Ezekiel 40–48 can be called a program of restoration. As such, it served a different purpose in subsequent years than did Isaiah 40–55. The latter presents glimpses of God's future with Israel that suggest audacious new ways of viewing the vocation of those chosen to be witnesses in the world to God's universal purpose. In addressing the same basic problems of exile, sin, restoration of righteousness, and faithful leadership, yet doing so in such different ways, Ezekiel and Second Isaiah can best be seen as complementing each other, though the contrast between their messages was so great that at times they were used by opposing sides in battles for political control.

Due to the opaqueness of poetic imagery, Second Isaiah's image of the Servant of the Lord has been interpreted in many different ways at different periods of history and by different communities. Therefore, our description of the world within which the image of the Servant was born and of the issues it addressed is merely the starting point in the task of interpreting Isaiah 52:13–53:12. Other essays in this volume will carry the task further. What our initial exploration contributes to all such efforts, however, is the rich image of the Servant of the Lord, seen sometimes as individual, sometimes as community, whose life reveals important lessons about God's vocational plan for those who choose the path of faithfulness and obedience. There are two important aspects to that plan, and they must be attended to in proper order. The first aspect involves the healing of those called to be God's people. The second aspect concerns the vocation for which the healing equips that people, the vocation of being the witnesses through whom knowledge of God's will can be proclaimed to all peoples and the light by which God's salvation may reach the ends of the earth. Given the richness of the image of the Servant of the Lord, there is little wonder that the history of its subsequent interpretation has been so creative and so diverse.

2

Basic Issues in the Interpretation of Isaiah 53

Henning Graf Reventlow

◆

The so-called Servant Songs in the second part of the Book of Isaiah belong to the most debated texts of the Old Testament.[1] The discussion on the manifold problems which these poems pose has been going on ever since B. Duhm in his commentary on the Book of Isaiah[2] as the first scholar to isolate a series of four Songs (Isa. 42:1–4; 49:1–6; 50:4–9; 52:13–53:12) from the surrounding material, including the basic question of whether Duhm was right at all in separating the "Songs"[3] from their context. The theme of our colloquy focuses our attention on the fourth Song, Isaiah 52:13–53:12. In the interest of brevity we will refer to this passage as Isaiah 53. But to understand the content and significance of Isaiah 53, it is also necessary to consider its place in the series of the four Servant Songs. Let us anticipate that we follow the majority of modern

---

1. Useful histories of research are given by C. R. North, *The Suffering Servant in Deutero-Isaiah,* 2d ed. (London: Oxford University Press, 1956), Part I, 6–120; Postscript, 220–39; H. H. Rowley, "The Servant of the Lord in the Light of Three Decades of Criticism," in *The Servant of the Lord and Other Essays on the Old Testament,* 2d ed. (Oxford: Blackwell, 1965), 3–60; D. Michel, "Deuterojesaja," in *TRE* (1981), 8:521–26; H. Haag, *Der Gottesknecht bei Deuterojesaja* (Darmstadt: Wissenschaftliche Buchgesellschaft, 1985). After the colloquy the following contributions on Isaiah 53 appeared: B. Janowski and P. Stuhlmacher, eds., *Der leidende Gottesknecht: Jesaja 53 und seine Wirkungsgeschichte,* Forschungen zum Alten Testament 14 (Tübingen: J. C. B. Mohr [Paul Siebeck], 1996), contains a complete bibliography on the Old Testament, selected bibliographies on ancient Judaism and the New Testament by W. Hüllstrung and G. Feine, 251–71; S. Sekine, *Identity and Authorship in the Fourth Song of the Servant: A Redactional Attempt at the Second Isaianic Theology of Redemption,* Annual of the Japanese Biblical Institute 21 (1995): 29–56; 22 (1996): 3–30; L. Ruppert, "'Mein Knecht, der Gerechte, macht die Vielen gerecht, und ihre Verschuldungen — er trägt sie,'" n.s., *BZ* 40 (1996): 1–17

2. *Das Buch Jesaja,* Göttinger Handkommentar zum Alten Testament III, 1, 1st ed. (Göttingen: Vandenhoeck & Ruprecht, 1892; 4th ed., 1922 = 5th ed., 1968, reprinted).

3. Even this signification is not adequate to the form and content of the pieces.

scholars in regarding Duhm's proposal to take the four Songs as a separate source as still valid, although some of Duhm's reasons for doing so are connected with typical presuppositions of his time, in that he saw in the prophetic personality an especially high value. Modern attempts at blending the songs with the context[4] are not very convincing. That similar proposals return at regular intervals[5] is, however, understandable, since the term "Servant of Yahweh" occurs also outside the Songs and there clearly has a collective sense, meaning Israel as the people of God (41:8–10; 44:1f., 21; 45:4; 48:20). This collective understanding of the Servant has been the ruling interpretation in Judaism since Rashi (1040–1105) and is also shared by Christian scholars who are not prepared to follow Duhm. It seems to find support in 49:3 in the third Song, where "Israel" appears in apposition to "Servant." The adherents of Duhm explain this occurrence as a gloss. This conclusion is appropriate, as it is obvious that the Servant in the third Song receives an office for Israel (49:5f.). The same can be said about the fourth Song, where the "we" speaking in the first-person plural in the main part of the Song (53:1–10a) clearly is to be distinguished from the (already deceased) Servant, the fatal destiny of whom the "we" is deploring. So it can be concluded that in the Song the Servant is an individual.[6]

Taking the Servant Songs as a separate textual group does not mean that we regard them as originating from the same author and having been written at the same time. Nearly all commentators agree that this cannot be the case, since the second and third Songs are spoken by the Servant himself in the first-person singular, whereas in the central part

---

4. The best known is T. N. D. Mettinger, *A Farewell to the Servant Songs: A Critical Examination of an Exegetical Axiom* (Lund: Gleerup, 1983); for criticism see H.-J. Hermisson, "Voreiliger Abschied von den Gottesknechtsliedern," *TR* 49 (1984): 209–22. In Mettinger's wake see also F. Matheus, *Singt dem Herrn ein neues Lied: Die Hymnen Deuterojesajas*, SBS 141 (Stuttgart: Katholisches Bibelwerk, 1990); A. Laato, *The Servant of YHWH and Cyrus*, ConBOT 35 (Stockholm: Almqvist & Wiksell International, 1992), 16–21; idem, "The Composition of Isaiah 40–55," *JBL* 109 (1990): 207–28. This position was already taken in a "minority vote" by K. Budde, *Die sogenannten Ebed-Jahwe-Lieder und die Bedeutung des Knechtes Jahwes in Jes 40–55: Ein Minoritätsvotum* (Gießen: Töpelmann, 1900).

5. Besides Mettinger, Matheus, and Laato, who took this position recently, also Michel ("Deuterojesaja") might be mentioned, who sees in the "Servant" a group in Israel, trying in his solution to combine a collective and an individual interpretation (527f.).

6. This can also not be refuted by a reference to the "nations" and "kings" in 52:15 as the audience, as they belong to the traditional scenario of the royal imagery connected with the Servant. They are not the speakers in 53:1, against M. Weippert, "Die 'Konfessionen' Deuterojesajas," in *Schöpfung und Befreiung*, Festschrift C. Westermann, ed. R. Albertz, W. Golka, and J. Kegler (Stuttgart: Calwer Verlag, 1989), 110.

of the fourth a group speaking in the first-person plural discusses its own previous misunderstanding of the Servant's role. So we can conclude that the fourth Song is later than the foregoing three and was added when the author was already deceased.[7] Also, most modern interpreters[8] are inclined to regard the unknown prophet whom we call Second Isaiah as the author of the first three Songs, though these three also differ in style. The first Song (42:1–4) is a divine proclamation, spoken in the heavenly court, in which the Servant is called to his office, whereas in 49:1–6 and 50:4–9 the prophet speaks on his own behalf. An observation which recently has gained more attention, however, is that the frame of the fourth Song (52:13–15; 53:11b–12) is in style and speaker closely connected with the first Song: In both texts it is Yahweh himself who outlines the office and reward of his Servant.[9] This shows that in their final form the Songs are a clearly defined group of texts. It is likely that the Songs existed initially as an independent unit before being combined with other material originating from the prophet.

There are also clear indications in content that the fourth Song looks back to the third. The third Song, spoken by the Servant himself, contains in 50:6 utterances which belong to the standard formulations of the complaint psalms, colored by special expressions in which the Servant stresses patience and humility: "I gave my back to those who struck me/and my cheeks to those who pulled out the beard." These words have clear parallels in 53:7, where it is said that the Servant humbled himself and kept silent when harshly treated, followed by the simile of the sheep borne to the slaughter and the ewe before her shearers. But whereas in the third Song the complaint is followed by expressions of confidence from the Servant that Yahweh will come to his help (50:7–9),[10] the ut-

---

7. Already K. Elliger, *Deuterojesaja in seinem Verhältnis zu Tritojesaja*, BWANT IV, 11 (Stuttgart: Kohlhammer, 1933), 6–27, noted the stylistic differences between the first three and the fourth Song. Though his attribution of the fourth Song to Trito-Isaiah is not tenable, his observations still hold.

8. An exception is J. van Oorschot, *Von Babel zum Zion*, BZAW 206 (Berlin: de Gruyter, 1993), 195f.

9. B. Janowski, "Er trug unsere Sünden: Jes 53 und die Dramatik der Stellvertretung," in Janowski and Stuhlmacher, *Der leidende Gottesknecht*, 31f. (see above, n. 1), observes that the fourth Song opens in 52:13a with a formulation looking back to the opening formulations of the first Song in 42:1–4. According to Janowski, the הנה in 50.9 also points back to the הן in 42:1a and marks a disconnection to the הנה in 52:13a (32f.; cf. 36).

10. Formulated in the language of the law court, but not really meaning that the Servant will actually be accused; see C. R. North, *The Second Isaiah* (Oxford: Clarendon Press, 1964), 203f.

terances of the speakers in the fourth Song contain the confession that they had not comprehended what was going on and that the man of despised appearance had actually been the one who had given his life for their salvation. So Isaiah 53 is, in a way, a commentary, especially on the third Song. But it presupposes an already developed situation: The Servant has been killed (so it seems) and the speakers are left alone, looking back and only now discerning the relevance of all that had been going on before their eyes.

It cannot be our intention here to give a wholesale exposition of the fourth Song. But it will be useful to mention some special problems connected with it. One is the apparent contrast between the frame and the central part of the Song. It begins in 52:13 with the announcement by Yahweh himself in the first-person singular that "my Servant" will prosper and rise to a high rank. Looking back at his disfigured appearance and the disgust caused by it among the people (v. 14), he is declared to be destined for a powerful position in which whole peoples and mighty kings will be startled by seeing him (v. 15). Still more curious: Even after his death a prosperous future is announced for him, containing all the well-being that a normal Israelite could aspire to: seeing children, expecting a long life,[11] and even being promised abundant spoils from battle.[12] That he shall share the booty with the "many" (53:12)[13] is probably a metaphor indicating that he will be integrated again into the community from which he was separated by his illness and suffering.[14] Some scholars see an unbridgeable disparity between the frame and the central part of the Song. Some seek a solution by declaring the frame, or large parts of it, secondary.[15] A similar theory regards the central part as the orig-

---

11. The first two words in v. 11 are a sense unit (poetically a double-stress colon), the following two another.

12. Obviously a picture; see also 49:2, where the equipment of the Servant with weapons is described. This is no mere coincidence, but obviously a planned connection. Doubtful is the explanation of H.-J. Hermisson, "Das vierte Gottesknechtslied im deuterojesajanischen Kontext," in Janowski and Stuhlmacher, *Der leidende Gottesknecht,* 18f., who sees in the "booty" of the Servant the success of the whole salvation plan of Yahweh mentioned in Isaiah 52:10b and also 42:1, 4; 49:6.

13. For the emendation see E. Kutsch, *Sein Leiden und Tod — unser Heil: Eine Auslegung von Jesaja 52, 13–53, 12,* BibS 52 (Neukirchen-Vluyn: Neukirchener Verlag, 1967), 37f. = idem, *Kleine Schriften zum Alten Testament,* BZAW 168 (Berlin: de Gruyter, 1986), 190f.

14. See H.-J. Hermisson, "Der Lohn des Knechts," in *Die Botschaft und die Boten,* Festschrift H. W. Wolff, ed. J. Jeremias and L. Perlitt (Neukirchen-Vluyn: Neukirchener Verlag, 1981), 286.

15. So, for instance, E. Haag, "Die Botschaft vom Gottesknecht," in E. Haag et al., eds., *Gewalt und Gewaltlosigkeit im Alten Testament,* QD 96 (Freiburg, Basel, Vienna: Herder, 1983), 166–72.

inal Song and the frame as a more recent addition.[16] This may actually be the case, but would not explain the present composition which the redactor must have viewed as coherent. This, of course, is complicated to a modern observer: The apparent break between the death of the Servant (53:8f.) and the auspices for a happy future during his lifetime in 53:10–12 gave rise to the assumption that real death was not meant, but only the proximity to death typical for the formulations in the complaint psalms.[17] It is true that in the period of the Babylonian exile the idea of the resurrection of the dead was still undeveloped, but in exceptional cases we find descriptions of assumption from the earth, as with Elijah (2 Kings 2) or Enoch (Gen. 5:24). But in all this the intentionally imprecise, poetic language shows that we cannot analyze the text as if it were a scientific report. We can add that an artificial structure seems to reign in the whole Song between frame and middle part: The frame contains the same basic motives (the raising of the Servant out of baseness and suffering and the sense of his death as vicarious suffering for the "many") as the middle part.[18]

A central topic in the fourth Servant Song which covers the middle part of the confession of the "we" and still finds an echo in the concluding Yahweh-speech in 53:11b–12b is the speakers' interpretation of the suffering of the Servant on their behalf. They declare that they did not understand how all the torments inflicted upon him and borne with utmost patience were a vicarious suffering for their own sins. Again, the different pictures used show that no exact description of the pains is intended. It is important to stress this, as the New Testament scholars

---

16. J. Vermeylen, "Isaïe 53 et le ralliement d'Ephraim," in *"Wer ist wie du, HERR, unter den Göttern?"* Festschrift O. Kaiser, ed. I. Kottsieper et al. (Göttingen: Vandenhoeck & Ruprecht, 1994), 347, sees the speeches of Yahweh in 52:13–15, 53:11aβ–12 as a later interpretation of the central part, the "we"-speech in 53:1–11aα. Similarly L. Ruppert, "'Mein Knecht, der Gerechte,'" 7ff. Sekine, *Identity and Authorship in the Fourth Song of the Servant*, 21–22, sees seven stages of a redactional process which formed the present text.

17. See J. A. Soggin, "Tod und Auferstehung des leidenden Gottesknechtes," *ZAW* 87 (1975): 346–55; W. A. M. Beuken, *Jesaja deel II*[B] (Nijkerk: Callenbach, 1983), 241; R. N. Whybray, *Thanksgiving for a Liberated Prophet*, JSOTSup 4 (Sheffield: Department of Biblical Studies, University of Sheffield, 1978). See the critical review by H.-J. Hermisson, *TLZ* 106 (1981): 802–4. Also J. van Oorschot, *Von Babel zum Zion*, BZAW 206 (Berlin: de Gruyter 1993), 193, evades the supposed absurdities of the text by a collective understanding of the Servant, mentioning Whybray. See also Ruppert, "'Mein Knecht, der Gerechte,'" 9.

18. See K. T. Kleinknecht, *Der leidende Gerechtfertigte*, WUNT 2, 13 (Tübingen: Mohr [Siebeck], 1984), 49. P. R. Raabe, "The Effect of Repetition in the Suffering Servant Song," *JBL* 103 (1984): 77–81, stresses the repetition of the same catchwords in the description of the Servant's humiliation and exaltation.

who deny any influence of Isaiah 53 on the earliest understanding of the vicarious death of Jesus point to the fact that, whereas the expression ὑπέρ ὑμῶν (ἡμῶν) is the characteristic expression for indicating the connection between Jesus' suffering and the sins of the first Christians (see 1 Cor. 15:3; 1 Pet. 3:18), no formulation with ὑπέρ can be detected in the Septuagint text of Isaiah 53 (only διά and περί).[19] But the use of metaphorical language in 53:4–6, 8bβ, and 10aβ shows that the speakers had passed through a quite new experience: There was no institution and therefore no institutional language describing the unheard-of occurrence that the suffering of a single man could have the power of removing the consequences of the guilt of a whole group of people. This was a liberating event without a model. Therefore the "we" had to use metaphors to paint its likeness in the picture of sickness: He had borne their infirmities, carried their pains (53:4a). In this also the metaphor of taking a burden upon one's shoulders is used (53:4, 11, 12) in different formulations, as well as the picture of a man heavily wounded — he was pierced by their transgressions, crushed by their iniquities, and his wounds brought healing for them (53:5a, bβ) — and the picture of legal punishment — his chastisement had caused their weal (53:5bα). Even Yahweh himself is mentioned as the one who effected the torments of his Servant: He put the guilt of all to hit upon him (53:6b). This is especially unheard-of, even if one is prepared to accept that the idea of an atoning death was well known in the ancient world.[20] The last metaphor in the context has attracted the notice of most exegetes: In v. 10aβ, which is already the turning point of the statements in that the announcement of the future happiness of the Servant follows immediately, we find the words *sym 'šm*. This formulation has often been interpreted in the sense of a cultic offering.[21] Actually the word *'šm* can mean a special offering, but only in comparatively late strata of the Priestly source (Lev. 5:14–16,

---

19. See G. Barth, *Der Tod Jesu Christi im Verständnis des Neuen Testaments* (Neukirchen-Vluyn: Neukirchener Verlag, 1992), 58.

20. See M. Hengel, *The Atonement: The Origins of the Doctrine in the New Testament* (London: SCM; Philadelphia: Fortress Press, 1981), 19–32.

21. See, among others, G. Fohrer, "Stellvertretung und Schuldopfer in Jes 52, 13–53, 12," in idem, *Studien zu alttestamentlichen Texten und Themen (1966–1972)*, BZAW 155 (Berlin: de Gruyter, 1988), 24–43, and recently A. Schenker, "Die Anlässe zum Schuldopfer Ascham," in idem, *Studien zu Opfer und Kult im Alten Testament*, FAT 3 (Tübingen: J. C. B. Mohr, 1992), 63f.; Sekine, *Identity and Authorship in the Fourth Song of the Servant.*

17–19, 20–26; 6:10, etc.).[22] The original sense must be sought in connection with the restitution of damages due to a misdeed (Gen. 26:10; 1 Sam. 6:3–4, 8, 17, etc.), for which the offender has to give an equivalent.[23] So no cultic offering can be meant here.[24] This can also be said of the expressions in the framing parts: The statement which closes the whole poem and gives a sort of summarizing argument why the Servant deserves a reward (53:12b) contains the famous formulation that "he bore the sin of many." It remains as indistinct as the parallel clause that he "made intercession for the transgressors."[25]

So it is not possible to detect a fixed terminology in the poem. It is characteristic of poetry that the language used, the pictures coming to the fore, are fluid. So the poetic expressions in Isaiah 53 serve to give color to a situation which can neither be fitted into an institutional *Sitz im Leben* nor for which the people could draw upon any experiences preserved in the traditions handed down in Israel's long historical memory.

Another much-disputed question is: Who are the "many" of which the final verse speaks? Are they the same as the "we" who talk in the middle part of the Song? It is striking that the term "many" appears no fewer than five times in the frame of the poem (Isa. 52:14, 15 [adjective for "peoples"], 53:11c, 12a, b), and where it stands in an absolute position no parallel expression gives a clear indication of their identity. The only thing that seems clear is that the final redactor regarded the "many" as identical with the "we" in the central part of the poem. If the frame is later this is less certain. The "we" appear as a smaller group, and so the thesis that they are Israel or — more likely — a group of Israelites who were spectators when the Servant suffered and died, seems to be well founded.[26]

---

22. See K. Elliger, *Leviticus*, HAT I, 4 (Tübingen: Mohr [Siebeck], 1966), 76f.; D. Kellermann, "*ʾšm*," TWAT (1973), 1:467f.

23. See Elliger, *Leviticus;* see also R. Knierim, "*ʾašm*," THAT, 1:251–57; Kellermann, "*ʾšm*," 465; B. Janowski, "Er trug unsere Sünden: Jesaja 53 und die Dramatik der Stellvertretung," in idem, *Gottes Gegenwart in Israel* (Neukirchen-Vluyn: Neukirchener Verlag, 1993), 320f.; idem, in Janowski and Stuhlmacher, *Der leidende Gottesknecht*, 40–43; and L. Ruppert, "'Mein Knecht, der Gerechte,'" 4f.

24. Following B. Janowski, *Sühne als Heilsgeschehen*, WMANT 55 (Neukirchen-Vluyn: Neukirchener Verlag, 1982), esp. 144; C. Breytenbach, *Versöhnung: Eine Studie zur paulinischen Soteriologie*, WMANT 60 (Neukirchen-Vluyn: Neukirchener Verlag, 1989), 202–5, stresses that the pre-Pauline Christian tradition did not yet understand the death of Christ as an offering, nor did Paul himself.

25. NRSV. North, *The Second Isaiah*, 65, translates, "standing in the place of the transgressors." The sense of the root *pgʿ* (hiphil) seems to be in this case "to intercede for somebody" (different from the same word in 53:6); see P. Maiberger, "*pgʿ*," TWAT (1989), 6:506.

26. See Vermeylen, "Isaïe 53," 349. H. W. Hertzberg, "Die 'Abtrünnigen' und die 'Vielen':

All these uncertainties are typical of poetry. Poetry thrives on allusions, on impressions which touch the feeling, never using explicit
definitions, but rather hints referring to a knowledge hidden in the
subconscious of the hearers. The audience can identify the traditional
language in the frame — that "royal terminology" is used here has been
observed by many scholars — but this does not mean that the Servant
must be a king (see also Jer. 1:10). Hearers can detect themselves in
the "we" and find out that the "we" somehow must be the same as the
"many" (even if this is not correct in the strict sense, if one considers
the redactional process resulting in the present text), because the vicarious suffering of the Servant happened in the place of the punishment
deserved by themselves as the "many." If it is true that the term "many" is
inclusive in the sense of "all,"[27] we can conclude that the vicarious suffering of the Servant in the amplified and thereby final form of the fourth
Song is valid not only for a certain group but, as it seems, at least for
all Israel. There is no real advantage in asking for the original identity
of the Servant spoken about in a poem that might have consisted only
of the central part, 53:1–9.[28] His accomplishment is congruent with the
commission the Servant received in the first two Songs, which was also
directed to the peoples, although this was an active mission to be effected
by the word, whereas in the fourth Song it is the passion that is efficient,
an attitude seemingly without any activity of its own. But exactly in its
passivity the Servant's attitude does signify the deepest intensity of readiness, of obedience to the plans of God: For the Servant willingly took
the punishment of the sinners upon him and "did not open his mouth"

Ein Beitrag zu Jes 53," in H. Kuschke, ed., *Verbannung und Heimkehr*, Festschrift W. Rudolph
(Tübingen: Mohr [Siebeck], 1961), 102ff., tried to show that the "many" are the peoples. Against
him, among others, are H.-J. Hermisson, "Israel und der Gottesknecht bei Deuterojesaja," *ZTK* 79
(1982): 23f.; O. H. Steck, "Aspekte des Gottesknechtes in Jes 52, 13–53, 12," *ZAW* 97 (1985):
36–58 (quote from p. 40), also published in idem, *Gottesknecht und Zion*, FAT 4 (Tübingen: Mohr,
1992), 22–43 (quote from p. 26).

27. See J. Jeremias, "πολλοί," *TWNT*, 6:536–45.

28. Therefore we do not enter into a discussion of the hypothesis of Vermeylen, "Isaïe 53," 349,
about the group speaking here, which he seeks to identify as "Ephraim," meaning the northern
tribes. The idea seems to be rather far-fetched. Another attempt is the thesis of A. R. Ceresko,
"The Rhetorical Strategy of the Fourth Servant Song (Isaiah 52:13–53:12): Poetry and the Exodus-
New Exodus," *CBQ* 56 (1994): 44ff., who tries to identify the Servant with a prophet killed by
the Babylonians for political reasons. This interpretation was already inaugurated by J. W. Miller,
"Prophetic Conflict in Second Isaiah: The Servant Songs in the Light of Their Context," in *Wort,
Gebot, Glaube*, Festschrift W. Eichrodt, AThANT 59 (Zürich: Zwingli-Verlag, 1970), 77–85.

(53:7a),[29] though personally innocent (v. 9b). This idea is continued by the two pictures of the lamb carried to the slaughter (cf. Jer. 11:19) and the sheep silent before its shearers (v. 7b).

The unheard-of character of this experience led to the use of the special terminology in the fourth Song, especially the metaphorical language circumscribing in pictures what happened. Close parallels to the form cannot be found, though psalm language has been used in parts of it.

Does this mean that Isaiah 53 is an "erratic block" in the Old Testament that "remained left behind without being understood until the days of the New Testament"?[30] This judgment contains two elements, the first of which deserves closer inspection in connection with our theme.[31]

The first observation, for which we can build upon the results of recent redactional-critical research, is the extent of contextual exegesis of the Servant Songs which is evident in the second and third part of the Book of Isaiah itself. To begin with we have already noted that the fourth Song is itself a sort of commentary on the third Song, explaining what happened to the Servant after the disgraceful events mentioned there (50:6). Now that his way has come to a fatal end, the eyes of the observers, possibly even of the enemies who participated in the persecution, have been opened; so they are able to understand what happened, albeit through pictures just approximating the deeper sense. If we look at the context of the whole series of Servant Songs, they are not as isolated as Duhm regarded them. It has become clear that the problem of the individual versus the collective understanding of the Servant mainly depends upon how one can distinguish between text and interpretation.[32] Taking as starting point the assumption that the Servant Songs originally were an independent source[33] and at a certain point of the development were integrated into the main source containing the other Deutero-Isaianic material,[34] the final form of the text is the result of a longer process dur-

---

29. The second occurrence in v. 7b might be an addition (see *BHS*), if not an intended framing.

30. K. Koch, "Sühne und Sündenvergebung um die Wende von der exilischen zur nachexilischen Zeit," in idem, *Spuren des hebräischen Denkens: Beiträge zur alttestamentlichen Theologie,* Gesammelte Aufsätze 1 (Neukirchen-Vluyn: Neukirchener Verlag, 1991), 203.

31. See also Janowski, "Er trug unsere Sünden," 325, n. 64.

32. See M. Sæbø, "Vom Individuellen zum Kollektiven: Zur Frage einiger innerbiblischer Interpretationen," in Albertz, Golka, and Kegler, *Schöpfung und Befreiung,* 116–25.

33. So recently, among others, O. H. Steck, "Aspekte des Gottesknechts in Jesaja 52, 13–53, 12," 37 (quote appears on p. 22 of Steck, *Gottesknecht und Zion*); idem, "Die Gottesknechts-Texte und ihre redaktionelle Rezeption im Zweiten Jesaja," in *Gottesknecht und Zion,* 151.

34. See O. H. Steck, "Aspekte des Gottesknechts in Deuterojesajas 'Ebed-Jahwe-Liedern,'" *ZAW*

ing which the Songs were commented upon several times and adapted
to later situations. So the first Song in 42:1–4 has been explained by
42:5–7, which still does not mention a name, but according to R. G.
Kratz[35] has King Cyrus of Persia in view. It can be seen together with
other texts which also speak about Cyrus,[36] one of which (51:4f.) seems
to be connected with the third Song. So the great king, still a single person, is identified in this layer with the Servant; the Servant Songs are
understood as speaking about him. Later on[37] a second redaction understands the first two Songs in a collective sense, identifying the Servant
with Israel or Zion (42:8f.; 42:18–42 [43:8]; 49:7–13 [49:3 gloss]).[38] In
the course of this interpretation further additions were inserted into the
book.[39] Also Isaiah 60–62 seems to have been added in connection with
this reworking. As we already observed, this collective understanding was
very influential in the history of exegesis, but we should see that it does
not represent the original sense of the Songs![40]

So far the actualizations mentioned paid attention almost exclusively
to the first and second Songs. The third and, above all, the fourth Song
were not in the same way open to a re-use, as the aspect of suffering,
above all a vicarious suffering, blocked the development of new ideas.
Therefore it is not a surprise that the fourth Song especially seems isolated at first sight, the immediate context, as regards the content, showing

---

96 (1984): 372–90; also published in *Gottesknecht und Zion*, 3–21; idem, "Aspekte des Gottesknechts
in Jesaja 52, 13–53, 12" (see above n. 26); idem, "Beobachtungen zu den Ziontexten in Jes 51–
54: Ein redaktionsgeschichtlicher Versuch," *BN* 46 (1989): 58–90 = *Gottesknecht und Zion*, 96–125;
idem, "Die Gottesknechts-Texte"; idem, "Gottesvolk und Gottesknecht in Jes 40–66," in *Volk Gottes,
Gemeinde und Gesellschaft*, JBTh 7 (Neukirchen-Vluyn: Neukirchener, 1992), 51–75.

35. R. G. Kratz, *Kyros im Deuterojesaja-Buch*, FAT 1 (Tübingen: Mohr [Siebeck], 1991), esp. 141.
Steck in his recent articles follows Kratz in his judgment.

36. For details see Kratz, *Kyros im Deuterojesaja-Buch*, 175.

37. The dating of the different layers by Kratz — Steck is prepared to follow him also in this
aspect — is hypothetical and even partly doubtful. The same can be said about the distribution of
verses, semi-verses, and so forth in the sources, which cannot be debated here. The basic insights
regarding the intentions of the actualizations following one upon the other can, however, be regarded
as valid.

38. Hermisson, in Janowski and Stuhlmacher, *Der leidende Gottesknecht*, 18 (cf. n. 68), takes the
word as a possibly genuine part of the text: then the Servant would represent the true Israel.

39. For details see Kratz, *Kyros im Deuterojesaja-Buch*, 206f.; table on p. 217, column V.

40. A collective understanding is the consequence of a total integration of the Songs into the
context, as with Mettinger, *A Farewell to the Servant Songs*, and Matheus, *Singt dem Herrn ein neues
Lied* (see above, n. 4). It is, however, also possible with the presupposition that the Songs are a
separate, even a late addition in the book, as with van Oorschot, *Von Babel zum Zion*, 189–96, who
sees the Servant as Israel, his mission directed to the peoples.

no obvious connection with it.[41] If at all, it is the promises in the framing verses that the Servant would be exalted which are remembered; these can be readily transferred to the Servant Israel,[42] unlike the references to suffering in the central part which are our main topic in this article.[43] And where this is the case,[44] we have to do with scattered allusions to the wording of single sentences without catching the sense of the whole. What one can say is perhaps that a later group who stood behind Isaiah 66:1–4 (5) and regarded themselves as the true 'bdym (65:13–16) interpreted their own situation in the light of the persecuted 'bd and might therefore have inserted Isaiah 52:13–53:12 at its present place.[45] It seems as if K. Koch was right in maintaining that it was not understood until the time of the New Testament.

What we can do, however, is to look for parallels in the Old Testament which might have prepared the way for this deeper understanding. As we saw, the cultic sphere does not contain the soil in which these ideas could grow, for the pictures we meet are taken from daily life outside the cult. Closer to the ideas of Isaiah 53 is the motif of the suffering righteous. L. Ruppert more than twenty years ago published a comprehensive examination of the motif in the Old Testament and in intertestamental Judaism.[46] We can say that it belongs to the genre of the complaint

---

41. For some correspondences in Isaiah 52–54 on the level of keyword connections, see P.-É. Bonnard, *Le Second Isaïe, son disciple et les éditeurs,* EtB (Paris: Gabalda, 1972), 288; J. W. Olley, "'The Many': How Is Isa 53, 12a to Be Understood?" *Bib* 68 (1987): 350f.; and Vermeylen, "Isaïe 53," 346.

42. See Isa. 49:7; 55:5; and Kratz, *Kyros im Deuterojesaja-Buch,* 211f.; and Steck, "Gottesvolk," 65, 68ff. (on Isaiah 56–59). The same is valid for the occurrence of "servants" in the plural form, which is first mentioned in Isaiah 54:17, which — according to W. A. M. Beuken, "The Main Theme of Trito-Isaiah 'The Servant of YHWH,'" *JSOT* 47 (1990): 67 — looks back to Isaiah 53:10. The theme returns according to him also in most other passages of Trito-Isaiah in one or the other form. Beuken's view is doubtful.

43. O. H. Steck, "Beobachtungen zu den Ziontexten in Jes 51–54," 87 = *Gottesknecht und Zion,* 121, finds in Isaiah 52:7–12; 54:1, 4–8 connections to Isaiah 52:13–53:12, "because the fourth Ebed-Song is laid claim to for behavior, destiny and welfare of the innocent lady Zion," but these associations are rather far-fetched.

44. For relevant observations in Trito-Isaiah see O. H. Steck, *Studien zu Tritojesaja,* BZAW 203 (Berlin: de Gruyter, 1991), index.

45. This is the thesis of J. Blenkinsopp, "A Jewish Sect of the Persian Period," *CBQ* 52 (1990): 5–20. But it remains uncertain. Blenkinsopp himself offers the alternative that the group read the fourth Song with reference to itself, but was not responsible for inserting it (13).

46. L. Ruppert, *Der leidende Gerechte: Eine motivgeschichtliche Untersuchung zum Alten Testament und zwischentestamentlichen Judentum,* FB 5 (Würzburg: Echter, 1972); idem, *Der leidende Gerechte und seine Feinde* (Würzburg: Echter, 1973); idem, *Jesus als der leidende Gerechte?* SBS 59 (Stuttgart: Katholisches Bibelwerk, 1972). See already J. J. Stamm, *Das Leiden des Unschuldigen in Babylon und Israel,* AThANT 10 (Zürich: Zwingli-Verlag, 1946); E. Gerstenberger and W. Schrage, *Leiden:*

psalms and seems to have its origin there, though it might be asked if one of the existing samples can be dated with security in the preexilic period.[47] The suffering individual praying in such a psalm feels persecuted by his enemies, though he knows himself innocent, a righteous man. The speaker describes his suffering, asks reproachfully why he is left alone, and cries to his God for help. In the background stands the firm conviction that God will redeem the righteous believer, and often at the end of such a psalm we already find an affirmation of confidence anticipating the release. So far as we have a private person speaking here, it seems as if his suffering and his deliverance have only personal aspects. But that he can call his brothers and all fellow worshipers attending the service to join him in the praise of God (e.g., Ps. 22:23–27) shows that his salvation is not just his private experience, but a proof that the God of the whole community is present with his saving power and prepared to help whenever the righteous are persecuted and in danger. This righteous individual is exemplary for all members of the community who are obedient to God's will and faithfully "hoping in him," and there is a sort of solidarity between this individual and the whole. That God has intervened on his behalf gives the believing community the confidence that it is not left alone. In the postexilic period we find exclusive groups who call themselves the "poor," "low," and "oppressed" ones forming conventicles of a pious elite, which regard themselves as the true believers in contrast to the multitude of ordinary members of the people living in distance from their God. In this situation the solidarity seems already to have disappeared. Some reformers like Ezra and Nehemiah later tried to restore the unity of the people by administrative measures, such as obliging the assembly to obey the Torah (Nehemiah 8), to sign a covenant (Neh. 10:1ff.), and to end mixed marriages (Ezra 10:6ff.; Neh. 13:23ff.),

---

Biblische Konfrontationen (Stuttgart: Kohlhammer, 1977); D. J. Simundson, *Faith under Fire: Biblical Interpretations of Suffering* (Minneapolis: Augsburg Publishing House, 1980); Kleinknecht, *Der leidende Gerechtfertigte;* H. D. Preuss, "Die Frage nach dem Leide des Menschen—ein Versuch biblischer Theologie," in *Altes Testament und christliche Verkündigung,* Festschrift A. H. J. Gunneweg (Stuttgart: Kohlhammer, 1987), 52–80.

47. Ruppert, *Der leidende Gerechte,* 52, is prepared to reckon with an early date for Psalm 58 alone, but one has to see that the reasons given are in those cases rather subjective. According to E. Zenger, in E. Zenger et al., *Einleitung in das Alte Testament* (Stuttgart: Kohlhammer Verlag, 1995), 251, the oldest psalm collections originated in the exilic period. This seems to presuppose that at least part of the psalms were older.

but it is obvious from later developments that they were only partially successful.

A further step seems to be taken when it is the representative of the whole community who is suffering. This is the case in the royal psalms of complaint and thanksgiving (e.g., Psalms 18; 20; 21; 144). When the king is threatened, the whole community is in danger, and the foreign enemies imperil peace and even the very existence of the people. So the destiny of the king and the future of the people are closely intertwined. This connection is also visible when the whole community has to suffer punishment for the king's sin, as in the case of David's census which was castigated by the pestilence that killed seventy thousand people, according to the Deuteronomistic report (2 Sam. 24:15). It has to be remembered that individual and community belong together very closely in biblical thinking.

The prophet, too, participates in the destiny of his people in a special way. We can observe this participation in the Book of Jeremiah in the laments of the prophet. The main mission of the prophets is to proclaim Yahweh's message to the people, mostly a message of judgment. But there are also laments, which are more than a vehicle of indictment clothed in a poetic form. In some passages we find laments in the mouth of Jeremiah, in which he seems to react against the message of judgment coming from the mouth of Yahweh to be proclaimed to the people. Thus in Jeremiah 8:18, 21, 22b, 23[48] he feels personally involved in the destiny of his people and mourns its defeat. Another example is the intercession of the prophet on behalf of his people in Jeremiah 14–15, in which he speaks the communal lament (Jer. 14:2–9, 19–22).[49] In 7:16, 14:11f., and 15:1, the intercession is forbidden the prophet,[50] but this is a sign that it belonged to his normal duties. It was already G. von Rad who remarked that intercession is one of the most original functions of a prophet.[51] Intercession and lament are closely connected; they show how the prophet

---

48. See Kleinknecht, Der leidende Gerechte, 35; W. L. Holladay, Jeremiah, Hermeneia (Philadelphia: Fortress Press, 1986), 287–95. Whereas Holladay treats the speaker as the prophet Jeremiah himself, according to R. P. Carroll, Jeremiah, OTL (London: SCM Press; Philadelphia: Westminster Press, 1986), 235, it is the personified city that speaks.

49. See Holladay, Jeremiah, 421ff., esp. 426.

50. We must not decide here about the question of whether the verses are original or Deuteronomistic (so Carroll, Jeremiah, 320, on 15:1; in 14:11f. he follows a rather unlikely understanding [Jeremiah, 327]).

51. G. von Rad, "Die falschen Propheten," ZAW 51 (1933): 114.

in his office is involved in the destiny of his people. There are also passages in Jeremiah which present him as suffering for his message: Such utterances are contained in his so-called confessions,[52] which show him intently involved in his commission, in experiences with the God who sends him, with the consequences he has to bear as a messenger who has to announce bad news to his people, and with the obstinacy of his hearers, which makes the fulfillment of the menaces unavoidable. Setting aside the complicated problem of which parts of the context are possibly original words of the prophet and which Deuteronomistic framing, one could perhaps say that the "confessions" as we have them now in our Bible paint the prophet as a messenger suffering together with his message — that means suffering even with God himself, who commissioned him to deliver this announcement of destruction.[53] The narratives in Jeremiah 37–43 also show the prophet suffering because of his prophetic office; the prophet is personally involved in the failure of his message. He is shipwrecked with the shipwrecking of the word he has to proclaim in the name of God.[54] This is not vicarious suffering but it is a suffering close to the Servant's experience.

There is still another prophetic passage to be mentioned, to which W. Zimmerli directed attention nearly thirty years ago.[55] It is the symbolic act of the prophet Ezekiel described in Ezekiel 4:4–8. Originally the text spoke about Ezekiel's lying on one side for a certain time, thereby bearing symbolically the guilt of Israel. The passage interrupts the connection between two older symbolic acts signifying the siege of Jerusalem (4:1–3, 9–11), and so, it is secondary in the context. Whether it comes from the prophet himself or is a later addition by a pupil is uncertain. It parallels Isaiah 53 with the formulation in v. 5b: "And so you shall bear the punishment of the house of Israel." The exact date of origin of the passage is uncertain, but it is clear that the expanded

---

52. There is an enormous amount of secondary literature on the "confessions" of Jeremiah. For an overview see S. Herrmann, *Jeremia: Der Prophet und das Buch*, ErFor 271 (Darmstadt: Wissenschaftliche Buchgesellschaft, 1990), 129–39.

53. See also T. Polk, *The Prophetic Persona*, JSOTSup 32 (Sheffield: University of Sheffield, Department of Biblical Studies, 1984), esp. 127–62.

54. See G. Wanke, *Untersuchungen zur sogenannten Baruchschrift*, BZAW 122 (Berlin: de Gruyter, 1971), 155f.; see also Kleinknecht, *Der leidende Gerechtfertigte*, 37.

55. W. Zimmerli, "Zur Vorgeschichte von Jes 53," in Congress Volume, Rome 1968, VTSup 17 (Leiden: E. J. Brill, 1969), 236–44 = idem, *Studien zur alttestamentlichen Theologie und Prophetie*, Ges. Aufsätze II (Munich: Chr. Kaiser Verlag, 1974), 213–21.

form, differentiating between two periods for lying on both sides (390 or 40 days, representing the punishment of Israel on one side, Judah on the other side), is still younger. Zimmerli states that the use of the same formula "bear the guilt" in Ezekiel 4 and Isaiah 53 might be an indication that the picture of the suffering messenger of God stood in the background as a pattern for both passages.[56] We would then have a tradition which might actually have influenced Jesus' understanding of his own mission, earlier than the idea of the offering which became alive for the first Christians after the cross and resurrection.

There is still another passage that might be seen in the wake of Isaiah 53, though the understanding of it is totally uncertain. It is the enigmatic oracle announcing a mourning in Jerusalem over "the one whom they have pierced" (Zech. 12:10f.), a person which we cannot identify because no details are given. Maybe we are dealing with a historical figure living in the period after the reconstruction of the temple, one who was murdered. But the situation seems different from Isaiah 53, as no redemptive sense is attributed to this death. Also the terminology is completely different.

Only after all these considerations can we observe that the idea of substitution is also at the basis of offering. There are some traces in the Old Testament that originally a human offering was made in extraordinary situations (see 2 Kings 3:27, for saving the capital of Moab during a dangerous siege; possibly also in the background of Genesis 22). Later an animal could serve as a substitute for the guilty individual or community.[57] Offering the life of the animal could soothe the wrath of the deity; this is an idea widely known in the ancient world and parts of the modern world. But this whole area of religion is distant from Isaiah 53 and should not be confused with this passage.

Looking at the role of Isaiah 53 in biblical theology it can be said that its main importance did not emerge until the time of the New Testament. As M. Hengel has shown,[58] in the intertestamental period the

---

56. Steck, *Aspekte des Gottesknechts in Jes 52,13–53,12*, 56 = *Gottesknecht und Zion*, 41, n. 62, however, remarks that in Ezekiel 4 it is not said that guilt or punishment is taken away. It is not clear what the prophet or his pupils intended by the symbolic action.

57. For details of the idea of substitution in offerings, see Janowski, *Sühne als Heilsgeschehen*, 215–21.

58. M. Hengel, *Atonement.*

passage played no role.[59] That it emerged exactly then seems to be connected in my opinion to the wide range it shows in circumscribing the vicarious role of the Servant. Possibly during Jesus' own career and/or later when the early Christians tried to describe Jesus' mission it became feasible to use the mission of the Servant as an adequate type, because the loose pictorial description of the Servant's role offered a wide range of mental connections. These connections offered the insight that here was a paradigmatic sufferer, who went his way in obedience to the will of God until death, for the salvation of all. Whether Jesus himself gained this insight or his followers after the cross and resurrection I leave open for the moment — although I already have expressed my opinion on the subject.[60]

This article was meant to lead to the borders of the New Testament and not to enter into it. As a scholar specializing in the Old Testament it was my intention to cover the material that might throw light on the debate going on between New Testament scholars. This is a service we can perform to encourage progress in the field of biblical theology.

---

59. This might be restricted in the sense that later Jewish martyrology developed the idea of a connection between a violent death as a result of one's belief and resurrection. See, among others, G. W. E. Nickelsburg, *Resurrection, Immortality and Eternal Life in Intertestamental Judaism* (Cambridge: Harvard University Press, 1972); W. J. Heard, Jr., "Maccabean Martyrology" (Ph.D. diss., Aberdeen, 1987). See also D. Seeley, *The Noble Death: Graeco-Roman Martyrology and Paul's Concept of Salvation*, JSNTSup 28 (Sheffield: Sheffield Academic Press, 1990).

60. See *Epochen der Bibelauslegung* (Munich: Beck, 1990), 1:58.

3

Isaiah 53 and the Restoration of Israel

R. E. CLEMENTS

◆

It is helpful to begin by summarizing briefly some fundamental, if necessarily provisional, conclusions regarding the literary and historical setting of the four Servant passages in Isaiah 40–55. To do so in the wake of the publication of Mettinger's short essay bidding farewell to them is to suggest that he has succeeded in removing some unlikely lines of interpretation, but has done little to remove the more fundamental questions as to the significance of these passages.[1] His primary aim has been to remove from discussion the radical attempt of Bernhard Duhm to interpret these passages in historical and literary isolation from their present setting in Isaiah 40–55.[2] Yet already J. Lindblom had argued for a similar position and sought to interpret the Songs very closely in relation to their context.[3] Overall there is no doubt that the main lines of scholarship since the 1930s have been in the direction of seeking an interpretation which does not rely upon the kind of radical literary dislocation of the Songs that Duhm proposed.[4]

Some Basic Perceptions and Assumptions

We may begin by setting out the following basic perceptions:

---

1. T. N. D. Mettinger, *A Farewell to the Servant Songs: A Critical Examination of an Exegetical Axiom*, Scripta Minora (Lund: CWK Gleerup, 1983).

2. Bernhard Duhm, *Das Buch Jesaja*, Göttinger Handkommentar zum Alten Testament III, 1, 1st ed. (Göttingen: Vandenhoeck & Ruprecht, 1892, 4th ed., 1922 = 5th ed., 1968, reprinted).

3. J. Lindblom, *The Servant Songs in Deutero-Isaiah*, LUÅ, n.s., avd. 1, vol. 47, no. 5 (Lund: CWK Gleerup, 1951); idem, *Prophecy in Ancient Israel* (Oxford: B. H. Blackwell, 1962), 268ff.

4. See H. H. Rowley, "The Servant of the Lord in the Light of Three Decades of Criticism," in *The Servant of the Lord and Other Essays on the Old Testament*, 2d ed. (Oxford: B. H. Blackwell, 1965), 4–7.

1. There is no sufficient evidence to demonstrate that any of the four Servant passages needs to be ascribed to an author, or authors, different from, and chronologically separate from, the rest of Isaiah 40–55.

2. In light of this statement the degree to which these four passages are themselves to be regarded as standing significantly apart from, and therefore not directly related to, the rest of Isaiah 40–55 is questionable. In most respects their character, form, and subject matter show them to be integral to the material in these sixteen chapters. We can note in passing that recent studies have drawn attention to the links between these sixteen chapters and the earlier (chaps. 1–39) and later (56–66) parts of the book of the prophet Isaiah.[5] The extent to which this changed perspective has relevance for understanding the mission and work of Yahweh's Servant is not our immediate concern.

3. There are undoubtedly difficulties of translation, chiefly within the fourth passage (Isa. 52:13–53:12). Nevertheless the major problems of interpretation are not resolved by resort to a revised, and more radical, translation of the text, even though there are clearly significant difficulties for the translator.[6]

4. The primary problem for the interpretation of the figure of the Servant lies in the highly individual portrayal of the Servant's suffering set out in the final Song (Isa. 52:13–53:12) and the significance of this suffering for those who are identified by the use of the first-person "we" in the fourth Song.

5. Elsewhere in Deutero-Isaiah Yahweh's Servant is identified as the collective figure of Jacob-Israel (Isa. 41:8–9, Jacob/Israel; 44:1, 2 [Jacob/Jeshurun], 21, etc.). In the MT of Isaiah 49:6 the Servant is

---

5. W. A. M. Beuken, *Jesaja,* IIIA/B (Nijkerk: Callenbach, 1989); H. G. M. Williamson, *The Book Called Isaiah: Deutero-Isaiah's Role in Composition and Redaction* (Oxford: Clarendon Press, 1994); O. H. Steck, *Studien zu Tritojesaja,* BZAW 203 (Berlin and New York: de Gruyter, 1991).

6. See D. Winton Thomas, "A Consideration of Isaiah LIII in the Light of Recent Textual and Philological Study," *ETL* 44 (1968): 79–86; M. Dahood, "Phoenician Elements in Isaiah 52:13–53:12," in *Near Eastern Studies in Honor of William Foxwell Albright,* ed. H. Goedicke (Baltimore: Johns Hopkins University Press, 1971), 63–73; R. N. Whybray, *Thanksgiving for a Liberated Prophet,* JSOTSup 4 (Sheffield: JSOT Press, 1978).

addressed as "Israel," and this would support the corporate interpretation of the figure from directly within the second of the Servant passages.

This last fact, combined with a recognition of the close links between the Songs and their immediate context (Lindblom; Mettinger), would appear to be decisive for a collective understanding of the figure. Yet the textual reliability of Isaiah 49:6 does not appear to be above question, and extensive debate has hinged precisely on the issue of whether the context must be regarded as determinative for the complex portrait given in the fourth Song. In this the highly specific descriptions of suffering have led even such otherwise convinced advocates of a collective view as H. H. Rowley to recognize some fluctuation between collective and individual viewpoints.[7] We are compelled to reckon either with a remarkable compression of images of violence and injustice inflicted onto one single person, leading to his death, or to some exceptional poetic, or psychological, representation of a community's experience.

The literary background to all four passages concerning the identity of the Servant would undoubtedly support the claim that we are faced here with a figure who fulfils some form of representational collective role. Yet this leads to problems for the interpreter in understanding what kind of historical background has given rise to so impressive a picture of an individual's fate. Moreover, it leaves open many details regarding what precisely has happened to the Servant and how his fate is understood to benefit the onlookers, who are themselves not more fully identified. To a considerable extent the mystery of the Servant's identity is closely intertwined with the questions of the identity of those for whom his sufferings bring deliverance and of how his death can deliver the onlookers from guilt and disease (Isa. 53:4–5). What is implicit in the affirmation that his sufferings are counted as an "offering for sin" (Heb. 'ašam; Isa. 53:10)?

The claim that the sufferings endured by an individual are effective in bringing healing and forgiveness to a larger group is what lends the portrait of the Servant much of its uniqueness. The very notion of sacrificial offering is brought directly into the human sphere and incorporated into

---

7. Rowley, "The Servant of the Lord in the Light of Three Decades of Criticism," 51–60.

the understanding of how human experiences, which have no overt cultic intention, may yet be cultically efficacious.

What we are faced with therefore in the task of interpretation is understanding how the individual role of the Servant can link the distinctively personal experiences which are ascribed to him with the corporate identity of the Servant-Israel. There is evidently some degree of differentiation between the Servant and the community he serves, even though they share much of an inherited Servant imagery. The solution would appear to lie in a recognition that one leading figure in a community may serve as its representative, so that he, or she, may at times be wholly identified with it, while at other times standing out in opposition to it.

Individual and Collective Interpretations

By looking at certain representational roles in other areas of Hebrew literature we may hope to find some explanation for the fluctuation between the experience of the individual and the community which appears in the Songs. In this fluctuation the fate of one individual in some way both embodies, yet redeems, the fate of the larger group. We might have been tempted to conclude that all we are encountering is a very extended and forceful use of a literary figure of speech in which the group is personified. This would then make the text a close parallel to the description of the fate of Babylon which the prophet describes in terms of the humiliation and abuse inflicted on a well-brought-up young woman (Isa. 47:1–15). Yet few scholars have found such a literary explanation convincing, since, in the fourth Servant Song, the individual experience appears too exceptional, and the details of the suffering too precise, for a straightforward poetic device to have led to its creation. Some deeper ideological or institutional understanding of an individual's representative role appears to underlie the portrait of the suffering of the Servant in this passage.

Three major fields of ancient Israel's traditions have suggested themselves. We shall then look, in turn, at the roles of kingship, prophecy, and the Deuteronomic portrait of Moses, all of which appear to have some useful parallels and features by which the portrait of the suffering

Servant may be understood. Before doing so, however, it is as well that we should remove from the discussion what appears largely to have been a false trail in the path of exegesis. This relates to the attempt, most closely associated with the name of H. Wheeler Robinson,[8] to accept that Israelite thinking displayed a characteristic so fundamentally different from our own that the individuality of a person was merged into that of the group to which he or she belonged.[9] This could be described as a concept of "corporate personality" and was held to be a manifestation of "primitive thinking." It based itself upon the suggestions of L. Lévy-Bruhl and a related school of anthropologists and rested on a theory about the nature of self-awareness and self-identity in the thought world of antiquity.[10]

From both the anthropological and theological perspectives, a claim that people of antiquity embraced a fundamentally different mode of thinking from our own cannot be sustained.[11] To a degree the very concept of community representation is at issue here, since awareness of a fundamental distinction between the individual and the group was important for an understanding of how the group could be set under the authority and power of a representative leader. Although the theory of "corporate personality," as applied to the Hebrew Bible, had the merit of drawing attention to the way in which social groups could share a common interest and feel a sense of a shared destiny, it erred by seeking to explain this characteristic by a different psychology. It assumed that primitive communities suffered from blurred and poorly defined perceptions, rather than recognizing that different communities experienced differing pressures which controlled the interaction between the group and the individual. As a way of drawing attention to the varied social forces at work in a community the idea had a certain value, but as a claim that a different kind of mentality was the cause it resorted to implausible theorizing.

---

8. See H. Wheeler Robinson, *Corporate Personality in Ancient Israel*, rev. ed. with a new introduction by C. S. Rodd (Edinburgh: T. & T. Clark, 1981), 37–41; originally published as "The Hebrew Conception of Corporate Personality," in *Werden und Wesen des Alten Testaments*, ed. P. Volz, F. Stummer, and J. Hempel, BZAW 36 (Berlin: A. Töpelmann, 1936).

9. Robinson, *Corporate Personality in Ancient Israel*, 32–34.

10. See J. W. Rogerson, *Anthropology and the Old Testament* (Oxford: B. H. Blackwell, 1978), 46–65.

11. See Rogerson, *Anthropology and the Old Testament*, 55–56.

The Royal Servant

We may turn then to consider the institution of kingship as a background to the Servant Songs. In general, the Book of the prophet Isaiah,
to a greater degree than any other book in the canon, is deeply affected
by questions relating to the Davidic kingship.[12] I. Engnell, in an original
adumbration of the theory that royal features, largely connected with the
ritual function of the king, had been woven into the portrait of the Servant of Yahweh, drew heavily upon aspects of the Mesopotamian royal
cultus.[13] This heavy dependence upon supposed ancient Near Eastern
parallels cast a shadow of uncertainty over such an interpretation. Yet
O. Kaiser has been able to explore a more distinctively Israelite development of the notion that kingly traits color the portrayal of the Servant
and his experience.[14]

One strong reason for thinking of such a royal background to the
portrait of the Servant lies in the fact that, of all the institutional personages of ancient Israelite society, the divinely chosen and appointed
king appears to have exercised most strongly a representative function on
behalf of the nation.[15] Insofar as early Israel gave voice to an ideology
of the state, it did so in terms of claims of royal divine election. Nor is
there any doubt that the issue of the divinely elect status of the Davidic
dynasty was a central issue which served to shape the early prophetic
pronouncements of the prophet Isaiah.[16]

In a closely connected manner it is evident that the disasters of the last
days of the kingdom of Judah, which initiated the period of the Babylonian exile, fell particularly heavily upon the representatives of the Davidic
royal line. The tragic fates which befell in succession Josiah, Jehoahaz, Jehoiakim, Jehoiachin, and his uncle Zedekiah occupy a prominent place in
prophecy and contributed to the confusion and horror at Judah's down-

12. See A. Laato, *Who Is Immanuel? The Rise and the Foundering of Isaiah's Messianic Expectations*
(Åbo, Finland: Åbo Academy Press, 1988); P. D. Wegner, *An Examination of Kingship and Messianic
Expectation in Isaiah 1–35* (Lewiston, N.Y.: Edward Mellen Press, 1992).

13. I. Engnell, "The '*Ebed* Yahweh Songs and the Suffering Messiah in Deutero-Isaiah," *BJRL*
31 (1948): 54–93.

14. O. Kaiser, *Der königliche Knecht: Eine traditionsgeschichtlich-exegetische Studie über die Ebed-
Jahwe-Lieder bei Deuterojesaja*, FRLANT 70 (Göttingen: Vandenhoeck & Ruprecht, 1959).

15. S. Mowinckel, *He That Cometh: The Messiah Concept in the Old Testament and Later Judaism*,
trans. G. W. Anderson (Oxford: B. H. Blackwell, 1956).

16. See R. Kilian, *Die Verheissung Immanuels, Jes 7,14*, Stuttgarter Bibelstudien 35 (Stuttgart:
Katholisches Bibelwerk, 1968).

fall. That there took place a period of anxious reflection is highlighted by the extraordinarily high expectations which, in the face of all the facts of experience, still clung to these last representatives of a discredited and failing institution. This tension between the traditional expectations surrounding Judah's prestigious royal family and the experienced realities of history are to be seen both in prophecy and in the guarded, and seemingly contradictory, implications of the Deuteronomic reporting of the end of the monarchy (2 Kings 25:27–30).

It is wholly plausible that the fate of such kingly figures should have provoked deep spiritual reflection in the mind of a prophetic herald seeking to make sense of the events which overtook the last representatives of Judah's long-surviving royal dynasty. In particular the experience of Jehoiachin, in his prolonged Babylonian imprisonment, must have given cause for thinking afresh about the divine significance of such a fate. From within the Deutero-Isaianic corpus of material the enigmatic pronouncement of Isaiah 55:3–5 concerning the future of the Davidic dynastic promise is itself more than a little ambiguous concerning the significance of this piece of political theology for the renewal of Israel.

So the fate of Judah's last kings, when linked to the hope of restoring one of the surviving royal heirs to a major position in a renewed Israel, could well have exercised a formative role in shaping the figure of the suffering Servant. Royal personages had suffered grievously at the hands of their Babylonian enemies, and yet the dynasty had not been totally eclipsed. It could indeed be regarded as both stricken and abused, yet replete with hope that it would "prolong its days" and "see his offspring" (Isa. 53:10). If this is the case, then the conventional ideology in which the king embodied the hopes and divine blessing which were promised to the nation more generally can be readily understood. For many the idea of a restored independent nation without a king must have appeared an impossibility.

The Servant as Prophet

The second line of interpretation that has provided a strong basis for the fluctuation between the individual and the collective features of the Songs is to be found in the role of prophecy, and of particular prophets, within the life of Israel as a community. Already the Deuteronomic pre-

sentation of prophecy set out in 2 Kings 17:23 views the prophet as a
rejected figure who has spoken the truth from God, but who has been
refused a responsive hearing. Already we are well on the road toward
recognition of the prophet as a martyr figure who suffers for the truth.
Moreover, in the written collection of the canonical prophets each is
firmly presented as one who addresses the nation of Israel in its entirety.
He stands between God and the nation so that even the lines of political
demarcation between Judah and Israel become more than a little blurred.

The use of the autobiographical first-person form in the second and
third Songs, and to a more limited extent in the fourth also, strongly
points toward accepting that the experiences of individual prophets,
and most emphatically of that prophet whom we have come to know
as Deutero-Isaiah, have heavily influenced the Servant's portrait in the
fourth Song.[17] By this time it certainly appears that a sufficiently strong
pattern had become established among prophetic circles which viewed
the true prophet as a rejected and oppressed figure. This pattern has
markedly shaped the presentation of the call narrative of Isaiah 6:1–13
which has, in turn, exercised a far-reaching influence across the remainder of the book. The prophet speaks God's truth, but is refused a hearing
and becomes mocked and despised by those whom he addresses. Yet he
knows in advance that he will be rejected, mocked, and set aside by
the audience, and they, in turn, are hardened in their rebellion against
God. They become blind and deaf (see Isa. 42:18–20; 43:8), whereas the
prophet becomes isolated and outcast (see Isa. 8:11–15) until such time
as the judgment falls.

This interpretive pattern has certainly colored the presentation in Jeremiah, in which the impossibility that the prophet could fulfill any role
as intercessor and deliverer in the manner of Moses or Samuel is emphatically stressed (Jer. 15:1). We know almost nothing of the details of
experiences which befell the author of Isaiah 40–55, but the preserved
record of such a prophet as Jeremiah indicates that suffering and rejection could become a necessary accompaniment of a prophet's work,
leading ultimately to the eventual renewal of the community. A major
impulse toward the preservation of a written, and ultimately canonical,
collection of prophecies foretelling judgment on Israel lay in the experi-

---

17. Mowinckel, *He That Cometh*, 248–53; Whybray, *Thanksgiving for a Liberated Prophet*, 79–92.

ence of rejection and isolation which befell the major prophets who had foretold Israel's and Judah's downfall. These experiences gave rise to the idea of the true prophet as a martyr figure.

Yet the prophet remained an individual, and it still remains difficult to understand how the variety of misfortunes and ignominies heaped upon the suffering Servant, according to the fourth Servant Song, could have befallen one single person. We should be led to think of the experiences of several prophets being poetically brought together and vested into one typified "ideal" prophet. But such a line of interpretation does not help much in clarifying how the prophet could suffer at the hands of his people, be rejected by them, and yet, at the same time, recognize that his sufferings avail to bring them deliverance. The language employed in the fourth Song draws heavily upon cultic rites which go beyond what might typically have been regarded as the role of a prophet (so especially v. 10). Even the language of intercession, and the intercessory role accorded to the prophet in the Songs, appears insufficient to account for the declaration that the surrendered life of the Servant may serve as a "sin-offering" (Heb. *'asam*).

Moses and the Servant

There does, however, remain a central figure of Israelite tradition whose portrait in the biblical literature combines a significant number of kingly and prophetic features. This fact at least suggests that the undoubtedly unique figure of the suffering Servant was not without biblical parallel. The exilic age, after the debacles of 598 and 587 B.C.E., led to a profound magnification of the role of Moses in the formation of Israel as a nation (so the Deuteronomic literature generally, but most especially Deuteronomy 1–11; 29–34). The influence of G. von Rad has reawakened interest in the influence of the historical figure of Moses upon the portrait of the Servant of the Lord in Isaiah 40–55.[18]

That some connection existed was adumbrated, but later abandoned, by Ernst Sellin.[19] The suggestion proposed here is not that a direct intention existed to use the historical traditions about Moses as the prototype

---

18. G. von Rad, *Old Testament Theology*, vol. 2: *The Theology of Israel's Prophetic Traditions*, trans. D. M. G. Stalker (Edinburgh and London: Oliver & Boyd, 1965), 261–62.

19. Rowley, "The Servant of the Lord in the Light of Three Decades of Criticism," 10–11.

for the suffering Servant, but rather that essentially the same theological concerns which helped to shape the Deuteronomic portrayal of Moses have shaped those of the suffering Servant. More precision is devoted to showing Moses as a righteous individual who stood over against his people, yet who nevertheless suffered with them and on their account. Thereby this portrait could undoubtedly lead to the idea that the death of the righteous one was made necessary by the unrighteousness of the many. At the same time this signal experience of injustice could achieve renewal and sanctification, which made such a death a "sin-offering." The argument hinges firmly on recognizing that such an offering became necessary as a means toward restoring the holiness of the community, rather than serving as legal substitution of one victim for another.[20]

From a historical and literary perspective it is all too easy to overlook the extent to which the record and presentation of the person and work of Moses occurred relatively late in the development of Israelite historiography. All the indications appear to be that the earliest drafts of the so-called Deuteronomic History began in typical ancient Near Eastern fashion as a hagiographic type of royal chronicle. Then, in a major recasting, the hagiographic royal annals which celebrated the rise and authority of the royal house of David were transformed into a chronicle of the Mosaic origins of the nation of Israel and its steady fall from grace as progressive generations flouted the laws which Moses had given. The hero-kings became villains and a new mysterious and all-commanding superhero was introduced as the lead figure of the entire story. This figure was Moses.[21]

Both the introduction to the Deuteronomic law and its epilogue place the most exceptional degree of emphasis upon the role of Moses, recasting and enlarging upon two aspects of the earlier tradition which had previously appeared incidental. This is all the more surprising in view of the almost total absence of Moses from the central Deuteronomic law code in chapters 12–26. It is significant that the sole reference to him in this code comes only implicitly in the regulations governing prophecy (Deut. 18:15–22).

---

20. See the objections to such an idea expressed in Whybray, *Thanksgiving for a Liberated Prophet*, 29ff.

21. See G. W. Coats, "Legendary Motifs in the Moses Death Reports," *CBQ* 39 (1977): 34–44; idem, *Moses: Heroic Man, Man of God*, JSOTSup 57 (Sheffield: JSOT Press, 1988).

In the introduction to the code the foremost feature of the role ascribed to Moses is that of the greatest and most efficacious of the intercessors who had intervened with God on Israel's behalf. He had thereby rescued the nation from certain judgment and oblivion by putting his own life on the line and surrendering even his own hope of survival in order that Israel might be spared.[22]

A second, and even more surprising, feature is the emphasis placed in Deuteronomy upon Moses as the victim who, on account of Israel's rebelliousness, was denied the privilege of participation in the nation's entry into the promised land. He had to die, having seen the land, but without having set foot upon a single meter.

This portrait of Moses as intercessor and victim has certainly arisen in the light of the events that befell Judah in the first half of the sixth century B.C.E. The fate of the nation's leader is a fate with which others can identify and in which they may see some of their own misfortunes mirrored. Clearly the motif of Israel's rebelliousness has passed through various interpretive stages, but, in its Deuteronomic expression, is used to highlight the innate untrustworthiness of Israel's claims to loyalty.[23] The nation appears as irretrievably immersed in faithless self-doubt and complacent self-deception. Only Moses stands apart, to the extent that God offers to build a new nation from this one figure alone! Yet this cannot be, since Moses has committed himself wholly to the Israel that exists, with all its wayward tendencies.

The most surprising, and theologically unexpected, feature of this heroic and grand action on the part of Moses lies in the tradition which insists that, in spite of his courageous faith, Moses must die outside the promised land, in the same manner that the generation which had listened to the demoralizing warnings of the spies had had to perish. The one concession granted to Moses is that he should at least view the land from afar (Deut. 32:52).

So in the Deuteronomic portrait of Moses it is not only the guilty who must perish in the fires of judgment, but many of the innocent. It undoubtedly appeared to many that "the way of the LORD is unfair"

22. E. Aurelius, *Der Fürbitter Israels. Eine Studie zum Mosebild im Alten Testament*, ConBOT 27 (Stockholm: Almqvist & Wiksell, 1988), 41ff.

23. G. W. Coats, *The Murmuring Motif in the Wilderness Traditions of the Old Testament: Rebellion in the Wilderness* (Nashville: Abingdon Press, 1968).

(Ezek. 18:25). The very arbitrariness and unreality of Ezekiel's doctrine of the individual's freedom to repent (Ezek. 18:23) draws attention to this sense of grievance. Misfortune not only befell the wicked, but struck out aimlessly and mercilessly in many directions.

All the greater interest attaches therefore to the unexpected epilogue to the Song of Moses, which generally emphasizes the justness of the doctrine of retribution. God addresses Moses with a harsh and unexpected judgment:

> You shall die there on the mountain that you ascend and shall be gathered to your kin, as your brother Aaron died on Mount Hor and was gathered to his kin; because both of you broke faith with me among the Israelites at the waters of Meribath-kadesh in the wilderness of Zin, by failing to maintain my holiness among the Israelites. (Deut. 32:50–51)

The reason given is surprising, since it draws upon the conceptual field of holiness and the cult, which is quite distinct from the juridical ideas of retributive justice.[24] In spite of his successful intercessory role, Moses fell victim to the nation's sin in that he too had failed to maintain the divine holiness among the people. Sin in such a field of thinking was not simply an individual's failure, but a community experience which had consequences that could not be averted. The innocent were drawn into suffering along with the guilty. Kaminsky rightly draws attention to the fact that it is a more willful and glaring sin, carrying similar consequences, which is highlighted as the offense of the unfortunate Achan in Joshua 7. The rules concerning warfare appear only at the edge of the action which brought destruction upon Achan and his entire family. His behavior had disrupted and nullified the holiness which served as a protective envelope upholding Israel. When the envelope was intact, Israel could expect to receive remarkable divine blessings and victories. However, when the rules of holiness were broken, the divine power was believed to be withdrawn, and dire consequences ensued.

In the light of this perspective we can understand why it was important that the sufferings of the Servant of Yahweh in Isaiah 53 should act as an *'ašam* — a sin-offering. That the context is drawn primarily from

---

24. J. S. Kaminsky, *Corporate Responsibility in the Hebrew Bible*, JSOTSup 196 (Sheffield: Sheffield Academic Press, 1995).

cultic ideas and imagery is already indicated by the assertion that the Servant delivers the community (indicated by "us," "we," and "our" in Isa. 53:3–5) from "diseases" and "infirmities" (v. 4) besides "transgressions" and "iniquities" (v. 5).

The entire experience of defeat and exile had sentenced Israel to "die among the nations in an unclean land" (see Amos 7:17). Only by recovering its status as a "holy nation" (Exod. 19:5f.) could there be a renewal of life and a recovery of a life-giving relationship with Yahweh as God. Yet the very agency and means by which holiness had, in past years, been assured to Israel, namely, the temple of Yahweh in Jerusalem, had been destroyed and rendered ineffective. Without the temple there could be no sin-offering to guarantee the continuance of a holy relationship to Yahweh. The ravages of guilt and disease, understood as the threats and misfortunes from which divine holiness brought deliverance, could no longer be held at bay. Yet now Deutero-Isaiah introduces his boldest of assertions, that God will accept the sufferings of the Servant-Israel, perhaps largely focused on the specific sufferings of the unnamed prophet himself, as the 'ašam by which the restored nation will be purified.

Two passages from the Book of Ezekiel enable us to grasp this background of cultic ideas which have served to shape the language. The first is in Ezekiel 11:16, where the prophet insists that, during the period in which Israel was threatened with the uncleanness of the lands and countries into which they had been driven, God himself would be "a sanctuary for a little while." The language is vague and indeterminate. It amounts to an assertion that God would make a unique, though temporary, provision for those Judeans who had been driven into foreign lands, into a realm of danger and uncleanness. There they were no longer under the umbrella of holiness that the temple had secured for them when they had been in Jerusalem. God had withdrawn the presence of the divine glory from the temple and left it to its destroyers, but for those driven far off into strange lands, a temporary sanctifying presence of God would be granted.

The second passage occurs as Ezekiel looks ahead to the time when these scattered former members of Israel will return out of the unclean lands into which they had been taken to live in their own land. There God would "sprinkle clean water" upon them in order to remove all the uncleannesses with which they had been tainted during their years of

exile (Ezek. 36:25). Although the cultic imagery differs from that of Isaiah 53, the underlying ideas are essentially the same as in Isaiah 53:10:
God will make special provision to restore the survivors of Israel to the
status of a holy nation. The land would again become holy as traditional
assertions had claimed before the disasters of 587 B.C.E.

Seen in such light the flow of imagery and ideas in Isaiah 53 is wholly
coherent and consistent, so that the uniqueness of the idea that a human
life could serve as a sin-offering belongs within the context of Israel's
need again to become a holy people. Since there could be no authorized
sin-offering by which the people could be protected from sin and disease
while the Jerusalem temple lay in ruins with its altars desecrated, Yahweh
would make special provision. The sufferings of Servant-Israel would be
the offering by which the relationship of all the scattered nation with
Yahweh would be renewed. Israel would once again be returned to the
sphere of blessing and divine protection, which its own sins had nullified
in the past. Just as a sin-offering was needed so that Aaron could be con-
secrated to the office of high priest, so the sufferings of Israel among the
nations would count as an offering that the ruined temple in Jerusalem
could no longer provide.

Much of the difficulty concerning the idea of vicariousness has arisen
on account of a rigid preoccupation with juridical notions and the attempt to understand the language of Isaiah 53 against a background of
legal practice. Against such the language appears both alien and strained.
Yet once the language is understood in its proper cultic setting it makes
excellent sense. Plunged into the uncleanness of living among the nations, Israel could do little to escape the threat posed by disease and guilt.
Yet without the temple cultus to make atonement to remove the effects
of such guilt, Israel appeared helpless and faced an impossible dilemma.
Guilt-ridden and threatened by disease, it had no avenue through which
to secure atonement, since unauthorized offerings would simply have
added to the nation's disobedience. Now in this remarkable prophetic
insight, Isaiah 53 asserts God's unique resolution. Until the regular sin-
offerings could be restored, the Servant-Israel's own suffering among the
nations would be the sin-offering by which that nation's guilt would be
cleansed and its diseases carried away.

The incident in Acts 8:26–40 in which the Ethiopian eunuch alludes
to Isaiah 53:7–8 quite correctly understands the concern of the Isaianic

context with uncleanness and the threat of alienation. The Ethiopian was doubly excluded from the cultic community of ancient Israel on account of his physical defect (Deut. 23:1) and his Ethiopian origin (see Isa. 45:14). Yet the context adumbrated the promise of a new path to holiness and wholeness which the eunuch deeply coveted. Philip then shows that this renewal had now become possible and real through the death of Jesus and proceeded immediately to lead the eunuch to Christian baptism. The eunuch's uncleanness and alienation were removed. It seems impossible that, both in the original Isaianic setting and in that of Acts 8:26–40, before the beginning of the Christian mission to the Gentiles, the importance of a larger cultic background was not intentionally being drawn upon. God had provided a new form of sin-offering through the sufferings of a righteous Servant, by which uncleanness could be removed.

As to the identity of the Servant in Isaiah 53 the fundamental issues that we noted at the outset of this survey still remain. These concern the seeming fluctuation between the collective identification of the Servant of the Lord, in association with such titles as Israel and Jeshurun, and detailed description of the fate of an individual prophet-teacher. On this issue it certainly appears that we must accept and accommodate such fluctuations and tensions without destroying, or denying, the reality of both aspects. An individual may embody and represent the destiny of a nation, as we see in the Deuteronomic emphasis upon the representative role of Moses, the obedient leader who nevertheless suffers along with his people. The overall balance of the four Servant Songs, however, points strongly in the direction of some form of typified collective identification of the Servant as those Israelites who had been forced to suffer in exile. Their fate was the fate of individuals, yet also, in a real sense, they embodied the fate of a nation, since the central thrust of Isaiah 40–55 appears designed to uphold the claims of those taken into exile to be the true and faithful Israel.

The second issue, concerning the sense in which the sufferings of the Servant are understood to be vicarious and to bring deliverance to the community he represents, can be answered more adequately. Once the proper cultic background to the language is understood, then the supposed difficulties of the concept of vicariousness recede.

In what sense can a human being remove the sins of a community?

Just as the Deuteronomic history treats the death of Moses as an action which had become necessary because of Israel's sins in the wilderness, so the Servant suffers both for, *and with*, the community he represents. Moses too had done no less. The shared background of ideas in Isaiah 53:10 and Deuteronomy 32:50–51 consists of notions of holiness and wholeness by which a community is protected. Those, like Achan, who threaten that holiness must suffer for what they have done.[25] Yet Moses, too, even though he had challenged the disobedience which Israel chose to pursue, became a victim of the broken holiness which resulted. Since there had to be a sin-offering to effect restoration once the holiness of the people was infringed, Isaiah 53 insists that the Servant's misfortunes will provide that essential offering.

Conclusion

That the imagery of a suffering Servant whose misfortunes lead to redemption and eventual triumph has a complex origin should not occasion surprise. In a number of respects the notion lacks precise definition, and it represents a confluence of imagery and ideas embracing both prophetic and cultic traits. Nevertheless, comparison with the near-contemporary development of the redrawn portrait of Moses as intercessor and national leader (Deut. 9:6–29, 32:48–52) and with the insistence in Ezekiel that Israel must be washed from the uncleanness of its existence in exile provides a rewarding fresh understanding. God provides the very sin-offering by which Israel can be healed, cleansed, and forgiven.[26]

---

25. Kaminsky, *Corporate Responsibility in the Hebrew Bible*, 67–95.

26. For more information see O. Eissfeldt, "The Promises of Grace to David in Isaiah 55:1–5," in *Israel's Prophetic Heritage: Essays in Honor of James Muilenburg*, ed. B. W. Anderson and W. Harrelson (London: SCM Press, 1962), 196–207; P. D. Hanson, *Isaiah 40–66*, Interpretation Commentaries (Louisville: Westminster/John Knox Press, 1995); C. Houtman,"De dood van Mozes, de knecht des Heren: Notities over en naar aanleiding van Deuteronomium 34:1–8," in *De Knecht: Studies rondom Deutero-Jesaja, dooe collegas en oud-leerlingen aangeboden aan Prof. Dr. J. L. Koole* (Kampen: J. H. Kok, 1978); D. T. Olson, *Deuteronomy and the Death of Moses: A Theological Reading*, Overtures to Biblical Theology (Minneapolis: Fortress Press, 1994); and J. W. Rogerson, "The Hebrew Conception of Corporate Personality: A Re-examination," *JTS*, n.s., 21 (1970): 1–16.

4

On Reading Isaiah 53
as Christian Scripture

Roy F. Melugin

I am honored to be asked to contribute an essay in this volume — a volume which was stimulated by the Baylor colloquy on Isaiah 53 and Christian origins. I share enthusiastically the conviction of most presenters at the conference that Isaiah 53 is of importance to a Christian understanding of the vicarious suffering of Jesus. Yet it seems to me that the conference's tendency to limit itself to the impact of Isaiah 53 on Christian *origins*, as intellectually legitimate as that concern may be, perpetuates a hermeneutic which is unnecessarily restrictive in the use of Isaiah 53 for the upbuilding of the life of the Christian community.

Questions such as the following appear to me to be much too limited: Did Isaiah 53 shape the self-consciousness and the understanding of the personal calling of the historical Jesus? Or did that connection originate in the early church after the time of Jesus? To what extent are New Testament affirmations of the vicarious nature of Jesus' death clearly shaped by Isaiah 53? Questions such as these are extraordinarily difficult to resolve — so difficult indeed that there may never be anything like a scholarly consensus as to their answer. If this is true, how can we realistically expect pastors to follow this scholarly discussion and to benefit for the sake of the nourishment of their flock? How fruitful for the life of the church is a hermeneutic far too esoteric for pastors to use? Furthermore, I ask, is a hermeneutic so singularly focused on *origins* sufficient for dealing with the possible use of Isaiah 53 for the enrichment of the church? Are there other hermeneutical approaches which deserve serious consideration?

I should like to propose a hermeneutic rather different from the one
underlying much (if not most) of the Baylor colloquy — a hermeneutic which I believe would better serve the church in its use of Isaiah 53
as Christian scripture. As much as I respect the scholars who operate
primarily with the historical-critical paradigm, it appears to me that we
cannot move very far forward in using scripture to nourish the church
if our discipline remains committed almost exclusively to a paradigm
with origins in the Enlightenment and centered on what texts meant
in their original settings. Although I would not for the slightest moment doubt the continuing value of historical criticism for theologically
oriented biblical interpretation, I do *not* think that it should remain the
primary interpretive paradigm. Indeed, as I shall argue, other interpretive
paradigms can enrich us greatly in the reading of Isaiah 53 as Christian
scripture. It is to some of these hermeneutical issues that I turn.

I

Let me begin with some simple observations from the reading of Isaiah
52:13–53:12 (hereafter called Isaiah 53 for brevity). The poem opens
with someone speaking about "my servant" (52:13–15). Undoubtedly it
is Yahweh who speaks. Yahweh promises that the Servant will be lifted
up and made high. Many nations will be startled,[1] and kings will shut
their mouths. For they will see what had not been told to them, and they
will understand what they had not heard.

Then a group, calling themselves "we," begins to speak: "Who has believed what we have heard? And to whom has the arm of Yahweh been
disclosed?" (53:1). Then the "we-group" begins to talk about a "he": "For
he grew up before *him* like a young plant, like a root out of dry ground"
(53:2). Are the "we" saying that "he" (the Servant) grew up before "him"
(Yahweh) like a young plant? Or do these third-person singulars have
different referents? It is by no means easy to tell. In any event, the "we"
say that "he" had no "form" or "splendor" that "we" should look at "him"
or beauty that "we" should desire "him" (53:2). "He" was indeed despised and rejected. But, says the "we-group," "he" has borne (*nś'*) "our"

---

1. See the discussion in David Clines, *I, He, We, and They: A Literary Approach to Isaiah 53*,
JSOTSup 1 (Sheffield: JSOT Press, 1976), 14.

sickness, carried (*sbl*) "our" pains. All "we" like sheep have gone astray, "we" have turned, each one, to his own way, and Yahweh has made fall on "him" the iniquity (*'āwôn*) of "us" all.

There are many questions which could be asked: Who is the Servant? Israel? Remnant Israel? Israel of the future as opposed to Israel of the past? A prophet? The prophet Deutero-Isaiah? A revivified figure of the past, such as Moses? Who are the "we"? The gentile kings? Israel? Is the Servant as *'āšām* a "guilt offering"? Or does *'āšām* refer to a noncultic responsibility to discharge guilt? Does the language about the Servant's grave refer to a literal death, or have we to do with metaphor?

I shall not attempt to answer these questions here, partly because the language of Isaiah 53 is too cryptic to allow for a univocal understanding of textual meaning, and partly because this is an essay dedicated to hermeneutics rather than to exegesis. Moreover, I do not consider answering such questions to be of the highest priority, for what I believe to be quite good hermeneutical reasons. A text from scripture cannot be confined to its "original meaning(s)" if it is to be used as sacred text to shape the lives of Jewish or Christian communities many generations after the text was produced. Indeed, for a biblical text to function as scripture, it must be able to speak to communities of faith in contexts quite different from the setting in which it originated.

What might it mean to read Isaiah 53 in contexts rather different from its original setting? David J. A. Clines once proposed a hermeneutic in which the language in Isaiah 53 *does* something rather than simply *talks about* something. Language does not merely *refer* to something; it *creates* a "world" which the reader is invited to enter. Isaiah 53 is not to be viewed objectively from the outside as a spectator sees but must be construed instead as articulator of a "world" in which one participates. One is not a subject speaking about an object (the text); one is rather a participant in the "world" created by the text. Thus one's life is shaped by participating in the text and its "world."[2]

When a literary work appears in the public arena, the umbilical cord is cut between the text and its producer, Clines argues.[3] Its meaning is by no means limited to whatever its author had in mind. Thus we must

---

2. Clines, *I, He, We, and They*, 53–56.
3. Clines, *I, He, We, and They*, 53–60.

be open to the multiple meanings which the use of Isaiah 53 can create. When Philip uses Isaiah 53 to preach Christ to the Ethiopian eunuch, what is involved (says Clines) is not a reapplication of a text which once had a somewhat different meaning but rather the application of "one of the vast variety of meanings which the text itself can create."[4]

Clines is moving in the right direction. Reading Isaiah 53 as Christian scripture can take place only if the text is able to have a career of its own, not completely fettered to its "original meaning" in the exile. Moreover, Clines is right in pointing to the role of Isaiah 53 in constructing a symbolic world in which believers can reside and take on their identity in relationship with God.[5] Whether the Servant, as originally understood, was or was not Israel, whether the "we" who were healed by "his" stripes were or were not originally understood to be Gentiles — questions such as these pale into relative insignificance compared with the power to which the text may be put in creating a dynamic relationship between God and people.

Yet Clines misleads us somewhat by appearing to focus almost exclusively on what the *text* does and not enough on the role of the text's users in the construction of meaning.[6] Indeed, Clines sometimes speaks as if the text were a "verbal icon"[7] which moves through time unaffected by context, as if whatever multiple meanings one might find were inherent in the *text* and *its* activity rather than in ways in which users of the text *read* it. Underneath what Clines seems to say about what the text does appear to be telltale signs of what interpreters do. When the author of the Book of Acts presents Philip as using Isaiah 53 to preach Christ, does the preaching take shape exclusively on the basis of how the *text* acts upon this first-century interpreter? Scarcely! The text of Isaiah 53 and the traditions of the early Christian community, together with the experiences of Philip (or the author of the Book of Acts) in that community, have all worked together to shape Philip's interpretation and usage of Isaiah 53. Or when Paul says that Christ "died for our sins according to the scriptures" (1 Cor. 15:3) he was not *simply* reading Isa-

---

4. Clines, *I, He, We, and They*, 53–60.
5. See also P. Ricoeur, *Essays on Biblical Interpretation* (Philadelphia: Fortress, 1980), 95–104.
6. See S. Fish, *Is There a Text in This Class? The Authority of Interpretive Communities* (Cambridge: Harvard University Press, 1980), 1–17.
7. I have borrowed this term from Ricoeur, *Essays on Biblical Interpretation*, 100.

iah 53 (if indeed Isaiah 53 was the text to which he was referring); his reading of Isaiah 53 was surely colored by church traditions about Jesus and by Paul's own experiences both in Judaism and the church. All these surely contributed to Paul's use of Isaiah 53.

Isaiah 53 must be used figuratively in the construction of a symbolic world in which the Christian community might live. As Richard Hays has so ably argued, Paul uses scripture figuratively in the life of the Christian community.[8] Paul saw the church as God's eschatological community — a community in which the promises of God were being fulfilled.[9] Figures such as Abraham prefigured the community of faith in Jesus Christ, to cite one of Hays's major examples.

The Christian community should use Isaiah and Isaiah 53 in such a fashion. Obviously the Christian community can see Jesus Christ *prefigured* in the nameless Servant of Isaiah 53. The Christian community can quite appropriately see the Servant's stripes as the means by which "we all" are healed (Isa. 53:5), and see them as prefigurative of Jesus Christ. The assertion that "all we like sheep have gone astray" but that God had laid on the anonymous Servant the "iniquity of us all" can also be read as prefiguration of Christ Jesus. The depiction of the nameless Servant led speechless to a lamb's slaughter (Isa. 53:7) may too be read as prefiguration of Christ. That the Servant had a grave (53:9) and that he is lifted up (52:13) may also be read as prefiguration of Christ. Indeed, Isaiah 53, with all of its rich imagery, may be read as an elaborate prefiguration of Jesus Christ. Of course such meanings were not current in ancient Israel in the sixth, fifth, or fourth centuries B.C.E.; they are readings of Isaiah 53 which are distinctively Christian. But Christian liturgy and theology would be greatly impoverished without such uses of Isaiah 53.

Isaiah 53 need not be used exclusively christologically, however. The portrayal of the nameless Servant can also profitably be read as prefiguration of Christian disciples. Christians are taught, after all, to bear the cross. Cannot the entirety of the Christian community be seen figuratively as the Servant of Isaiah 53? Are not all Christians called upon to bear the pains of others, to suffer chastisement that makes others whole?

---

8. Richard B. Hays, *Echoes of Scripture in the Letters of Paul* (New Haven and London: Yale University Press, 1989).

9. Hays, *Echoes of Scripture in the Letters of Paul*, 105.

Are Christians not called to be willing to be led to slaughter without protest, to be cut off from the land of the living, to be stricken for the sins of others?

In the United States a large population of people were made slaves and, when freed, were oppressed by a battery of segregation laws specifying where these African Americans could eat, go to the toilet, and attend school. In 1955, when a seamstress named Rosa Parks refused to give up her seat on a bus to a white passenger, a dynamic new movement of protest began under the leadership of Martin Luther King. The protest was nonviolent; the protesters were called upon to love their oppressors. They were willing to go to jail, they were willing to be knocked to the ground with powerful fire hoses, they were willing to suffer the bombing of their homes and churches, they were willing even to be assassinated — all without violent response.

What they did fits a symbolic world constructed by using Isaiah 53 in the church. These African Americans suffered and died for the sins of their oppressors. My grandmother was a segregationist; so was my uncle. My father had tendencies in that direction. And I, who hated segregation and professed my love for African Americans, discovered to my consternation that at an unconscious level I possessed prejudices against blacks. Indeed, I came to know that these black people who had suffered and died had suffered and died for my sins.

II

I am quite aware that this is not a conventional essay in biblical studies, one revolving primarily around historical-critical method. The hermeneutic of this article is not a hermeneutic of detached, impartial explanation of textual meaning in antiquity, but rather a hermeneutic concerned with the use of scripture for personal transformation generation after generation, up to and including our own. It is indeed the thesis of this essay that interpretation and reinterpretation of scripture in the church is more basic and fundamental to the church's appropriate use of scripture than the reconstruction of original meanings in the contexts in which biblical texts were generated.

1. Let me be clear that I am profoundly appreciative of the value of

historical-critical approaches to the interpretation of the Bible. That historical criticism enables us to envision texts in their contexts in antiquity is of immense value — even for theologically minded interpreters of the Bible. *One* of the confessions Christians make, after all, is that God acts in history. Thus a method which helps us interpret biblical texts in their historical settings is of definite theological importance.

At the same time, there are distinct limitations upon what a historical-critical approach can accomplish. First of all, as I have argued at greater length elsewhere,[10] we have learned from Hayden White that historians cannot simply describe the past.[11] Historians almost always find more in their sources than they can incorporate into their reconstructions of the past; they must choose what to include and what to exclude. But their sources are at the same time not sufficiently full. As a result, each historian must bring *to* his or her narrative of the past certain perspectives from which to fill in gaps.[12] According to White, the historian must "emplot" the past by deciding the principles by which to join individual items from the historian's sources into a connected narrative whole.[13] What this means is that history writing is to a very large extent the construct of the historian and is by no means simply discovery of the past.

One faculty member's report of "what happened" at a committee meeting may differ so sharply from the report of another colleague that an outsider might wonder whether both persons were reporting the same event. It might be possible to verify or falsify aspects of these two reports of the committee meeting by appealing to the critical judgment of other persons who had attended. But it is also likely that other persons in attendance would describe many differences in the two reports as differences in perception, as different ways in which each of the two reporters "emplotted" the meeting. The two reporters may have construed the motivations of participants in the meeting differently, perhaps because they held divergent views of human nature or perhaps because they had known the other participants in different ways, or perhaps for still

---

10. R. F. Melugin, "Prophetic Books and the Problem of Historical Reconstruction," in Stephen Breck Reid, ed., *Prophets and Paradigms*, JSOTSup 229 (Sheffield: Sheffield Academic Press, 1996), 74–77.

11. Hayden White, *Tropics of Discourse: Essays in Cultural Criticism* (Baltimore and London: Johns Hopkins University Press, 1978).

12. White, *Tropics of Discourse*, 51.

13. White, *Tropics of Discourse*, 61–75.

other reasons. What is important to recognize is that even a past event in our own culture which is readily accessible to us will almost surely be construed differently by different interpreters. This means that any historical reconstruction of an event is to no small degree the creation of the historian. No matter how diligently the historian may try to filter out personal biases, his or her construal of the past event will nevertheless be shaped by that historian's culture and by that historian's own personal history.

The problem of historical reconstruction becomes even more difficult when we deal with cultures from antiquity which are quite different from our own, especially since we have available to us only a small number of sources to use in reconstructing the history of a culturally remote past. Historical-critical interpretations of Isaiah 53, for example, are usually dependent upon hypotheses about the literary history of the Book of Isaiah. We obviously lack hard data about the history of the growth of the book; thus we are reduced to theories which typically contain rather large doses of speculation. Was Isaiah 52:13–53:12 originally an independent unit of tradition,[14] or was it originally a part of its present literary context?[15] Form criticism is helpful in identifying genres, but it is less certain whether individual "genre-units" were originally independent units of tradition or whether the "genre-units" began as components of a larger body of text.[16] Such questions are extremely difficult to resolve, for we have only the tiniest bit of data which give us clear information as to how prophetic books were put together. Indeed, virtually all the hypotheses which scholars spin about the formation of prophetic books come from the fertile imagining in which the scholars themselves engage.

As far as I can see, similar difficulties exist for attempts to reconstruct the history of the formation of the Gospels. To be sure, a comparison of the Gospels shows us that the four evangelists had earlier sources, perhaps both oral and written, from which they drew. But exactly what these

---

14. See, e.g., J. Begrich, *Studien zu Deuterojesaja*, TBü 20 (Munich: Chr. Kaiser Verlag, 1963), 62–65.

15. J. Muilenburg, "The Book of Isaiah, Chapters 40–66," in *The Interpreter's Bible* (New York and Nashville: Abingdon, 1956), 5:384–93, 614–31.

16. Many years ago I argued that Isaiah 40–55 was constituted by units of speech which can be identified as to their genre. I therefore dubbed them "genre-units" (R. F. Melugin, *The Formation of Isaiah 40–55*, BZAW 141 [Berlin and New York: de Gruyter, 1976], 77–82). Whether the individual "genre-units" were originally independent units of tradition seems to me a question which is still unresolved, despite my attempts in that monograph to propose a solution.

sources were remains a matter of scholarly debate. Was Mark the earliest Gospel? The recent scholarly discussion of this issue, provoked especially by William R. Farmer, shows that the synoptic problem is by no means settled.[17] Can it ever be clearly resolved? Or are the sources too meager for settling the issue with a high degree of probability? Although I am not a New Testament scholar, my familiarity with the fragility of most redaction-historical reconstructions of texts in the Hebrew Bible suggests to me that analogous difficulties stand in the way of any permanent settlement of the debate concerning the synoptic problem.

I am also less persuaded than some (e.g., Farmer) about the prospects of recovering the historical Jesus. In his essay in this volume, Farmer considers it likely Jesus himself understood his mission in terms of Isaiah 53. He rejects the argument that Isaiah 53 and its theology of vicarious suffering came to be applied to Jesus only after his death. The narratives of the Last Supper in Matthew 26:26–34 and Mark 14:22–31 portray Jesus as having said "this is the blood of the covenant which is poured out for many for the forgiveness of sins" (Matt. 26:28)||"this is my blood of the covenant which is poured out for many" (Mark 14:24). Jesus' assertions that his blood is "poured out for many" are rooted, according to Farmer, in Isaiah 53's statements that the Servant "made bare his *nephesh* unto death" (my translation) and "bore the sin of many" (Isa. 53:12).

It is certainly plausible that these narratives about the Last Supper portray an event which actually took place. It is also plausible that Matthew 26:28 and Mark 14:24 drew upon Isaiah 53, for the affirmation that Jesus died for "many" could easily have been formulated because of what is said in Isaiah 53. Furthermore, it is quite conceivable that the Servant's giving his *nephesh* has influenced what is said in Matthew and Mark about the blood of Jesus, especially since blood was understood to carry within it the power of life.

Some of my difficulties with arguments such as Farmer's have to do with convincing myself that what is plausible is also probable. It is one thing to suppose that the Gospels preserve the memory of a supper and quite another to consider it probable that these memories have preserved an event which actually took place.[18] It is also one thing to observe

---

17. W. R. Farmer, *The Synoptic Problem: A Critical Approach* (New York: Macmillan, 1964).

18. Farmer recognizes that he is dealing with questions of probability rather than certainty. He and I differ, as best I can tell, in that he believes that it is probable that the narrative of the Last

some similarities between Isaiah 53 and what Jesus is reported as having done and said at this supper and quite another to argue that the short phrase "for many," together with the narrative's language about vicarious suffering, are adequate grounds for arguing that there is a very strong probability that Matthew 26:28 and Mark 14:24 are dependent on Isaiah 53 and that a strong theological argument can be made on the basis of that historical dependency.[19] If Farmer were arguing for reading Isaiah 53 and the Last Supper narratives *canonically*, without making arguments that Matthew 26:28 and Mark 14:24 were *generated* as a result of reading Isaiah 53, I would have no problems whatsoever. But if the argument rests on *historical* probability, I am less comfortable than Farmer in using them to make theological arguments.

2. Fortunately, we possess alternatives to historical criticism and the fragility of many of its results. What David Clines has shown is that historical-critical analysis is by no means the only, or even the most useful, approach to biblical interpretation. His insistence that language *does* something and does not simply *refer to* (or "speak about") something[20] fits in well with modern philosophical proposals about what language does.[21] When Clines argues that Isaiah 53 is not to be viewed objectively as a spectator behaves but can be used to construct a "world" in which one can live and be transformed, he follows the modern philosophy of language and its recognition that language is also performative or transformational in function rather than used primarily to represent reality. For example, the pronouncement, "I baptize you in the name of the Father, and of the Son, and of the Holy Spirit," does not explain or

---

Supper depicts an event which actually occurred, whereas I am somewhat less persuaded of the narrative's historicity. While I do not consider its historicity to be *im*probable, it seems to me that a great deal of the narrative *might* be the result of later traditioning processes.

19. I incline somewhat to the likelihood that Matthew 26:28 and Mark 14:24 (as well as Matt. 20:26–28||Mark 10:43–45 and 1 Cor. 15:1–3) were formulated on the basis of Isaiah 53, despite the fact that Matthew 26:28 and Mark 14:24 use the verb ἐκχέω ("pour out"), while Isaiah 53:12 (MT) employs the *hiphil* of ʿrh ("make bare") and the LXX of Isaiah 53:12 uses *paradidōmi* ("hand over"). Thus we must be cautious about the degree of likelihood we embrace.

20. Clines, *I, He, We, and They*, 53.

21. J. L. Austin, *How to Do Things with Words* (New York: Oxford, 1962); and J. R. Searle, *Speech Acts: An Essay in the Philosophy of Language* (Cambridge: Cambridge University Press, 1970). Clines also indicates dependence upon E. Fuchs, *Hermeneutik*, 4th ed. (Tübingen: Mohr, 1970); G. Ebeling, *The Nature of Faith* (London: Collins, 1961); R. W. Funk, *Language, Hermeneutic, and Word of God* (New York: Harper and Row, 1966); A. C. Thiselton, "The Parables as Language-Event: Some Comments on Fuchs's Hermeneutics in the Light of Linguistic Philosophy," *SJT* 23 (1970): 437–68; and idem, "The New Hermeneutic," in I. H. Marshall, ed., *New Testament Interpretation* (Exeter: Paternoster, 1976).

describe a baptism but rather *does* something, namely, *performs* a baptism. This language is indeed performative or transformational rather than representational or descriptive of reality precisely because its function is to transform a person's status by incorporating her or him into the Christian community. Commands or exhortations are also transformational in character, for their prime function is to transform behavior rather than to represent or describe reality.

When Clines contends that Isaiah 53 is a performative text whose meaning is not limited to what its author had in mind, he implies that it is a text which can be reinterpreted again and again in order that its users may *do* something with it, namely, that in new contexts they may *re*construct a "world" in which *they* may participate and find meaning for their lives. A number of years ago Walther Zimmerli argued that promises in the Bible could regularly be reinterpreted to address new circumstances.[22] Indeed, he contended, promises once fulfilled could again and again be interpreted as promises yet to be fulfilled. For example, the promise of the land, once seen as fulfilled in the days of Joshua, was reinterpreted as a promise yet to be fulfilled — in the return of the exiles from captivity in Babylon (Isa. 40:3–5), in the hopes for fulfillment following the destruction of Jerusalem in 70 c.e., and in the hopes of modern-day Jews connected with the ability to live in Palestine and to have access to the holy sites in Jerusalem's old city,[23] to mention but a few examples. Biblical promises, though originally limited to certain horizons of expectation, can readily be extended to embrace new horizons. Promises, originally focusing on one cluster of events in one period of time, are words which have performative force; they carry with them over a long history of usage a capacity to be reinterpreted. And in the periodic reinterpretation which takes place, the promises themselves are used to transform and to retransform communities of faith as they responsibly interpret promises in ways never envisioned when the promises were originally made.

Christian usage of Isaiah 53 takes place within this kind of hermeneutic. No interpretation of Isaiah which is limited to its sixth-century context can possibly be fully adequate for usage of Isaiah 53 in the Chris-

---

22. Walther Zimmerli, "Promise and Fulfillment," in *Essays on Old Testament Hermeneutics,* ed. Claus Westermann, trans. James Wharton (Richmond: John Knox, 1963), 89–122.

23. A. J. Heschel, *Israel: Echo of Eternity* (New York: Farrar, Straus, & Giroux, 1971), 5–38.

tian community. Paul Hanson's splendid reconstruction of the role of
Isaiah 40–55 in the shaping of a new symbolic world for Israelites whose
previous "world" had been shattered by the exile to Babylon is an excellent portrait of the past which can enable us to see the performative
force of the language of Isaiah 40–55 in ancient Israel (see his essay in
this volume). But we cannot regard the function of these texts in exilic
or early postexilic times as sufficient for the use of Deutero-Isaiah in
shaping the symbolic world of Christian communities.

Despite the prevalence of a historical-critical paradigm in the discussions which took place at the Baylor colloquy, nearly everyone seemed to
embrace the appropriateness of Christian reinterpretations of Isaiah 53.
Indeed, those who maintained that Jesus himself used Isaiah 53 to shape
his understanding of his own mission have in effect embraced a performative hermeneutic, whether they realize it or not; for they argue that
Jesus reinterpreted a text originally designed for an exilic or early postexilic setting when he used it to give shape to his own mission. But then,
paradoxically, they turned to a different paradigm — to a hermeneutic
devoted to the reproduction of original meaning. Their theology readily
allowed the reinterpretation of Isaiah 53 for performative purposes in the
life of Jesus, but then, inconsistently, they seemed to consider the *origin*
of the use of Isaiah 53 in interpreting the vicarious suffering of Jesus to
be of utmost theological importance. This is why they considered Morna
Hooker's more skeptical conclusions regarding the impact of Isaiah 53
on the New Testament understanding of the atoning death of Jesus to be
problematic for present-day Christian biblical theology.

I view these theological preoccupations with origins to be a product
of a hermeneutical paradigm created in the Enlightenment and not a
hermeneutic rooted in the Bible itself. As I have observed elsewhere,
the ways in which biblical books were formed shows that their authors/
redactors saw no need to point out the different settings in which the
materials they used originated.[24] Redactors of the Book of Isaiah undoubtedly realized that they were preserving words which originated in
a variety of settings different from their own, but they felt no compulsion explicitly to identify the differences in original setting. Why could

---

24. R. F. Melugin, "Figurative Speech and the Reading of Isaiah 1 as Scripture," in R. F. Melugin
and M. A. Sweeney, eds., *New Visions of Isaiah*, JSOTSup 214 (Sheffield: Sheffield Academic Press,
1996), 284–86.

they simply juxtapose these traditions and fail to inform us of their original settings? They did so, I think, because they were using language performatively. They could use and reuse those earlier traditions to construct symbolic worlds in which the life of communities of faith could be shaped and transformed in new contexts. In like manner Gospel writers could make use of earlier traditions without explicitly distinguishing between earlier and later materials in their literary product. Indeed, the hermeneutic of those who produced biblical books seems to be primarily performative or transformational in character. The compulsion to explain origins appears to be a largely unbiblical idea which came to us from the Enlightenment.

3. Let us suppose — for the sake of the argument at least — that there is not a single passage in Paul or the Gospels that clearly depends on Isaiah 53 for its understanding of the vicarious suffering of Jesus.[25] If that were to turn out to be true, we would not thereby need to conclude that Isaiah 53 could have no significant role in helping Christians gain a rich understanding of what vicarious suffering — and especially the vicarious suffering of Jesus — is all about. First of all, the Old Testament is a part of Christian scripture, and it contains powerful testimonies about God's purposes for Israel and for all humanity, including testimonies to an as yet unfinished history of salvation.

Second, there are strong family relationships between what Isaiah 53 says about vicarious suffering and what is said on that topic in the New Testament, whether the given New Testament texts explicitly cite, allude to, or even echo Isaiah 53.[26] That is to say, Isaiah 53 and all other biblical texts which speak about vicarious suffering are in the Christian *canon* of scripture, and that fact alone bids us place these texts into lively dialogue with one another.

Third, such an intertextual dialogue can be a dialogue, not simply to reconstruct historical dependencies of certain texts upon Isaiah 53, but to put them into a larger, richer *canonical* intertextual dialogue. This kind of dialogue, which does not revolve primarily around the question of origins, is to be undertaken for the performative purposes of constructing a

---

25. Although I argued above that it seems to be somewhat likely that certain NT texts were influenced by Isaiah 53 in their understanding of the vicarious suffering of Jesus, my purpose *here* is to make a *canonical* argument which disputes the *theological necessity* of asserting the influence of Isaiah 53 in the formation of NT affirmations about the vicarious suffering of Jesus.

26. For a discussion of intertextual echo, see Hays, *Echoes of Scripture in the Letters of Paul*, 29–33.

symbolic world which embraces a vision of vicarious suffering. And, in the embracing of that vision, persons even today can enter that symbolic world and reimagine or reconfigure themselves as persons who understand themselves both as having been vicariously suffered *for* through the wondrous grace of God *and* as having taken on as their calling an intention to be persons who are willing to suffer for others, that God's grace may become incarnate *in* them and their suffering.

III

I close with some reflections about the moral significance of the exegetical practices of the scholarly community. Questions about the exegetical practices of the church's biblical scholars are moral questions, because the exegetical practices in which we engage serve as role models for theological students who are the church's future pastors. I am coming more and more to believe that scholarly preoccupation with questions of redaction history and other complex problems can do a great deal to inhibit the preachers we train from using the Bible seriously in their preaching. Historical criticism often raises extremely complex and esoteric questions: Who is the Servant? Israel? An individual? Which particular individual or kind of individual? Is Isaiah 53 a part of a particular layer of redaction to be distinguished from other layers of redaction?[27] Did Jesus himself see his calling as shaped by Isaiah 53? Or does redaction history suggest that Isaiah 53 first affected the New Testament traditions only after the death of Jesus?

We in the scholarly community seem to be modeling questions such as these to be of utmost importance in our discipline. But many of these questions are much too complex for anyone but experts to deal with. Are we not in effect unintentionally sending signals to ordinary pastors that they cannot be significantly involved in the most central issues of biblical interpretation? Moreover, are not most of the complex historical-critical issues we discuss far removed from the great existential issues of life and death which pastors' flocks must deal with every day? Parishioners *are*

---

27. For a recent attempt to reconstruct the redaction history of Isaiah 40–55 and the layer to which Isaiah 53 belongs, see J. van Oorschot, *Von Babel zum Zion: Eine literarkritische und redaktionsgeschichtliche Untersuchung*, BZAW 206 (Berlin and New York: de Gruyter, 1993), 178–96.

concerned with suffering and forgiveness. But they are rarely interested in which particular layer of redaction was the first to apply the Servant's suffering to Jesus. We should indeed not be surprised that our exegetical concerns are not frequently of interest to pastors. Thus I ask: is it morally responsible for so many of our questions to be so esoteric and so far removed from important existential issues?

The hermeneutic which I have proposed here is not simplistic. It requires sophisticated skills in literary analysis to construct the kind of symbolic world I have in mind. Its accompanying performative hermeneutics are rooted in the work of Wittgenstein, Austin, and Searle. Yet if an ordinary pastor cannot play the interpretive game with the sophistication of the scholar, the game I have in mind is still not too esoteric to play. It is furthermore a game which has to do with the most fundamental questions of self-identity in the presence of God.

In sum: I am proposing a redefinition of the task of biblical scholarship in service to the church. Complex historical replication of the past as a central paradigm will not be able to resurrect the Bible as a lively and powerful revelatory text in our time. Interpretation which invites people to participate in a symbolic world shaped by imaginative biblical interpretation *can*. The task I have in mind will surely require a certain amount of historical imagination, but the most important imaginative task is to create anew a world in which the church can live and be nourished.

5

Jesus and Isaiah 53

OTTO BETZ

◆

Two Different Views

For the past fifty years, two sharply opposed views of the use of Isaiah 53 in the New Testament have been offered. Both remain quite influential. The first is well represented by the study of H. W. Wolff, "Jesaja 53 im Urchristentum,"[1] in which the author understands the ministry of Jesus against the background of the Hebrew Bible. Jesus applied to himself Isaiah's Song of the Suffering Servant. It was the will of his heavenly Father that the Son must suffer and save his people from their sins (see Matt. 1:21). H. W. Wolff supported this conclusion by pointing to passages in which Jesus alluded to Isaiah 53, such as Mark 9:12b, 31; and Luke 22:37. Most important, however, are Mark 10:45 and 14:24: "The Son of Man will give his life as a ransom for many" (see Isa. 53:10, 12); and, at the Last Supper, the statement that Jesus' covenant blood "is poured out for many" (see Isa. 53:12).[2] Following this tradition, the Jerusalem church,[3] Paul (Rom. 4:25; 10:16; 15:21; 2 Cor. 5:21; 1 Cor. 15:3),[4] and 1 Peter 2:22–25[5] proclaimed Christ's death on the cross as the fulfillment of Isaiah 52:13–53:12 (hereafter Isaiah 53).

---

1. H. W. Wolff, "Jesaja 53 im Urchristentum" (Ph.D. diss., Halle, 1942; 2d ed., Berlin, 1950; 3d ed., 1952). The fourth edition (Gießen: Brunnen Verlag, 1984) offers a valuable introduction by P. Stuhlmacher (7–11) in which further discussion and research on Isaiah 53 and its possible influence on Jesus is presented.

2. Wolff, "Jesaja 53 im Urchristentum," 55–70. H. W. Wolff brings some good arguments against the form-critical approach of R. Bultmann to the Jesus tradition in the Synoptic Gospels.

3. Wolff, "Jesaja 53 im Urchristentum," 86–92.

4. Wolff, "Jesaja 53 im Urchristentum," 93–99.

5. Wolff, "Jesaja 53 im Urchristentum," 99–103.

These argents did not convince R. Bultmann. According to him, Wolff could neither prove with certainty that Jesus identified himself with the suffering Servant, nor demonstrate that the early church and Paul interpreted the death of Christ in the light of Isaiah 53, for the influence of the fourth Servant Song can be seen in later writings only, such as 1 Peter.[6] In her famous book *Jesus and the Servant*,[7] M. Hooker, after a careful examination of the relevant New Testament passages in her own sophisticated way, has reached the same negative results and thus, independently, she confirmed the conclusion drawn by R. Bultmann.

A Constructive Approach to the Problem

I want to handle the theme "Jesus and Isaiah 53" in another way, in what I term a *constructive*, mainly *traditionsgeschichtliche*, way of expounding the scriptures: (1) In addition to the Hebrew and Greek of Isaiah 53, I shall look at the Aramaic rendering of this difficult text. (2) I shall carefully consider the speculative methods of interpretation used in this Aramaic version because Jesus and the writers of the New Testament could have dealt with Isaiah 53 in a similar way. (3) I want to examine some heretofore largely neglected statements of both Jesus and Paul in which I see allusions or echoes of Isaiah 53. (4) In this article I shall also concentrate on a topic which has not yet been dealt with in connection with Isaiah 53's use in the New Testament, namely, the term *shemū'ah* ("report") in Isaiah 53:1. Let me make a few remarks concerning this kind of constructive approach under the headings of the four-point outline just given.

1. If we are to examine the problem whether the historical Jesus really decided to follow the way of the suffering Servant, we must do so by investigating the words in which he may have made allusions to Isaiah 53. We must go behind the Greek text in our Gospels and consider both the underlying Hebrew (Masoretic) text and also the Aramaic rendering of Isaiah 53. Since Jesus also taught the people in Aramaic the *Targum Jonathan to the Prophets* must be consulted. One has to admit, however,

---

6. R. Bultmann, *Theologie des Neuen Testaments*, 5th ed. (Tübingen: Mohr, 1965), 31–33.
7. M. D. Hooker, *Jesus and the Servant* (London: SPCK, 1959).

that this Targum in its extant written form is quite late. As I shall show, however, much of its content and its way of interpreting the Hebrew original can be presupposed for both Jesus and Paul. Isaiah was a favorite prophetic book in the time of Jesus, especially because of its messianic predictions in Isaiah 1–12 and its message of comfort and joy in Isaiah 40–66. This we can see from the many texts of Qumran, especially the two Isaiah scrolls, and the 4QPesharim. In the New Testament, as well, this prophetic book is frequently quoted and alluded to. It so happens that we do not have fragments of an Isaiah Aramaic Targum from Qumran. However, Isaiah 53 was an unusual and quite difficult text with regard to both its language and its content, and we conclude that it was translated into Aramaic quite early. Moreover, its translation would have offered some kind of explanation as well; for otherwise it could not have been understood when read as a Haphtarah in the synagogue worship service. All these requirements are met by the Aramaic text of Isaiah 53 in *Targum Jonathan*. It is of unusual length, because it is much more elaborate than the Greek translation in the LXX. The Aramaic translation is given as a speculative interpretation, quite different from our way of translating an Old Testament text.

2. When examining the passages in the New Testament Gospels and Epistles in which Isaiah 53 may have been used, I want to take into consideration this "targumic" method of dealing with this difficult but very important passage of scripture. The criteria for such a use, such as (*a*) quotations, (*b*) allusions, and (*c*) echoes, together with the emphasis on linguistic evidence provided by M. Hooker, are quite helpful. In addition, however, we must reckon with the possibility that a given New Testament statement without any trace of linguistic evidence could, nevertheless, have been strongly influenced by the content of Isaiah 53. The substance of this text was certainly well-known to Jesus and the early Christians, despite the fact that its vocabulary was somewhat outmoded and difficult. Sometimes M. Hooker seems to hold that Isaiah 53 must be quoted in some particular way if we are to conclude that it has influenced the New Testament. I do not think that this is the way to understand the influence of Isaiah 53. We must reckon with the probability that the whole Song with its theme of the vicarious suffering of the Servant is in the mind of Jesus and the early Christians. In what follows I want to indicate some of the grounds for concluding that both Jesus and

Paul used Isaiah 53, sometimes quoting a phrase and sometimes alluding to one.

As Hengel has pointed out, Isaiah 53 was the best biblical prophecy for the proclamation of the "Word of the Cross" and for defending before the Jews the scandalous message of the ignominious death of the Messiah and Son of God.[8] The text played an important role in the debate between Christians and Jews. We learn this from the *Dialogue* between Justin Martyr and the Jew Tryphon, in which Isaiah 52:10–54:6 is quoted by Justin in full (*Dial.* 13). I think that there is no other passage in the Bible which so clearly reveals both the common root of Judaism and Christianity and also the decisive difference which separates them. We can see this from the interpretation of Isaiah 53 (*a*) in the *Targum Jonathan to the Prophets,* and (*b*) in the New Testament. In neither of them is the Servant of the Lord understood collectively as a symbol for the true Israel. Rather, in both the Servant is related to the person of the Messiah. But the result of their interpretation is very different. For the Targumist, the Servant of Isaiah 53 does not suffer at all. He appears rather as the victorious Messiah who will bring the exile of the Israelites to an end by defeating their political enemies. He will make these enemies suffer under his blows as Israel is suffering now under their yoke; the Servant will be successful throughout (see Isa. 52:13: *yaskīl ʿabdī yārūm wenissāʾ*). But for Jesus, the evangelists, and the apostles it is the messianic Servant himself who will suffer vicariously for the many. Strangely enough, the methods of interpretation used by both sources are quite similar.

3. The number of New Testament passages which are influenced by Isaiah 53 has to be increased considerably. There are words and formulas which point to this prophetic text in an abbreviated way. Among them are the Greek words δεῖ="must" and the verb πάσχειν="to suffer." Besides these is the formula that Jesus has "to be delivered" (παραδοθῆναι) into the hands of men (Matt. 17:22; Mark 14:41; see Mark 10:33; Matt. 26:2, 45; Gal. 2:20; Rom. 4:25; 6:32; 1 Cor. 11:23). I shall reexamine below some of the passages, treated by H. W. Wolff, and in addition I

---

8. M. Hengel, "Some Considerations about Isaiah 53 and Earliest Christianity" (statements for the Isaiah 53 colloquium at Baylor University, Waco, Texas, 23–25 February 1996). See also his article, "Jesus, the Messiah of Israel: The Debate about the 'Messianic Mission' of Jesus," in W. R. Farmer, ed., *Crisis in Christology: Essays in Search of Resolution* (Livonia, Mich.: Dove Booksellers, 1995), 217–40.

shall deal with the words of Jesus (Matt. 6:17–19; 13:16f.; 26:13; Mark 10:38), and with teachings in the Pauline corpus (1 Cor. 1:18, 24; 2:2; 2 Cor. 5:16–21; Rom. 1:16; Phil. 2:6–11).

4. The special theme of this article will be the *gospel* (εὐαγγέλιον) in Isaiah 53. In my view the term "gospel" and its content are derived from and substantiated by the Song of the Suffering Servant. The *rabbis* considered the "gospel" *to be the very heart* of the Christian doctrine. In their eyes the noun εὐαγγέλιον appeared to be a kind of distorted equivalent to the Torah, and Jesus appeared to them to be the embodiment of this new, heretical, teaching of the Gospel. They could render the solemn statement of Matthew 5:17 in the following way: "I, the *euangelion*, did not come to take away from the law, but to add to it."[9] And they made funny wordplays on the Greek noun εὐαγγέλιον calling it *'awaen gillayōn*="Scroll of Doom" or *'awon gillayōn*="Scroll of Sin."

Isaiah 53 and the Gospel of Jesus and Paul

There is no doubt that *Jesus* proclaimed the "Kingdom of God" as good news. This Kingdom will break into the world in the near future (Matt. 6:10); moreover, it begins to become realized through the mighty deeds of Jesus (Matt. 12:28). M. Hooker is quite right with her assumption that Jesus, in proclaiming the good news of the Kingdom, was highly influenced by the message of chapters 40–66 in the Book of Isaiah. There we find the verb *bisser*=εὐαγγελίζεσθαι (Isa. 40:9; 52:7; 60:6; 61:1). The Hebrew noun *besorah*=εὐαγγέλιον is not yet used there for the good news of the final salvation. Matthew, however, can sum up the preaching of Jesus by the formula "Gospel of the Kingdom" (εὐαγγέλιον τῆς βασιλείας, 4:23; 9:35; 24:14), which I think was coined by the first evangelist in analogy with the rendering of Isaiah 40:9 and 52:7 in *Targum Jonathan*. There the good news of the messenger (*mebasser*) expressed in the phrases, "Behold your king!" (Isa. 40:9) and "Your God has become king!" (52:7), are translated by the phrase, "Revealed is the kingdom of your God!" (*'itgeliath malkūthā' d'aelāhā'*). Matthew took an additional step by introducing the noun "gospel" (εὐαγγέλιον) for Jesus' message

---

9. See H. L. Strack and P. Billerbeck, *Kommentar zum Neuen Testament aus Talmud und Midrasch,* 4 vols. (Munich: Beck, 1922–26), 1:242.

of the Kingdom. We do not find its Hebrew equivalent, *besorah*, in Isaiah 40–66 (MT) or in the texts of Qumran. The corresponding Aramaic noun, *besoretha'*, is not used in the *Targum Isaiah* 40:9 and 52:7, and the Greek εὐαγγέλιον does not appear in Isaiah 40–66 of the Septuagint. Like Matthew, Mark puts εὐαγγέλιον on the lips of Jesus (1:14f.; 8:35; 10:29; 13:10; 14:9), while Luke in his Gospel merely has the verb εὐαγγελίζομαι. The following questions must be asked: (1) Did Jesus actually use *the noun* εὐαγγέλιον, as Matthew, Mark, and the rabbis say that he did? (2) What is the *possible source for this noun*? From which biblical (Old Testament) passage may this key word of Christian preaching have come? We have to turn to the writings of Paul in order to find an answer to the second question.

The εὐαγγέλιον of Paul and the Gospel (*besoretha'*) of Isaiah 53:1[10]

Much has been written on the term "gospel" (εὐαγγέλιον) in the New Testament, but the source for this term has not been brought out clearly. It is my contention that it was derived *from* Isaiah 53:1, and from that source only. For Paul, Isaiah was one of the most important prophets. It was through Isaiah that God foretold the Gospel of his son (Rom. 1:2). This can be seen in the first place from passages such as Romans 10:16; 1:16f.; and 1 Corinthians 1:18, 24; 2:2.

In Romans 10:16a Paul makes an important statement about the reception of his preaching. He says: "But they have not all heeded the gospel." As scriptural proof for this frustrating experience he quotes Isaiah 53:1a: "For Isaiah says: 'Lord, who has believed what he has heard from us?' " (LXX: ἀκοῇ ἡμῶν, MT: *shemu'atenu*). The juxtaposition of these two halves of the verse from Romans 10:16 shows that the Pauline verb ὑπακούειν has its scriptural equivalent in πιστεύειν of Isaiah 53:1, and the Pauline noun εὐαγγέλιον in the noun ἀκοή=*shemū'ah*. This means that Paul understands this noun in the same way as the Targumist who translates *shemua'tenu* by *besōrethana'*="our gospel." But the reason for this is different. For the Targumist the report on the Servant was good news and the gospel of a victory. As a result of the Targumist's

---

10. See P. Stuhlmacher, *Das paulinische Evangelium* (Göttingen: Vandenhoeck & Ruprecht, 1968).

very explicit and sophisticated exegesis of Isaiah 53, the messianic Servant will be successful. For Paul, Isaiah 53 tells of good news because the messianic Servant, represented and actualized in the person of Jesus of Nazareth, suffered vicariously and died for us (1 Cor. 15:3); he was made sin for us, that we might become righteous before God (2 Cor. 5:21). In Romans 10:16 Paul did not quote Isaiah 53:1 in an atomistic way — simply to prove the unbelief of the Jews — without having the vicarious suffering of the Servant in his mind.[11] I want to show that although he cited only Isaiah 53:1a, Paul thought of the whole verse and of the whole chapter of Isaiah 53 as well.

We now turn to Romans 1:16 and to 1 Corinthians 1:18 (see 1:24). In these two passages Paul alludes to *the second half of Isaiah 53:1,* which the Apostle did not quote in Romans 10:16. In 1 Corinthians 1:18 Paul says of the "Word of the Cross": "For us who are being saved it is the power of God." Similarly, in Romans 1:16 he affirms: "I am not ashamed of the gospel, because it is the power of God for salvation for everyone who believes" (see 2 Tim. 1:8). How can Paul prove this bold assertion of the saving power of the gospel? Of course, he has experienced the power during his mission. In addition, he can point to the scriptures. According to Isaiah 53:1 the report about the Servant, which one has to believe (*he'emin*), is the revelation of the power of God: "Who has believed our report, to whom has the arm of the Lord been revealed?" The comparison between 1 Corinthians 1:18 and Romans 1:16, both setting forth the theme of the respective letters, reveals the important fact that the "gospel" of Christ (Rom. 1:16) is identical with the "Word of the Cross" (1 Cor. 1:18), which had been foretold in the Song of the Suffering Servant. The power, revealed in the word of his gospel, became for Paul the truth which sustained his apostolic ministry (2 Cor. 6:7). That is why Paul decided "to know nothing . . . except Jesus Christ and him crucified" (1 Cor. 2:2). On the other hand he knew that the word of the cross "is folly for those who are perishing" and that his preaching on

---

11. M. Hooker, *Jesus and the Servant,* 116f., holds that Paul, although quoting Isaiah 53:1 in Romans 10:16, did not have the whole Song and the suffering of the Servant in mind; he simply referred to the disbelief of the Jews. But such an atomistic use of scripture is very unlikely for Paul when he quotes Isaiah 53:1; for "the gospel," mentioned in Romans 10:16, is identical with the "Word of the Cross" in 1 Corinthians 1:18. The unbelief of the Jews appears in a much stronger form in Isaiah 6:9f.; see John 12:39f.

Christ crucified became "a stumbling block to Jews and folly to Gentiles" (1 Cor. 1:23; 1:18).

As long as Paul was still a Pharisee trying to destroy Christian faith (Gal. 1:23), he had the same false understanding of the cross of Jesus. His view was affected at that time by the judgment of God, mentioned in Deuteronomy 21:23: "Cursed be everyone who hangs on a tree" (Gal. 3:13). To proclaim as Messiah (Christ) such a cursed and hanged man (*taluy*) was a blasphemy in the eyes of Paul the Pharisee. The new understanding and saving faith was given to him on the Damascus road, where the exalted Christ appeared to his persecutor and opened his eyes. I have shown[12] that the crucial passage, 2 Corinthians 5:16, which was misunderstood by W. Bousset, R. Bultmann, and many others, has to be evaluated in the light of Isaiah 53, in which a similar change of mind and "Damascus event" experience is confessed by those who report on the vicarious suffering of the Servant (Isa. 53:3f.). By seeing Jesus as the exalted Messiah, Paul realized that Jesus did not suffer martyrdom and death because of his own guilt — this would mean "to regard him according to the flesh" (2 Cor. 5:16). Rather "he died for all" (2 Cor. 5:15), for our sake God "made him to be sin who knew no sin [see Isa. 53:9b], so that in him" we might become the righteousness of God (2 Cor. 5:21). Christ redeemed us from the curse of the Law (Gal. 3:13), because he bore the curse of God which we had deserved.

The Pre-Pauline Character of Paul's εὐαγγέλιον

This understanding and confession of the cross of Jesus as a saving event, as a vicarious sacrifice of Christ's life, and as the formation of the gospel, all *according to Isaiah 53*, was *pre-Pauline*. Paul says this especially in 1 Corinthians 15:1–5. There he applies the exegetical terminology of the rabbis to the fact that he has received (παραλαμβάνειν=*qibbel*) the gospel which he handed over (παραδίδομαι=*masar*) to the Corinthians (v. 1f.). This means that the gospel which Paul himself had *seen* on the Damascus road and was therefore given to him *through a revelation of*

---

12. See my article, "Fleischliche und geistliche Christuserkenntnis nach 2. Korinther 5,16," in *Jesus, der Herr der Kirche*, WUNT 52 (Tübingen: J. C. B. Mohr, 1990), 114–28; O. Hofius, "Erwägungen zur Gestalt und Herkunft des paulinischen Versöhnungsgedankens," *ZTK* 79 (1980): 186ff.

Christ (Gal. 1:12; 1 Cor. 9:1), was *heard* and confirmed also *by the apostles in Jerusalem* (Gal. 2:2). The content of the apostolic gospel, mentioned in 1 Corinthians 15:3f., consists of three basic facts of the Christ-event: his *atoning death, burial, and resurrection.* They are foretold and reported in the same sequence in Isaiah 53:4f. (atoning death), 53:9 (burial), and 53:11 (coming to life). In addition, the *appearances* of the risen Lord (1 Cor. 15:4–8) should be linked with Isaiah 52:15; the *gospel* as the proclamation (1 Cor. 15:1f.) occurs in *Targum Isaiah* 53:1. Romans 4:24f. alludes to the Targumic version of Isaiah 53:5, while Romans 4:25 may be a pre-Pauline creedal statement, as well as the so-called Christ hymn in Philippians 2:6–11, which is shaped by the structure of Isaiah 52:13– 53:12. The gospel of Christ's vicarious sacrificial death (see 1 Cor. 5:7) had its cultic "setting in life" in the celebration of the Eucharist, where the death of the Lord had to be proclaimed (1 Cor. 11:23–26).

The Gospel of Jesus and Isaiah 52:14f.; 53:1, 4f.

Can we establish a continuity between the gospel of Paul and of the earliest church and the message of Jesus?[13] *Can we link Isaiah 53 with the historical Jesus?* Did Jesus identify himself with the suffering Servant, despite his messianic self-consciousness? Did he speak of a εὐαγγέλιον, whose content was similar to that of the gospel of Paul?

This use of εὐαγγέλιον is suggested by both Matthew and Mark. In the story of the anointing at Bethany (Matt. 26:3–13; Mark 14:3– 9; see John 12:1–8), Jesus praises the deed of the woman and declares solemnly: "Truly, I say to you, wherever this gospel [τὸ εὐαγγέλιον τοῦτο] is preached in the whole world, what this woman has done will be told in memory of her" (Matt. 26:13; Mark 14:9). The act of an anticipatory anointing of Jesus is probably historical, because it does not agree with the report of the women buying spices on the morning of Easter and going to the tomb for anointing the body of Jesus (Mark 16:1). The story of anointing is told by Matthew and Mark in such a way that Isaiah 52:14; 53:1 are reflected. As I have explained else-

---

13. R. Bultmann and J. Becker deny such a connection between Jesus and the gospel of Paul (*Paulus, der Apostel der Völker* [Tübingen: Mohr, 1989], 112–31).

where,[14] there is an extensive play on the difficult phrase *mishḥat me'ish mar'ehu* (Isa. 52:14) which is usually understood: "His appearance was so marred, beyond human dignity"; the noun *mishḥat* is derived from the verb *shiḥet*="to pervert, to ruin, to mar." *Mishḥat*, therefore, could also mean "waste" (ἀπώλεια), according to the judgment of the disciples in Matthew 26:8, or "burial" (ἐνταφιασμός, v. 12) in the explanation of Jesus (*m+shahat*="pit"). The large Isaiah scroll from Qumran (1QIsaᵃ) reads *mashahti* for *mishḥat*. This suggests the following meaning: "I have anointed his face more than that of [any other] man"; this is precisely what the woman at Bethany wanted to do. Thus we see that the key words of this story in Matthew 26:3–13 could have been suggested or confirmed by the strange word *mishḥat* in Isaiah 52:14.

From these considerations we can draw the following conclusion: If Isaiah 52:14 had such a strong influence on the story of the anointing of Jesus at Bethany, then the noun "gospel" in the concluding statement of Jesus (Matt. 26:12f.) most probably refers to Isaiah 53:1 (see Rom. 10:16). It must have had a content similar to that of the gospel of Paul, for the good news (εὐαγγέλιον), in which the anointing of the body of Jesus for burial will be preached, had to concern his death. Because it is proclaimed as a gospel, offering salvation, this death must have an atoning effect: Christ, the Son of God, died for our sins. Therefore this gospel will be preached in the whole world (Matt. 26:13). Actually, this was stated by the Apostle with reference to the gospel: Quoting from Isaiah 52:7, Paul could praise the efforts ("feet") of the messengers who proclaim the good news (εὐαγγέλιον, Rom. 10:15); he confirmed them by the words of Psalm 19:4: "Their voice has gone out to all the earth" (Rom. 10:18).

This exegesis of Matthew 26:3–13, made in connection with Isaiah 52:14; 53:1, may appear to be rather speculative and even fanciful. However, a similar verse-by-verse use of Isaiah 52:14–53:1 can be found in John 12:32–38, which follows the Johannine version of the anointing of Jesus at Bethany (12:3–8). John 12:32 contains in the first place a clear allusion to Isaiah 52:13: The Servant "will be lifted up" (ὑψωθήσεται). Together with his glorification (δοξασθήσεται, Isa. 52:13 LXX), this

---

14. "Jesu Evangelium vom Gottesreich," in *Jesus, der Messias Israels*, WUNT 42 (Tübingen: J. C. B. Mohr [Paul Siebeck], 1987), 250f.

prediction of the vindication of the Son of Man plays an important role in the Fourth Gospel and corrects the Jewish rejection of the *taluy*, the man hanged upon a tree. The strange verb "to draw" (ἑλκύειν, see John 6:44), which has a soteriological meaning in John 12:32, may have its Hebrew equivalent in the verb *mashakh*=to draw. It could be another speculative reference to the phrase *mishhat me'ish* in Isaiah 52:14: After his resurrection and exaltation Jesus will "draw all men" (*mashakh kol 'ish*) into the realm of salvation. In 12:38 the Fourth Evangelist takes a further step in his exegesis and use of Isaiah 52–53; for there he quotes the whole verse Isaiah 53:1: "Lord, who has believed our report, and to whom has the arm of the Lord been revealed?" He wants to explain the fact that the Jews did not believe in Jesus, despite the many signs which he had done before their eyes. These signs reveal the "arm of the Lord." In the Targum of Isaiah 53:8 miracles are mentioned which will be done in the messianic age; we are not told of these in the Hebrew text.

The traces of Isaiah 52:14 and the speculative use of the word *mishhat* (*me'ish mar'ehu*) can also be discovered in the *Sermon on the Mount*. So Jesus himself appears to be the source of this kind of interpretation. We may see this in the authentic saying of *Jesus on fasting* (Matt. 6:16f.): "When you fast... do not look dismal [σκυθρωπός][15] like the hypocrites, for they disfigure their faces [v. 16]. But when you fast, anoint your head and your face." In this saying Jesus takes up the criticism of Isaiah 58:5–9, where a self-centered practice of fasting is criticized. He transforms the wording and creates a briefer and more provocative saying condemning pious hypocrisy; this he does by alluding to Isaiah 52:14. In Isaiah 58:5 we read: "Is it [a fast] to bow down his head like a rush and to spread sackcloth and ashes under him?" The answer is: "Let the light break forth like the dawn!" (Isa. 58:8). In Matt. 6:16f. Jesus calls fasting with a self-centered attitude hypocrisy and characterizes it by the strange expression *"disfiguring the face,"* which corresponds with Hebrew *shihet mar'ehu* in Isaiah 52:14. Jesus, however, recommends that one *anoint the face* (in Hebrew: *mashah mar'eh*), an expression we find in the Isaiah Scroll 1QIsa[a] for 52:14. The saying of Jesus on fasting seems to be

---

15. This strange word may be compared with *Targum Isaiah* 52:14. The appearance of the Israelites in exile among the nations was "dark" (*hashokh*).

independent of the gospel of his suffering and atoning death, but it is the background of the Christian practice of fasting. According to Mark 2:20, Jesus said: "The days will come, when the bridegroom is taken away from them, and then they will fast on that day." The expression "being taken away" (ἀπαρθῇ) is an echo of Isaiah 53:8 (*luqqaḥ;* LXX: αἴρεται ἀπὸ τῆς γῆς).

Isaiah 52:15 most probably served as a background for the saying at Matthew 13:16f. (Luke 10:23f.):[16] Being eyewitnesses of the work of Jesus, his disciples can see what "many prophets and righteous men longed to see." (Luke 10:24 has "prophets and kings" — Luke may have the more original version. According to Isaiah 52:15 "many nations" and "kings" shall see what has not been told them.) Matthew states that the Kingdom, the eschatological rule of God, is beginning to be realized through the mighty deeds of Jesus (Matt. 12:28). He reveals the significance of the healing activity of Jesus by quoting Isaiah 53:4: "This was to fulfill what was spoken by the prophet Isaiah: He took our infirmities and bore our diseases" (Matt. 8:17). Matthew certainly knew the spiritual meaning of Isaiah 53:4: Bearing and taking away our sicknesses actually refers to the vicarious suffering of the Servant because of our sins. For Jesus, healing the diseases and forgiving the sins actually belong together. This becomes clear from the story of the healing of the paralytic (Matt. 9:1–9) in which the Son of Man is acting in the place of God, "who forgives all your iniquity and heals all your diseases" (Ps. 103:3). Those saving deeds of Jesus justify the proclamation of the Kingship of God and of the realization of the eschatological hopes (Isa. 52:7); they "reveal the arm of the Lord" (Isa. 53:1), his helping and saving righteousness (Isa. 56:1; Matt. 6:33). They bring freedom from sin, which is the main requirement for entering the Kingdom. Matthew (1:21) explains the name Jesus=*Jeshū'a* in the spirit of Isaiah 53: "For he will save his people from their sins."

Salvation from sin is somewhat different from forgiveness of sins, which can be granted to those who repent and believe. But the people of God have gone astray and turned away from God. They do not even recognize their error and disobedience. They cannot understand how much

---

16. W. Grimm, *Weil ich dich liebe: Die Verkündigung Jesu und Deuterojesaja,* ANTJ 1 (Bern: Herbert Lang, 1976), 112–14.

they really need God, but try to live their lives independently. The attempt to save them from their sins requires an act *extra eos,* a sacrifice for those who are still sinners — vicarious suffering (*Existenzstellvertretung*) for those who do not even want it. This was done by the Servant of the Lord who suffered and gave his life for those "who have turned everyone to his own way" (Isa. 53:6) and who esteemed him stricken for his own guilt and transgression (Isa. 53:4). In order to save God's people from their sins, Jesus had to give his life as a ransom and vicarious sacrifice. Paul could understand the preaching of the gospel of God as a priestly service, in which he offered the nations the sacrifice of Jesus as a well-pleasing gift (Rom. 15:16).

Matthew sees a strong affinity between the *gospel of the Kingdom,* which Jesus proclaimed to the Jews, and the *gospel of Christ,* which the apostles preached to the whole world. In both Gospels the saving power and righteousness of God is revealed. The "Word of the Cross," however, tells how the promise contained in the name "Jesus" and the prophecy of Isaiah 53 were fulfilled. While the Targumist derives from this text the good news that the Messiah will save Israel from its enemies and bring its exile to an end, the apostles understand from Isaiah 53 that Jesus has saved them from their sins and will do away with the dominion of sin and death.

The exegetical route toward gaining these different results is quite similar. It arises from the difficulty of the Hebrew text of Isaiah 53 and the twofold meaning which the interpreters discovered in some of its words. This twofold meaning enabled them to establish their different beliefs in the saving ministry of the Messiah. The Christian theologians had to cope with the "scandal" of the cross of Christ. Therefore, they emphasized the necessity and soteriological effect of the suffering and death of the Servant. The Targumist wanted to separate the Messiah from suffering and make him successful in all his actions: Through his victories over kings and nations he will liberate Israel from the oppression of foreign powers and by his teaching he will bring all of them under the dominion of the Law. On the other hand, Paul understands Christ as the Second Adam, who through his obedient death offers all men freedom from the bondage of sin and of death and from the yoke of the Law.

Christ's Way to the Cross:
Isaiah 53 in Mark 10:38, 45; 14:22–24

H. W. Wolff and other New Testament exegetes pointed to Mark 10:45 and Mark 14:22–24 in their attempt to prove that the historical Jesus himself actually related Isaiah's prophecy of the suffering Servant to his messianic ministry. Jesus became the pioneer and perfector of our faith, because he determined to give his life as a ransom for many (Mark 10:45; see Isa. 53:10, 12) and shed his blood for the forgiveness of sins (Mark 14:24; see Isa. 53:12). According to the classical form-critical evaluation of these sayings, however, their authenticity can no longer be accepted. For example, according to R. Bultmann they must be considered to be creations of the post-Easter church.

But these words, I am convinced, must be attributed to Jesus himself. Both sayings are quite revolutionary, contradicting the way of the world (Mark 10:42–44) and the traditional understanding of Jewish messianic hopes (see Dan. 7:13f.): The Son of Man declares his intention to serve, instead of being served as the ruler appointed by God (Dan. 7:14), and to give his life as a ransom for many (Mark 10:45). This key word of Jesus, "the many," and the equally revolutionary prophecy of the suffering Servant, I am convinced, have their scriptural background in Isaiah 53. Jesus seems to allude to Isaiah 53 in at least two respects: that the Servant will give his life (*naphshō*) as an *'asham* (guilt-offering, 53:10), and that he poured out his soul to death and bore the sin of many (*rabbim*, 53:12). M. Hooker[17] has rightly rejected the linguistic equation of λύτρον with Hebrew *'asham*=guilt-offering in Isaiah 53:10, for λύτρον is the money to be paid for the release of a slave or a prisoner of war; its Hebrew equivalent is *kopher*. Therefore, W. Grimm[18] has pointed to Isaiah 43:3f. as the more likely background for Mark 10:45, which he considers to be an authentic saying of Jesus. In Isaiah 43:3, God promises to give (*natan*) Egypt as a ransom (*kopher*) for Israel, with Cush and Seba in exchange. Then he says: "Because you are precious in my eyes and honored and because I love you, I give a man [*'adam*, "men" in RSV] in return for you

---

17. Hooker, *Jesus and the Servant*, 77. Ransom is no offering. In Isaiah 53:10 *'asham* means the effort of clearing the obligation of debt, caused by the guilt of the many (R. Knierim, *THAT* 1:251–57).

18. Grimm, *Weil ich dich liebe*, 231ff.

[*taḥteyka*], peoples in exchange for your life." Isaiah 43:3f. offers quite
a few parallels to Mark 10:45; most important is the promise of God
to give a man in exchange for Israel, which has the sense of *Existenzstellvertretung.*[19] Moreover, the surprising offer to serve instead of being
served is found in Isaiah 43:23f.: God has not forced Israel to serve him;
on the contrary, Israel has "burdened down" God by their sins (43:24).
Therefore, W. Grimm has made a valuable discovery. S. Kim[20] has also
declared that Isaiah 53 should not be dismissed as a possible background
for Mark 10:45, especially because of the "many," a term that is characteristic of Isaiah 53. I too think that the term *'asham* should not be taken
as a serious obstacle to making this connection. For neither the LXX nor
the Targum was concerned about a precise rendering of this word.

I want to support the view that Mark 10:45 is influenced by Isaiah 53
by pointing to Mark 10:38. For in this saying Jesus also alluded to Isaiah 53:10. He asked the two sons of Zebedee: "Are you able to drink
the cup that I drink, or to be baptized with the baptism with which I
am baptized?" This dark prediction of Jesus, indicating his willingness to
suffer by the metaphor of "baptism" (of death), belongs, I think, together
with Mark 10:45. They have a common scriptural background: Mark
10:45 is dependent on Isaiah 53:10aα, Mark 10:38 on Isaiah 53:10aβ.
Why did Jesus use this strange metaphor of "baptism" in his veiled announcement of his atoning death? In Luke 12:49f. "baptism" is linked
with the fire which Jesus will cast on earth, probably meaning the final
purification of the polluted world; baptism, too, serves the purpose of
providing purity. In Isaiah 53:10aα the prophet says: "It pleased God to
bruise him [i.e., the Servant] through sickness [*dakke'o*]." The LXX renders this: "And the Lord wants to cleanse him from disease"; the Targum
has: " . . . to refine and to purify the remnant of Israel." They both understand the rare verb *dikka'*="to bruise" in an Aramaizing way and interpret
dekhā' (*zakkē'*)="to cleanse," to mean "to restore levitical purity." In my
opinion Jesus formed the metaphor, "baptism [of death]," by taking both
meanings of this verb together: Whoever is "bruised" is free from the

19. P. Stuhlmacher, "Existenzstellvertretung für die Vielen: Mk 10, 45 (Mt 20, 28)," in *Werden und Wirken des Alten Testaments,* Festschrift C. Westermann (Göttingen: Vandenhoeck und
Ruprecht, 1980), 412–27; reprinted in *Versöhnung, Gesetz und Gerechtigkeit* (Göttingen: Vandenhoeck
und Ruprecht, 1981), 27–42.
20. S. Kim, *The Son of Man as the Son of God,* WUNT 30 (Tübingen: J. C. B. Mohr [Paul
Siebeck], 1983), 53–61.

bondage of sin (Rom. 6:7); his death may be a "baptism," an atonement for his sins (*Sanh.* 6:2). Thus, the vicarious death of an innocent agent of God will wash away the sins of many. This becomes clear from Isaiah 53:10 and 53:11. The meaning of the suffering of the Servant, the saving effect of his death, is shown by the sequence of these two verses. The same is true for Mark 10:38 and 10:45. In Isaiah 53:11 God declares that his righteous Servant will rightwise ("justify," NKJ) the many; this explains why his violent death had been necessary and determined by God (Isa. 53:10). In a similar way Jesus explains in Mark 10:45 the soteriological meaning of his death, which in Mark 10:38 remains unclear: His "baptism" (of death) is necessary and decided by God because it will save and cleanse many people from their sins (see Gal 1:4).

It is interesting that in his *Dialogue with Tryphon the Jew* 13:1–9, Justin Martyr quotes the Song of the Suffering Servant in full length (Isa. 52:10–54:6). He calls the ministry of the Servant, taken over by Jesus and completed by his vicarious death on the cross, a "saving bath" (σωτήριον λουτρόν) for those who do not want to be cleansed by the blood of he-goats and sheep. He states that true cleansing is by faith through the blood of Christ and his death (13:1). This "bath of repentance and knowledge of God" (13:1), proclaimed by Isaiah, constitutes Christian faith. This is the baptism (βάπτισμα) and water of life (ὕδωρ τῆς ζωῆς) which can cleanse (καθαρίζειν) those who repent (14:1). The washing (λουτρόν) with water makes merely the flesh and the body clean (14:1); but the soul needs to be washed from evil inclination (14:2).

This "baptismal" interpretation of Isaiah 53 may be influenced by the word of Jesus on his baptism (of death, Mark 10:38) and by the soteriological explanation of his death in the ransom saying, Mark 10:45. For Justin the λύτρον (ransom) character of Christ's death becomes effective through the σωτήριον λουτρόν, the saving cleansing of the soul in the blood of Christ, a cleansing that those who repent receive with baptism into Jesus Christ. Justin's arguments and his use of Isaiah 53 may be guided by the interpretation of Christian baptism given in Romans 6, despite the fact that Justin does not use the expression "baptism of death" or "being baptized into death."

I think that Paul knew the saying of Jesus in Mark 10:38 as well as the soteriological interpretation of Christ's death in Mark 10:45 and in the Eucharistic words of Mark 14:24. In Romans 6 he applies the

metaphor "baptism (of death)" to those who want to have eschatological communion with Christ; Jesus had done this in Mark 10:38b: "Are
you able to be baptized with this baptism, with which I am baptized?"
For Paul declares that to be baptized into Christ Jesus means to be baptized into his death (Rom. 6:3), to be buried by baptism into death (6:4),
and to be united with him in a death like his (6:5), and that the old
self was crucified with him (6:6). This baptism into Christ and into his
death differs from the real death meant by Jesus in his question at Mark
10:38 and suffered by him on the cross. Paul wants it to be understood
metaphorically as a *death to sin* (Rom. 6:6–11), followed by a new life
to God (6:11) free from the enslavement of sin (6:6). Christ died for
us on the cross, "while we were yet sinners" (Rom. 5:8); "while we were
enemies, we were reconciled to God by the death of his Son" (Rom.
5:10). But Christian existence means communion with Christ's death,
which is achieved through baptism into his death. For this communion
with his death communicates the fruit of his sacrifice, the forgiveness
of sins. Paul's idea of healing, life-giving communion through the sufferings and death of Christ may have its scriptural foundation in the
statement at Isaiah 53:5: "With his wound [*baḥaburato*] we are healed."
The word *ḥaburah*="wound," "stripe," meant in the New Testament age
especially "company, association," *ḥaber* meaning "the colleague," "partner." The Targum translates this part of Isaiah 53:5 in the following
way: "And through our gathering to his words our sins will be forgiven to
us," which means that communion with the Law-teaching Messiah will
make us free from sin. Thus the noun *ḥaburah* is understood as "company." Paul probably took up both meanings: "wound" and "company."
For in Philippians 3:10 he mentions the "communion [κοινωνία] of his
[Christ's] sufferings," in which he participates as an apostle. Baptism into
Christ Jesus offers such a communion with the death of Christ and with
its healing effect, which means freedom from sin.

Such a communion with his atoning, life-giving death Jesus offered
to his disciples at the last Passover meal. He did this symbolically in
advance. In the Eucharistic words he indicated that he takes over the role
of the suffering Servant, making atonement for their sins through his
vicarious death. While the meaning of Mark 10:38, 45 was determined
by Isaiah 53:10, during the Last Supper *Jesus enacted Isaiah 53:12:* He
identified himself with the Servant who "poured out his soul to death"

and "bore the sins of the many." That is why Jesus in the Eucharistic words spoke of his body and of his blood and illustrated the surrender of them with the gifts of bread and wine. For he will bear the sins "in his body on the tree" (1 Pet. 2:24; see Isa. 53:12c) and "pour out his life (soul) to death" (Isa. 53:12b) by pouring out his blood for the sins of the many "for the forgiveness of sins" (Matt. 26:27).[21]

---

21. Even the distribution of the symbols for the body and the blood is indicated in Isaiah 53:12a, for in that text the verb *ḥilleq* (διαμερίζειν), "divide," appears twice, referring to the distribution to the people and to things acquired through the sacrifice of the Servant.

6

Did the Use of Isaiah 53 to Interpret His Mission Begin with Jesus?

MORNA D. HOOKER

Introduction

It was 1956 when I finished typing the final copy of my M.A. dissertation, which appeared in book form a long three years later as *Jesus and the Servant*.[1] Forty years on is an appropriate time to look back, and so I am particularly grateful for this opportunity to take stock and to think again about a topic which has lost none of its fascination and importance. I have to warn you, however, that having done so, I am, by and large, unrepentant. I have no intention of recanting! To the question posed in the title of this lecture, I have to reply that I can find no convincing evidence to suggest that Isaiah 53 played any significant role in Jesus' own understanding of his ministry.

But let us begin with what no one will deny: that for centuries Christians have read Isaiah 53 in the light of their knowledge of Christ's ministry and death and of their experience of the forgiveness which has come through him. Isaiah 53 is by no means the only text that has been read through what we may term christological spectacles. Looking back, all sorts of passages — Isaiah 7:14, for example, or 35:5–6 — seem to Christian eyes and ears to be clear "messianic" prophecies; Old Testament scholars usually see things differently. But Isaiah 53 has, above all other passages, seemed to be the most relevant and divinely inspired: here, apparently, we have a vision of one man suffering vicariously for the sins

---

1. *Jesus and the Servant* (London: SPCK, 1959).

of others. What Christian can read that moving passage in Isaiah 53 and fail to say "Amen"?

But therein lies our problem. Isaiah 53 seems *so* appropriate, *so* apposite, that we find it difficult to rid ourselves of the assumption that its relevance was seen from the very beginning — even, perhaps, that it was read as a prophecy of a suffering messiah by the Jews themselves. Isaiah 53 has become part of our Christian culture, and its relevance is reinforced every year when we hear its words sung to the music of Handel's *Messiah*. We have, in a sense, been brainwashed into thinking that, because Christians have found that their reading of Isaiah 53 expressed the deepest truth about Jesus, he too must have seen in it a description of his own calling. The very suggestion that it could have been otherwise has seemed to some an undermining of Christian faith itself. How, asked one commentator, could the church continue to believe about Jesus what he did not know to be true about himself?

Well, the answer to that question is "very easily." The judgments of history are not to be despised because those who were involved in the original events did not know everything that would result from them. When, at the end of the so-called Battle of Britain, Winston Churchill said of those who had flown the Spitfires and defended British shores against enemy attack, that "never in the course of human history have so many owed so much to so few," he was summing up what a grateful nation felt they had achieved. It is unlikely, however, that any of those pilots had thought of what they were doing in those terms: they had simply seen a job to be done and done it. Perhaps you will think that with Jesus it was different. But was it? When the Fourth Evangelist spoke of him as the eternal word made flesh, he was surely not suggesting that this was how the earthly Jesus had thought of himself; and when the fathers of the church drew up the creeds, they were certainly articulating their own beliefs, not his. It is true that the Christian church must look for *continuity* between Jesus and their own beliefs about him: if the church uses Isaiah 53 of Jesus, then it can only be because it believes that Jesus behaved in such a way, and that God worked through his ministry and death and resurrection in such a way, that Isaiah 53 is an *appropriate* text to use of him. But if we take the incarnation seriously, then it is not necessary to trace the use of this passage back to Jesus himself. Unfortunately, however, Christians do not always take the incarnation seriously!

They frequently attribute to him complete knowledge, and in doing so, strip him of his trust in God, and his obedience to God's will, a trust and obedience which he maintained even when he did not know where they would lead him.

So let us be clear that if I question Jesus' use of Isaiah 53, it is not because I wish to question the church's affirmation that the passage *can* be read in the light of Jesus' death and be found meaningful. I would suggest, however, that to do so is an example of what we these days call "reader response" — the response of *Christian* readers to a text. The question with which I am concerned is a historical one: did Jesus himself see the passage as particularly significant for his own role? But there are two related questions that we shall also need to consider: one concerns the way in which Isaiah 53 was read by Jews in the time of Jesus; the other is the question as to when it was that Christians first saw the relevance of that passage. It is with this latter question that I begin. For convenience' sake, I shall continue to refer to the passage as Isaiah 53, even though, of course, the crucial text begins in 52:12.

Clear Quotations

Let us begin by glancing at those passages in the New Testament where we have clear quotations of Isaiah 53. By these I mean passages where there is no possible doubt that Isaiah 53 is being quoted. In seven out of the eight passages, as though to dispel all doubt, the quotation is introduced by an introductory formula, such as "it is written." The first, "he took our infirmities and bore our diseases," in Matthew 8:17, is particularly interesting, because it is applied in what seems to us a surprising way — not to Jesus' sufferings and death, but to his miracles of healing. But why not? Matthew's quotation is not taken from the LXX of Isaiah 53:4, which speaks of the Servant as "bearing our sins," but it is in fact a fair translation of the original Hebrew, which speaks of afflictions and pain. Taken out of its original context, and used as a proof text, the quotation is an entirely appropriate one for Jesus' miracles of healing. It is only because we have grown accustomed to Isaiah 53 being used of Jesus' death that we are surprised by this passage; it is, in fact, a far more appropriate passage to have used of the miracles than the quotation of Isaiah 42:1–4 found in a similar context in Matthew 12:17–21.

The quotation of Isaiah 53:12 in Mark 15:28, where it is used of Jesus' crucifixion between two thieves, is surely a later addition to Mark's text. Note, however, that it is not used to explain the *meaning* of Jesus' sufferings, but simply as a proof text: scripture was fulfilled in the fact that Jesus was put to death *in the company of* wrongdoers. The same verse is used, in a similar way, in Luke 22:37, but this time, the wrongdoers are Jesus' own disciples. The implication, in both contexts, is that Jesus himself is innocent.

The Fourth Evangelist also has one clear quotation; it comes in John 12:38, and is from Isaiah 53:1: "Lord, who has believed our report?" The same quotation is used by Paul, in Romans 10:16. Both authors use it in the same way, as a reference to Israel's failure to respond to the gospel. Also in Romans we have a quotation of Isaiah 52:15 in 15:21, again with reference to Paul's ministry, but this time the quotation and application are both positive, for the Gentiles *have* responded to his gospel.

The longest quotation is found in Acts 8:32f., and consists of the second half of Isaiah 53:7 and the first three lines of v. 8. That reference to the first three lines is significant, since the quotation consists of a description of the Servant's sufferings, and breaks off at precisely that point where the passage begins to speak of their interpretation:

> As a sheep is led to the slaughter,
> And as a lamb before its shearers is dumb
> so he opens not his mouth.
> In his humiliation, justice was denied him.
> Who can describe his generation
> For his life is taken up from the earth.

There is nothing here about the sin and iniquities which are mentioned immediately before and immediately after these words in Isaiah 53. *Why?* "There was no need," suggest some commentators, "because these verses would represent the whole chapter: Luke expected his readers to think of it all." Really? Did they *know* the rest of the chapter? And if they did, and Luke meant them to think of it all, why is it that he chose these particular verses? If he had been trying deliberately to avoid the theme of atonement, he could not have done better! Is it not odd

that the ideas which seem so important to us are not quoted? At the very
least, that suggests that these ideas were not so important to Luke. The
passage is quoted without any reference to the meaning of Jesus' death;
like the verse quoted in Luke 22:37, it serves as a simple proof text.

The final quotation is found in 1 Peter 2:22-25, where we have scattered phrases from vv. 9, 4, 12, 5, and 6 of Isaiah 53. This is, of course,
a rather different use of Old Testament material, and perhaps we ought
not to include it among the quotations at all. It is not introduced with
a formula, and the phrases quoted are certainly not consecutive: rather,
they are woven into the argument — or perhaps we should say into the
hymn, since this passage is clearly hymnic in form. But their source is
clear, and there are several phrases which are closely parallel to the LXX,
so we may perhaps include it among the clear quotations. The fascinating
thing about this passage in 1 Peter is its purpose: the author is appealing
to slaves to be submissive to their masters and to put up with undeserved
punishment. For this, he says, they have been called, because Christ himself suffered for them, leaving them an example, in order that they might
follow in his steps. How he did this is then spelled out in terms of Isaiah 53. But having begun with the appeal to Christ's sufferings as an
example to be followed, he progresses to the idea that they have atoning
value — an idea which, strictly speaking, is not relevant to his argument.
Here, in this final passage, then, we at last find an example of Isaiah 53
being used in the way in which, as Christians, we *expect* it to be used. Is
this perhaps *the* significant moment in the exegesis of that passage, when
it was first interpreted of the *meaning* of Christ's death?[2]

We find this remarkable fact, therefore: that in none of the seven passages where a quotation from Isaiah 52-53 is introduced by a formula
indicating that a citation from scripture follows is that quotation interpreted *of the meaning* of Jesus' death. In other words, it is not used here
in the way we expect — the way which seems so self-evident to the later
church. It is used once of his miracles, and two or three times as a proof
text concerning the fact of his death; it is used several times of reaction
to the gospel. It is only by cheating a little, and including 1 Peter 2,
where the allusion to Isaiah 53 is so clear as to be beyond reasonable

---

2. In fact, as we shall see later, there appears to be an earlier allusion to Isaiah 53 in another
passage dealing with Jesus' death, at Romans 4:25.

doubt, that we find a passage where the prophet's words are understood in terms of what Jesus' death achieved. The importance we attach to that last passage will, of course, depend very largely on the answers we give to questions regarding the date and authorship of that epistle. But I am more intrigued by another question, and that is this: is it significant that it is precisely here, where Isaiah 53 is not being used as a "proof text," that we find it being used *creatively* for the first time? We have moved here beyond simple appeal to "what is written" to the exploration of its *significance.*

Now of course, it may be that we shall find evidence for the use of Isaiah 53 elsewhere, in phrases that echo that passage, and we must return to consider that possibility before we conclude. But I want to turn now to consider the central question which has been put to me: did *Jesus* interpret his own mission in terms of Isaiah 53?

Jesus

Asking any historical question about Jesus is, I need hardly say, fraught with difficulties. We need, then, to consider first of all two questions regarding our assumptions in handling the material. One way of proceeding is to begin by considering the question of the authenticity of the teaching attributed to Jesus by our evangelists. If one takes a somewhat negative approach to that question, then one is almost bound to come to a negative conclusion regarding his use of Isaiah 53; most of the possible allusions will have been eliminated, not on the grounds that they do not echo that great passage, but because they are not considered to be authentic words of Jesus. Not surprisingly we find Bultmann following that path, and coming to a negative conclusion as a result. The method I adopted forty years ago was to give the material the benefit of the doubt and to treat it as authentic, in order that all the evidence should be considered, and that still seems to me the best way to proceed, even if it is not fashionable. Had I come to a positive conclusion I would then, of course, have had to consider the nature of the tradition. In fact, I came to a negative conclusion, in spite of including everything: but my negative results were not based on negative assumptions regarding authenticity.

The other methodological question concerns the relationship between the Synoptics. Forty years ago, there was no need for me to justify the assumption of Markan priority. Today, and certainly in present company, I must at least explain that I still believe Markan priority to be the most likely hypothesis, and that I am unpersuaded by the arguments of those who support other views. But again, fortunately, it seems to me that assumptions for or against any theory are largely irrelevant to this particular inquiry. I mention this, *not* because I think it would be helpful for us to discuss the matter, but simply to justify the fact that I am ignoring it.

So what is the evidence for the use of Isaiah 53 in the so-called passion predictions attributed to Jesus himself? Many commentators assume that Jesus' conviction that he must suffer *must* have been based on Isaiah 53, because there is no other passage to explain it. No other passage? The Old Testament scriptures are full of the sufferings of the righteous! Could he not have read the Psalms? Did he not know Daniel? Is it not significant that he spoke, not of the sufferings of the Servant, but of the Son of Man? There is no justification for assuming, as has so often been done, that Jesus believed himself to be the Messiah, preferred the title Son of Man, but understood his role to be that of the Servant. That kind of piecing together of Jewish hopes and predictions belongs to the period of the church, when he was seen as the fulfillment of all the scriptures, and when Christian writers built up a kind of identikit picture[3] of Old Testament promises, juxtaposing images and ideas from various sources. So I say again, where is the evidence *in these sayings* for the use of Isaiah 53 by Jesus? The only word reminiscent of the LXX of Isaiah 53 is παραδίδωμι, used in Mark 9:31 and 10:33 and parallels in a sense very different from the sense in which it is used in Isaiah 53:12. Nor do these passion predictions take up the idea of vicarious suffering. If we are looking for an Old Testament background against which to understand these sayings, we should take the hint we are offered in the reference to the Son of Man, and look to Daniel 7, rather than Isaiah 53.

The other saying attributed to Jesus which is often said to show the influence of Isaiah 53 is Mark 10:45 (= Matt. 20:28). But the similarities are superficial. The verb διακονέω is never used in the LXX to translate עָבַד, and λύτρον, which is often traced to אָשָׁם in Isaiah 53:10, is

---

3. An identikit picture is built up by the police by piecing together smaller pictures — a nose, a chin, etc. — answering to witnesses' descriptions.

never used for that word, and has a quite different meaning. The LXX text of Isaiah 53:10 is in fact very different from both Mark 10:45 and from the Hebrew, for it reads "if you [presumably the listeners] offer a sin-offering" — i.e., περὶ ἁμαρτίας. Of the three words traced to Isaiah 53, only πολλῶν (used there three times) is relevant, and that is a term which is used frequently elsewhere. I do not find this evidence persuasive.

Isaiah 53

My work on Jesus and the Servant has come under attack, as is well known, by those who remain convinced that Jesus must have seen himself in terms of the Servant of Isaiah. What seems so obvious to us, it is said, must surely have been obvious also to him. But I have also come under what can be described as "friendly fire," from those who believe that though I was right in arguing that Isaiah 53 was not a particularly important text for him, I had not gone far enough! I should, I was told, have examined the assumptions that Old Testament scholars make about that text, as well as the assumptions that New Testament scholars make about *their* material.

Two scholars, Norman Whybray[4] and Harry Orlinsky,[5] have suggested that Christian scholars have misunderstood Isaiah 53. They have both argued that the passage is not, in fact, a description of vicarious suffering at all; Whybray, indeed, has argued that the Servant was not even understood to have died, and that the references to his apparent "death" should be understood rather as meaning that he came close to death. He points to some interesting parallels in other prophetic passages and in the Psalms, but it has to be said that on neither point does he seem to have persuaded many others that his interpretation of the passage is correct.

Obviously if Orlinsky and Whybray were correct, we should have an explanation as to why what appears to us to be the unique theme of Isaiah 53 was for so long ignored. The idea was not taken up and used because it was not there in the first place! So it is worth asking what

---

4. *Thanksgiving for a Liberated Prophet*, JSOTSup 4 (Sheffield: Department of Biblical Studies, University of Sheffield, 1978).

5. *Studies on the Second Part of the Book of Isaiah*, VTSup 14 (Leiden: E. J. Brill, 1967).

their evidence is. At this point, we have to raise the question as to what
we mean by the word "vicarious." In English, the term is unfortunately
ambiguous; my *Oxford English Dictionary* understands it, firstly, to refer
to that which "takes or supplies the place of another thing or person,"
and so to mean someone who acts as a substitute; in theological contexts, this is generally interpreted in terms of Christ suffering in the
place of sinners. This is the concept that our German colleagues refer
to as "exclusive place-taking" (*exkludierende Stellvertretung*), and this is
how Isaiah 53 has traditionally been understood. But there is a second
definition in my dictionary, which takes the word to refer to an action
"performed or achieved by... one person on behalf of another," and so
to mean someone who acts as a representative, and this, I think, is what
is referred to in German as "inclusive place-taking" (*inkludierende Stellvertretung*).[6] The point made by Orlinsky and Whybray is not that the
Servant does not suffer, but that he does not suffer *instead of* others (as
their substitute); rather, he suffers *alongside* them (as their representative).
They point to the fact that in Isaiah 40:2, Israel is said to have suffered
"double for all her sins"; if that passage is relevant to Isaiah 53, and if
the speakers in that chapter are understood to be Israel, as seems most
probable, then the Servant cannot be said to have suffered *instead of* Israel. There is no question of the guilty onlookers getting away scot-free.
This cannot, then, be "substitutionary" suffering.

What, then, is meant by the kind of statement we find in v. 5?

> He was wounded for our transgressions,
> crushed for our iniquities.

Orlinsky and Whybray point to the fact that in Hebrew the preposition
is מִן, not בְּ, while in Greek we have διά. The most natural meaning,
in both languages, is that the transgressions and sins are understood to
be causal:

> He was wounded *because of* our transgressions,
> crushed *because of* our iniquities....

In other words, the Servant suffered *as a result of* the sins of others. This
is certainly not vicarious in the substitutionary sense; after all, it could be

---

6. See Daniel Bailey's article, pp. 237–241.

said of the Jews who perished in the Holocaust, that they were wounded because of Hitler's transgressions, crushed as a result of his iniquities. In other words, it was his wickedness which led to their suffering. The Servant's sufferings were also the result of the misdemeanors of others. In his case, however, we do not have someone who suffers *instead of* his guilty compatriots, but rather someone who *shares* in their sufferings, even though he himself, unlike them, is innocent.

But what of a statement such as we find in v. 4, that the Servant bore our infirmities and carried our diseases, or in v. 12, that he bore the sin of many? Once again, if we remember that the Servant was not the only person to be suffering, these statements read rather differently from the way in which they are normally interpreted. The so-called Servant did not escape suffering, even though he was innocent; on the contrary, he seems to have borne the brunt of the suffering. The suffering which he endured belonged by right to his people. What we have is not "vicarious suffering," *if* by that we mean substitutionary suffering — the anomalous "exclusive place-taking" which is without parallel in Old Testament thought; rather we have an example of "*inclusive* place-taking" or of what we in English normally term "representation."

If this is a correct interpretation, then what is being said in this chapter is, first of all, that the Servant suffers *as a result of the sins of others.* The onlookers thought him guilty, but now that he has been vindicated by God, they realize that he was innocent. He suffered, not because of his own sins, but because of theirs. If we forget our Christian presuppositions, and read the text in that light, it comes across in a new and interesting way, and perhaps explains some of the readings of both the LXX and the Targum.

So far so good. But at this point I find myself parting company with Orlinsky and Whybray, because it seems to me that they have played down too much what the Servant's sufferings *achieved.* We still have to explain v. 5b:

> upon him was the punishment that made us whole,
> and by his bruises we are healed,

as well as the enigmatic statement in v. 10 about the אָשָׁם, and the statement in v. 10 that the righteous one will make many righteous. There is no doubt that the sufferings of the Servant are understood here, both in the Hebrew and in the LXX texts, to have had atoning power, even though the text of v. 10 is uncertain and obscure. It is no longer simply that the sins of others have caused the Servant to suffer: now his sufferings lead in turn to their restoration and forgiveness. Once again, however, [there is no need to interpret this in terms of "substitution": there are many ways in which the sufferings of one person can save a whole community.]

Nevertheless, the work of these two scholars reminds us that the meaning of Isaiah 53 is by no means as obvious as Christians have often assumed. In addition, the Hebrew is, to say the least, difficult: much of it is obscure or unintelligible, and the Septuagint, like the Targum, often seems to say something rather different. Taken together, these facts may explain to some extent why there is so little reference to the idea of "vicarious suffering" in Judaism, and why the Christian community was so slow to exploit this passage.

What I find of particular interest in all this, however, is that the idea which Otfried Hofius[7] *denies* to Isaiah 53 and finds in the New Testament application of the passage is, in my view, present in the original also. What we have in Isaiah 53 is much better described as *representative suffering* rather than *vicarious suffering:* as *inclusive* place-taking rather than *exclusive* place-taking. But before we explore the implications of that idea, let us return to Jesus.

Explanation

Isaiah 53 was, it is often said, the obvious text for Jesus to use. Why, then, is there so little evidence that it was in fact important for him? Perhaps because what seems to us, after the event, to be the obvious text was not necessarily the obvious text at the time. The important question for us to ask, therefore, is not necessarily about the original meaning of the Hebrew, but rather: "How was this passage read in the first century

---

7. "Das vierte Gottesknechtslied in den Briefen des Neuen Testamentes," *NTS* 39 (1993): 414–37. The article was one of those referred to by Daniel Bailey in his contribution to the colloquium. Hofius argues that in Isaiah 53 itself the Servant's sufferings are interpreted as substitutionary ("exclusive place-taking"), and that it was our New Testament writers who transformed the meaning by understanding it as "inclusive place-taking." I suggest, on the contrary, that the "representative" interpretation has its roots in the original text.

C.E.?" Now one of the remarkable things about Isaiah 53 is that Jewish exegesis of this chapter in the period between its composition and the first century C.E. seems virtually to ignore the idea that one person's suffering can have atoning power for others.[8] It is, of course, possible that the idea was used, and that the literature in which this happened has not come down to us, but certainly we have no evidence to suggest that this was so. Later Jewish literature shows the influence of some of the themes found in Deutero-Isaiah, but not of this particular idea. It has frequently been said that the Qumran literature picks it up, but once again it is echoes of the Servant passages in general, rather than of this particular idea, that are to be found there. So how was the chapter understood? One problem in answering this question is the problem of the Targum: does its very strange interpretation of the chapter indicate the way that the passage was understood in the first century C.E., or does it reflect a process of anti-Christian rewriting? If the former, it suggests that the sufferings described in that chapter were not being interpreted in a positive way; if the latter, it offers us no help at all in understanding first-century Jewish interpretation, since we cannot recover the original text. If the early Christian community ignored for so long what appears to *us* to be the key theme of Isaiah 53, was this perhaps because in the Jewish milieu of the first century this was *not* the key theme? If we are to understand the thoughts of first-century men and women, we need to put ourselves into their shoes, and not try to make them wear ours.

But there is another way in which we muddy the waters, and that is by our constant reference to the Servant "Songs" or to the "suffering Servant" or even to the "Servant" — each of these words being, of course, spelled with a capital *S*. It is necessary to remind ourselves that in the first century C.E. no one talked about "Servant Songs," or even about "Deutero-Isaiah." The question "Did Jesus think about himself as 'the Servant'?" (with a capital *S*) is a meaningless one. To the author of Isaiah 53, "my servant" (without a capital) had seemed an appropriate way of describing one who had been utterly obedient to God; to others, it had seemed an appropriate way of describing men such as Moses and David. In time, it seemed an appropriate way for the church to describe

---

8. Evidence for the idea of vicarious atoning suffering itself (quite apart from possible influence by Isaiah 53) is equally scant. See Sam K. Williams, *Jesus' Death as Saving Event: The Background and Origin of a Concept*, HDR 2 (Missoula, Mont.: Scholars Press, 1975), 121–35.

Jesus. But there was no notice in the "Jobs Vacant" column of the papers reading "Wanted: the Servant of the Lord"; no expectation that there would be a Servant who would suffer; there was simply a description of one who had been faithful to God and who had therefore been termed God's "servant."

I suggest, then, that the reason that Jesus did not model himself on the so-called suffering Servant of Isaiah 53 was because it was by no means the obvious passage of scripture to which he would turn. During his ministry, he proclaimed the forgiving love of God, which welcomed repentant sinners back without condition: particular acts of "atonement" were apparently unnecessary. As he faced death, he appears to have seen his role in terms of the one like a son of man in Daniel 7, who stood for the righteous saints, persecuted because of their faithfulness to God. The Psalms, too, provided a description of what happened to those who were faithful to God; Isaiah 53 *may* have been part of this pattern, but apparently added nothing to it. And beyond death, Jesus trusted in God for vindication, in accordance with the promise contained in all these Old Testament texts. If Mark 10:45 and 14:24 are authentic sayings, then it seems that Jesus may have seen his death as an event comparable to the Exodus, bringing into existence a new people of God: certainly this seems to have been the way in which all the evangelists interpreted it.[9] There was, in a sense, no need for him to link his death specifically with the notion of atonement for sin. It was his followers who took that step, because it corresponded with their experience of forgiveness.

Let us return, then, to those clear quotations of Isaiah 53 with which we began, since now, I suggest, the apparently perverse way in which they are used should no longer surprise us. I have already suggested that the quotation from v. 4, used of the miracles in Matthew 12, is entirely appropriate, provided that we forget the LXX rendering. The use of proof texts, without reference to the notion of vicarious suffering, in Mark 15, Luke 22, and Acts 8 no longer surprises us: the verses quoted are sufficient explanation of Jesus' suffering. The use of Isaiah 53:1 in John 12 and Romans 10 of the Jews' refusal to respond to the gospel is an obvious one, as is the more positive use of Isaiah 52:15 in Romans 15. And what we have in 1 Peter 2 is perhaps an indication of the way in which

---

9. See Matt. 20:28; 26:28f.; Luke 9:31; 22:24–30; John 18:28; 19:33.

the use of Isaiah 53 developed: first it is used to show that Jesus' suffering was innocent; then a second theme appears, as the same passage is used to show how the Servant's suffering brings healing and forgiveness to others.

Is this passage in 1 Peter the beginning of the second stage of Christian exegesis of Isaiah 53? Or was that stage already begun by Paul? Are there echoes of Isaiah 53 in his writings? Who first used Isaiah 53 to interpret Jesus' death as an atonement for sin?

Paul

Now it seems to me that there is one clear echo of Isaiah 53 in Paul, and that is in Romans 4:25: an interesting passage which is often said to be pre-Pauline, though I can see no good reason for denying it to Paul himself. Forty years ago I did not appreciate the importance of this verse: I followed C. H. Dodd in assuming that Paul's language here was rhetorical,[10] and many other commentators have interpreted the passage in the same way. Thus Grayston writes: "The formula was constructed to be verbally memorable rather than theologically precise."[11] I would argue now that Paul has in fact chosen his language with care, and with an eye to theology rather than rhetoric: Christ, he says, was delivered up on account of our trespasses; he was raised for our justification or "rightwising."[12] This antithesis corresponds with what he says elsewhere in his letters about Christ's identification with the situation of sinners and our identification with his — an identification which he spells out in different passages in various ways: he speaks, for example, of Christ being made sin, becoming a curse, being born under the Law, coming in the likeness of sinful flesh for our sake, in order that we might share his righteousness, receive blessing, be set free from the Law, and receive adoption as the children of God.[13] Christ shares our condemnation in order that we might share his vindication by God, a vindication which was made

---

10. C. H. Dodd, *The Epistle of Paul to the Romans* (London, 1932), 70. Hooker, *Jesus and the Servant*, 195 (p. 123, n. 1).

11. Kenneth Grayston, *Dying We Live* (London: Oxford University Press, 1990), 92.

12. The two uses of διά are formally parallel, but the first is causal, the second final.

13. 2 Cor. 5:21; Gal. 3:13f.; 4:4f.; Rom. 8:3f., 14–20.

known when he was proclaimed as Son by the resurrection of the dead.[14] In other words, what Paul says in Romans 4:25, where he links Christ's death with our sins, and his resurrection with our justification, is understandable in the light of the idea that some of us refer to as "interchange in Christ,"[15] an idea which is widespread in his writings: Christ shares our situation — the situation of those who are born of Adam — but transforms it by his obedience, so that those who, through baptism into his death and resurrection are now *in* Christ, share *his* vindication and *his* righteousness. The one who is innocent shares the suffering and death which are deserved by Adam's descendants, and his vindication is shared by those who acknowledge him as Lord. These ideas are summed up admirably in the words of Romans 4:25, "he was delivered up because of our trespasses; he was raised for our justification" (δικαίωσις). But the explanation as to *why* his death and resurrection are effective "for us" is found only in the context: the meaning of 4:25 is spelled out in chapters 5, 6, and 8. The language of 4:25 is echoed in the argument about Adam and Christ in 5:12–21, where Paul emphasizes that it was the *trespass* of Adam which led the many to sin and to die, and the grace of God in Christ which made them *righteous*.[16] In chapter 6, Paul spells out *how* this happens: believers are baptized into Christ and share his death (vv. 3, 5–11); they also share his risen life and his righteousness (vv. 4, 6–7, 12–14). This is why there is now no condemnation for those who are in Christ (8:1). It is clear, as we read on, that 4:25 is based on a belief that Christ shares the death of those who are "in Adam," and that those who are "in him" share his righteousness before God.

The language of Romans 4:25 — παραδίδωμι and δικαίωσις — echoes Isaiah 53:11f. But what is said in Romans 4:25 is very close also to the interpretation I have been offering of the *meaning* of Isaiah 53, which should be understood, I have suggested, in terms of representation rather than substitution, of "inclusive" rather than "exclusive place-taking." Thus Isaiah 53:5: "He was wounded because of

---

14. Romans 1:3f.

15. I have explored various facets of this idea in essays collected in *From Adam to Christ* (Cambridge: Cambridge University Press, 1990). See also M. D. Hooker, "A Partner in the Gospel: Paul's Understanding of his Ministry," in *Theology and Ethics in Paul and His Interpreters*, ed. Eugene H. Lovering Jr. and Jerry L. Sumney (Nashville: Abingdon, 1996).

16. Note the frequent occurrence of παράπτωμα (vv. 15 [bis], 16, 17, 18, and 20) and the root δικαιό- (vv. 16, 17, 18 [bis], 19, 21).

our transgressions; and with his bruises we are healed." Paul: "Christ was delivered up because of our trespasses; and through his resurrection we are brought into a right relationship with God." In Romans 4:25, then, we have not only distinct echoes of the *language* of Isaiah 53:11f., but similarities in thought; this passage clearly meets the criteria I suggested should be applied to possible echoes of Old Testament texts.

So is this one reference to Isaiah 53 accidental? Or is it an indication that it was Paul who first exploited the idea of atoning suffering in that passage? Was that chapter the raw material out of which his understanding of atonement in terms of an interchange between Christ and the believer was built?[17] If so, why is it only in Romans that the link becomes clear? And why has the passage left so few traces elsewhere? Or did Paul develop the idea and *then* see the relevance of Isaiah 53? These are the questions which intrigue me, and I am particularly glad that this colloquium is concentrating on the writings of Paul. To the question that has been put to me, "Did the use of Isaiah 53 to interpret his mission begin with Jesus?" I remain convinced that the answer is "No." To the question "Where, then, *did* it begin?" I am far more ready than I was forty years ago to suggest that it may well have been with Paul.

---

17. There are interesting echoes of this idea of interchange outside Paul, and one of them is in 1 Peter 2:24, in the exposition of Isaiah 53: "He himself carried our sins in his body up to the tree, so that, freed from sins, we might live for righteousness." Significantly, however, this passage does not express the theme that is essential to the idea of "interchange" — namely, that of *sharing*. The author does not say or imply that Christ shared our human death, or that we share his righteousness — simply that Christ dealt with our sins by his death so that we might live for righteousness. The passage reads like an echo of Paul's ideas, minus the idea that everything takes place through our union with Christ; cf. 1 Thess. 5:10: "Christ dies for us, so that . . . we might live *with him.*"

7

Isaiah 53 in Acts 8

A Reply to Professor Morna Hooker

MIKEAL C. PARSONS

Introduction

In her influential book *Jesus and the Servant* (and in her reflections at
this conference nearly forty years after her ideas were first put forward),
Prof. Morna Hooker argues that "Jesus himself was not profoundly influenced by the Servant passages in particular."[1] To reach this conclusion,
Professor Hooker engages in a detailed exegesis of the relevant NT passages, as well as exploring the general background and meaning of the
Servant Songs of Deutero-Isaiah. One of the passages she deals with is
the quotation of Isaiah 53 in Acts 8. I would like to take up her interpretation of that passage and offer an alternative way of reading that text.
I am not attempting at this point to topple Professor Hooker's overall
thesis, but rather to clarify and refine her interpretation of one of those
passages which led to her conclusion. Reassessing her exegesis of this one
passage, however, does raise the question regarding her interpretation of
other passages, which could ultimately lead to a reassessment of her total
argument.[2]

Though the general ideas of this essay were expressed in the seminar discussion, the paper was not
formally presented but rather emerged as a response to the proceedings of the conference, "Isaiah 53
and Christian Origins," especially to Morna Hooker's keynote address, "Did Jesus Use Isaiah 53 to
Interpret His Mission?"

1. Morna Hooker, *Jesus and the Servant: The Influence of the Servant Concept of Deutero-Isaiah in
the New Testament* (London: SPCK, 1959), 163.

2. I am of the opinion that only by a combination of a detailed passage-by-passage analysis
and a coherent theory of early Christian use(s) of Jewish scriptures can one begin to undertake to
dismantle the overall thesis proposed by Hooker.

Hooker's Interpretation of Acts 8

About the use of the Servant motif in Acts, Hooker concludes: "The account of the beliefs of the early Christians which is given in the Acts of the Apostles does not suggest that the primitive community ever thought of Jesus as 'the Servant' of Deutero-Isaiah."[3] She reaches this particular conclusion on the basis of her reading of the titles παῖς (3:13, 26; 4:27, 30) and ὁ δίκαιος (Acts 3:14; 7:52; 22:14) and especially on the use of Isaiah 53 in Acts 8. About that passage she writes:

> [I]n Acts 8 we find a quotation from Isaiah 53 actually applied to the sufferings and death of Christ. While it is evident from the context, however, that Philip interpreted the passage as a description of the Passion of his Lord, this by no means implies that he must have in mind an equation of the nature: Jesus=the Servant. For it must be stressed once again that the words which are quoted speak only of the *fact* of the sufferings and death of the Servant, and do not mention their *significance*. These facts, however, are precisely those features which were already present in the primitive kerygma, and which needed no passage from the Old Testament to suggest them. The significance of the quotation, therefore, must lie, not in any interpretation of the meaning of Christ's death, but in the fact that it is a foreshadowing of the events of the Passion. (150–51)

Hooker refers to the use of Isaiah here in Acts 8 as a "'proof text' from the Old Testament that these things could — and did — happen to the Messiah" (151).

Hooker arrives at her "proof text" conclusion from a careful exegesis of Acts 8. She notes that Acts 8 provides "clear evidence for the use of Isaiah 53 in connection with Jesus' sufferings by at least one of the earliest members of the Church" (113). She continues, however, with these words: "Thus, while it is clear that Philip was ready to interpret this chapter of Jesus, there is no proof that it was a passage of particular importance" (113). She quite rightly notes that the quotation of Isaiah 53 in Acts 8:32–35 consists of the last three lines of Isaiah 53:7 and the first three lines of 53.8. Curiously missing are the references to vicarious suffering in

---

3. Hooker, *Jesus and the Servant*, 150. Subsequent page references in text are to this volume.

Isaiah 53 just prior to ("and the Lord laid on him the iniquity of us all" —
Isaiah 53:6) and just after ("because of the iniquities of my people he was
led to death" — Isaiah 53:8) the material quoted. Hooker concludes:

> The exact verbal agreement with the LXX suggests that he was
> quoting from a written source, and not from memory, so that the
> choice is not a haphazard one. It seems that the significance of Isa-
> iah 53 lay, for the author of Acts at least, not in the connection
> between suffering and the sin of others, but in the picture of hu-
> miliation; thus yet again the chapter is used as a proof text of the
> necessity for Christ's Passion, and not as a theological exposition of
> its meaning. (114)

Two conclusions Hooker draws here are deserving of further analysis:
(1) Luke begins and ends the quotation of Isaiah 53 where he does to
avoid making explicit reference to the vicarious suffering of the Servant;
and (2) Acts 8 is to be taken as a "proof text" and not as a "theological
exposition" of the necessity of Christ's suffering. I will return to both of
these points in the analysis of Acts 8 which follows.[4]

Reevaluating the Role of Isaiah 53 in Acts 8 and Beyond

I begin the analysis of Acts 8:25–40 by probing its literary structure.
Most scholars agree that a chiastic structure shapes the unit, though they
disagree about its details. The most significant aspects of any chiasm
usually lie in the outer frame, on the one hand, and the center of the
chiasm on the other. This passage is no different. On the outer ring,
vv. 25 and 40, the chiastic structure is clear (following the Greek word
order, but translated into English):

v. 25	A		they returned to Jerusalem
	B		to many villages of the Samaritans
		C	they [Peter and John] preached
v. 40		C′	he [Philip] preached
	B′		to all the cities
A′			until he came to Caesarea

---

4. Most of the following material in this section has been taken from my forthcoming narrative
commentary on Acts in a series edited by Alan Culpepper and Werner Kelber.

Likewise, most formal analyses locate at the center of the chiasm the citation from the OT and the eunuch's questions. The quotation of Isaiah 53:7–8 is the only time in Acts when the narrator quotes the OT directly, apart from the lips of an individual character. Hooker is misleading on this point when she attributes the citation of Isaiah 53 to the eunuch and not to the narrator of Acts: "It is strange that this first quotation should be found in the mouth of an unconverted Gentile, and not a Christian preacher, or even a Jew" (113). Her conclusion is even more off-base: "It cannot, therefore, be taken as evidence that this passage of scripture was central in the Christian preaching of the time" (113). In fact, as the only OT passage explicitly cited by the narrator, and as the middle citation of three important lengthy OT quotations in the entire Book of Acts (cf. the quotation of Joel 3 in Acts 2 and Isaiah 6 in Acts 28), this passage does have great significance for Acts as a whole. But what exactly is its significance?

The Eunuch in Late Antiquity

To answer this question, we return to the beginning of Acts 8:25ff. The rest of the opening unit is given over to a description of the man whom Philip meets, "an Ethiopian, a eunuch, a minister of the Candace, queen of the Ethiopians, in charge of all her treasure" (8:27). Each of those words conveys very important cultural information about this character.[5] Of these descriptors, the most important is that the man is a eunuch.

But what did the term "eunuch" mean in late antiquity? Some evidence does exist for the view that eunuch is simply a royal title. Genesis 39:1 reports that "Joseph was brought down to Egypt; and Potiphar an officer [εὐνοῦχος] of Pharaoh...." Potiphar was, of course, married, so "eunuch" here probably refers to his standing in Pharaoh's court. Some early Christian writings developed the notion of eunuch as a reference to those who remain celibate. Athenagoras wrote in *A Plea for the Christians:* "If to remain a virgin and *abstain from sexual intercourse* [εὐνουχία] brings us closer to God ..." (33.3; cf. Clement of Alexandria, *Stromata*, 3.1; Matt. 19:12c[?]). Nonetheless the overwhelming number of instances of

---

5. For a discussion of the significance of Ethiopia both as a geographical and ethnic descriptor, see Clarice Martin, "A Chamberlain's Journey and the Challenge of Interpretation for Liberation," *Semeia* 47 (1989): 105–35.

"eunuch" from the classical period to late antiquity refer to eunuch in the *physical* sense as one who was sexually mutilated (see Philostratus, *Life of Apollonius*, 6.42; Lucian, *Saturnalia*, 12) or, much more rarely, born with a congenital defect (see Aristotle, *Generation of Animals*, 2.7.25).

How is the reader to understand the word here in Acts 8? Clearly the nuance of celibacy is not at work here, and no interpreter has ever argued such. There is some debate about whether the word "eunuch" here should be taken literally to refer to castrated or mutilated persons (*castrati*) or whether it simply refers to the title of a court official. The advantage to this latter view is that the Ethiopian may be viewed as a Jewish proselyte returning home from temple worship and dutifully reading Isaiah. Even more important for some is that if the Ethiopian eunuch is a Jewish proselyte, then Cornelius is still the first Gentile admitted for baptism.

Several factors mitigate against this view and in favor of understanding "eunuch" in its physical sense. First, the status of the Ethiopian as a high-ranking official is established in 8:27 quite apart from the use of the term "eunuch." He was a "minister of the Candace, queen of the Ethiopians, in charge of all her treasure." The use of the term "minister" (δυνάστης) is interesting here. The only other occurrence in Luke and Acts is in the Magnificat where Mary pronounces that God has "brought down the mighty ones [δυνάστας] from their thrones and exalted those of low degree" (Luke 1:52). Furthermore, he has the wealth at his disposal to be driven in a chariot (see 8:27, 38) and to possess an expensive Greek scroll of Isaiah. To reduce the term "eunuch" to mean nothing more in this context than a "high-ranking official" is to render it redundant.

More likely then is the view that the Ethiopian eunuch here is a physically mutilated man. His service as a close advisor to a queen, the Candace, makes it likely he was castrated, since male attendants for royalty were often castrated (see Herodotus, 8.105; Esther 2:3, 14; 4:4–5).[6] Further, for the remainder of the story the official is referred to, not as an Ethiopian (an exotic dark-skinned fellow) or as a "minister or official"

---

6. Eunuchs had great influence and power in the royal courts of Assyria and Persia because of their undivided loyalty to the reigning monarch. They were valued and needed because they had no family heirs (not, as in much popular thought, because they posed no sexual "threat"). Only eunuchs could be trusted to stand outside the nepotism and intrigue created by the competition in the palaces among the many princelings. It was their lack of kinship heirs which made them the leading palace officials in Persian, Hellenistic, and Roman times.

(signifying power and wealth), but simply as the "eunuch" (8:34, 36, 38, 39). If this is his dominant, defining characteristic, then two questions emerge. What was the status of eunuchs in the Mediterranean world of late antiquity? How would Luke's readers have understood this text in light of the larger cultural script for eunuchs?

Eunuchs in antiquity "belonged to the most despised and derided group of men."[7] One of Herodotus's characters, Hermotimus, a eunuch, took revenge on the man who had castrated him and sold him as a slave into the court of Xerxes, calling the activity "the wickedest trade on earth" (8.104–6). Elsewhere, Lucian of Samosata tells of a supposed eunuch vying for a chair of philosophy in Athens. His assumed status as a eunuch (he claimed to be a eunuch to avoid charges of adultery) led to an invective by one of his opponents, who claimed that it was "an ill-omened, ill-met sight if on first leaving home in the morning, one should set eyes on any such person [a eunuch]." Eunuchs, he claimed, "ought to be excluded... not simply from all that but even from temples and holy-water bowls and all the places of public assembly" (*The Eunuch*, 6–11).

This attitude was also prevalent among Greek-speaking Jews of the first century. Josephus wrote:

> Shun eunuchs and flee all dealings with those who have deprived themselves of their virility and of those fruits of generation, which God has given to men for the increase of our race; expel them even as infanticides who withal have destroyed the means of procreation. (*Ant.* 4.290–91)

Why were eunuchs thus demonized and ostracized in antiquity? In part, the answer lies in their ambiguous sexual identity. To quote Lucian again, a eunuch "was an ambiguous sort of creature like a crow, which cannot be reckoned either with doves or with ravens"; he was "neither man nor woman but something composite, hybrid and monstrous, alien to human nature" (*The Eunuch*, 6–11). Josephus comments along similar lines: "For plainly it is by reason of the effeminacy of their soul that they changed the sex of their body also. And so with all that would be deemed

---

7. See Scott Spencer, "The Ethiopian Eunuch and His Bible: A Social-Science Analysis," *Biblical Theology Bulletin* 22 (1992): 156. The idea of the importance of the social status of the eunuch for understanding the function of the Isaiah 53 citation in Acts 8 was sparked by this article.

a monstrosity by the beholders" (*Ant.* 4.291). Likewise Philo of Alexandria claims that eunuchs were "men who belie their sex and are affected with effemination, who debase the currency of nature and violate it by assuming the passions and the outward form of licentious women" (*Spec. Leg.* 1.324–25). In a culture where honor was gender-based, to be sexually ambiguous was to blur clear-cut gender roles and expectations and thus to bring shame upon oneself and one's community.[8]

Further, in Jewish thought, eunuchs, by belonging neither to the cultural expectations of male nor female, had violated purity codes.[9] Like amphibians who lived in two worlds but belonged to neither, eunuchs were considered unclean (see Leviticus 11). In addition, the physical body was thought to mirror the corporate social body, so a physical body that was damaged or mutilated had the potential of defiling the social body.[10]

This was especially true in Judaism in which the physically defective, like eunuchs, were forbidden both entry into the temple and interaction with the larger social body: "No one whose testicles are crushed or whose penis is cut off shall be admitted to the assembly of the Lord" (see Deut. 23:1). The Ethiopian eunuch, as Scott Spencer has noted, "embodied impurity as much as he exhibited shame. His ambiguous sexual identity ('neither male nor female') denied him a distinctive place on the purity map of the social body, even as his defective genital anatomy depicted his polluted map of the physical body."[11] It is this kind of person whom Philip is directed by the Spirit to approach (8:29) — a man excluded, because of his physical condition, from participation in Jewish worship at the temple in Jerusalem, a man understood by Luke's readers to be a social outcast, living on the threshold in terms of his sexual identity, his religious identification, and his socioeconomic status.

---

8. See Bruce J. Malina and Jerome H. Neyrey, "Honor and Shame in Luke-Acts: Pivotal Values of the Mediterranean World," in *The Social World of Luke-Acts: Models for Interpretation,* ed. Jerome H. Neyrey (Peabody, Mass.: Hendrickson, 1991), 41–44.

9. See Spencer, "The Ethiopian Eunuch and His Bible," 158–59. See also by the same author, *The Portrait of Philip in Acts: A Study in Roles and Relations,* JSNTSup 67 (Sheffield: JSOT Press, 1992), 168–72.

10. See Jerome H. Neyrey, "The Symbolic Universe of Luke-Acts: 'They Turn the World Upside Down,'" in *The Social World of Luke-Acts: Models for Interpretation,* ed. Jerome H. Neyrey (Peabody, Mass.: Hendrickson, 1991), 278–85.

11. Spencer, "The Ethiopian Eunuch and His Bible," 159.

The Eunuch's Bible[12]

Why, then, was the eunuch reading from Isaiah, and more specifically Isaiah 53? On the general question of "why Isaiah?" we may note that the repeated references to Ethiopia (Isa. 18:1; 45:14) and the explicit reference to eunuchs in Isaiah 56:1–8 would make the scroll of Isaiah of special interest for an Ethiopian eunuch. The social location of the eunuch discussed above is a crucial key for interpreting the specific citation of Isaiah 53:7–8 within the social and literary world of Acts.

The passage of scripture which the eunuch was reading was, as Hooker notes, a verbatim quotation of a Greek version of Isaiah 53:7–8: "As a sheep led to the slaughter or a lamb before its shearer is dumb, so he opens not his mouth. In his humiliation, justice was denied him. Who can describe his descendants? For his life is taken up from the earth" (Acts 8:32–33). As Hooker points out, the passage quoted here takes up just after the reference to the Servant's vicarious suffering and ends just before a similar note in Isaiah 53:8. The passage as it stands in Acts tends rather to emphasize the "humiliation" of the unnamed sufferer and perhaps also his vindication.

The key word here is "humiliation" (ταπείνωσις), found in the middle of the citation. In later Christian literature (see *1 Clement* and *Hermas*), this word is taken more in terms of Christian "humility," that is, as an example of a Christian virtue, enacted through rituals of penitence and fasting. Only rarely, however, does the word apply in antiquity to personal immorality (see, e.g., Propertius 1.10.27–28), and should not be so understood here. Rather, the reference to ταπείνωσις here is to a "social position within Mediterranean society" which "was severely reprobative."[13] A passage from Lucian's *Somnium* is illustrative of the social ostracism conveyed by ταπείνωσις (see also Pollux *Onomasticon* 5.162–64). In this dream, Lucian is warned that should he choose a career in sculpture (rather than education) he will

> be nothing but a laborer, toiling with your body and putting in it your entire hope of a livelihood, personally inconspicuous, getting meager and illiberal returns, lowly in disposition [ταπεινὸς

---

12. The title of this section is derived from Spencer's article cited above.
13. See Willi Braun, *Feasting and Social Rhetoric in Luke 14,* SNTSMS 85 (Cambridge: Cambridge University Press, 1995), 50.

τὴν γνώμην], an insignificant figure in public, neither sought by your friends nor feared by your enemies nor envied by your fellow-citizens, nothing but just a laborer, one of the swarming rabble, ever cringing. (*Somnium*, 9)

Should, however, Lucian choose the life of education (*paideia*), his social fortunes will be reversed. If not, then his lot is surely one of an outcast:

On the other hand, if you turn your back upon these men so great and noble, upon glorious deeds and sublime words, upon a dignified appearance, upon honor, esteem, praise, precedence, power and offices, upon fame for eloquence and felicitations for wit, then you will put on a filthy tunic, assume a servile appearance ... with your back bent over your work; you will be a groundling, with groundling ambitions, lowly in every manner [πάντα τόπον ταπεινός] ... you will make yourself a thing of less value than a block of stone. (*Somnium*, 13)

It is not surprising, then, that the eunuch, whose access to wealth is tenuous at best and ironically dependent upon a socially debased position, should be drawn to this figure in Isaiah who, like the eunuch, is described as being in a state of "humiliation" and to whom, like the eunuch, "justice was denied" (Acts 8:33).

Furthermore, this figure in Isaiah is not only socially marginalized, but also depicted as unclean or polluted.[14] The Isaianic figure is identified as a slaughtered lamb and a shorn sheep (Acts 8:32). Both similes on the Jewish map of purity evoke images of pollution. Dead bodies, whether animal carcasses or human corpses, were unclean and taboo to the touch (see Lev. 11:24–40; 21:1–4). Likewise, priests were required to follow certain regulations regarding shaving their bodies: "They shall not make bald spots upon their heads, or shave off the edges of their beards" (Lev. 21:5; cf. also Num. 6:1–21; see Acts 21:21–26). Again, the eunuch in Luke's narrative could have closely identified with the Isaianic figure since both are depicted as ritually unclean. He, too, is like a lamb before its "cutter," reduced to silence in humiliation (Acts 8:32–33).

---

14. On the dimension of cultic purity of the fourth Servant Song, see Hanson's essay in this volume.

Within Judaism there existed the eschatological vision of Isaiah that eunuchs and foreigners and other outcasts would be reincorporated in the end days: "To the eunuchs who keep my sabbaths, who choose the things that please me and hold fast my covenant, I will give, in my house and within my walls, a monument and a name better than sons and daughters; I will give them an everlasting name that shall not be cut off" (Isa. 56:4–6). For the present, however, this vision of the future stood as a cruel reminder of the gulf between his heart's desire and the harsh social reality of exclusion from temple worship which we must assume he had just experienced (see 8:27).

The eunuch had just come from his trip to Jerusalem for worship, where he no doubt was forbidden from entering the temple (Deut. 23:1). When Luke shows that nothing hinders the eunuch from being baptized, ritually cleansed, and incorporated into the body of Christ, he undoubtedly intends a thinly veiled antitemple polemic. What is held out as a promise in the (distant?) future but denied by the current practices of the temple cult, is offered freely by the representative of the Way, whose founder and community had radically redrawn the Jewish purity map not only of places (see the preceding passage on the Samaritans in Acts 8:4–8), but now also of persons. The status of the socially despised and ritually polluted eunuch is ritually transformed by the act of Christian baptism.

But the passage from Isaiah, as understood by Luke, does not limit its vision to a description only of the Servant's debased status. The first hint of reversal may come in the phrase concerning the Servant cited in Acts 8:33, often translated "justice was denied him" while some prefer the translation "judgment was removed from him" (on Luke's use of "judgment," see Luke 10:14; 11:31–32). The next phrase is likewise ambiguous: "Who can describe his generation?" Is this a lament over the fact that the Servant is cut off from his descendants or a note rejoicing over the "indescribable generation" too many to number? The case for the last phrase in the scripture citation, "for his life is taken up from the earth" (8:33), having a double meaning is much stronger. Here again, the reference may be either to the figure's death or to his "lifting up" in exaltation, symbolized in Jesus' ascension in Acts 1:9.[15]

---

15. Or as Luke Johnson puts it: "The LXX can be read by the Messianist who confesses a resur-

This double entendre of "lifting up" as both death and exaltation may sound on first hearing as distinctly Johaninne. But Luke also understands the death and exaltation of Jesus as inextricably tied into one event, despite the fact that he narrates the death, crucifixion, and ascension separately. The death, resurrection, and ascension, however, are not separate, unrelated episodes for Luke, but rather three aspects of one event. Two key texts justify this conclusion. In the Lukan transfiguration scene, Jesus is depicted as conversing with Moses and Elijah about "his departure [ἔξοδος], which he was about to accomplish in Jerusalem" (Luke 9:31). Now either this singular "exodus" refers to the entire death-exaltation transit, or it refers to only one of those events. If it refers only to the final departure in Luke 24:50–53, then one is left with the tension created by the passion predictions which clearly speak of his "death" as the event which must be "fulfilled in Jerusalem" (see Luke 18:31–32), while Luke 9:31, on this reading, claims that what "must be accomplished" in Jerusalem is Jesus' final departure.

On the other hand, if the "exodus" refers only to his death, then the final departure scene in 24:50–53 is superfluous, and there is tension between this passage and 9:51 in which we are told that "the days drew near for him to be taken up." In fact, I have argued elsewhere that the word "taken up" (ἀνάλημψις) used in Luke 9:51 is itself a word that carries a double entendre in the semantic currency of late antiquity and is best seen as a reference to the entire death/resurrection/exaltation of Jesus.[16] Thus it is not difficult to imagine that a writer who has already closely aligned the death and exaltation of Jesus (see Luke 9:31, 51; Acts 1:2), and for whom the larger theological pattern of reversal is well-known in Luke and Acts (see Luke 1:48; 3:5–6; 14:11; Acts 2:32–33), would see a double entendre in the Greek of Isaiah 53 and end his quotation by reversing the despised status of the Servant with reference to his exaltation through death, his "being lifted up from the earth"!

---

rected prophet as 'life is lifted from the earth'" (*The Acts of the Apostles*, Sacra Pagina 5 [Collegeville, Minn.: Liturgical Press, 1992], 156).

16. See Mikeal C. Parsons, *The Departure of Jesus in Luke-Acts: The Ascension Narratives in Context*, JSNTSup 21 (Sheffield: Sheffield Academic Press, 1987), 128–33. In these pages, I also argue for a similar understanding of ἀνελήμφθη in Acts 1:2. For a reference to ἀνάλημψις meaning "death," see *Pss. Sol.* 4:18. For other examples from late antiquity on the meaning of ἀνάλημψις as "passing away" and "taken up," see P. A. van Stempvoort, "The Interpretation of the Ascension of Luke and Acts," *NTS* 5 (1959): 32–33.

It becomes clear, upon close reading, that the specific citation of Isaiah 53 in Acts 8, rather than being a kind of place-holding proof text (in whose place nearly any OT prophetic text could stand), accomplishes two critical points for Luke. The eunuch is attracted to this figure described in Isaiah 53:7–8. To have included references to the Servant's vicarious suffering would have served as an obstacle to the eunuch's identification with the social location of the sufferer. Thus, for historical verisimilitude, these verses are cited.[17] Furthermore, these verses allow Luke to recapitulate the suffering/vindication of Jesus the Servant in an economical space. To have gone beyond the reference, "and his life is taken up from the earth," would have destroyed the death/exaltation schema.

Intertextual Echoes in Acts 8

So now we can present an alternative to Hooker's view that Luke began and ended the Isaiah quotation where he did in order to avoid references to vicarious suffering. Luke may have wished to avoid these references, but not because he was reticent to contemplate or uninterested in the suffering vocation of the Servant; rather, Luke avoids citing those parts of the passage because it would have detracted from the relevance of the passage for drawing the eunuch to identify with the Servant, and it would have disrupted the humiliation/exaltation schema which Luke found in the rhetorical ambiguity of the Greek of Isaiah 53:7–8.

The allusion to vindication, to be sure, is implicit, and so the ambiguous nature of the scripture requires a Christian interpreter. The eunuch asks: "About whom, pray, does the prophet say this, about himself or about someone else?" So Philip "opened his mouth [see 8:32b!] and beginning with this scripture he told him the good news of Jesus" (8:34–35). This good news, no doubt, included the vindication as well as the suffering of Jesus (see Acts 2:23–24; 3:13–15) and what may have been ambiguous in the scripture is now made clear in its Christian exposition. If, however, the reference were left simply to the kerygmatic "good news" of the death and resurrection, then Hooker's objection would still hold true:

---

17. Ironically, Hooker does not explore why this text might be appropriate for the eunuch to be reading, but simply acknowledges that "behind this story there may lie a genuine recollection that this was the chapter which the eunuch happened to be reading" (*Jesus and the Servant,* 113).

These early chapters of Acts speak only of the historical fact of Christ's death; they do not dwell on his sufferings, or point out the parallel with the Servant Songs. Nor do they trace any connection between Christ's death and the forgiveness of sins, which we would expect if an identification of Jesus with the Servant were intended: for while the forgiveness of sins was proclaimed as part of the kerygma from the very beginning, it is not suggested that this forgiveness was dependent upon Christ's death. (110)

Philip's interpretation, however, does not stop simply with an appeal to the general kerygmatic "good news" of Jesus' death and exaltation. There is an important intertextual echo which takes the reader back to the last chapter of Luke's first volume. The phrase in Acts 8:35, "beginning from" (ἀρξάμενος ἀπό), is a verbatim verbal echo of the same phrase in Luke 24:27, "beginning from [ἀρξάμενος ἀπό] Moses and from all the prophets," the only other place in all of Luke-Acts in which this phrase ("beginning from") is used in connection with scripture.

Let me begin here by applying Richard Hays's criteria for determining allusions and echoes in Paul's letters to Acts 8:35 and Luke 24.[18] Though Hays's criteria were crafted in terms of OT citations and allusions in Paul's letters, I think they apply as well here for the following reasons: (1) the Gospel of Luke was *available* to the author and his original readers; (2) given the verbatim repetition of ἀρξάμενος ἀπό and the rhetorical stress placed on both passages in their narrative context, the *volume* is quite explicit; (3) the *recurrence* of parallels and patterns from Luke in Acts is well-known; (4) the *thematic coherence* is likewise strong: Luke 24 is an amplification of the shorthand of Acts 8; (5) it is *historically plausible* that Luke intended this intertextual echo and that his readers, at least upon subsequent readings, would have recognized it; (6) in terms of the *history of interpretation*, modern scholars, at least, have consistently pointed out the parallels between the stories of the road to Emmaus and the Ethiopian eunuch and suggested interpreting the two

---

18. Examining the adequacy of Hays's criteria was a subtheme of this conference. Though some might object to referring to an echo to Luke in the Book of Acts as "intertextual" because they form one continuous narrative, I have argued elsewhere that Luke and Acts are two independent but interrelated works, and thus "intertextual echo" is a fitting term; see Mikeal C. Parsons and Richard I. Pervo, *Rethinking the Unity of Luke and Acts* (Minneapolis: Fortress, 1993). On the absence of Hays's article in this volume, see the editors' note on p. 5.

passages in light of each other;[19] and (7) the suggested intertextual echo does illuminate the surrounding text and fits well within Luke's rhetorical argument about the gentile mission, thus providing an aesthetically *satisfying fit.*

But what specifically is the context of the phrase in Luke 24? In this story, the resurrected Jesus has joined two disciples on their journey home. Cleopas and his companion have complained that the crucifixion of Jesus, "a prophet mighty in deed and word," had left them in utter despair: "We had hoped that he was the one to redeem Israel" (24:21). The resurrected, but as of yet unrecognized, Christ chastises them: " 'O foolish ones, and slow of heart to believe all that the prophets have spoken! Was it not necessary that the Christ should suffer these things and enter into his glory?' And beginning with Moses and all the prophets, he interpreted to them in all the scriptures the things concerning himself" (24:25–27). Here clearly, Jesus' exposition of scripture, beginning with Moses and all the prophets, exposes the divine necessity of the Christ's suffering. But what was the purpose of this suffering?

This point is made clear a little later in Luke 24:44–47, in a passage which parallels 24:25–27. Here the risen Christ commissions his disciples: " 'These are my words which I spoke to you, while I was still with you, that everything written about me in the law of Moses and the prophets and the psalms must be fulfilled.' Then he opened their minds [cf. Philip opening his mouth in 8:35] to understand the scriptures and said to them, 'Thus it is written that the *Christ must suffer* and on the third day rise from the dead, and that *repentance and forgiveness of sins should be preached in his name to all nations*'" (24:44–47). For Luke the divine necessity of Christ's suffering was both for the redemption of Israel (24:21) and so that the Gentiles (ἔθνη, "nations") might hear the good news of repentance and forgiveness of sins!

Through the use of an intertextual echo, Philip's preaching of the good news, beginning with this scripture (Acts 8:35), is given content by the precursor text in Luke 24. Isaiah 53 is part of those scriptures which testify to the divine necessity of Christ's suffering for the redemption of Israel and for the sake of the repentance and the forgiveness of sins of

---

19. See, e.g., Joseph A. Grassi, "Emmaus Revisited (Luke 24:13–35 and Acts 8:26–40)," *CBQ* 26 (1964): 463–67, and many of the commentaries.

the Gentiles.[20] Hooker is certainly right (contra Betz) that Isaiah 53 does not hold any unique place in the preaching of Acts about the suffering of Christ. But Isaiah 53 (contra Hooker) is indeed *one* of the texts that Luke had in mind when he referred to Christ's suffering according to the scriptures. In fact, it is the only one he explicitly cites!

Conclusion

What then are we to say about the use of Isaiah 53 in Acts 8? Over against Hooker (who, we should remember, argues that in Acts 8 Luke carefully avoids making reference to the vicarious suffering of the Servant), we have argued that the citation begins and ends where it does in a way that is appropriate to the argument: the eunuch identifies with the humiliated and polluted servant, and Luke has found in this particular passage, especially in the double entendre "he was lifted up," a useful humiliation/exaltation schema, and one that is reenacted when the eunuch is baptized by Philip.

Further, over against Hooker's insistence that the citation of Isaiah 53 in Acts 8 is nothing more than a "proof text," I have argued that the intertextual echo to Luke 24 gives the "theological exposition" of Christ's suffering that Hooker claims is missing. With rhetorical subtlety, Luke attributes both *factuality* and *significance* to Christ's suffering. To be sure, Isaiah 53 is not the only text Luke has in mind in Luke 24:25–27 and 24:44–46, but Isaiah 53 *is* part of the prophetic pattern of suffering that informs the early church's (or at least Luke's) understanding of the significance of Christ's suffering.

The conclusion of the Acts 8 passage comes, then, as no surprise. Convinced of the truth of Philip's message, the eunuch lets forth with the refrain of an unhindered gospel that runs throughout Acts: "Look, here is water! What hinders me from being baptized?" (cf. Acts 10:47; 28:31). Until now, there were barriers that could have stood in the way of his undergoing religious initiation rites; perhaps he could not be circumcised and, in any case, he could not be a proselyte to Judaism. But

---

20. This "forgiveness of sins" is part of what Tom Wright calls the "new exodus" enacted by Jesus (see his article in this volume).

now because of the "good news about Jesus" proclaimed to him by Philip, nothing prohibits his transformation being ritualized through Christian baptism. The suffering of Christ, the humiliated, polluted, yet exalted Servant, continues to bear fruit!

8

Response to Mikeal Parsons

Morna D. Hooker

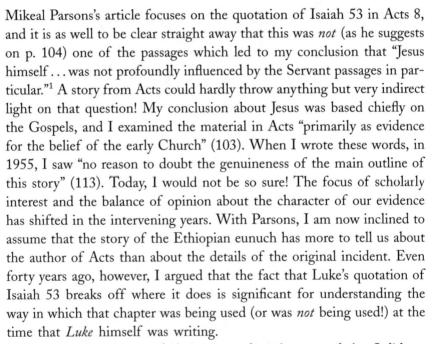

Mikeal Parsons's article focuses on the quotation of Isaiah 53 in Acts 8, and it is as well to be clear straight away that this was *not* (as he suggests on p. 104) one of the passages which led to my conclusion that "Jesus himself ... was not profoundly influenced by the Servant passages in particular."[1] A story from Acts could hardly throw anything but very indirect light on that question! My conclusion about Jesus was based chiefly on the Gospels, and I examined the material in Acts "primarily as evidence for the belief of the early Church" (103). When I wrote these words, in 1955, I saw "no reason to doubt the genuineness of the main outline of this story" (113). Today, I would not be so sure! The focus of scholarly interest and the balance of opinion about the character of our evidence has shifted in the intervening years. With Parsons, I am now inclined to assume that the story of the Ethiopian eunuch has more to tell us about the author of Acts than about the details of the original incident. Even forty years ago, however, I argued that the fact that Luke's quotation of Isaiah 53 breaks off where it does is significant for understanding the way in which that chapter was being used (or was *not* being used!) at the time that *Luke* himself was writing.

Again, in the interest of clarity, it needs to be stressed that I did *not* suggest that "Luke begins and ends the quotation of Isaiah 53 where he does *to avoid* making explicit reference to the vicarious suffering of the Servant."[2] Parsons repeats this statement on p. 118, and it rep-

---

1. Morna D. Hooker, *Jesus and the Servant* (London: SPCK, 1959), 163. Subsequent page references in text are to this volume.
2. Mikeal C. Parsons, "Isaiah 53 in Acts 8: A Reply to Professor Morna Hooker," in this volume, p. 106, italics mine.

resents a grave distortion of my position. To speak of Luke carefully
avoiding "making reference to the vicarious suffering of the Servant"
suggests a deliberate rejection of a particular interpretation of Isaiah 53.[3]
I have always questioned whether that interpretation was known to Luke.
Moreover, that Luke *chose* some lines from Isaiah as apposite to his purpose does *not* mean that he consciously *rejected* others. He had to begin
and finish his quotation somewhere! My argument was that he included
those lines which seemed to him particularly relevant to his purpose, and
ignored those that did not.

We turn to a consideration of the passage itself. Parsons begins by
noting (p. 107) that I was "misleading" in saying that the citation of
Isaiah 53 is found "in the mouth of [the eunuch]."[4] He is, of course,
right — it is Luke who is telling the story, and who therefore quotes
the passage; the point I was making referred to the story itself, where
Isaiah 53 was being read by the eunuch. It is an unimportant quibble,
but one which obscures something more significant, which is that we
need to distinguish between the events related in the narrative and the
interpretation of the storyteller. Here it is Parsons who slips up, for my
conclusion that this particular story provides no "evidence that [Isaiah 53]
was central in the Christian preaching of the time"[5] is not, as he suggests,
"off-base"! The phrase "of the time" referred quite clearly to the time of
the incident itself, not to the time of the author of Acts. It is Parsons's
criticism which is "off-base," because he has failed to read what I wrote
with sufficient care. Even if (as I was — perhaps naively! — supposing)
the story is based on a historical encounter, it cannot be taken as evidence
that Isaiah 53 was an important text in the preaching of the early church.
What was important for Luke is another matter altogether — though
Parsons and I are clearly in agreement in seeing him as making positive
choices about which lines from Isaiah 53 should be included.

Unfortunately, however, in his discussion of "The Eunuch in Late Antiquity" and "The Eunuch's Bible," Parsons does not always make it clear

---

3. Cf. the argument which is often put forward suggesting that Luke has deliberately rejected
the implication of the saying recorded in Mark 10:45 because he preferred the version of the saying
which he himself uses in a different context in Luke 22:27. Such an interpretation goes far beyond
what we may justifiably deduce from the evidence. We do not know that Luke *rejected* the Markan
saying; he may well have had very good reasons for wishing to *include* the alternative version.

4. Hooker, *Jesus and the Servant*, 113.

5. Hooker, *Jesus and the Servant*, 113.

whether he is interpreting the story at the historical level or in terms of
Luke's redaction. He appears to begin with the former question, but ends
with the latter, and in particular with the question as to why Luke should
have linked the eunuch with these particular verses in Isaiah 53. I find his
explanation that a eunuch might have felt an affinity with the portrait of
the sufferer in Isaiah 53, and that this is why Luke chose to quote certain verses from that chapter and to omit others, an attractive one. It is,
however, somewhat puzzling that Acts 8:27 gives no hint that the eunuch
had been prevented from worshiping in the temple:[6] a statement that his
trip to Jerusalem had been fruitless would have picked up the theme of
Acts 7 and would have contrasted admirably with the eunuch's strangely
worded question regarding baptism in 8:37. The absence of any hint that
the eunuch had been unable to join in the worship in Jerusalem makes
me uneasy about Parsons's explanation.

In the last section of his article, Parsons turns to a discussion of
"Intertextual Echoes in Acts 8." He quotes here another passage from
my book[7] — a passage, incidentally, which was written about the introductory chapters of Acts, and not about Acts 8, though it is true that
what I said about Luke not specifically linking the forgiveness of sins
with Christ's death applies also to that chapter. Parsons seeks to make
the link between the quotation of Isaiah 53 and the proclamation of the
forgiveness of sins by means of what he terms an "intertextual echo." Although this particular term is used because of his views concerning the
relationship between Luke and Acts, his argument here does not depend
upon that theory. The suggestion is that the phrase ἀρξάμενος ἀπό in
Acts 8:35 is a conscious echo of the same phrase in Luke 24:27. Since
Luke and Acts were written by the same author (something that Parsons
does not deny), many of us are more likely to conclude that the phrase
was used in two very similar contexts simply because it was the natural
one for Luke to use. However, if we grant that this is a conscious echo,
what follows? We are asked next to make a link between the appeal in
Luke 24:25–27 to Moses and the prophets as confirmation of the necessity for Christ's sufferings and the parallel statement in 24:44–47, which
also refers to Moses and the prophets, and which concludes that "it is

---

6. Parsons, "Isaiah 53 in Acts 8," 110.
7. Hooker, *Jesus and the Servant*, 110.

written that the Christ is to suffer and to rise from the dead on the third day, and that repentance and forgiveness of sins is to be proclaimed in his name to all nations, beginning from Jerusalem." In neither of these statements are we told which passages from "Moses and the prophets" are in mind. Parsons's argument appears to be that the phrase ἀρξάμενος ἀπό in Acts 8:35 is intended to remind us of Luke 24:25–27, that Luke 24:25–27 is parallel to 24:44–47, where forgiveness is mentioned, and that we thus have a link between the quotation of Isaiah 53 in Acts 8 and the proclamation of forgiveness in Luke 24:44–47. He might have strengthened his case by pointing to the use of the phrase ἀρξάμενος ἀπό in Luke 24:47 ("beginning from Jerusalem") — but maybe that is simply more evidence that this was a typical Lukan phrase, rather than an "intertextual echo"![8] When Isaiah 53 is quoted in Acts 8, therefore, we are apparently intended to link that with the idea of forgiveness, even though Luke has carefully (in Parsons's interpretation, not mine!) avoided referring to this idea in order not to detract from his main concern, which is to show how appropriate the portrait of the sufferer was to the eunuch's own situation.

In his conclusion, Parsons refers to the author of Acts as using "rhetorical subtlety."[9] The phrase is an apt one! The subtlety is such, I suggest, as to strain our credulity. We are asked to believe that Luke has in mind (and intends his readers to have in mind) a passage in the Gospel in which the fulfillment of scripture is linked with the forgiveness of sins and which is very similar to another passage earlier in the same chapter which speaks of the fulfillment of scripture (but not of forgiveness) and where, in speaking of the exegesis of scripture, we find the phrase "beginning from," a phrase which is used in Acts 8. Strangely, although Parsons has provided a plausible reason as to why Luke has not included any reference to "vicarious suffering" in Acts 8, he attempts at the very same time to show that it is, after all, lurking beneath the surface. These two interpretations are incompatible. *Either* Luke wants his readers to link Isaiah 53 with forgiveness *or* Luke has chosen to begin and end his citation where he does because if he had included more, this would have obscured his argument. Parsons cannot have it both ways!

8. The phrase is used three times altogether in Luke, and three times in Acts.
9. Parsons, "Isaiah 53 in Acts 8," 118.

In his final summing-up, Parsons once again wrongly attributes to me the view that "in Acts 8 Luke *carefully avoids* making reference to the vicarious suffering of the Servant";[10] strangely, though he says that he is arguing "over against" this view, it seems to be the one he himself espouses, since he has earlier said. "Luke may have wished to avoid these references [to vicarious suffering], . . . because [citing them] would have detracted from the relevance of the passage for drawing the eunuch to identify with the Servant, and it would have disrupted the humiliation/exaltation schema which Luke found in the rhetorical ambiguity of the Greek of Isaiah 53:7–8."[11] It is, of course, the *reason* for the omission of certain lines which is in dispute. The suggestion I made was simply that Luke had not noticed their relevance. The explanation Parsons puts forward is that Luke *deliberately* omitted them because they detracted from his main theme.

Parsons's argument regarding the "intertextual echo" cannot be regarded as convincing evidence that Isaiah 53 was, after all, important for Luke's "understanding of the significance of Christ's suffering."[12] On the contrary, by providing a plausible explanation for the use of these particular verses from Isaiah in this particular context, he has undermined the usual argument that this story demonstrates the importance of Isaiah 53 for the church's understanding of the death of Christ, that the omission of the key verses was accidental, and that Luke intended us to bear the whole Old Testament passage in mind. The attraction of the passage was apparently not even that it was an obvious proof text (as I have argued), but that it corresponded to the *eunuch's* condition! If he is right, then he has provided further evidence that the church came only slowly to see the relevance of this great passage to its message about the forgiveness of sins.

---

10. Parsons, "Isaiah 53 in Acts 8," 118, italics mine.
11. Parsons, "Isaiah 53 in Acts 8," 115.
12. Parsons, "Isaiah 53 in Acts 8," 118.

9

Jesus' Death, Isaiah 53, and Mark 10:45

A Crux Revisited

RIKKI E. WATTS

Introduction

In 1959 C. K. Barrett and Morna Hooker independently published material that raised serious objections to the prevailing consensus that Jesus' understanding of his suffering was largely shaped by Isaiah 53's account of the suffering Servant.[1] In her deservedly celebrated book, Hooker argued that in order unequivocally to demonstrate such a link it must be shown that statements concerning the necessity of Jesus' sufferings not only exhibit linguistic and conceptual parallels with Isaiah 53 and related passages, but that such parallels were also unique to those passages. Although allowing that the Gospels contained "a considerable number of possible references to the oracles of Deutero-Isaiah," Hooker found no "sure reference to any of the Servant Songs...in those passages where Jesus speaks of the *meaning* of his death: there is no evidence that either he or the evangelists had the suffering of the Servant in mind."[2] On the contrary, much more likely is the possibility that the suffering motif was

---

This essay, based on an expanded section of my Ph.D. thesis (see n. 10 below), was given at the "International Colloquy on Isaiah 53 and Christian Origins," Baylor University, February 1996.

1. C. K. Barrett, "The Background of Mark 10:45," in *New Testament Essays: Studies in Memory of T. W. Manson*, ed. A. J. B. Higgins (Manchester: Manchester University Press, 1959), 1–18, and M. D. Hooker, *Jesus and the Servant* (London: SPCK, 1959). Hooker cites F. Jackson and K. Lake, *The Beginnings of Christianity*, vol. 1, pt. 1 (London: Macmillan, 1920), 381–92, as the first serious challenge, supported later by F. C. Burkitt, *Christian Beginnings* (London, 1924), 38–39, and H. J. Cadbury in Jackson and Lake, *Beginnings*, 5:364–70.

2. Hooker, *Jesus and the Servant*, 148–50.

derived from reflections upon the career of the Son of Man in Daniel 7.[3] Barrett's article concentrated solely on Mark 10:45 but came to similar conclusions. Finding no clear linguistic links with Isaiah 53, he argued that the motif of service was too widely known in the OT to evoke specifically the Servant and that the suffering pattern instead probably derives from the Maccabean background to Daniel 7's Son of Man.

There is no question that Hooker and Barrett have exposed the tenuous nature of many of the assumptions and the weakness of many of the arguments propounded by supporters of the Isaiah 53 theory. However, their works have been criticized for dealing with sayings in a piecemeal fashion, treating linguistic parallels in isolation, and to varying degrees failing to take into account that the whole is commonly greater than the sum of the parts.[4] To this we might add that even when a saying is regarded in its totality, it must also be located within the broader context of the evangelist's presentation of Jesus' ministry. In this regard Hooker was right to recognize the profound influence of "Deutero-Isaiah" on Jesus, even if we might question whether this influence was taken seriously enough. At the same time, a number of recent developments warrant a new examination of the data (see below).

In this essay I will argue that insufficient attention has been paid either to the hermeneutical framework provided by Mark's Gospel as a literary whole or to those indications which the Markan Jesus offers as to the provenance of his descriptions of his future suffering. Further, the examination of linguistic parallels has often neglected the mixed nature of Markan citations of and therefore perhaps allusions to the OT, the highly allusive fashion in which Mark's Jesus often appeals to OT texts, the often idiosyncratic or less common translational choices evident in Isaiah LXX, and the phenomenon of semantic change which raises questions about the validity of relying solely on the LXX to determine linguistic parallels. When all of these factors are considered, the case for an allusion to Isaiah 53 in the passion predictions and Mark 10:45 is rather stronger than Hooker or Barrett suggests. As both Hooker and Barrett dealt with the words as they stand in Mark's Gospel, and given the limits of this

---

3. M. D. Hooker, *The Son of Man in Mark* (London: SPCK, 1967), 103–47.

4. E.g., J. Jeremias, review of *Jesus and the Servant*, by M. D. Hooker, *JTS* 11 (1960): 142f.; R. T. France, "The Servant of the Lord in the Teaching of Jesus," *TynBul* 19 (1968): 28f.; C. G. Kruse, *New Testament Foundations for Ministry: Jesus and Paul* (London: Marshall, Morgan & Scott, 1983), 44f.

article, I will do the same, thereby confining myself to comments on the sayings of Jesus as Mark presents them. The question of how much of this derives from the historical Jesus will have to be held in abeyance.

Method: The Markan Jesus and the OT

At the outset, several characteristic features of the Markan Jesus' use of the OT should be noted. First, there is the phenomenon of semantic change. For example, most scholars including Hooker agree that Mark 3:27 alludes to Isaiah 49:24 even though there is no direct verbal correspondence — the LXX uses γίγας whereas Mark's Jesus uses ἰσχυρός.[5] In other words, since the conceptual parallels are deemed strong enough and unique to both passages, the absence of direct linguistic parallels is not considered sufficient grounds to disqualify the allusion. This is important since both Barrett and Hooker base their argument against an Isaiah 53 allusion in Mark 10:45 primarily on the lack of clear verbal parallels.

Moreover, the data are actually more subtle than this. Although the substantive form of γίγας renders גִּבּוֹר sixteen times in the LXX, its synonym, ἰσχυρός, is used twice as often. The translator of Isaiah has apparently chosen a less common rendering, but this is not uncharacteristic.[6] By the late first century C.E., however, not only is γίγας absent from the NT and many contemporaneous writings, but also, in the one place in the NT where an OT text containing γίγας appears — the allusion to Ezekiel 39:20 in Revelation 19:18 — it is rendered by ἰσχυρός.[7] This suggests that semantic change ruled out γίγας as a viable translational option, and hence the synonym ἰσχυρός was used — which in any case was the more common LXX choice. The point here is that merely consulting the LXX of Isaiah fails to take into consideration either the idiosyncratic translation tendencies evident in that book or the effects of semantic change whereby the earlier Septuagintal choice of a word might no longer be a valid option in the first century.

---

5. See Hooker, *Jesus and the Servant*, 73. However, ἰσχύοντος occurs in 49:25 LXX.

6. E.g., ἀνοίγω to render קָרַע in 63.19, ψυλλίζω for בָּזַע in 37:22 and 49:7.

7. See G. B. Caird, *A Commentary on the Revelation of St. John the Divine* (London: A. & C. Black, 1966), 247. γίγας does, however, occur in the patristic writings with the sense of giant or heretic; see G. W. H. Lampe, ed., *A Patristic Greek Lexicon* (Oxford: Clarendon, 1961), 315.

The allusion to Isaiah 49:24 in Mark 3:27 raises a second consideration: the nature of the Markan Jesus' explanatory comments. There are very few occasions when Mark's Jesus gives some indication of the *significance* of his saving or delivering actions.[8] Interestingly, one such explanation seems to occur in each of Mark's three basic sections (see below) and concerns respectively Jesus' exorcisms in 3:27, his suffering in 10:45, and the significance of the cup in 14:24. The highly allusive character of 3:27 and at least part of 14:24 is undisputed — from Mark's point of view, Jesus was apparently given to enigmatic ways of speaking. If the absence of clear linguistic parallels is characteristic of the explanatory statements in 3:27 and 14:24, then we should perhaps expect something similar for 10:45.

Third, as Kee has noted, many of Mark's allusions to or citations of the OT are mixed or combined. That is, the OT is used in a "synthetic" manner. Analogously with, for example, *4QFlorilegium* (4Q174), two seemingly unrelated OT texts are integrated to present a new assertion (e.g., Mal. 3:1 with Exod. 23:20 [?] and Isa. 40:3 in Mark 1:2f.; Isa. 42:1, Ps. 2:7, and perhaps Gen. 22:2, 12, 17 in Mark 1:11; Isa. 56:7 and Jer. 7:11 in Mark 11:17).[9] Again, it might not be surprising if Mark 10:45 reflects a similar approach.

These data together suggest that (*a*) on the basis of the nature of the Markan Jesus' explanations elsewhere, we might reasonably expect 10:45 to be highly allusive; (*b*) it might well combine allusions to several previously unconnected OT texts; and (*c*) the absence of clear linguistic parallels is not sufficient grounds to rule out an allusion, and even less so where only one OT passage offers a comparable picture.

The Markan Horizon: The Broader Context of Mark 10:45

The next matter concerns the importance of Mark's theological horizon. The point here is that to isolate a statement from Mark's overall theological framework is to ignore a key hermeneutical indicator. Mark almost

---

8. Statements concerning judgment are rather clearer, e.g., 4:12; 7:6–7; cf. 11:17; 12:10–11.

9. H. C. Kee, "The Function of Scriptural Quotations and Allusions in Mark 11–16," in *Jesus und Paulus*, ed. E. Earle Ellis and E. Grässer (Göttingen: Vandenhoeck & Ruprecht, 1975), 175ff. Given our focus here it should be noted that Kee, 183, concludes, "There are no sure references to Isaiah 53."

certainly intends his literary-theological structure to provide the delimiting interpretative context for those sayings of Jesus which he chooses to record. In this regard, Hooker's observation that Jesus seems to have been strongly influenced by the message of Deutero-Isaiah, although generally shared by a number of commentators, has found detailed support in two recent works, namely, the Ph.D. thesis of the present author, and later, in a book and an essay by Joel Marcus.[10] In both cases it is argued that Mark's Gospel reflects the Isaianic schema of a New Exodus (hereafter NE).

This is borne out not only in terms of ancient literary technique, in which opening sentences were widely understood to lay out the author's program,[11] but also in the light of the Deutero-Isaianic imagery which so thoroughly pervades not only Mark's prologue but also subsequent chapters.[12] The basic threefold structure of Mark's Gospel (after the prologue: 1:16–8:21/26; 8:22/27–10:45/52; 10:46/11:1–16:8) also coheres with the Exodus rubric of deliverance from bondage and journey to the place of Yahweh's presence:

Exodus:	deliverance from Egypt	journey through the desert	Sinai
Isaianic NE:	deliverance from Babylon	journey along the "way"	Jerusalem
Mark:	deliverance from Satan	journey along the "way"	Jerusalem

As far as Mark 10:45 is concerned, both Marcus and I have also argued that Mark's "way" section seems shaped by the Isaianic "way"

---

10. R. E. Watts, "The Influence of the Isaianic New Exodus on the Gospel of Mark" (Ph.D. diss., Cambridge, 1990), published as *Isaiah's New Exodus and Mark,* WUNT II, 88 (Tübingen: Mohr Siebeck, 1997); J. Marcus, *The Way of the Lord: Christological Exegesis of the Old Testament in the Gospel of Mark* (Louisville: Westminster/John Knox, 1992), and idem, "Mark and Isaiah," in *Fortunate the Eyes That See: Essays in Honor of David Noel Freedman in Celebration of His Seventieth Birthday,* ed. A. B. Beck et al. (Grand Rapids: Eerdmans, 1995), 449–66. See also M. A. Beavis, *Mark's Audience: The Literary and Social Setting of Mark 4.11–12,* JSNTSup 33 (Sheffield: JSOT Press, 1989), 110, and R. Schneck, *Isaiah in the Gospel of Mark, I–VII,* BDS 1 (Vallejo, Calif.: BIBAL, 1994).

11. See D. Earl, "Prologue-Form in Ancient Historiography," *ANRW* 1:22, 842–56.

12. So, e.g., Isaiah 40 and Malachi 3 in Mark 1:2–3; on εὐαγγέλιον, see P. Stuhlmacher, *Das paulinische Evangelium,* vol. 1: *Vorgeschichte* (Göttingen: Vandenhoeck & Ruprecht, 1968), 191–206; on the rending of the heaven and Isaiah 42 in the voice, see Watts, "Influence," 49–58; and on the summary of Jesus' preaching in 1:15, see B. D. Chilton, *God in Strength,* SNTU 1 (Freistadt: F. Plöchl, 1979), 86–95. Further, e.g., O. Betz, "Jesu Evangelium vom Gottesreich," in *Das Evangelium und die Evangelien,* WUNT 28, ed. P. Stuhlmacher (Tübingen: J. C. B. Mohr [Paul Siebeck], 1983), 55–77, R. Guelich, "'The Beginning of the Gospel' Mark 1:1–15," *BibRes 27* (1982): 5–15; W. L. Lane, *The Gospel of Mark,* NICNT 2 (Grand Rapids: Eerdmans, 1974), 43; and H.-J. Steichele, *Der leidende Sohn Gottes: Eine Untersuchung einiger alttestamentlicher Motive in der Christologie des Markus Evangeliums,* BU 14 (Regensburg: Pustet, 1980), 52ff.

to Jerusalem.[13] In Isaiah, this "way" also exhibits a sapiential aspect. Part of what is at issue in these chapters is a debate between Yahweh and his "blind" servant Israel over Yahweh's right to effect her salvation as he chooses, which in this case centers on Yahweh's staggering and offensive choice of Cyrus as his agent.[14] It is Israel's refusal to accept this choice — perhaps due to expectations of a new Moses or new David — that results in the delay of the majority of the Isaianic New Exodus (hereafter Isaianic NE) promises. Thus in chapters 49–55, given Israel's idolatrous refusal to accept Yahweh's plan, a new but unnamed "servant" Israel is commissioned (49:1ff),[15] whose utterly misunderstood career (Isa. 53:1ff.; cf. 52:12) and "death" is apparently closely tied to the realization of the now postponed full restoration of the nation.[16]

The parallels between Mark and Isaiah are obvious. Just as Yahweh's promise to lead "blind" Israel along a way it does not know (Isa. 42:16) indicates that Israel's deliverance will not be in keeping with its expectations, so in Mark the "blind" disciples are led along a "way" they do not understand, as indicated by their response to the three passion predictions.[17] Similarly, just as in Isaiah the misunderstood death of the enigmatic "servant"[18] is ironically revealed to be the NE "way" in which wise Yahweh will finally effect Israel's restoration, so also Mark's "way" to Jerusalem is characterized by the repeated instruction that Israel's es-

---

13. Respectively, "Influence," 102–12, and "Mark and Isaiah."

14. For this see R. E. Watts, "Consolation or Confrontation? Isaiah 40–55 and the Delay of the New Exodus," *TynBul* 41 (1990): 41–49.

15. R. F. Melugin, *The Formation of Isaiah 40–55* (Berlin and New York: de Gruyter, 1976), 70f.; H. G. M. Williamson, "The Concept of Israel in Transition," in *The World of Ancient Israel*, ed. R. E. Clements (Cambridge: Cambridge University Press, 1989), 146f.; B. J. van der Merwe "Pentateuchtradisies in die prediking van Deuterojesaja" (diss., Groningen, 1955; cited in H. C. Spykerboer, "The Structure and Composition of Deutero-Isaiah" [diss., Groningen, 1976], 52).

16. Watts, "Consolation," 49–59; see also J. F. A. Sawyer, *From Moses to Patmos* (London: SPCK, 1977), 115; W. J. Dumbrell, "The Purpose of the Book of Isaiah," *TynBul* 36 (1985): 126; R. J. Clifford, *Fair Spoken and Persuading: An Interpretation of Second Isaiah* (New York: Paulist, 1984), 181; A. R. Ceresko, "The Rhetorical Strategy of the Fourth Servant Song (Isaiah 52:13–53:12): Poetry and the Exodus-New Exodus," *CBQ* 56 (1994): 42–55; cf. H. E. von Waldow, "The Message of Deutero-Isaiah," *Int* 22 (1968): 284f. This might also help explain why aspects of Isaiah 53 are attributed to the Messiah in *Tg. Isa.* 53; see further S. H. Levey, *The Messiah: An Aramaic Interpretation. The Messianic Exegesis of the Targum*, HUCM 2 (New York: Hebrew Union College, 1974), 63–67; B. D. Chilton, *The Glory of Israel: The Theology and Provenience of the Isaiah Targum*, JSOTSup 23 (Sheffield: JSOT Press, 1982), 86–96.

17. Watts, "Influence," 108–11; cf. Marcus, "Mark and Isaiah," 452ff.

18. The term "servant" is used to refer to the enigmatic figure/s that seems to be the subject of at least Isaiah 50:4ff. and 52:12–53:12.

chatological hopes are to be realized through the death of her Messiah (e.g., 10:45; 14:24; cf. 1:2–3).

All this suggests that Mark intends his audience to use the Isaianic NE as the primary frame of reference. Consequently, if there is any doubt concerning the source or significance of a given allusion, then the first port of call ought to be those Isaianic texts which concern the NE.

Mark 9:12: The OT Context of Mark 10:45

Although Barrett earlier argued that the background to Jesus' suffering is Maccabean martyrology, to which Daniel 7 points,[19] his argument ignores the one indication that the Markan Jesus himself gives as to his understanding of his suffering, namely, Mark 9:12. The introductory formula πῶς γέγραπται (cf. δεῖ in Mark 8:31) almost certainly refers to what Jews and Protestants now regard as the OT,[20] which one would then expect to be the source of the language πολλὰ πάθῃ καὶ ἐξουδενηθῇ.

Recognizing that there is no direct OT prophecy of a suffering Son of Man, Hooker nevertheless argues that ἐξουδενηθῇ refers to the suffering Son of Man in Daniel 7.[21] While it is true that Jesus uses Son of Man as a self-designation which prima facie indicates a Daniel 7 background, we have also seen that Mark's Jesus is not averse to combining otherwise "unrelated" OT texts or motifs. That this is probably the case here is suggested by two pieces of data. Conceptually, a suffering Son of Man is hardly the point of the Daniel 7, being at most only implied, and, linguistically, neither ἐξουδενέω nor any of its synonyms describes either the Son of Man or the saints in either the LXX or the other Greek versions. The case for Daniel 7 is not strong.

Several psalms in which some form of the ἐξουδεν- stem occurs have also been proposed, for example, Psalms 21:7 (LXX, using the nominal; cf. Mark 15:24, 34) and 118:22, 141 (LXX, with the nominal and par-

---

19. See, e.g., Barrett, "Background," 12f.; Hooker, *Jesus and the Servant,* 158f.

20. See, e.g., E. E. Ellis, *The Old Testament and Early Christianity* (Tübingen: Mohr, 1991).

21. M. D. Hooker, *The Gospel according to St. Mark,* BNTC (London: A. & C. Black, 1991), 220, assuming that Son of Man is both a title and an allusion to Daniel 7. On aspects of the present debate, see, e.g., C. F. D. Moule, "'The Son of Man': Some of the Facts," *NTS* 41 (1995): 277–79; M. Casey, "Idiom and Translation: Some Aspects of the Son of Man Problem," *NTS* 41 (1995): 164–82; T. B. Slater, "One Like a Son of Man in First-Century c.e. Judaism," *NTS* 41 (1995): 183–98.

ticiple).[22] In each case there is some connection with a despised sufferer who appeals for assistance. However, apart from a typological approach none of these texts has a sense of future necessity, and neither are they related to the Isaianic NE. This fact in itself does not necessarily disqualify them, but on the other hand, that LXX Isaiah commonly offers idiosyncratic renderings suggests another option — Isaiah 53 — which is absolutely central to the Isaianic NE. All three Greek versions unanimously reject LXX Isaiah 53:3's irregular choice and adopt the otherwise standard Septuagintal translation of בָּזֹה,[23] that is, ἐξουδενέω.[24] Mark seems not to regard 9:12 as a direct quotation and therefore may feel no compulsion to conform it to a specific LXX text. Indeed, it may be that he, or his tradition, instead considers ἐξουδενέω to be the more typical or common Greek word for the underlying Hebrew (cf. 3:27). If so, Mark's term might well indicate an allusion not to the LXX but the Hebrew of Isaiah 53.[25] Although the evidence is less than clear-cut, at least an allusion to Isaiah 53 combines the motifs of prophetic necessity and the Isaianic NE and so displays an intrinsic coherence with the overall Markan agenda — such is not the case with the other candidate texts.

There is also πολλὰ πάθῃ. Only Psalm 21 (LXX) and Isaiah 53 extensively describe the sufferings of their respective subjects. Psalms 117 (LXX) and 118 (LXX) have brief accounts, while Daniel 7 at least notes that the saints suffer (Dan. 7:25), but at most only implies suffering for the Son of Man. Conceptually speaking, the Daniel 7 option is again not strong. However, when we examine the linguistic issues from the perspective of semantic innovation the data become clearer.

In striking contrast to the NT, πάσχω is rarely found in the LXX, with only a few occurrences having Hebrew counterparts in the OT:

22. E.g., R. H. Gundry, *Mark: A Commentary on His Apology for the Cross* (Grand Rapids: Eerdmans, 1993), 485. Psalm 117:22 (LXX) has also been proposed, but when Mark elsewhere cites this text he uses the LXX's ἀποδοκιμάζω (12:10; cf. 8:31).

23. See E. C. D. Santos, *An Expanded Index for the Hatch-Redpath Concordance to the Septuagint* (Jerusalem: Dugith, Baptist House, n.d.), 23; Hooker, *Jesus and the Servant*, 94. As noted earlier, בָּזֹה in Isaiah 37:22 and 49:7 is translated by the unusual φαυλίζω.

24. R. T. France, *Jesus and the Old Testament* (repr., Grand Rapids: Baker, 1982), 123f.; see C. E. B. Cranfield, *The Gospel according to St. Mark*, CGTC (Cambridge: Cambridge University Press, 1959), 298. Gundry, *Mark*, 485, excludes the evidence of the later versions because they are not pre-Christian, but fails to appreciate that they provide important indications of the trajectory of semantic change.

25. While Mark apparently uses the LXX, he is clearly not bound by it, and will go his own way when it suits; see, e.g., Mark 1:2f., and Mark 4:12. See the arguments of Chilton on the Targumic background to Jesus' language, *God in Strength*.

Amos 6:6; Esther 9:26; Zechariah 11:5; Ezekiel 16:5; and Daniel 11:17. Of these, only in Amos 6:6, where πάσχω renders the *niphal* of חָלָה, does it have the sense of "to be weak, sick" and thus "to be in pain, to suffer." The LXX in fact uses a variety of other verbs to render the considerable semantic range of חָלָה. In order of frequency they are ἀρρωστέω, πονέω, ἀσθενέω, μαλακίζομαι, ἐνοχλέω, ματριάζω, and φλεγμαίνω.[26] What is noteworthy is that while various nominal forms of these verbs occur in the NT, the only verbs that carry over are ἀσθενέω and ἐνοχλέω,[27] and they tend to be quite specific, respectively, "to be weak, sickly" and "to cause trouble, to annoy." The idea of suffering in general, however, is conveyed by πάσχω. These data indicate a process of semantic change whereby πάσχω, although earlier meaning "to experience" either good or ill and infrequently used in the OT, in the NT has come to be the common word for the more general concept of suffering.[28] In other words, πάσχω appears to be the contemporary Greek equivalent of חָלָה, where the latter means "to suffer or endure."

In considering the candidate texts above, it is significant that none of the Psalms nor Daniel 7, whether in the Hebrew, the LXX, or the other Greek versions, has any of the relevant verbal or substantival forms of חָלָה or its Greek counterparts. The only text which does contain such forms is Isaiah 53, which has not one but three points of contact: two substantives and a *hiphil* form of חָלָה — חֳלִי (v. 3), חֳלָיֵנוּ (v. 4), and הֶחֱלִי (v. 10) — while the LXX has μεμαλάκισται (v. 5) and μαλακίαν (v. 3; cf. πόνος in v. 4). Aquila reads ἀρρωστία, Symmachus ἐπίπονος, and Theodotion μαλακία in 53:3, Symmachus νόσος in 53:4, and Aquila (Eus.) ἀρρωστία in 53:10. If πολλὰ πάθη is intended to evoke a particular OT passage, it is hard to see how Isaiah 53 could not be the primary candidate.[29]

When these data are put together with Mark's Isaianic NE horizon,

---

26. K. Seybold, *TDOT* 4:402, who also notes the nominal forms: ἀρρωστία, μαλακία, νόσος, πόνος, ἁμαρτία, and τραῦμα.

27. The word ἀρρωστέω occurs in Matthew 14:14 in D, and several uses occur in Philo, Josephus, and early Christian literature; see BAGD.

28. See BAGD, 633f., and W. Michaelis, *TDNT* 5:907ff.

29. See D. J. Moo, *The Old Testament in the Gospel Passion Narratives* (Sheffield: Almond, 1983), 91. Gundry, *Mark*, 485, rejects an allusion to Isaiah 53:3 because atonement is not mentioned, and Mark nowhere else appeals to Isaiah 53:3. But the first argument is irrelevant since the fact of Jesus' suffering, not its purpose, is in view, and the second somewhat strangely implies that Mark must allude to OT texts at least twice.

then the convergence of the various lines of evidence suggests that the conceptual and linguistic backgrounds to Mark 9:12 are to be found in Isaiah 53. Again, that Mark's Jesus should join two previously unconnected ideas — Son of Man and Isaianic "servant" imagery — is not surprising.[30] If this assessment is correct, then we might expect the other suffering sayings to derive from the same source.

The Passion Predictions

The characteristic actions described in the three passion predictions are, respectively, πολλὰ πάσχω, ἀποδοκιμάζω, ἀποκτείνω, and μετὰ τρεῖς ἡμέρας ἀνίστημι (8:31); παραδίδωμι, ἀποκτείνω, and μετὰ τρεῖς ἡμέρας ἀνίστημι (9:31); and παραδίδωμι, κατακρίνω θανάτῳ, ἐμπαίζω, ἐμπτύω, and μαστιγόω (10:33–34). Because we are dealing with allusions rather than quotations and assuming some coherence between Mark 9:12 and the predictions, we will look for parallels with the texts examined above.

Taking the actions seriatim, πολλὰ πάσχω (8:31), as I have argued, is most probably an allusion to Isaiah 53. The word ἀποδοκιμάζω occurs in Mark 12:10's citation of Psalm 117:22 (LXX) and, in the context of being handed over to death but being resurrected (see Ps. 117:18), might allude to that psalm[31] — another example perhaps of combining ideas, although being a matter of only one word suggests that it belongs instead to the larger motif of the righteous sufferer.[32] The word ἀποκτείνω (8:31 and 9:31) is unattested in any of our texts, but the concept is reiterated in 10:33's κατακρινοῦσιν αὐτὸν θανάτῳ. Although both Psalm 21:16 and 117:18 (LXX) have single references to death (εἰς χοῦν θανάτου κατήγαγές με and τῷ θανάτῳ οὐ παρέδωκέν με), Isaiah 53

---

30. "The process in all of this is the interpretation of Scripture by Scripture, but with an eschatological aim that sees in Jesus the fulfillment of what can be discerned only when the synthesis of unrelated passages has been achieved" (Kee, "Function," 177). The combination of Son of Man language with other OT figures and motifs in intertestamental literature suggests that the assumption that all the content of Mark's Son of Man predications must originate in Daniel 7 be treated with caution; see, e.g., J. VanderKam, "Righteous One, Messiah, Chosen One, and Son of Man in 1 Enoch 37–71," in *The Messiah*, ed. J. H. Charlesworth (Minneapolis: Fortress, 1992), 169–91.

31. M. Black, "The 'Son of Man' Passion Sayings in the Gospel Tradition," *ZNW* 60 (1969): 1–8; Gundry, *Mark*, 429, 446.

32. On the similarities between Isaiah 53 and the thanksgiving psalm genre, to which Psalm 117 (LXX) belongs, see R. N. Whybray, *Thanksgiving for a Liberated Prophet: An Interpretation of Isaiah Chapter 53*, JSOTSup 4 (Sheffield: JSOT Press, 1978), 132ff.

with its three points of contact (see θάνατος in vv. 8, 9, 12; LXX) clearly places greater emphasis on the matter. Moreover, that this "death" is explicitly the result of "judgment"[33] (see κατακρινοῦσιν in Mark 10:33) is found only in Isaiah 53:8 (וּמִמִּשְׁפָּט מֵעֹצֶר, cf. the LXX, κρίσις).[34] Παραδίδωμι (9:31 and 10:33f.) occurs in the request for deliverance in Psalm 118:121 (LXX), but Mark's Jesus is predicting the opposite. Schaberg has proposed that 9:31's παραδίδοται εἰς χεῖρας and μετὰ τρεῖς ἡμέρας ἀναστήσεται echoes Daniel 7:25.[35] Full discussion of this suggestion is not possible here. A reasonable case can be made for the first phrase — somewhat less for the second — but even this is not particularly strong. However, even if one does not wish to rule out the possibility of a Daniel 7 influence, again it is in Isaiah 53 that παραδίδωμι is more prominent (vv. 6, 12, LXX). Further, while being handed over to death is not immediately evident in Daniel 7,[36] it is clearly the case with the "servant."[37] Μετὰ τρεῖς ἡμέρας ἀνίστημι is not found in any of the proposed OT sources (see Hos. 6:2), but both Psalm 21 (LXX) and Isaiah 53 express some expectation of subsequent deliverance.[38] Finally, while none of the terms ἐμπαίζω, ἐμπτύω, and μαστιγόω appears in our texts, the last two are found in Isaiah 50:6's description of the sufferings of the "servant" (μάστιγας and ἐμπτυσμάτων) and thus exhibit an intrinsic coherence with Isaiah 53, perhaps even suggesting that Mark's Jesus saw both texts as describing the one figure.[39]

---

33. See, e.g., Whybray, *Thanksgiving*, 99f.

34. See C. R. North, *The Suffering Servant in Deutero-Isaiah* (London: Oxford University Press, 1948), 149f.; C. Westermann, *Isaiah 40–66*, trans. D. M. G. Stalker (London: SCM, 1969), 264; D. J. A. Clines, *I, He, We, and They — A Literary Approach to Isaiah 53*, JSOTSup 3 (Sheffield: JSOT Press, 1976), 17f.; Whybray, *Thanksgiving*, 99f.; cf. J. D. W. Watts, *Isaiah 34–66*, WBC 25 (Waco, Tex.: Word, 1985, 1987), 220ff.

35. J. Schaberg, "Daniel 7, 12 and the New Testament Passion-Resurrection Predictions," *NTS* 31 (1985): 209ff.; cf. C. C. Caragounis, *The Son of Man*, WUNT 38 (Tübingen: J. C. B. Mohr [Paul Siebeck], 1986), 199.

36. The literary context — the previous account in Daniel 6 and its parallel in Daniel 3 (see A. Lenglet, "La structure littéraire de Daniel 2–7," *Bib* 53 [1972]: 169–90), and the brutal nature of the fourth beast — could indicate that "being handed over" means death.

37. Moo, *Passion*, 92–96; cf. Caragounis, *Son*, 197. Hooker, *Son*, 94, disallows an allusion here since it is merely "the natural word to use in the context" (which may also explain its use in Isaiah 53). If an allusion was intended, what other word would Mark's Jesus use?

38. See Whybray, *Thanksgiving*, 79ff., 120; and N. H. Snaith, for whom the Song's primary focus is the Servant's vindication and triumph ("Isaiah 40–66: A Study of the Teaching of the Second Isaiah and Its Consequences," in *Studies on the Second Part of the Book of Isaiah*, ed. N. H. Snaith and H. M. Orlinsky, rev. ed., VTSup 14 [Leiden: Brill, 1977], 207).

39. See Moo, *Passion*, 88f. Gundry, *Mark*, 576, sees the reversed word order and the "remarkable" omission — since it appears in Mark 14:65 — of ῥαπίσματα as discounting an Isaiah 50:6 (LXX)

To sum up, while there are various single linguistic connections with one or another of the candidate texts — and therefore to assume only one OT influence is probably mistaken — Isaiah 53 not only has on several occasions more numerous points of contact with a specific expression, but is also by far the dominant text overall. This fact on its own suggests that Isaiah 53 is again the formative text. That this conclusion conforms so well with the evidence of Mark 9:12, with Mark's overall Isaianic NE horizon, and with the significance of the "death" of the "servant" for the Isaianic NE, only serves to confirm the suspicion that Isaiah 53 is the primary conceptual influence on the Markan Jesus' understanding of his death. If so then what we have is once again the conjunction of two motifs: the Son of Man and the suffering of the Isaianic "servant" figure. In this regard, if for the sake of argument we allow that Mark's Jesus was among the first to see a suffering Son of Man in Daniel 7, the linguistic and conceptual parallels indicate that he derived the majority of the descriptive details of this suffering from Isaiah 53 and 50.[40]

This raises the question of whether Mark's Jesus is creatively elucidating a unique reading of suffering within the Son of Man motif — but then why should he do so using language and concepts primarily clustered around the "servant" texts in Isaiah? — or is he, as the general "Deutero-Isaianic" color of his ministry might suggest, being equally creative in attributing a more determinative role for the enigmatic suffering "servant" figure of Isaiah? I will return to this question later.

Mark 10:45

In spite of Mark's Jesus three times predicting the fact of his death, the ransom saying at the climax of Mark's "way" section is his first comment on the purpose of his death. Although Hooker and Barrett have argued against an Isaiah 53 influence, the material presented up to this point strongly suggests the contrary. Before reassessing the evidence some points need to be reviewed. First, since we are again dealing with an al-

---

allusion. But having provided the first and the third words, Mark's Jesus may feel no compulsion to provide a complete list.

40. E.g., Hooker, *Son*, 95, who concedes that "the predictions do correspond broadly with the picture of Isa 53." On this method of integrating texts, see in particular L. Hartmann, *Prophecy Interpreted* (Uppsala: CWK Gleerup, 1966).

lusion, as in the case of Mark 3:27, linguistic considerations based on the LXX alone should not be determinative. Second, we should also not be surprised if again we find a combination of a number of ideas from the OT. Third, all three passion predictions follow a consistent pattern of (a) prediction (8:31; 9:31; 10:32f.), (b) failure to understand (8:32–33; 9:32; 10:35–41), and (c) subsequent teaching (8:34–38; 9:35–37; 10:42–45); and therefore 10:45 should not be divorced from the thrust of the passion predictions overall. That is, 10:45 is not just about the nature of leadership but also serves to summarize and cap off the teaching on Jesus' suffering. Fourth, since we are talking of the same event, we may assume that Mark (or the Markan Jesus) intends 10:45 to be interpreted in the light of the context he has already provided. In other words, it is reasonable to assume that the stated purpose of Jesus' death is related either to the implied suffering of the Son of Man or, more likely perhaps on the basis of the evidence so far, to the explicit suffering of the Isaianic "servant." Although we should not allow it to prejudice our examination, it is the case that while the notion of "purpose" is absent from Daniel 7 the "servant's" suffering in Isaiah 53 is not only integral to the Isaianic NE but is closely related to its fulfillment.[41]

Taking v. 45a first, the central issue is the idea of "service." Both Hooker and Barrett have rejected an Isaiah 53:10ff. allusion since δι-ακονέω is not only never used to render the root עבד in the LXX, but, as Hooker noted, the service in Isaiah is directed toward God whereas in Mark it is toward others.[42] Perhaps recognizing that the concept of self-giving service is nowhere found in Daniel 7, Barrett argued instead that the idea of service arises out of the nature of Jesus' ministry.[43]

By way of response, in contrast to the word's frequent use in the NT and as Barrett rightly notes, διακονέω is simply not attested anywhere in the LXX and its cognates occur either not at all or only rarely and late (e.g., 1 Macc. 11:58; 4 Macc. 9:17).[44] In other words, by NT times either the δουλ- or διακον- stems, or both, had undergone a semantic shift with διακον- appropriating some of the former's functions, such

---

41. See n. 16 above.

42. Hooker, *Jesus and the Servant*, 74f., 185 n. 6; followed, apparently, by Gundry, *Mark*, 591.

43. "Background," 9, apparently responding to the "literary influence" (i.e., Isaiah 53) theory; see Jackson and Lake, eds., *Beginnings*, vol. 1, pt. 1, 381–92.

44. If the διακ- stem was common in the LXX but not used in the so-called Servant Songs then Barrett's case would have been more persuasive.

that διακονέω became a viable, and sometimes perhaps even a prefer-able, rendering of the LXX's δουλεύω.[45] But why διακονέω in v. 45? A number of proposals have been suggested — for example, the active-passive structure of 10:45 rules out δουλεύω since it does not form the passive[46] — but there is the additional factor of NT usage.

Although διακονέω and δουλεύω and their substantives are appar-ently near-synonyms (or at least contiguous),[47] Paul for example prefers δουλ- when describing his "service" oriented toward Christ,[48] but uses διακον- when discussing his "service," still in Christ, but oriented toward others — conceivably the more extreme term (δουλ-) being felt appro-priate solely for service toward God. While only a trend, Mark 10:45's διακονέω might reflect this tendency.

This raises the objection that the "servant's" service is oriented toward God, not others. But this opposition is more apparent than real since the "servant" also serves the "many" (53:11, LXX: εὖ δουλεύοντα πολλοῖς), and in Mark Jesus' death is in obedience to God (14:36).[49] While it is true that the Isaianic "servant" is God's servant, this should not obscure the fact that the "servant" also ministers not only to Israel, whom he is to restore, but also to the nations to whom he is to be a light and a covenant (e.g., Isa. 42:1b–4, 6b; 49:6, 8b, 9a; 53:12).[50] The two types of service are merely facets of the one servant calling: to be Yahweh's "servant" means "to serve the many" and thus διακονέω in 10:45 could happily be a nuanced allusion to this fact.

---

45. That Symmachus chooses a third option — λατρεύω — in Isaiah 53:11 only accentuates the fact that semantic fields were altering (cf. Jer. 8:2 in Acts 7:42). There might also have been cultural factors such that whereas the idea of subjugation in δοῦλος (in religious contexts) might have been acceptable for Jews, for Gentiles the connotations might have been less appropriate or, perhaps more likely, διάκονος entailed a more nuanced sense of personal service; see H. W. Beyer, *TDNT* 2:81.

46. A. J. B. Higgins, *Jesus and the Son of Man* (London: Lutterworth, 1964), 42.

47. R. T. France, "The Servant of the Lord in the Teaching of Jesus," *TynBul* 19 (1968): 34. On synonyms see M. Silva, *Biblical Words and Their Meaning*, rev. ed. (Grand Rapids: Zondervan, 1994), 120–29; cf. the synonymous parallelism of Mark 10:43 and 44.

48. Respectively, e.g., Romans 13:4; 15:8; 2 Corinthians 3:6; 5:18 (cf. 1 Tim. 4:6); Romans 14:18; 16:18; and 1 Thessalonians 1:9 (cf. Paul's self-designations in Rom. 1:1; Phil. 1:1; etc.). See further Galatians 4:8; Matthew 6:24 (par.); Acts 20:19. Possible exceptions are 2 Corinthians 11:23 and 2 Corinthians 4:5 (but even here "for Jesus' sake"; cf. 1 Cor. 9:19), but the latter is clearly rhetorical (cf. Gal. 1:10), and the former concerns hardships endured in order to minister to the Corinthians; see BAGD, ad loc.

49. See France, "Servant," 34 n. 40.

50. See Watts, "Consolation," 50–56, and the literature cited therein. In regard to the texts cited, it needs to be remembered that first-century readers would not be engaged in a critical reconstruction of the text, as is the case in, e.g., North, *Suffering*.

Finally, Barrett's proposal that the service idea emerges from the nature of Jesus' life fails to give due weight to the thoroughgoing OT background, not only of Mark in general but also of Mark's Jesus and particularly his suffering as indicated by 9:12 and the passion predictions. Indeed, Barrett almost admits as much when he goes on to list the many OT examples of servants of God. The problem with these examples is that they do not belong to the sphere of Israel's eschatological hopes and their service is directed toward God — in Isaiah 53 the service is directed toward "the many" — and is not characterized by dying for others.[51] What figure is there in the OT who is closely associated with the Isaianic NE and whose "service" involves his suffering "for the many," if not the "servant" of Isaiah 53?

Turning to v. 45b, there are three fundamental issues: the idea of being given over to death, the meaning of λύτρον ἀντὶ..., and the significance of πολλῶν, which largely depends on the answers to the preceding two matters. Although Barrett readily admits the obvious parallelism between δοῦναι τὴν ψυχὴν αὐτοῦ and הֶעֱרָה לַמָּוֶת נַפְשׁוֹ (Isa. 53:12), he seeks to blunt its force by reconstructing the Hebrew on metrical grounds, thereby eliminating לַמָּוֶת.[52] However, there is no evidence that Mark, or Mark's Jesus, was working with an excised text, and in any case the LXX, the later Greek versions, and the Targum support the MT as we have it now. Not only so, but δοῦναι τὴν ψυχὴν αὐτοῦ closely parallels another Isaianic expression, תָּשִׂים אָשָׁם נַפְשׁוֹ (53:10).[53] Again, remembering that the Markan Jesus has used highly allusive language and the thoroughgoing Isaianic NE background to date, that the two closest, if not only, conceptual OT parallels occur in Isaiah 53 strongly suggests that it is the source of this idea.

On the second matter, Hooker and Barrett reject the common assertion that λύτρον alludes to אָשָׁם arguing with some vigor that the words were never connected.[54] Granting the lack of a connection in most cases, that the literalistic Aquila uses λύτρωσις to render אָשָׁם in Leviticus 5:18

---

51. "Background," 9.

52. "Background," 5. The significance of Hooker's comment, *Jesus and the Servant*, 248, that "these words mean little more than ... 'he gave up the ghost,'" is unclear since this still means "he died" and the context suggests that he does so for others.

53. France, "Servant," 34; Moo, *Passion*, 122ff. Barrett, "Background," does not discuss this possibility.

54. Hooker, *Jesus and the Servant*, 76f.; Barrett, "Background," 5f.

and 25 (cf. 7:1) suggests that some dilution of otherwise unqualified claims might be in order. Nevertheless, Barrett proposes that the origin of this language is to be traced through the example of the Maccabean martyrs (2 Macc. 7:37f.; 4 Macc. 6:27ff.; 17:22; 18:4)[55] back to the offer of Moses (Exod. 32:30), whose death (Deut. 34:5-8) is understood in later rabbinical tradition as atonement for the sin of the golden calf or the sin at Peor (see b. Soṭa 14a).[56] But since, as noted earlier, Jesus in Mark 9:12 construes his suffering in terms of the OT, a direct link with Maccabees is ruled out and an indirect one through the implied suffering of Daniel 7 — provided one first accepts that Mark and his Jesus understood Daniel in modern critical terms — is hardly strong.

The example of Moses is more promising since it is not only of OT origin but also concerns an exodus in which the nation's deliverance is being threatened by its idolatrous propensities, and in which Yahweh's agent, Moses, offers to make "atonement" for the nation to secure its continued salvation.[57] The parallels with the "servant" in the Isaianic NE suggest that there is more to this than immediately meets the eye. But in terms of Barrett's argument, it seems strange to reject Isaiah 53 due to the absence of clear linguistic connections and then to propose Exodus 32 whose only parallel with Mark is the root כפר.[58] Even this link is far from certain, however, since although the LXX renders the nominal כֹּפֶר with λύτρον, the verb כִּפֶּר, which occurs over a hundred times, is never translated by λυτρόω.[59] More important, it is not obvious that Moses offers his life as a substitute for Israel, but instead he identifies himself with them: if they are to die, then he will share their fate. Exodus 32:30ff. is, at the critical juncture, still a long way from the explicit thrust of Mark

55. "Background," 12f.; see further E. Lohse, Märtyrer und Gottesknecht: Untersuchungen zur urchristlichen Verkündigung vom Sühntod Jesu Christi, 2d ed., FRLANT 64 (Göttingen: Vandenhoeck & Ruprecht, 1963), 38–112.

56. C. K. Barrett, "Mark 10.45: A Ransom for Many," in New Testament Essays (London: SPCK, 1972), 22f. See further Lohse, Märtyrer, 113–203; M. Hengel, The Atonement: The Origins of the Doctrine in the New Testament, trans. J. Bowden, with substantial additions by the author (Philadelphia: Fortress, 1981), 60ff., but also his cautions regarding the righteous sufferer and martyr-prophet motifs; J. Jeremias, TDNT 4:854; and O. Piper, "Unchanging Promises: Exodus in the New Testament," Int 11 (1957): 19.

57. See further, B. S. Childs, Exodus, OTL (London: SCM, 1974), 571; J. I. Durham, Exodus, WBC 3 (Waco, Tex.: Word, 1987), 432f.

58. See Mark 10:45 in F. Delitzsch, Hebrew New Testament (Berlin, 1882).

59. There appears to be no instance in Edwin Hatch and Henry A. Redpath, A Concordance to the Septuagint and Other Greek Versions of the Old Testament, 3 vols. (reprint, Grand Rapids: Baker, 1983), 2:890.

9:12 and 10:45. Nevertheless, the parallels with Isaiah 53's account of
the "servant" suggest that the Moses story inspired a later prophet who
was also wrestling with the problem of an idolatrous Israel, again on the
verge of another exodus, but that this time Yahweh's agent not only identifies with the people but "dies" on their behalf.[60] Interestingly enough,
the prevailing Isaianic flavor of the passion predictions and Mark 9:12
point us to this very passage.

On the other hand, Hooker recognizes that λυτρόω (translating גָּאַל)
is particularly linked to the Isaianic NE redemption (Isa. 35:9; 41:14;
43:1, 14; 44:22–24; 52:3; 62:12; 63:9; see פָּדָה in 51:11).[61] However,
since גָּאַל and פָּדָה are never used of the "servant," the connection cannot be extended to his activity.[62] But such a radical disjuncture between
the redemptive action of Yahweh and his agent of that salvation, the
enigmatic "servant," is surely overdrawn. No doubt it is Yahweh who ultimately redeems his people, but is it not the case that he does so through
the agency of his "servant"? This at least seems to be the point of the
literary arrangement of Isaiah 52–54 with which chapters 40–55 reach
their climax.[63] Chapter 52, using language reminiscent of the Exodus,
summons Zion to prepare to depart Babylon.[64] Chapter 54 describes
the goal of the Isaianic NE redemption in terms of the glorious and
reconciled daughter Zion rejoicing over the miraculous increase of her

---

60. On Moses and the "servant," see A. Bentzen, *Messias, Moses redivivus, Menschensohn* (Zürich, 1948), 64ff., cited in W. D. Davies, *The Setting of the Sermon on the Mount* (Cambridge: Cambridge University Press, 1964), 117f.; von Waldow, "Message," 284; E. J. Woods, "Jesus and Beelzebub: The Meaning of 'Finger of God' within Luke 11:14–26" (D.Litt. et Phil. diss., University of South Africa, Pretoria, 1989), 22f., 48; and now especially the detailed analysis of G. P. Hugenberger, "The Servant of the Lord in the 'Servant Songs' of Isaiah: A Second Moses Figure," in *The Lord's Anointed*, ed. P. E. Satterthwaite et al. (Grand Rapids: Baker; Carlisle: Paternoster, 1995), 129ff. There is also the strong OT tradition ascribing the title "servant of God" to Moses (e.g., Exod. 14:31; Num. 12:7f.; J. Jeremias, *TDNT* 5:663; cf. 681). It is difficult to tell if later rabbinic reflec-tions on Moses' death (Deut. 34:5–8) were in response to Christian claims, to the end of temple sacrifice (i.e., analogous to the rise of *Aqedah* theology; P. R. Davies and B. D. Chilton, "The Aqedah: A Revised Tradition History," *CBQ* 40 [1978]: 514–46), or the result of independent reflection on Exodus 32.

61. Hooker, *Son*, 144; also H. Ringgren, *TDOT* 2:354f.

62. Hooker, *Jesus and the Servant*, 76ff.; cf. O. Procksch and F. Büschel, *TDNT* 4:328–56; D. Hill, *Greek Words with Hebrew Meanings* (Cambridge: Cambridge University Press, 1967), 58–80. Contrary to Barrett, "Background," 7, even if the motif of the eschatological ransom of Israel is widespread, the Markan framework surely indicates that he intends an Isaianic background.

63. Again n. 16 above. On the centrality of the restoration of Jerusalem — the focus of these chapters — in Isaiah's schema of eschatological redemption, see Dumbrell, "Purpose."

64. Westermann, *Isaiah*, 248; Melugin, *Formation*, 164–67; Ceresko, "Rhetorical," 48.

offspring.[65] It is here, too, that we find the first mention of "servants" (plural; Isa. 54:17),[66] which apparently signifies the success of the mission outlined in 49:6. That chapter 53 ties the two together strongly suggests that the "death" of the "servant" is integral to Israel's redemption.[67]

This literary reading receives additional confirmation from Ceresko's recent demonstration that Isaiah 53's language of suffering derives both from the descriptions of Israel's pre-Exodus suffering and the related covenant curses of Deuteronomy 28.[68] He concludes that the "Song ... describes the Servant bearing in his own person the effect of these curses," and continues, "[H]e thus effects the 'healing' his people require (53:5d)."[69] Yahweh accomplishes the transition from Isaiah 52 to 54 by causing his "servant" to bear the covenant curse "for many," and so "the whole people is now free to enjoy the great gift — the land."[70]

In terms of the language often used in this context, it appears, according to Isaiah 53, that Yahweh is going to redeem Israel (גָּאַל; see פָּדָה, λυτρόω) by making his "servant" an אָשָׁם (53:10). This relationship is significant not only because it represents an apparently new synthesis of two commonly used restorational concepts — redemption and compensation — but also because the oft-stated hard and fast distinction between the two is frequently cited as the basis for rejecting an allusion to Isaiah 53 in Mark 10:45. But if our reading is correct, the association of these two ideas is integral to the Isaianic formulation of the NE.

Hooker is therefore correct to relate λύτρον to Yahweh's redemptive action. But given the above this hardly disqualifies an allusion to Isa-

---

65. J. F. A. Sawyer, *Isaiah*, DSB (Philadelphia: Westminster, 1986), 2:150ff.; Westermann, *Isaiah*, ad loc.

66. Watts, "Consolation," 55; W. A. M. Beuken, "The Main Theme of Trito-Isaiah 'The Servants of Yahweh,'" *JSOT* 47 (1990): 67–87.

67. Dumbrell, "Purpose," 111; cf. Clifford, *Persuading*, 181; and Melugin, *Formation*, 169, where "52,13–53,12 is an important bridge to the conclusion of the collection in chapters 54 and 55." M. A. Sweeney, *Isaiah 1–4 and the Post-exilic Understanding of the Isaianic Tradition*, BZAW 171 (Berlin and New York: de Gruyter, 1988), 85–87, although recognizing the link between Isaiah 52, 53, and 54, understands Isaiah 52 as already describing Jerusalem's restoration, but this seems instead to be the point of Isaiah 54; see Melugin, *Formation*, 164. *Tg. Isa.* apparently also links these chapters such that Yahweh's promises as outlined in 52:1–12 are fulfilled in 54:1ff. through his Messiah (52:13ff.); cf. 52:12 with 52:13; 53:8, 10.

68. Ceresko, "Rhetorical," 47ff.; cf. Hugenberger, "Servant," 129ff.

69. Ceresko, "Rhetorical," 50, 53; cf. Hugenberger, "Servant," 136–38.

70. R. J. Clifford, "Isaiah," in *Harper's Bible Commentary*, ed. J. L. Mays (San Francisco: Harper, 1988), 573, cited in Ceresko, "Rhetorical," 54. The Targum's messianic interpretation of Isaiah 53 further supports this causal link; cf. B. D. Chilton's notes in *The Isaiah Targum: Introduction, Translation, Apparatus, and Notes*, ArB 11 (Edinburgh: T. & T. Clark, 1987), 103ff.

iah 53 in Mark 10:45. Since Isaiah 53 apparently explains how Yahweh redeems Israel, it seems quite reasonable for Mark's Jesus to describe his death as a λύτρον when speaking of its purpose. In other words, Mark 10:45 may be said to be an exegetical summary of the Isaianic NE from the perspective of the "servant": the ministering "death" of true "servant" Israel, that is, Jesus,[71] in compensation for the sins of "the many" is the means by which Yahweh effects their redemption.

With these sorts of correlations in view, the background to "the many" is no longer as ambiguous as Hooker and Barrett suggest. Undeniably it reflects, as Hooker notes, the universalistic nature of Isaianic salvation in general,[72] and also, with Barrett, it is surely of a piece with the pervasive OT theme of the "one for the many."[73] But these observations only show that the ideas found in Isaiah 53 are not without precedent, while on the other hand surely Isaiah 53 is the premier eschatological example — indeed the only one — where both motifs occur together. Given the contextual markers noted so far there seems little reason to look elsewhere.

Consequently, as Mark 9:12 indicates, the background to all this is neither the Maccabean martyrs nor the rabbis, but the OT. Even if aspects of Isaiah 53's interpretation are unclear, where else, if not here, in the OT can we find any concept of a "serving" figure who, in an eschatological context, gives his life for "the many"?[74] The Isaianic NE horizon

---

71. On Jesus as true Israel, see Hooker, *Jesus and the Servant*, 68–73; cf. P. G. Bretscher, "Exodus 4:22–23 and the Voice from Heaven," *JBL* 87 (1968): 301–11.

72. Hooker, *Jesus and the Servant*, 78f.

73. Barrett, "Background," 7; A. Suhl, *Die Funktion der alttestamentlichen Zitate und Anspielungen im Markus-evangelium* (Gütersloh: Gerd Mohn, 1965), 119.

74. Whybray, *Thanksgiving*, has argued at length, and with considerable vigor, that vicarious suffering is not in view in Isaiah 53; cf. H. M. Orlinsky, "The So-Called 'Servant of the Lord' and 'Suffering Servant' in Second Isaiah," in N. H. Snaith and H. M. Orlinsky, *Studies on the Second Part of the Book of Isaiah*, rev. ed., VTSup 14 (Leiden: Brill, 1977), 1–133; and S. K. Williams, *Jesus' Death as Saving Event*, HDR 2 (Missoula, Mont.: Scholars Press, 1975), 107–11. Although it is impossible here properly to discuss Whybray's detailed case, some points may be noted. (*a*) Whybray assumes that since the exiles are suffering for their preexilic transgressions, the "servant" cannot be suffering in their stead (e.g., pp. 30, 58, 61, etc.). But Isaiah 40:1–2 announces Yahweh's forgiveness of the past. Instead, it is on account of the exiles' present unbelief and idolatrous rejection of Yahweh's announcement that the "servant" suffers; cf. W. A. M. Beuken, "MIŠPĀṬ: The First Servant Song and Its Context," *VT* 22 (1972): 1–30; Watts, "Consolation." (*b*) Whybray's method of comparing the poetic language of Isaiah 53 to usage elsewhere, while not inappropriate, fails to consider that the prophet might be seeking to give shape to new ideas but is constrained by the language available to him. In other words, surely the sense of the present context is the overriding concern rather than how terms might have been used elsewhere. After all, since the speakers' attitude is precisely that their salvation has been achieved in an utterly unexpected way, some allowance should be

of Mark and the influence of Isaiah 53 on both Mark 9:12 and the passion predictions make an allusion to Isaiah 53 in Mark 10:45 even more
likely.[75]

More recently, however, Werner Grimm proposed that Yahweh's offer
in Isaiah 43:3f. to give the nations in Israel's stead forms the primary
background to Mark 10:45.[76] He argued that neither לְרַבִּים nor בְּרַבִּים is
equivalent to ἀντὶ πολλῶν; that λύτρον is identical with כֹּפֶר, which is
not found in Isaiah 53;[77] and that Mark has δοῦναι instead of παρεδόθη
(Isa. 53:12).[78] On the other hand, כפר תחת and נתן נפשו, which most
likely underlie δοῦναι τὴν ψυχὴν and λύτρον ἀντί, are found in Isaiah
43:3f.: "I give [נָתַתִּי] Egypt as your ransom [כָפְרְךָ], Ethiopia and Sheba
in exchange for you [תַּחְתֶּיךָ], . . . people in return for you [תַּחְתֶּיךָ] and nations for your life [תַּחַת נַפְשֶׁךָ]."[79] Further, *Mekh.* 21:30; *Exod. Rab.* 11:2;
and *Sipre Deut.* 333 on 32:43 appeal to Isaiah 43:3f. in their portrayal
of the nations being cast into Gehenna in Israel's place (see *b. Berakoth*
62b and *Tg. Isa.* 43:2).[80] Mark's πολλῶν is, however, an allusion to

---

made for the stretching of earlier categories. On the other hand, not all is radically new: the linking
of sacrifice with Yahweh's victory is already integral to Israel's deliverance in the first Exodus, a pattern on which Isaiah 40–55 is predicated; see Exodus 32:30. (*c*) Whybray also rejects the idea of a
vicarious אשׁם in Isaiah 53:10a, since the Jews found the idea of human sacrifice repugnant. But is
Isaiah 53 speaking about human sacrifice any more than, e.g., 2 Macc. 7:37f.; 4 Macc. 6:27ff., 17:22;
18:4 (indeed, one may well ask where the ideas expressed in Maccabees originated; see M. Fishbane,
Biblical Interpretation in Ancient Israel [Oxford: Clarendon, 1985], 493, on the probable influence
of Isaiah 53 on Daniel); *Sanh.* 6:2; *Lev. Rab.* 20:7; or *Sipre Deut.* 333? Or is it possible, given that
we are dealing with poetry, that the language is metaphorical and means only that the "servant's"
innocent suffering was accepted by Yahweh "as" or "in the place of" an אשׁם? In any case, as Whybray observes (p. 126) the "speakers in Isaiah 53:4–6 . . . acknowledge that they themselves have been
restored to a full state of well-being in consequence of the experiences undergone by the Servant":
the "servant's" sufferings and deliverance are instrumental in their salvation and restoration.

75. M. Casey, *Son of Man: The Interpretation and Influence of Daniel 7* (London: SPCK, 1979),
206, rejects an Isaiah 53 allusion on the criterion of dissimilarity. But given the innovation inherent
in the early Christian confession of a crucified Messiah, perhaps some more room should be allowed
for creativity; see W. Grimm, *Weil ich dich liebe: Die Verkündigung Jesu und Deuterojesaja*, 2d ed.,
ANTJ 1 (Frankfurt am Main and Bern: Peter Lang, 1981), 65. Both J. Starcky, "Les quatre étapes
du messianisme à Qumran," *RB* 70 (1963): 492, and Hengel, *Atonement*, 58, have commented on
an Aramaic text which seems to interpret Isaiah 53 eschatologically, where a savior-figure "achieves
atonement for all the sons of his race," "teaches the will of God," delivers a word that "works to the
ends of the earth," and also apparently both suffers at the hands of his enemies and is involved in
"sorrows" (. . . ומכאבין ל) and . . . נגדי מכאביכה; cf. Isa. 53:4).

76. Grimm, *Verkündigung*, 231–77; cited approvingly by P. Stuhlmacher, "Vicariously Giving His
Life for Many, Mark 10:45 (Matt. 20:28)," in *Reconciliation, Law, and Righteousness: Essays in Biblical Theology*, trans. E. Kalin (Philadelphia: Fortress, 1986), 23, although he grants a greater influence
to Isaiah 53.

77. Grimm, *Verkündigung*, 235.

78. Grimm, *Verkündigung*, 236.

79. Reading אֶתֵּן אָדָם; cf. 1QIsa[a], 1QIsa[b], contrary to Westermann, *Isaiah 40–66*, 114.

80. Grimm, *Verkündigung*, 245f.

Isaiah 53.[81] Mark 10:45 then describes Jesus taking the nations' place as Yahweh's "ransom" for Israel, while Isaiah 53's πολλῶν shows that Isaianic NE redemption now includes the nations.

While Grimm clearly offers important insights, several points require qualification. First, although λύτρον is used twenty times in the LXX, it is used to render כֹּפֶר on only six of the latter's nineteen occurrences (it is almost twice as commonly used for nominal forms of the פדה/גאל word group, as Hooker had noticed with the verbal forms), and it never does so in either the LXX or the later Greek versions of Isaiah, where λύτρον appears once, and then for מְחִיר (45:13). In terms of the Isaianic context, the connection between λύτρον and כֹּפֶר is tenuous, let alone as strong as Grimm suggests. Second, the subjects of the verbs are different: in Isaiah 43 it is Yahweh who gives the nations, but in Mark 10:45 the Son of Man — Israel's representative — gives himself. While it is possible that this indicates identity between the Son of Man and Yahweh, at least in terms of purpose, it might also be that it is the change of subject and not an allusion to Isaiah 43 which explains the shift from Isaiah 53's παρεδόθη to Mark's δοῦναι. This does not necessarily rule out Grimm's attractive suggestion that the Son of Man now takes the place of the nations as Israel's *Lösegeld*, but it does mean that the matter is hardly clear-cut. Third, if in the context of the salvific death of a "messianic" figure πολλῶν alone is sufficient to indicate an Isaiah 53 allusion (vv. 10– 12),[82] then surely the same applies to נַפְשׁוֹ in Isaiah 53:10–12 — the same three verses that contain πολλῶν — and Mark's τὴν ψυχὴν αὐτοῦ.[83] Fourth, speaking conceptually, Grimm's rabbinical sources are quite late, and the idea of giving one's life is far clearer in Isaiah 53, which stresses "death" for "the many" in the context of "service" (53:11 and θάνατος in vv. 8, 9, 12; LXX).

In sum, Grimm's strongest linguistic parallel is the use of ἀντί, with additional support from a less common and non-Isaianic link between λύτρον and כֹּפֶר and a verb with a different subject (the significance of which change is ambiguous) — and these are parallels to a text which lacks the central motifs of "service" and "death." What then of ἀντί?

---

81. Grimm, *Verkündigung*, 236f.
82. Grimm, *Verkündigung*, 236f.
83. S. Kim, *The "Son of Man" as the Son of God*, WUNT 30 (Tübingen: J. C. B. Mohr [Paul Siebeck], 1983), 53f.

Grimm is undoubtedly correct in rejecting it as a direct translation of לָרַבִּים or בָּרַבִּים. But, given that we are dealing with an allusion and not a citation, is it not the case that the point in Isaiah 53 is that the "servant" suffers in the place of the others (v. 10)? If so, Mark 10:45's ἀντὶ πολλῶν seems an apt exegetical summary of the relationship between the "servant" and "the many" in Isaiah 53. And all this comes in addition to the preceding Markan Jesus' sayings, which strongly suggest a consistent Isaiah 53 background. Although a sudden shift to Isaiah 43 is certainly not impossible, it would be somewhat incongruous that the climactic explanation of the purpose behind the suffering should do so. While not wishing to exclude some Isaiah 43 influence, it must finally be admitted that the data do not appear to support Grimm's conclusion that it is the primary background to Mark 10:45.

Finally, the Isaiah 53 interpretation has been rejected as inappropriately joining "the title of an apocalyptic figure ... to the sufferings of a prophetic one."[84] Aside from whether the distinction between "apocalyptic" and "prophetic" is anachronistic, there is evidence that this combination was not quite so incongruous. 11QMelch (line 18) describes the messenger of Isaiah 52:7 as "the Anointed One" (cf. Isa. 61:1; 42:1)[85] "of whom Daniel said...," at which point the text breaks off. Milik and Vermes suggest Daniel 9:25,[86] but Horbury believes that Daniel 2:34f. or 7:13 is more appropriate.[87] The Similitudes of 1 Enoch is well-known for the pervasive influence of "servant" imagery on its descriptions of the Son of Man.[88] As Black observes, "the term 'the

---

84. Hooker, *Jesus and the Servant*, 96. Although applied to the passion predictions, e.g., 8:31; 9:12, 31; 10:33, it pertains here. The question arises: if inappropriate for Jesus, why then should Mark make such a connection (see below)? It is generally accepted that in the Gospels as they stand Son of Man has both Daniel 7 and messianic connotations; e.g., see N. Perrin, "The Creative Use of the Son of Man Traditions by Mark," *USQR* 23 (1967–68): 357–65; W. O. Walker, "The Son of Man Question and the Synoptic Problem," *NTS* 28 (1982): 374–88; M. Müller, *Der Ausdruck "Menschensohn" in den Evangelien: Voraussetzungen und Bedeutung*, ATD 17 (Leiden: Brill, 1984). On pre-Christian messianic connotations of the Son of Man, see W. Horbury, "The Messianic Associations of the 'Son of Man,'" *JTS* 36 (1985): 34–55.

85. J. A. Fitzmyer, "Further Light on Melchizedek from Qumran Cave 1," *JBL* 86 (1967): 40.

86. J. T. Milik, "*Milki-ṣedeq* et *Milki-reša'* dans les anciens écrits juifs et chrétiens," *JJS* 23 (1972): 97ff., 108, and G. Vermes, ed. and trans., *The Dead Sea Scrolls in English*, 3d ed. (Harmondsworth: Penguin, 1987), 301.

87. "Messianic," 42.

88. J. Jeremias and W. Zimmerli, *The Servant of God*, rev. ed. (London: SCM, 1965), 58ff.; J. Coppens, *Le Fils d'Homme Vétéro- et Intertestamentaire* (Leuven: Leuven University Press, 1983), 134f.; J. Theisohn, *Der auserwählte Richter*, SUNT 12 (Göttingen: Vandenhoeck & Ruprecht, 1975), 114–25; M. Black, *The Book of Enoch or I Enoch: A New English Edition with Commentary and*

Elect One' points...unequivocally to the elect Servant of Second Isaiah" (e.g., 48:4–6; cf. Isa. 42:6; 49:2–7; 60:10; 61:1f.; and *1 Enoch* 62:1; cf. 49:1ff.).[89] The constant humiliation of the kings and the mighty (46:4; 62:3; 62:1–9; cf. 46:6; 48:6) is reminiscent of Isaiah 49:7 and 52:14f., and not only does the "Elect One" slay the wicked with the sword of his mouth (62:2; cf. Isa. 49:2; 51:16), but he is a light to the Gentiles (48:4; cf. Isa. 42:6; 49:6; also Mark 13:10). Similarly, *b. Sanhedrin* 98a's later discussion of the timing of the Messiah's return cites Isaiah 59:20; 59:16; 48:11; and 60:22 alongside Daniel 7:13, while in *Midr. Ps.* 2:9, Isaiah 52:13 and 42:1, together with Daniel 7:13f., are applied to a messianic figure. Given, too, Hooker's affirmation of the "Deutero-Isaianic" background of Jesus' ministry,[90] the Markan Jesus' self-designation as Son of Man already implies a fusion of a prophetic conception of Jesus' ministry in general and the apocalyptic Son of Man figure. In the light of Mark's Isaianic NE hermeneutic, should it be so surprising that the suffering element, instead of deriving from Daniel 7, comes from those "servant" texts where the redemptive role of suffering in the Isaianic NE is most obvious?[91]

Conclusion

Taken in isolation, it is true that none of the individual words of Mark 10:45 unequivocally suggests Isaiah 53. However, Mark has not given us isolated words, but whole sentences which he has deliberately set within an overarching Isaianic NE motif. Further, the teaching concerns of Mark's "way" section, evident in the threefold predictions that the Messiah must suffer, parallels the Isaianic NE "way" of Yahweh's wisdom

---

Textual Notes, SVTP 7 (Leiden: Brill, 1985), 181–252. Hooker, *Son*, 33–48, omits any mention of these parallels.

89. Black, *Enoch*, 189.

90. *Jesus and the Servant*, 66, 67f., 73; cf. 95; *Mark*, 249. Also Grimm, *Verkündigung*, passim; H. Schürmann, *Gottes Reich — Jesu Geschick: Jesu ureigener Tod im Licht seiner Basileia-verkündigung* (Freiburg: Herder, 1983), 240.

91. "Wenn man aber im Zentrum der Verkündigung Jesus' Abhängigkeit von DtJes nachweisen kann, warum dann nicht auch in den Gottesknechtsliedern?" (Schürmann, *Reich*, 240), but with cautions, 241, 243, cf. B. Lindars, *Jesus Son of Man* (London: SPCK, 1983), 82. For Horbury, "Messianic," 42–47, creative textual integration is characteristic of messianic exegesis; on Jesus as the seminal mind behind Christian messianic exegesis, see C. H. Dodd, *According to the Scriptures* (London: Nisbet, 1952), 109f.; Hengel, *Atonement*, 59.

wherein Israel is to be redeemed through the unexpected suffering of the enigmatic "servant." I have also suggested that some misunderstanding has arisen because of a failure to appreciate several factors. First, Mark (or his tradition) probably intends Jesus' words to be understood as Greek translations of sayings which allude to the Hebrew rather than to the LXX (otherwise one might have expected him to conform them to the LXX, and after all Jesus spoke Aramaic). Second, the mixed or synthetic nature of Jesus' use of the OT advises against identifying one source and one source alone for his thought. Third, the phenomenon of semantic change along with an awareness of the idiosyncratic tendencies of the LXX Isaiah suggests some caution in relying solely on the LXX as a benchmark. When all this is taken into consideration, I have argued that there are more explicit parallels, conceptually and verbally, with the suffering of the "servant" figure of Isaiah 53 than with any similar grouping of characteristics ascribed to any other single OT figure in a given passage.[92] This is certainly so with respect to the Son of Man in Daniel 7, whose only explicit contact with Mark 10:45 is the title. Any ideas that his suffering for the many effects Israel's redemption have to be implied or imported as Barrett's and Hooker's proposals illustrate.[93] On the other hand, even those least enthusiastic about an Isaianic "servant" paradigm nevertheless admit that Jesus' passion predictions "correspond broadly" to Isaiah 53.[94]

This is not to suggest that Isaiah 53 is the only influence on the Markan Jesus' perception of his suffering and death. As noted earlier Mark also seems to present Jesus as "true Israel"; Hooker's proposal that the title Son of Man identifies Jesus as "the one true Israelite who is able to accept the mission and destiny of his people" seems to me to be correct.[95] My concern is that a Son of Man identification should not debar other OT figures. This brings us back to the earlier question of the relative importance of the two figures. Granted that Jesus clearly defines himself as Son of Man and assuming for the moment

---

92. See, e.g., also W. G. Kümmel, *Promise and Fulfillment: The Eschatological Message of Jesus,* trans. D. M. Barton, SBT 23 (London: SCM, 1957), 73, who rejects any idea of "servant" consciousness in Jesus.

93. Barrett, "Background," 9–15; and Hooker, *Son,* 27–30, 140–47; but see the criticisms of France, "Servant," 47ff.; Higgins, *Son,* 41–50; and Casey, *Son,* 205f.

94. Hooker, *Jesus and the Servant,* 95; cf. 74f.; and Barrett, "Background," 5.

95. *Son,* 193.

that this goes back to Daniel 7 — where else is Son of Man language combined with the reign of God (cf. Kingdom of God) if not here? — nevertheless the Markan emphasis on the Isaianic NE suggests that this represents no mere tinkering around the edges of an exegesis of the Son of Man, but probably reflects a thoroughgoing exegetical synthesis of Israel's redemptive hopes.

Finally, as discussed earlier, such an allusive, innovative, and creative hermeneutic is not without parallel. In Mark 3:27, Mark's Jesus apparently construes his exorcisms within the grid of the Yahweh-Warrior's activities on Israel's behalf (Isa. 49:24ff.). It is worth noting the substantial similarities between this saying and 10:45.

Both texts provide key insights into the Markan Jesus' self-perception and both occupy climactic moments in their respective sections. Both are crucial to interpreting the central concerns of those sections: Jesus' exorcisms and his passion. Both are placed on Jesus' lips, and both display the same allusive character. Both exhibit a similar, innovative hermeneutic. Hooker's observation on 3:27 is, therefore, apposite:

> Although there is no verbal correspondence between the Greek text and the LXX version of Isaiah 49.24f., the similarity in meaning is so great that there is little doubt that Jesus had this passage in mind when he spoke these words; nor is there any comparable picture elsewhere in the Old Testament.[96]

I respectfully submit that the application of these criteria to 10:45, especially given the larger Isaianic NE horizon of Mark's presentation and the other linguistic phenomenon mentioned, should result in a similar verdict concerning the influence of Isaiah 53. The pervasive impress of Isaiah 53 on Mark 9:12 and the passion predictions only serves to reinforce the suggestion.

For Mark, genuine Israel, and consequently the one who is truly "like a Son of Man," is none other than Jesus. At the same time, Jesus' strikingly unorthodox messianic self-understanding — that he is to die for the redemption of many — is of the one cloth with the misunderstood career of Isaiah's "servant," whose rejection, suffering, and "death" for the many is Yahweh's equally unorthodox means of effecting Israel's NE.[97]

---

96. Hooker, *Jesus and the Servant*, 73.
97. Elsewhere in the NT (e.g., Eph. 2:13–19; Heb. 4:16; 1 Pet. 3:18), Christ's death is regarded

This leaves one final question: if this is indeed what the Markan Jesus' words signify, why does the NT not make more of this motif?[98] Given the constraints of this essay I can only offer some brief suggestions. Implicit in many of the analyses to date is an understandable but perhaps misleading presumption that Mark would conform his "Jesus sayings" to the wording of the LXX where he sees a connection — hence the reliance on LXX parallels. No doubt Mark might do so in some cases, but it assumes of course that Mark himself not only recognized the source but also that he would be less interested in the actual words of Jesus as they came down to him than in a Septuagintal association. These matters are related. What if Mark was not aware of the precise source of the ideas, but recorded Jesus' words just as they had come to him simply because they represented in his tradition one of the few occasions on which Jesus gave some insight into his self-understanding? This would make more sense of the form of sayings like Mark 3:27 and 9:12. If so, as I have suggested earlier, Mark's Greek might not so much reflect the "conforming" lens of the LXX as it does his (or his tradition's) translational choice, in the light of contemporary usage, of an Aramaic tradition of Jesus' sayings which then goes back to the Hebrew OT (or perhaps some Targumic variation thereof).

A faithful attempt to record the words of Jesus, recognized as crucial to his self-understanding even if not fully understood, might also explain why allusions to Isaiah 53 might be present in the Gospels but not fully explicated. Hooker may then be right in affirming that 1 Peter is the first fully developed NT theology of Isaiah 53's vicariously suffering "servant." But this is not because it was the early church that first understood the texts in this way.

We have already suggested that part of the reason for the delay of the Isaianic NE — at the very least from the perspective of the Book

---

as reconciling us to God and as opening the way to his presence, both key motifs in the Isaianic NE; see G. Beale, "The Old Testament Background of Reconciliation in 2 Corinthians 5–7 and Its Bearing on the Literary Problem of 2 Cor. 6:14–7:1," *NTS* 35 (1989): 578ff.; Hengel, *Atonement*, 52; P. Stuhlmacher, "'He is our peace' (Eph. 2:14): On the Exegesis and Significance of Eph. 2:14–18," in *Reconciliation, Law, and Righteousness: Essays in Biblical Theology*, trans. E. Kalin (Philadelphia: Fortress, 1986), 187ff.

98. See, e.g., Moule's comment on the relative paucity of NT references to Isaiah 53: "Yet the only clearly redemptive-suffering passage in the Jewish scriptures is only sparingly used. Here is a phenomenon that still awaits explanation" (*The Birth of the New Testament*, 3d ed. [San Francisco: Harper and Row, 1982], 104).

of Isaiah overall if not chapters 40–55 themselves — seems to be Israel's inability to let go of her expectations, which were probably and understandably shaped by her social memory of the Exodus under Moses and the glorious reign of her warrior-king David. For instance, *Tg. Isaiah's* bifurcation of chapter 53, such that the suffering is assigned to Israel and the glorious victory to the Messiah (granted the difficulty of dating the material), and Mark's account of responses to Jesus' death (8:32; 15:29–32) together bear eloquent witness to the sheer inability of Israel's worldview in general to accommodate the notion of a suffering Messiah. Nor does Mark encourage us to think that the disciples were quickly disabused of this outlook. Is there any reason to expect that the early Jewish Christians should find it any easier to make the necessary paradigm shift? And if so, that they should quickly extend this hermeneutic to their reading of Isaiah 53?

The assessment offered here suggests that the genesis of this new exegesis of Isaiah 53 lay with Jesus, but as, for example, Mark's Gospel and Acts 1:6ff. make clear, the full implications of his characteristically enigmatic instruction were not appreciated by his uncomprehending disciples until after a period of subsequent reflection. This kind of response is hardly unknown. The history of ideas is replete with examples of creative thinkers, the implications of whose unique and extraordinarily perceptive insights provide decades if not centuries of grist for lesser mills as they struggle to catch up.

10

Isaiah and Matthew

The Prophetic Influence in the First Gospel

A REPORT ON CURRENT RESEARCH
BY ADRIAN M. LESKE

◆

Introduction

I was drawn to this research by three major concerns. First of all was
the conviction that the message of Jesus and the Gospels must be studied primarily from the perspective of the Jewish heritage. Since Jesus
grew up in a Jewish household and in a Jewish community it seemed
appropriate to approach his message and mission as presented in the
Gospels from that point of view, rather than reaching back piecemeal
into ancient Israel's literature for understanding of particular concepts.
Such a conviction means approaching the Gospels with a fairly thorough
understanding of Jewish history and literature, particularly from the time
of the exile onward, and looking for evidence of an underlying Jewish
contextual authenticity.

Second was the consideration of the Jewish nature of the Gospel of
Matthew. This Gospel is replete with Semitisms and OT quotations and
allusions. The integral nature of the ten so-called formula citations, as
well as the quotations of Jesus in Matthew's Gospel, shows not only that
the author himself was thoroughly familiar with the context of each of
the prophetic quotations but that he expected his readers would be also.
He often combined words from two different texts into one quotation in
order to alert the reader to the context of both (e.g., 2:6 [Mic. 5:1–2 and
2 Sam. 5:2]; 2:23 [Isa. 11:1 and 60:21]; 11:10 [Exod. 23:20 and Mal.
3:1]; 21:5 [Isa. 62:11 and Zech. 9:9]; 21:13 [Isa. 56:7 and Jer. 7:11]; 27:9

[Jer. 18:1–13; 19:1–12; and Zech. 11:12–13]).[1] His thorough knowledge of the OT scriptures is also indicated sometimes in subliminal messages. For example, in 3:4, to describe the Baptist's clothing, he uses words almost identical to the description of the garments worn by Elijah in 2 Kings 1:8, in order to alert the reader to recognize John as the returning Elijah (cf. 11:14; 17:13).[2] Similarly, in 27:41–43 he has characterized the chief priests, scribes, and elders with the very words used to describe the wicked in Psalm 22:8 and Wisdom 2:10–20 (an echo of Isaiah 53), in order to point out that these religious leaders in Jerusalem are actually the wicked who persecute the righteous Servant of Psalm 22 and Isaiah 53, that is, Jesus.

While most scholars recognize that this Gospel must have been written by a Jewish Christian primarily for Jewish Christians, most, since B. H. Streeter, have argued that the author re-Judaized the gentile Gospel of Mark and a saying source Q. Yet a close study of the Gospel itself shows no evidence of "re-Judaizing," but rather a fairly thorough Semitic background and understanding of the context of the many OT quotations and allusions found in it. Nevertheless, this idea of "re-Judaizing" has led scholars considering the Jewish nature of the First Gospel, because of Matthew's distinctive references to law and righteousness, to look for Matthew's Jewish influences in rabbinic Judaism, though that approach does not mesh too well with the distinctly antagonistic attitude toward Pharisaic Judaism found in this Gospel. Moreover, this supposedly catechetical approach not only makes Matthew the creator of many of the sayings of Jesus, but it also creates more problems than it solves. While the Gospel may show some general evidence of

---

1. H. C. Kee, "The Function of Scriptural Quotations and Allusions in Mark 11–16," *Jesus und Paulus: Festschrift für Werner Georg Kümmel zum 70. Geburtstag,* ed. E. E. Ellis and E. Grässer (Göttingen: Vandenhoeck & Ruprecht, 1975), 175–78, mentions the following conflated citations as characteristic of Mark's style: 1:2–3 (Exod. 23:20; Mal. 3:1; and Isa. 40:3); 1:11 (Isa. 42:1 and Ps. 2:7); 11:1–11 (Zech. 9:9 and Ps. 118:25–26); 11:17 (Isa. 56:7 and Jer. 7:11); 12:1–12 (Isa. 5:1–2 and Ps. 118:22–23); 13:24–26 (Isa. 34:4; Josh. 2:10; Ezek. 32:7–8; and Dan. 7:13–14); and 14:62 (Dan. 7:13 and Ps. 110:1). As well as other citations mentioned above, all of these are found in Matthew's Gospel. Zechariah 9:9 does not appear in Mark 11:1–11, but it does in Matthew 21:5. Mark 1:2–3 has every indication of being a conflated summary of quotations regarding the Baptist incorporated into the Isaian quotation, the arguments of Joel Marcus notwithstanding in his *The Way of the Lord: Christological Exegesis of the Old Testament in the Gospel of Mark* (Louisville: Westminster/John Knox Press, 1992), 13–16.

2. Mark 1:6 also contains this allusion to the garments of Elijah, but since Mark omits the whole pericope of Jesus' witness concerning John together with Jesus' provocative statement that John is Elijah (Matt. 11:14), the primary purpose of the allusion is lost.

style similar to later exegesis, the overwhelming influence in it is clearly prophetic.

Furthermore, as I studied the Jewish nature of Matthew's Gospel in relation to the other Synoptics, I became convinced that the greatest factor inhibiting real understanding of Matthew's message was approaching it from the perspective of the Two Source Hypothesis. I became convinced that one must study the First Gospel on its own merits as originating in a Jewish environment and responding to the Jewish message of a Jewish Jesus. Take, for example, Matthew 12:1–42. The various pericopes in this chapter form an integrated whole, illustrating the growing opposition and rigidity of the Pharisees over against Jesus as the Anointed One of Matthew 11:2 (Isa. 61:1), who is gathering the faithful to be part of the restored Kingdom of God. The two sabbath stories (12:1–8, 9–14) illustrate this purpose. The disciples pluck grain and eat because they *were hungry* (v. 1). Appeasement of hunger is a sign of the renewal of the covenant relationship and restoration of the Kingdom (Isa. 32:6; 49:10; 65:13; cf. 58:6–7, 10). It is the Kingdom which takes precedence over the ritual keeping of the law ("Something greater than the temple is here," v. 6). Similarly, the healing of the man with the withered hand is another sign of the coming of the Kingdom. The reference to rescuing a sheep on the sabbath (vv. 11–12) is important in the Jewish context because Jesus' purpose is the gathering of the lost sheep of the house of Israel (9:36; 10:6; 15:24; 18:10–14; cf. Isa. 40:10–11; 49:9–10; Zech. 10:2, 6–10). In spite of Pharisaic opposition the restoration of the Kingdom continues (v. 15). All this, Matthew points out, is to fulfill the role of the Servant (12:18–21=Isa. 42:1–4).

This activity is followed (v. 22) by the healing of the blind and dumb demoniac which, in a sense, continues the quotation of Isaiah 42, for in v. 7 the Servant's role is "to open the eyes that are blind," picking up the Isaianic motif of healing the blindness of God's chosen people and restoring them to faithful relationship (see Isa. 29:18; 35:5, 6; 42:16, 18, 19; 43:8). In contrast, the continued blindness of the Pharisees is seen in their readiness to condemn Jesus' healings as sorcery (v. 24). Jesus' response, "if it is by the Spirit of God that I cast out demons, then the Kingdom of God has come upon you," is a direct reference to Isaiah 42:1 and 61:1 (cf. Isa. 44:3; 59:21). The allusion to Isaiah 49:24–25 (vv. 29–30) is integral to the role of the Servant who is to *gather* the scattered of Israel (Isa. 49:5). So Yahweh promises (Isa. 49:25): "Even the captives of the mighty shall be taken and the prey of the tyrant be rescued, for I will contend with those who contend with you and I will deliver your children." Therefore, not to be *gathering* with Jesus is to be scattering (v. 30), to be aligning oneself with tyrants and oppressors, and to be contending with God. This is the blasphemy against the Holy Spirit which will not be forgiven (vv. 31–32). For this act the Pharisees are condemned — not for their opposition to Jesus, but for their opposition to the Spirit of God. For they are certainly not those described in Isaiah 59:21 (vv. 34–37). The only sign given to them is the sign of Jonah (vv. 38–42), who was sent to witness to Nineveh as illustration of Israel's role to be a light to the nations (Isa. 42:6; 49:6). But "something greater than Jonah, something greater than Solomon is here" — it is the Kingdom of God engendered by the Spirit which has come upon them (v. 28).[3]

All this in Matthew forms an integrated whole. But in the corresponding account in Mark 2:23–3:30, which follows roughly the same order, this development of the motif is lost. Most of the key indicators are omitted, so that even the allusion to Isaiah 49:24–25 retained by Mark (3:27) has lost its essential meaning. The stories in Mark have thus become a series of disconnected pericopes. The same is true of Luke to some extent. He places the sabbath stories before the choosing of the Twelve in 6:1–11, connects the blasphemy against the Holy Spirit with the somewhat conflicting phrase, "he who denies me before men will be denied before the angels of God" (12:9–10, a somewhat different version of Matt. 10:33), and places the story about casting out demons by Beelzebub and the seeking of a sign in 11:14–26, 29–32. To interpret Matthew through Mark and Q would be to destroy the integrity of the Matthean account.

Third, in a related study of important themes such as the poorman motif, justice and righteousness, messianic kingdom in 2 Isaiah and

---

3. Luke also records these two πλεῖον sayings (Luke 11:31–32), but they have lost their connection with the Spirit and Kingdom of God partially through his interpretive statement, "As Jonah became a sign to the men of Nineveh, so will the Son of Man be to this generation" (11:30). Consequently, there has been a tendency to interpret the μεῖζον πλεῖον sayings in Matthew as referring to Jesus as Son of Man/Messiah, e.g., W. C. Allen, *A Critical and Exegetical Commentary on the Gospel according to S. Matthew*, 3d ed. (Edinburgh: T. & T. Clark, 1912), 128; John P. Meier, *Matthew* (Wilmington, Del.: Michael Glazier, 1980), 129, 138; W. D. Davies and Dale C. Allison, *A Critical and Exegetical Commentary on the Gospel according to Saint Matthew* (Edinburgh: T. & T. Clark, 1991), 2:314, 357; Donald Hagner, *Matthew 1–13*, WBC 33A (Dallas: Word, 1993), 330, 335.

postexilic literature, I became convinced that the hopes for restoration expressed particularly in 2 and 3 Isaiah and how these hopes were developed in later prophetic writings were the basis of the message of Jesus as presented in Matthew's Gospel. So all this led to my present study.

The Contribution of Second Isaiah

Second Isaiah's message is a profound one — a vision of impending deliverance and restoration. It is a vision of Yahweh's everlasting love reaching out to exiled Israel, remembering their sins no more, calling them from death to life with a renewed purpose to live as his faithful people and thus to become a *people covenant* and a *light to the nations* (42:6; 49:6, 8). The people Israel were not only to gather the scattered of Israel and Judah together as God's children but were to be God's witnesses to the nations, because with Yahweh as their King they would dwell together forever in covenant faithfulness and in peace. As the nations watched, they too would be drawn to seek the same kind of relationship with Yahweh and to acknowledge him as the universal and only true God.

Many themes from Second Isaiah's plan of restoration become the focus of the message in the NT, particularly in Matthew's Gospel. Themes that come out in this Gospel more clearly than elsewhere include the proclamation of the good news that Yahweh will reestablish the Kingdom, not as the kingdom of Judah, or of David, but as the Kingdom of God. God himself will reign, he will be their shepherd (40:10, 11). The nation will return to the time prior to the monarchy, when God ruled as King over his covenant people. Israel, which has been the afflicted and dispossessed (*'ny w'byôn*), the one who mourns, will be comforted, redeemed, forgiven, will have reward and recompense, and will be filled with God's Spirit. They will experience God's justice and righteousness and will respond with *their* righteousness, because God's *torah*, his teaching, will be written in their hearts (51:7). Over and over again Israel is declared to be God's chosen one, his Servant, his Beloved, carried from the womb in order to perform the divine purpose. So God will heal them of their blindness, their deafness, their lameness; he will raise them from the dead to fulfill that purpose.

Up to the time of the exile Servant Israel had been like a sword in a sheath, like a polished arrow in a quiver waiting for the time to fulfill its purpose, not just to gather the scattered people, but to be a people covenant, a light to the nations that God's "salvation may reach to the ends of the earth" (49:5–8). For that reason the Servant will again see his seed and prolong his days; he will rise from the death of the exile so that *by his knowledge* (i.e., relationship with God) *the Righteous One will make many to be accounted righteous* (53:10–11). So in God's Kingdom, Servant Israel as a corporate entity is now to fulfill the role of David, and the everlasting covenant made with David is now transferred to the Servant, to those who are willing to give witness to the reign of God in their lives (55:1–5).

Continuation of Second Isaiah's Message by the Prophetic Minority

It becomes evident[4] that the message of Second Isaiah was carried on by a faithful prophetic minority, not only among those who soon returned to Judah, but also by those who long after looked to the fulfillment of the hopes and aspirations expressed by that prophet of the exile. This is evident particularly in the following textual traditions.

Third Isaiah

When the first disciples of Second Isaiah finally returned to Judah, the trees were not actually clapping their hands (Isa. 55:12–13). There was opposition from the Zadokite priesthood, resistance from the people already settled in Judah, and no hope for seeing an immediate fulfillment of Second Isaiah's restoration plan. The Righteous One, now more broadly defined as "the people of steadfast love" (*'nšy ḥsd*), the faithful, was perishing (Isa. 57:1). But in the disappointment and disillusionment that followed, the promises of the restoration and Israel's purpose were reaffirmed (chaps. 60–62).

The transfer of the everlasting covenant, originally made with David to the faithful of Israel, as a whole was taken very seriously. Thus Servant

---

4. As Paul D. Hanson has clearly shown in his *The Dawn of Apocalyptic* (Philadelphia: Fortress, 1975).

Israel is *anointed* (61:1) to bring good news to the afflicted, and the everlasting covenant is reaffirmed (61:8). The people are now the "crown of beauty" and a "royal diadem" in the hand of Yahweh who reigns (62:3). The faithful are described as the fulfillment of the messianic promise of Isaiah 11:1 — they are the "shoot" (*nṣr*) of God's planting (60:21) who will mature into "oaks of righteousness" (61:3). They will be known also as "the priests of Yahweh" and as "the ministers of our God" (61:6). Thus the responsibility for covenant faithfulness and fulfilling Israel's purpose is placed entirely into the hands of the righteous ones. Once again, therefore, they were to become a "kingdom of priests and a holy nation" (Exod. 19:6; cf. Isa. 62:12) under God's rule. They may still be the *suffering* Servant, those "crushed and afflicted in spirit," but God is with them (Isa. 57:15; 66:2 — picking up the terminology of 53:4).

Malachi

Some of this Isaianic influence is continued in Malachi, mostly in terms of an intense criticism of the Zadokite priesthood and the desire that the Levites will soon take over the priestly duties. Malachi looks forward to the day when the righteous will be vindicated and the wicked burned as stubble. The work finishes with the promise of the coming of the prophet Elijah to restore relationships, lest God smite the nation with utter destruction (4:5–6).

Zechariah 9–14

The struggles of the prophetic minority, those who carried on the hopes and ideals of Second and Third Isaiah, are cataloged again later by the author of Zechariah 9–14. His message is expressed as two major revelations received during different celebrations of the annual Feast of Booths. The first vision begins by portraying Yahweh as the great Warrior-King coming to fulfill the promises to his people of an expanded kingdom in which they will dwell in security and peace. This was a covenant promise recited every year at the three major festivals: "I will cast out nations before you and enlarge your borders" (Exod. 34:24). In the midst of these promises of God's rule over an expanded kingdom, the announcement is made: "Lo, your king comes to you; righteous and saved is he, afflicted and riding on an ass, on a colt the foal of an ass" (according to the MT). This announcement draws on two passages: Zephaniah 3:14–15, which speaks of God as the King in their midst, and Isaiah 62:11, which also comes out of a harvest-festival context (62:6–12). In the announcement in that context the faithful had been told: "You shall be a crown of beauty in the hand of Yahweh, and a royal diadem in the hand of your God" (62:3), and these people were to receive a new name: "The holy people, the redeemed of Yahweh" (62:12; cf. Zech. 14:5).

The king here (9:9–10) is not some future messiah or Davidide; rather, the faithful people represent the rule of God and are to replace the present corrupt priesthood and civic leaders (10:3). The faithful in these visions are referred to as "the house of Judah" (10:3; 12:4), or "clans of Judah" (12:5, 6), or "tents of Judah" (12:7). This is why the "king" is depicted as coming into Jerusalem riding on an ass, on a colt, the foal of a she-ass, just as Judah was depicted entering Shiloh for the Feast of Booths in Genesis 49:10–12. This "king" is described as *righteous, saved* (cf. Isa. 53:11; 57:1; 45:17, 22), and *afflicted* (Isa. 53:4, 7; cf. 41:17; 49:13; 51:21; 61:1; 66:2; cf. 57:15; Zeph. 3:12) — all terms used of the Servant in Isaiah. Further echoes from Isaiah in the following verses bear out the correspondence:

9:10: "He shall command peace to the nations"
(cf. Isa. 42:1, 6; 52:7)
9:11: "I have set your captives free" (Isa. 42:6–7; 49:9; 61:1–3)
9:12: "Today I declare that I will restore to you double"
(Isa. 40:2; 61:7; cf. 54:1–3)
9:13: "Arrow" and "sword" recalled (Isa. 49:2–4)
9:16: "They are the flock of his people" (Isa. 40:11)
"Like the jewels of a crown they shall shine on his land"
(Isa. 62:3)
9:17: Grain and new wine (cf. Isa. 62:8–9)

Thus chapter 9 is really a celebration of the Kingship of Yahweh, whose justice is represented not by a Davidic king, nor through the priesthood, but through the lives and actions of his faithful people. Yahweh will use the people, not only to bring peace and security, but to extend his gracious rule over all nations (9:11–17). Chapter 10 (vv. 2–4) describes how God will strengthen the house of Judah who "wander like sheep, afflicted for want of a shepherd" and make out of them the cornerstone (Isa. 28:16), the tent peg (Isa. 33:20; 54:3), the battle bow (cf. 9:13), and every commander (cf. Isa. 60:17).

The second vision begins (12:1) with virtually a quotation of Isaiah 42:5, with allusions in v. 2 to Isaiah 51:13–16, 17–23. In this vision it is God who reigns — he is the King, the Lord of hosts (14:16), to whom the nations will come to celebrate the Feast of Booths. In the struggle to achieve this reign, the house of Judah suffers but is ultimately victorious. It suffers because of the house of David and the inhabitant(s) of Jerusalem. These latter will repent of their deeds and are to be cleansed from their sin and impurity (12:10–13:1). The result will be that on that day, when they celebrate the Feast of Booths, their worship will no longer be regarded as under the exclusive privilege of the priesthood, but all will participate — worship will be entirely democratized (14:20–21; cf. Isa. 61:6; 66:21; cf. 65:1–12).

Jonah

In the Book of Jonah, the prophet Jonah is really a caricature of Israel, which fails to carry out its purpose to be a people covenant and a light to the nations as described in Second Isaiah. When commanded by God to do so, Jonah tries to go in the opposite direction and must undergo a death and resurrection experience in order to turn and carry out the divine purpose. Even then Jonah seems more concerned for his own comfort than for the welfare of all the people.

Daniel

The motif of Servant Israel representing God's rule before the nations takes on a different expression in Daniel 7. The corporate figure of the Servant becomes the more symbolic image of "one like a son of man," who stands for "the holy ones of the Most High" (7:18, 21, 22, 25; cf. v. 27). This corporate figure is "one like a son of man" in contrast to the oppressing nations, depicted as beasts. He "comes with the clouds of heaven" in contrast to the beasts, who come up out of the sea of chaos. The "holy ones" are those mentioned in Isaiah 62:12; 63:18; and

Zechariah 14:5 rather than "angels."[5] They are the people who remain faithful to "the holy covenant" (Dan. 11:28–30), the wise who shall make many understand (11:32; cf. Isa. 53:11). Under suffering and persecution the concern turns toward judgment of the kings and nations who oppress, and to vindication and power for the righteous. Ultimately, the righteous will shine like the brightness of the firmament (see Isa. 60:1–3), turn many to righteousness (Dan. 12:3; cf. Isa. 53:11), and possess the Kingdom of God forever.

Wisdom of Solomon

The work offers a picture of the "righteous poor man" (δίκαιος πένης, 2:10) who professes to have knowledge of God (2:13; cf. Isa. 53:11), who calls himself a child/servant of the Lord (παῖς κυρίου, 2:13), who "blesses the final times of the righteous" (μακαρίζει ἔσχατα δικαίων, 2:16) and boasts that God is his Father (2:16; cf. Isa. 63:16; 64:8), who is the righteous one, the son of God (2:18, ὁ δίκαιος υἱὸς θεοῦ). The Righteous One is a collective term for "the righteous ones" (3:1) whom God tested and found worthy (3:6) — "like a sacrificial burnt offering he accepted them" (3:6; cf. Isa. 53:8). The continuing stream of prophetic thought can be seen again in 3:8: "They will govern nations and rule over peoples, and the Lord will reign over them forever."

The Parables of Enoch (*1 Enoch* 37–71)

In these parables the author has taken various titles given to the Servant in the Isaian literature and combined them with the concept of the Son of Man in Daniel. Thus, "Chosen One," "Righteous One," "Anointed One," "that Son of Man" are titles used indiscriminately of an individual who becomes God's agent to vindicate the righteous, chosen, holy ones — titles used for the faithful generally. The corporate figure of Isaiah and Daniel has become an individual who acts on behalf of the righteous chosen ones and sits on God's throne in order to pronounce divine judgment on the oppressors, and thus to deliver the faithful from

---

5. In disagreement with John J. Collins, *The Apocalyptic Vision of the Book of Daniel* (Missoula, Mont.: Scholars Press, 1977), 123–26, and *The Apocalyptic Imagination* (New York: Crossroad, 1984), 83–85.

persecution, suffering, and martyrdom. These righteous and chosen ones will be saved and the dead raised on that day (51:1–4), and they will wear the garments of glory (62:15; cf. Isa. 61:10). They will form the congregation of the righteous established by the Son of Man (38:1; 45:1; 53:6) and dwell in peace in the presence of the Lord of the Spirits (39:6–7; cf. Wisd. 5:15–16). The author draws on many Isaianic concepts to describe both the faithful and the Son of Man and also demonstrates the influence of Daniel and Wisdom of Solomon in his descriptions of both.

All these writings give evidence of a prophetic stream of thought, a developing prophetic heritage carried forward through history by a faithful prophetic minority, despite persecution and oppression. This is the particular Jewish heritage of Jesus in the Gospel of Matthew. No other writing in the New Testament bears such strong evidence of the influence of the thought of Second Isaiah and how his hope of the restoration of God's reign after the exile was reaffirmed, reshaped, and transformed in the above writings as time went on. The mission and message of Jesus in Matthew's Gospel, therefore, must be considered in the light of this developing prophetic heritage.

The Prophetic Tradition in Matthew's Gospel

The Importance of Galilee

One must assume that this prophetic stream continued among the common people but not in Jerusalem/Judea, where the temple cult and the religious leadership of Sadducees and Pharisees were strong. The purest form of the prophetic influence would likely have existed some distance from Judea, where it could continue without too much pressure from Jerusalem. Galilee probably would have been an ideal place for such influence — separated from Jerusalem by Samaria, tinged with diaspora concerns regarding temple and Torah. It is possible that Nazareth gained its name from *nṣr*, the "shoot" of Isaiah 11:1; 53:2; 60:21 (cf. Matt. 2:23). That *nṣr* was used already at the time of Jesus of the faithful of Israel is clear from the Qumran psalms (1QH 6:15; 7:19; 8:5–10). The term "Nazorean" would have identified a person who followed in this prophetic tradition and sought to fulfill the role of faithful Israel as the "shoot of God's planting." This term refers to a movement rather than to a place.

Thus Jesus was often referred to as "Jesus the Nazorean" (Matt. 26:71; Luke 18:37; John 18:5, 7; 19:19; Acts 2:22; 3:6; 4:10; 6:14; 22:8; 26:9), and Paul was later called a "ringleader of the party of the Nazoreans" (Acts 24:5). Nazareth, therefore, may have been established by a group who wished to live out that role of true Israel. Later, however, its proximity to Sepphoris would have made it an unlikely base for any minority movement. The Pharisee party appears to have exerted the greater influence in Lower Galilee, and this may be why Matthew always refers to "their synagogues." Rather, Upper Galilee seems to have become the home of Jewish religious movements which regarded the priesthood in Jerusalem as corrupt. George Nickelsburg has pointed to Upper Galilee as the place of origin of *1 Enoch* and the *Testament of Levi,* and an anti-Jerusalem bias with a focus more to Mount Hermon than Mount Zion, suggesting reasons why Jesus revealed his mission at Caesarea Philippi (Matt. 16:13–28).[6] We find the same emphasis in Matthew — it is regularly to "the mountain" in Galilee to which Jesus leads his disciples and where he gives his revelation.

The Proclamation of the Kingdom in Word and Deed

Matthew speaks of Jesus' activity as *teaching, proclaiming* the good news of the Kingdom, and *healing* (διδάσκων, κηρύσσων, θεραπεύων — 4:23; 9:35). The good news of the Kingdom is that announced in Isaiah 40:9 and 52:7. The heart of Jesus' message throughout this Gospel is the restoration of the Kingdom of God — the direct rule of God over his people who have his teaching in their hearts (Isa. 51:7), and who are called to be a people covenant and a light to the nations (Isa. 42:6; 49:6, 8; cf. Matt. 5:13–16). Seen against the background of Isaiah 40–66, it becomes clear that the Beatitudes (5:3–12) which introduce the Sermon on the Mount are not a list of ethical requirements, but the proclamation of the good news to the faithful that the Kingdom has come to them. The various titles given to the faithful in Isaiah 40–66 are summarized in the Beatitudes, and the promises are announced as now having been

---

6. George W. E. Nickelsburg, "Enoch, Levi, and Peter: Recipients of Revelation in Upper Galilee," *JBL* 100 (1981): 575–600.

fulfilled.[7] This is the good news of the Kingdom proclaimed further in various parables throughout Jesus' preaching.

However, this proclamation is announced also in Jesus' actions, particularly his acts of healing recorded in chapters 8–9 and summarized in Jesus' response to John's disciples in Matthew 11:2–6. All these and other miracles are depicted as signs of the restoration of God's Kingdom, in fulfillment particularly of Isaiah 29:18–20; 35:5–7; 41:17–20; 42:7, 18–22; 61:1–3. The phrase "deeds of the Anointed One" (τὰ ἔργα τοῦ Χριστοῦ, 11:2) clearly points to Jesus fulfilling the role of the Servant, the Anointed One of Isaiah 61:1.

Law and Righteousness in the Prophetic Tradition and in Matthew's Gospel

In spite of the strong anti-Pharisaic bias in Matthew, NT scholars of the past have often presupposed that νόμος in Matthew was to be understood somewhat in a forensic sense in accordance with the rabbinical legal tradition. This has led to various problems of interpretation and a sense of conflict in Matthew's Gospel between the evangelist as redactor and the person of Jesus in their approaches to law. Or the understanding has given rise to an overemphasis on Jesus as the new Moses, as a lawgiver setting down new requirements in the Beatitudes (5:3–12) and requiring more scrupulous standards (5:20).[8] When understood against the prophetic background a strong contrast becomes clear between how the Pharisees understood *torah* and how the Matthean Jesus understood it. The prophets understood *torah* as meaning "teaching" rather than "law" in a forensic sense, particularly that teaching of God uttered by

---

7. For a fuller description see Adrian M. Leske, "The Beatitudes, Salt, and Light in Matthew and Luke," in *SBL 1991 Seminar Papers* (Atlanta: Scholars Press, 1991), 816–39.

8. See some of the discussions on law, for example, by Günther Bornkamm, "End-Expectation and Church in Matthew," and Gerhard Barth, "Matthew's Understanding of the Law," in *Tradition and Interpretation in Matthew*, ed. Günther Bornkamm, Gerhard Barth, and Heinz Joachim Held (Philadelphia: Westminster, 1963), 15–51, 59–164. Also see Georg Strecker, *Der Weg der Gerechtigkeit: Untersuchungen zur Theologie des Matthäus*, 3d ed. (Göttingen: Vandenhoeck & Ruprecht, 1962), 143–58; Reinhart Hummel, *Die Auseinandersetzung zwischen Kirche und Judentum im Matthäus Evangelium* (Munich: Chr. Kaiser Verlag, 1963), 31–75; R. G. Hammerton-Kelly, "Attitudes to the Law in Matthew's Gospel: A Discussion of Matthew 5:18," *BibRes* 17 (1972): 19–32; Robert Banks, "Matthew's Understanding of the Law: Authenticity and Interpretation in Matthew 5:17–20," *JBL* 93 (1974): 226–42; Alexander Sand, *Das Gesetz und die Propheten: Untersuchungen zur Theologie des Evangeliums nach Matthäus* (Regensburg: Verlag Friedrich Pustet, 1974), 33–67.

the prophets in their call to covenant faithfulness. In the prophetic literature *torah* and God's *word* are synonymous (Isa. 1:10; 2:3; 5:25; 8:16, 20; 24:3, 5; 30:9, 12; etc.). It is this prophetic teaching of faithfulness to the covenant relationship which is quite evident in Matthew whenever Jesus speaks about the law and/or the prophets (5:17; 7:12; 11:13; 22:40). Thus, Jesus is commonly addressed as "teacher" (διδάσκαλος) in the First Gospel. Only Judas the betrayer refers to Jesus as "rabbi" (26:25, 49).

The same problem arises with Matthew's use of "righteousness" (δικαιοσύνη, 3:15; 5:6, 10, 20; 6:1, 33; 21:32). There has been a tendency to interpret it forensically as meaning "right moral conduct" — the demand of God to live according to the norm of the law — as the word was used in rabbinic literature.[9] Yet a study of *ṣdq, ṣdqh* in the prophetic literature and the Psalms, particularly in the Isaiah corpus, reveals that "righteousness" is a relational term, often used in conjunction with such other relational terms as *'mûnh, 'mt, ḥsd,* and *rḥmym,* and has the general meaning of covenant faithfulness, both human and divine. Matthew's Gospel thus refers to both God's righteousness, for which the faithful hunger and thirst (5:6; 6:33), and human righteousness (5:10, 20; 6:1), by which they relate to God as Father and to one another in love, the commandment on which hang *all* the law and the prophets (22:40).

Jesus' Mission

In this prophetic context it becomes clear that Jesus' mission is (1) to exemplify in himself the role of Servant Israel to be a people covenant and a light to the nations; thus he is identified as such in the references to and quotation of Isaiah 42 at his baptism (3:17), in 12:18–21, and in the transfiguration (17:5). (2) His mission is also to gather the lost sheep of the house of Israel into the Kingdom of God and to train them in the ways of the Kingdom, in order to help Israel become what it had been chosen to be: a people covenant, a light to the nations. (3) Facing growing opposition, Jesus informs his disciples of the need for him, as exemplar of the Servant, to relive the whole history of Israel — even

---

9. See, for example, Benno Przybylski, *Righteousness in Matthew and His World of Thought,* SNTSMS 41 (Cambridge: Cambridge University Press, 1980), 105; Strecker, *Der Weg,* 150 53; David Hill, *Greek Words and Hebrew Meanings: Studies in the Semantics of Soteriological Terms* (Cambridge: Cambridge University Press, 1967), 129; Davies and Allison, *Critical and Exegetical Commentary,* 1:327, 453, 460, 500, 577, 661.

the death of the exile — in order for the resurrection to happen. Thus he must relive Isaiah 53 and the sign of Jonah. The significance of Jesus' death and resurrection in Matthew's Gospel is studied from this point of view. (4) Finally, he comes as the Son of Man to vindicate and to judge.

Christology in Matthew

In order to understand Matthew's Christology, it is necessary to see it against the background of the whole prophetic heritage as outlined above.[10] While the Gospel begins by emphatically proclaiming Jesus as "son of David, son of Abraham" (1:1), as the fulfillment of *all* messianic hopes, in response to Pharisaic criticism, the evangelist goes on to show that Jesus fulfills his messiahship primarily by assuming the role of God's Chosen One, Servant Israel, and relives Israel's history in microcosm (Matthew 2). He is identified as the Servant at his baptism (3:17; Isa. 42:1) and then undergoes testing in the wilderness (4:1–11), as Israel was tested. But whereas Israel in the past has failed, Jesus as Servant Israel succeeds. Matthew's quotation of Isaiah 42:1–4 in 12:18–21 emphasizes that it is as Servant Israel that Jesus always speaks and acts. Matthew's Jesus, however, uses the term "Son of Man" as a self-designation, not only because of its representative nature, but also because it has come to be the all-embracing title for the role of the Servant as this role has evolved and been transformed by the prophetic minority, reflected particularly in the Parables of Enoch (*1 Enoch* 37–71). Peter's answer at Caesarea Philippi to the question, "Who do men say that the Son of Man is?" (Matt. 16:13) is given with this understanding. "You are the Anointed One" refers to the use of that term in Matthew 11:2, where it is clearly a reference to Isaiah 61:1, and the phrase "son of the living God" alludes to Hosea 1:10, where this was a title to be bestowed on restored Israel. Thus, it is revealed to the disciples that Jesus is fulfilling the role of Servant Israel. So it is in this context (16:21) that Jesus reveals to them that he, the Son of Man, must now bring the Servant's role to completion. The exile for Israel had been an experience of suffering and death, but God had raised the nation

---

10. For my summary of that influence, see Adrian M. Leske, "The Influence of Isaiah on Christology in Matthew and Luke," in *Crisis in Christology: Essays in Quest of Resolution,* ed. William R. Farmer (Livonia, Mich.: Dove Booksellers, 1995), 241–69.

up to fulfill the divine purpose of bringing many to righteousness (Isa. 53:11; cf. 49:1–13). Israel's failure to carry out this mission had meant that Jesus needed to undergo suffering, death, and resurrection on behalf of the faithful, and thus to lead them to fulfill that original purpose, and to "make disciples of all nations" (28:19).

The impact of Isaiah 53 on Christology in Matthew cannot be seen in isolation, but must take into consideration the whole purpose of the Servant/Son of Man to be a living covenant and a light to the nations. Through coming as that Servant/Son of Man and giving himself as a "ransom for many" (Matt. 20:28) Jesus makes it possible for the faithful to follow his example and to fulfill Israel's purpose. Jesus' response to the sons of Zebedee in Matthew 20:20–28 further illustrates how Jesus saw his ultimate mission and how that mission relates not only to Isaiah 53, but also to the rest of the Isaianic message of the restoration of the Kingdom of God.

In order to understand fully the context of that response one needs to recall that Second Isaiah described the exile as Israel being "sold" to their oppressors because of their covenant transgressions (50:1; 52:3; cf. Judg. 2:14; 3:8; 4:2; 10:7; 1 Sam. 12:9; Ps. 44:13). But now that they have done double for all their sin, their iniquity is pardoned (Isa. 40:2), and Yahweh will now *redeem* them. They will soon return from exile because, as the prophet constantly tells them: "Your *Redeemer* [*g'l*] is the Holy One of Israel" (41:14).[11] This language draws from the legal tradition that when a person had been sold into slavery because of debt, someone of his own family could redeem him by paying a ransom price and thus restore him to honor (Lev. 25:48–49). Yahweh's kinship with Israel, which gives him that right, is emphasized repeatedly: God is both father and mother to Israel, whom he has "formed in the womb" for himself to be his Servant (43:21; 44:2, 21, 24; 45:10–11; 46:3–4; 49:5, 14–15), and also functions as husband (50:1–2; 54:4–8). The prophet reminds the exiles that God has redeemed them in the past, giving Egypt as their *ransom* (*kpr*) and Ethiopia and Seba in exchange. He will do it again, "because you are precious in my eyes and honored, and I love you. I give men in return for you, peoples in exchange for your life" (43:1, 3–4). So the exiles are

---

11. Yahweh is referred to as *Redeemer* thirteen times in Isaiah 40–66. The verb *g'l* is used another ten times.

urged to return along God's way as the *redeemed, the ransomed of Yahweh* (35:9–10; 44:22; 51:10–11).[12]

Yet the matter of the ransom price for Israel's redemption is of concern. But the prophet assures the people that God's hand is not shortened so that it cannot redeem (50:1–2). To the cry of the exiles, "You have made us like sheep for slaughter and scattered us among the nations, you have sold your people for a trifle, demanding no high price for them!" (Ps. 44:13), Second Isaiah responded: "Thus says Yahweh, 'You were sold for nothing, and you shall be redeemed without money!'" (52:3). For God has pleaded the cause of his people and has now taken away from them the "cup of staggering, the bowl of his wrath" (51:17–23). Jeremiah had spoken of God's judgment on Judah and the nations as drinking the "cup of God's wrath" (Jer. 25:15–31; 49:12), a theme continued by Ezekiel (23:31–33). Now that period was ended. The exiles would return shouting joyfully the good news of Zion: "Your God reigns!" (52:7). With this in mind Israel's experience of the exile is recalled, in Isaiah 53, as a suffering and death experience, a guilt-offering (*'šm*, 53:10) for their own transgression, from which God has raised them up to be his Servant and to fulfill their purpose of being a living covenant, a light to the nations (49:1–8), to "bear the sin of many" and "to make many to be accounted righteous" (53:11–12). Servant Israel, now having been redeemed by God, was now — through this death and resurrection experience — to become the means of redemption (or the ransom price) for the nations.

It is against this background that Jesus, exemplifying the Servant in himself and training his disciples to fulfill the role of Servant Israel, responds to the sons of Zebedee: "Are you able to drink the cup that I am to drink?" (20:22). It is that cup of God's wrath which had been taken away from Israel (Isa. 51:22), but because of the evidence of continuing transgression in opposition to Jesus' proclamation of the Kingdom, that cup is once more in the hands of Servant Israel in the person of Jesus (see 26:39). So Jesus will now complete the role of Servant, bear the nation's iniquities, and give his life as a *ransom* (λύτρον) *for many* (20:28) — "he bore the sin of *many*" in order to "make *many* to be accounted righteous"

---

12. The verbs *g'l* and *pdh* have virtually the same meaning and are used in synonymous parallelism also in Hosea 13:14 and Jeremiah 31:11, always in the context of God gathering his scattered people.

(Isa. 53:11, 12). Λύτρον is not the translation of 'šm in Isaiah 53:10 but rather picks up the whole Isaian concept of divine redemption. The verb λυτρόω was commonly used as the translation for both g'l and pdh in the LXX. Once again, God is giving a person in exchange for Israel's life (see Isa. 43:4), and the Son of Man is the atoning ransom price.[13] There can be no doubt that Isaiah 53 forms the basis of Matthew 20:28, but the proof is found in the context and meaning of Isaiah as a whole and not in the search for verbal similarities in the LXX version.

It is interesting to note that the account in Mark 10:35–45 is almost identical with Matthew 20:20–28. There is one significant difference, however. To the question about drinking the cup, Mark adds "or be baptized with the baptism with which I am baptized" (Mark 10:38). This addition would seem to indicate that Mark not only connects the reference to the cup primarily to the cup in the Lord's Supper (Mark 14:23–24, 36), but that he is also influenced by the Pauline baptismal theology of Romans 6:3–4. Mark thus seems to focus more on the death of Jesus as a sacramental act than on its connection with Second Isaiah. Luke turns the account into a more general reference to service (Luke 22:24–27) and omits any reference to the "ransom" concept for his gentile readers.

Conclusion

The influence of the Isaianic material in the Gospel of Matthew is profound. It is evident that the mission and message of Jesus had developed to a large degree from this material and how it evolved in the later prophetic literature. This Isaianic material is not only evident in Matthew but also, to a lesser degree, in Mark and Luke. Taking into consideration that Matthew was written for a Jewish Christian audience and Mark and Luke primarily for gentile Christians, who would not always appreciate the many allusions to the prophetic literature, that many allusions remain in more muted form speaks strongly for the authenticity of the more extensive quotations and allusions in Matthew. This raises once again the whole question of the relationship between the Synoptic Gospels. A fresh appraisal of the synoptic problem is necessary from the perspective of the influence of the prophetic literature on the New Testament.

---

13. See Leske, "Influence," 261; Hill, *Greek Words*, 53–81.

11

The LXX, 1QIsa, and MT Versions of Isaiah 53 and the Christian Doctrine of Atonement

David A. Sapp

◆

Does the Old Testament provide a clear foundation for the Christian doctrine of atonement? Isaiah 53 is at the center of the debate over this question because it is the one Old Testament text that, according to the evangelical Christian church, describes the death of a human individual for the sins of the world. This individual, called "the servant of the Lord," is not the nation Israel collectively personified, because Israel, also called the Lord's servant, needed redemption from her sin, and this person provides it (cf. Isa. 49:5–6).[1]

But why, if Isaiah 53 describes an individual redeemer, does the New Testament quote extensively from Isaiah 53, but never from the two key verses that sound most like atonement language, vv. 10–11? The Nestle-Aland *Greek New Testament* recognizes eight allusions to these two verses. But no quotations exist. This fact, along with the collective interpretation, has been used by some scholars to argue that neither Isaiah 53 nor the earliest Christian proclamation viewed the deaths of the Servant or of Jesus Christ as events that atoned for sin. Instead, according to this view, atonement theology related to Jesus arose only in later layers of New Testament tradition such as 1 Peter 2:24.

---

1. Isaiah 49 distinguishes between one servant of the Lord, Israel, who has turned from God (vv. 1–4), and another servant whom the Lord sends to bring Israel back to himself (v. 5). This latter Servant not only is sent to redeem Israel, but also to be a light to the Gentiles and to bring salvation to the ends of the earth (v. 6). The nation Israel would despise him, but he is chosen by the Lord (v. 7). Isaiah 53, similar to chapter 49, clearly distinguishes between an individual Servant-redeemer and "the many" whose sins he bears.

This debate, however, has not sufficiently recognized that the above two views rest on two different textual traditions of Isaiah 53, one Hebrew and the other Greek. A few scholars have pointed out that there are differences in the two versions — that the language of the Hebrew Masoretic Text (MT) of Isaiah 53, particularly in vv. 10–11, is more Christian-friendly and leans more toward atonement theology than the sometimes periphrastic translation of the Hebrew in the Greek version used by the early church, the Septuagint (LXX). But the extent of those differences is usually minimized along two avenues. First, since scholars generally view the theologies of the two texts as fundamentally similar, they usually attempt to reconcile them and read one as much like the other as possible. Second, those who view Christian atonement theology as a later phenomenon in the New Testament often argue almost solely on the basis of the Greek translation of Isaiah 53, acting as though the New Testament authors, who wrote in Greek and quoted the Old Testament in Greek, did not use their Hebrew Bibles or allude to it in their writings.

The present study will compare and contrast the theological tendencies of the Greek text of Isaiah 53, represented by the LXX, the oldest known Greek translation of the Hebrew (third–second centuries B.C.E.), and the Hebrew text of its oldest extant versions: the two Qumran Isaiah scrolls, 1QIsa[a] and 1QIsa[b] (second–first centuries B.C.E.), and the MT (fifth–tenth centuries C.E.). It will study the language of these versions in detail to discover significant theological differences, especially in vv. 10–11, beginning with v. 11b, where the Servant of the Lord is called "the righteous one." It will also compare differences between the two Hebrew traditions, the MT and Qumran, to discover whether one is closer to the LXX than the other and what significance if any that might have.

This study shows that at crucial points the LXX translators chose grammar, syntax, or vocabulary that reveal a divergent theological presupposition and consequently a different view of the fate of the Lord's Servant compared to the Hebrew versions. This has a major bearing on how the New Testament church, believing as it did in the atoning value of Christ's death, would have used the texts of the LXX and the Hebrew in its teaching and evangelizing of the Greek speaking world. The key to understanding the differences between the Greek and Hebrew versions of Isaiah 53 and solving the riddle of no New Testament quotations from

vv. 10–11b is not to gloss over the differences between the LXX and the Hebrew texts but to realize that the differences are actually greater than we have realized.[2]

The Hebrew Versions and Their Relation to the LXX

Before comparing the LXX to the Hebrew texts, we must ask, does it make any difference which Hebrew version we use? Are there any appreciable differences between the MT, 1QIsa^a, and 1QIsa^b that would make one significantly closer to the LXX than the others and thus more likely to have been the source of the LXX's translation? It is generally acknowledged that Qumran Hebrew is closer to the LXX than Masoretic Hebrew. In Isaiah 53 there is one clear example of this in v. 11a, where 1QIsa^{ab} and the LXX all have the word "light" (אור = φῶς), which the MT lacks. But do any of Qumran's differences with the MT constitute a theological as well as a textual difference? And do the Qumran Isaiah scrolls *in Isaiah 53 as a whole* lean more to the LXX or the MT?

Appendix A below lists and evaluates the key textual differences in Isaiah 53 between the Qumran Isaiah scrolls and the later Masoretic text tradition. The result of this evaluation is the following: The LXX tends to follow Qumran more than it follows the MT where the two Hebrew traditions differ. However, none of these textual variants is theologically significant. The differences in meaning are minor. Even the word "light" in v. 11a that Qumran includes and the MT lacks does not give an appreciable difference in meaning in the two texts. But in most of the instances in which the LXX agrees with *neither* Qumran *nor* the MT, the LXX's differences with both Hebrew traditions are *major* and represent a significant difference in meaning compared to the Hebrew.

The Qumran textual variants in Isaiah 53 compared to the MT are minor. Major differences appear only in the LXX's Greek translation as compared to *all three* Hebrew versions. The Qumran textual variants, therefore, generally speaking, are actually much closer to the MT than to the LXX. What happens when we widen the study to the rest of

---

2. Critical discussion of translation possibilities will be confined to footnotes so that the reader can follow the argument of the text unimpeded by translation analysis. Unpointed Hebrew will usually refer to Qumran, pointed Hebrew to the MT. A "(Q)" or "(MT)" will indicate the presence of word(s) or meanings only in the Qumran text(s) or the MT respectively.

Isaiah 53 where the Hebrew versions textually agree except for a few orthographic (spelling) differences? How will the LXX compare to the Hebrew there?

The Fate of the Servant: Isaiah 53:11b

The LXX and Hebrew of Isaiah 53:11b read as follows:

MT (1QIsa): יַצְדִּיק צַדִּיק עַבְדִּי לָרַבִּים

LXX: δικαιῶσαι δίκαιον εὖ δουλεύοντα πολλοῖς

The translation of the Greek text is fairly straightforward except for the nuance of the verb: "to justify [or "vindicate"?] the righteous one who serves the many well." The Hebrew text is also not difficult except for the syntax of the second word (צַדִּיק), which has received extensive debate. The best translation is to take it as a noun, "righteous one," just as the LXX has done.[3] Beyond this debate, three major differences exist

---

3. Three possibilities exist for the syntax of צַדִּיק. It could be (1) an adjective describing the Servant: my "righteous" Servant; (2) an adverb: the Servant justifies or vindicates "righteously"; or (3) a noun: "the righteous one." The *adverbial* usage is the least likely because it would be redundant and awkward next to its cognate verb "justify" ("justify righteously"), against Bo Reicke, "The Knowledge of the Suffering Servant," in *Das ferne und nahe Wort*, BZAW 105 (Berlin: Töpelmann, 1967), 189–90.

The *adjectival* usage, despite the clear sense it gives, is syntactically doubtful, because an adjective normally *follows* its subject (see Jer. 23:5, צֶמַח צַדִּיק, "a righteous branch;" Isa. 45:21, אֵל־צַדִּיק, "a righteous God"). But here the supposed adjective precedes its supposed subject (צַדִּיק עַבְדִּי), against Christopher R. North, *The Second Isaiah: Introduction, Translation, and Commentary to Chapters XL–LV* (Oxford: Clarendon, 1964), 232–33; Franz Delitzsch, *Biblical Commentary on the Prophecies of Isaiah*, trans. James Martin (Grand Rapids: Eerdmans, 1949), 336; and Alan Richardson, *An Introduction to the Theology of the New Testament* (London: SCM, 1958), 180.

The *substantival* use finds support from Karl Theodor Kleinknecht, *Der leidende Gerechtfertigte: Die alttestamentlich-jüdische Tradition vom 'leidenden Gerechten' und ihre Rezeption bei Paulus*, WUNT, 2d ser., vol. 13 (Tübingen: Mohr [Siebeck], 1984), 48, 51; James M. Ward, "The Servant's Knowledge in Isaiah 40–55," in *Israelite Wisdom*, ed. John G. Gammie et al. (Missoula, Mont.: Scholars Press, 1978), 129, 136 n. 16; and L. Ruppert, *Der leidende Gerechte: Eine motivgeschichtliche Untersuchung zum Alten Testament und zwischentestamentlichen Judentum*, FB 5 (Würzburg, 1972), 49.

The difficulty often cited with the substantival view is the lack of the Hebrew article "the" with the adjective "righteous." The absence of the article, however, is not uncommon in the Hebrew Bible when the context calls for a definite rather than indefinite meaning. Such is the case, for example, in Isaiah 24:16 and 26:7 where צַדִּיק lacks the article but clearly means "the righteous" collectively. The addition of "my servant" immediately after "righteous" in 53:11b functions like an article, identifying the particular righteous one to whom the prophet refers. This gives the sentence a *dual subject: "the righteous one, my servant*, justifies. . . ."

Proposals have also been made to delete or transpose צַדִּיק. The proposal to *delete* it (following three Isaiah manuscripts) as an erroneous insertion by a scribe due to haplography (reading the word "justify" twice except for the first Hebrew letter) is doubtful. Christopher R. North originally

between the two texts. The first two concern the subject, object, and meaning of *the verb* (first word in each clause). The third has to do with the relationship of "the many" (last word in each clause) to "the servant" (next-to-last word).

First, the subject of the sentence differs in the two languages. In the Hebrew the Servant performs the action of the verb. But in the LXX *the Lord* does. The LXX accomplishes this by using the normal Greek equivalent of the Hebrew verb, but in a different form. The Hebrew has the imperfect tense, "will justify" (יַצְדִּיק). But the LXX uses an aorist *infinitive*, "to justify/vindicate" (δικαιῶσαι). This makes "justify/vindicate" the last in a series of four infinitives that complement the phrase καὶ βούλεται κύριος, "and the Lord desires," at the end of v. 10. To find the subject of v. 11b, we must go back to the end of v. 10. This is the fundamental difference between the MT and LXX versions of vv. 10–11 that influences all the other differences.

Second, the object and meaning of the Greek and Hebrew verbs differ. To accomplish this difference, the LXX first alters the syntax of the Hebrew word צַדִּיק, "righteous one" (LXX: δίκαιον). In the Hebrew text "righteous one" is the *subject* of the verb. But in the Greek text "righteous one" is the accusative *object* of the verb. In the Hebrew texts the righteous *Servant* of the Lord docs something *for the many*. But in the Greek text the *Lord* (the subject of the sentence back in v. 10) does something *to the Servant*.

This change gives the Greek verb δικαιόω (= צָדֵק *hiphil*) a different nuance. The two basic options for the meaning of both the Greek and Hebrew verbs are "justify" (cause to be righteous, declare righteous, or give righteousness to) and "vindicate" (prove to be righteous). With the

took this view in his earlier study, *The Suffering Servant in Deutero-Isaiah: An Historical and Critical Study*, 2d. ed. (London: Oxford University Press, 1956), 126; followed by A. Gelston, "Some Notes on Second Isaiah," *VT* 21 (1971): 524–25. But North remarked in his later work, *The Second Isaiah*, 232: "We may not delete the word on the authority of three MSS…which themselves are more likely to have omitted it by homoioteleuton" (skipping over it inadvertently because it looks so much like the previous word).

Finally, the proposal to *transpose* the adjective and verb (switch places) is theologically motivated and lacks manuscript support. This view was proposed by Charles Cutler Torrey, *The Second Isaiah: A New Interpretation* (New York: Scribner's, 1928), 421–22, and followed by G. R. Driver, "Notes on the Psalms," *JTS* 36 (1935): 152, who then emends the verb צְדִּיק to the noun צֶדֶק. See also G. R. Driver, "Isaiah 52.13–53.12: The Servant of the Lord," in *In Memoriam Paul Kahle*, ed. Matthew Black and Georg Fohrer, BZAW 103 (Berlin: Töpelmann, 1968), 101; and D. Winton Thomas, "A Consideration of Isaiah LIII in the Light of Recent Textual and Philological Study," *ETL* 44 (1968): 86, and his textual notes to Isaiah 53:11 (note c) in the Hebrew Bible critical edition *BHS*.

change of "righteous one" from the subject to the object of the verb in
the Greek text, the verb no longer, as in the Hebrew, means "justify"
(give righteousness to) those who need righteousness (i.e., the many who
are sinners). It now means *"vindicate"* (prove to be righteous) one who
already is righteous (i.e., the Servant).[4]

Third, the LXX changes how a group of people called "the many"
(לָרַבִּים = πολλοῖς) relates to the Servant. In the MT "the many" is the
object of the verb "justify." But the LXX has given the verb ("vindicate")
a new object ("righteous one"). This leaves "the many" dangling, with no
verb to which to be attached. The LXX solves the problem by creating
a new verb. The LXX takes עַבְדִּי, "my servant," and retains its position
in apposition to "righteous one" (Hebrew: "the righteous one, [i.e.,] my
servant"). But it changes the stative noun "servant" into a verbal noun
or participle, "one who serves," and substitutes the adverb "well" for the
possessive pronoun "my" (εὖ δουλεύοντα).[5] This alters the description
of the Servant in this verse from one who is God's Servant to one *"who
serves the many well,"* which gives a further reason that the Lord desires
to vindicate him. "The many" are no longer the object of a specific action of the Servant that justifies them. They are the beneficiaries of his
general good service to Israel.

The LXX, through these grammatical and syntactical changes, has
given Isaiah 53:11b an entirely different meaning. The resulting sense
is: "the Lord desires [10c] . . . <u>to vindicate the righteous one who serves
the many well</u>." The sense of the Hebrew differs radically: "<u>the righteous

---

4. Reicke, "The Knowledge of the Suffering Servant," 188–90, argues that the verb should be
taken not only in the sense of vindication but also intransitively (with no object). See Claus Westermann, *Isaiah 40–66: A Commentary,* trans. David M. G. Stalker, OTL (Philadelphia: Westminster,
1969), 267. Reicke translates: the Servant "proves to be righteous for the many." This sense of
the verb צָדֵק, however, is reflexive in nature ("proves *himself* righteous") and belongs not to the
causative *hiphil* form of the verb in the text but to the intensive reflexive *hithpael.* The *hiphil* of
a stative verb like צָדֵק can, in fact, have an intransitive meaning. But the meaning is "act justly"
or "act righteously" (see Thomas O. Lambdin, *Introduction to Biblical Hebrew* [New York: Charles
Scribner's Sons, 1971], 212–13). In Isaiah 53, however, this is ambiguous, for it leaves the question
of how the Servant acts righteously on behalf of the many.

The more common causative sense of יַצְדִּיק with a direct object fits Isaiah 53 much better and
clears up the ambiguity: the Servant *"will cause [the many] to be righteous,"* meaning, he will *"justify"* them. The dative form of the object in both the Greek and Hebrew texts is required by their
respective verbs but has a direct-object equivalent in translation. Hebrew: "gives righteousness *to*
the many" (="justifies them," see BDB, 511 sec. 3.a.). LXX: "renders service *to* the many" (="serves
them").

5. The LXX translators have already encountered עַבְדִּי, "my servant," at the beginning of the
passage (52:13) and translated it correctly (ὁ παῖς μου).

one, my servant, will justify [give righteousness to] the many." *The LXX has made the Lord's vindication of the Servant and his righteousness the dominant theme in v. 11b, not the Servant's justification of sinners.*

This fundamental difference between the LXX and the Hebrew texts of v. 11b raises the question of whether the LXX has made similar theological shifts in other parts of the passage. Further examination reveals that the differences between the two texts begin much earlier in the passage.

The Fate of the Servant: Isaiah 53:4b, 8–11a, 12ac

In the LXX **v. 4b** anticipates the theme of 10c–11b by omission as well as by selection of vocabulary. The MT has: "And we considered him stricken, and (Q) smitten by God [מֻכֵּה אֱלֹהִים], and afflicted [bowed down, humbled, מְעֻנֶּה]." The LXX omits the reference to God: "And we considered him to be in distress and under a stroke (of misfortune) [ἐν πληγῇ] and under oppression [ἐν κακώσει]." The final word in the LXX suggests violent opposition by men, as opposed to humbling affliction allowed by God according to the final word of the Hebrew. At this early stage in Isaiah 53, the LXX has removed any suggestion of divine intent in the Servant's misfortune. It has portrayed the prophet and the people of Israel as *sympathetic* to the Servant's oppression by others rather than assuming divine retribution in that suffering.

The LXX makes a similar maneuver at the end of the passage in **v. 12a.** The LXX shifts from the Hebrew's first person, the divine "I," to the third person.[6] The Hebrew reads: "Therefore *I* [*the Lord*] will give a portion to him in/among the many/great" [לָכֵן אֲחַלֶּק־לוֹ בָרַבִּים]. But the LXX has: "Therefore *he* [*the Servant*] will inherit much" (διὰ τοῦτο αὐτὸς κληρονομήσει πολλούς).

Verse 8a contains a subtle shift in theme like that in v. 11. The Hebrew has: "By coercion/restraint and by judgment he [the Servant] was taken away." The LXX, however, instead of "coercion" (עֹצֶר), has "hu-

---

6. Isaiah 53 divides into two sections beginning at v. 7 as the text moves from the people's view of the Servant (marked by the national "we," the prophet speaking as one of the people) to a consideration of the Servant's death and the Lord's view of it. The Hebrew uses the divine "I," through which the prophet speaks for God, twice (8b, 12a) rather than the LXX's once (8b, "*my* people") in order to help mark this topical shift.

miliation" (ταπείνωσις). This shifts the focus of the sentence from the coercive actions of wicked people who have held the Servant for judgment to the humiliating effect of those actions on the Servant. The LXX then drops the conjunction "and" and adds the pronoun "his" to "judgment." This changes the connotation of "judgment" (מִשְׁפָּט = κρίσις) to "justice." The LXX then reads: "By humiliation his justice was taken away." The LXX has shifted its attention from the coercive, judgmental actions of the Servant's oppressors (Hebrew) to the *justice* they have denied him. And since justice has been denied the Servant, he is in need of vindication by the Lord.

Verses 8b–11a in the LXX go on to delineate the circumstances through which the Lord will vindicate the Servant. **Verse 8b** at first sight appears to make the task of vindication impossible. How can a dead man be vindicated? The LXX reads: "And who shall describe his generation? [8b] For his life is taken up [αἴρεται ... ἡ ζωὴ αὐτοῦ] from the earth; because of the lawless deeds of my people he was led to death [ἤχθη εἰς θάνατον]."[7] The Greek, however, considerably weakens the expressions of the Hebrew texts, which read: "For he was cut off (separated, excluded) from the land of the living [נִגְזַר מֵאֶרֶץ חַיִּים]; for the transgression of my (Q "his") people the stroke [of death] (was) upon him" (MT נֶגַע לָמוֹ; Q נוגע למו, "he was stricken"). The death of the Servant is clear in the Hebrew text. But compared to the Hebrew the LXX hedges. He was lead to the point of death. But was he subjected to it?

Verse 12c in the LXX seems to negate the above observation about v. 8b, for it appears to describe the death of the Servant more definitely than v. 8b. The LXX reads: "Because his soul was delivered up [παρεδόθη] to death." But the Hebrew text again is more definitive: "He poured out his soul [laid it bare, הֶעֱרָה][8] to death." The LXX uses the weaker passive voice where the Hebrew has employed the active causative *hiphil* verb. Compared to the stronger Hebrew text, the LXX of vv. 8 and 12c, but especially v. 8b, leaves some doubt as to whether the Servant was actually put to death or only led up to the point of possible death.

---

7. The LXX apparently takes the final Hebrew word as לָמוּת, "to death," instead of לָמוֹ, "upon him." *1 Clement* 16:9, instead of the passive tense of ἄγω ("he was led"), has the present of ἥκω ("he comes" to death), a difference that is not significant.

8. הֶעֱרָה is the *hiphil* perfect third *masculine* singular of עָרָה, "be naked or bare." The *hiphil* perfect third *feminine* singular form הערתה, which we do not have here, would make the feminine noun "soul" the subject of the sentence as in the LXX.

Anyone reading v. 8 from a Christian perspective would not see enough difference between the Greek and Hebrew texts to take either one as describing anything other than the death of the Servant of the Lord. The LXX can easily be taken this way despite its softened expressions compared to the Hebrew. When, for example, in Acts 8:30–35 the Ethiopian eunuch read Isaiah 53:7–8 (presumably in Greek) ending with "his life is taken up from the earth" and asked Philip for an explanation, Philip "opened his mouth" and "beginning from this scripture preached Jesus to him" (i.e., his death and resurrection and their implications).[9]

The next two and a half verses in the LXX (9–11b) cast considerable doubt, however, on whether the LXX translators saw in the Hebrew text of v. 8 and following a prophecy of the Servant's death. The biggest differences between the LXX and MT begin at v. 9a.

Verse 9a reads as follows:

MT: וַיִּתֵּן אֶת־רְשָׁעִים קִבְרוֹ וְאֶת־עָשִׁיר בְּמֹתָיו

1QIsa[a]: ויתנו את רשעים קברו ועת עשיר בומתו

LXX: Καὶ δώσω τοὺς πονηροὺς ἀντὶ τῆς ταφῆς αὐτοῦ καὶ τοὺς πλουσίους ἀντὶ τοῦ θανάτου αὐτοῦ

The Hebrew of v. 9 translates: "[9a] And he [the Servant, continuing the third person from 8b; Q[a] "they"] will make his grave with [אֶת] the wicked and with [אֶת] the rich in [בְּ] his death [Q[a]; MT "deaths"],[10] [9b] although he did no wrong, and no deceit was in his mouth." Despite the Servant's innocence, his oppressors execute and bury him like a criminal.

The LXX, however, has understood אֵת not as the preposition "with" but as the direct-object marker.[11] It has also taken the verb נתן in its

---

9. David Daube, *The New Testament and Rabbinic Judaism* (London: School of Oriental and African Studies, 1956; repr., Peabody, Mass.: Hendrickson), 434, notes: "In Rabbinic language, 'to open one's mouth,' *pathah piw*, as a rule shortened into 'to open,' frequently denotes 'to open a lecture on Scripture' or even 'to lecture on Scripture.'" Luke is saying that Philip began to explain the good news of Jesus to the eunuch beginning with Isaiah 53:7–8 *and* the whole passage of which it is a part, Isaiah 53.

10. במתו (Q) could possibly be from בָּמָה, "his grave/sepulchre" (see John D. W. Watts, *Isaiah 34–66*, WBC 25 [Waco, Tex.: Word, 1987], 226, and *BHS* note c). But see North, *Second Isaiah*, 231, and translation p. 65.

11. The אֵת reads better as the preposition "with" than the more common direct-object marker (as in v. 12 twice). Note BAGD, 87: אֵת expresses closer association than עִם," hence "together

most basic sense of "give" rather than "make." The resulting thought, "he gives (to) the wicked his grave," makes no sense, because the Servant, forcefully carried to the slaughter by wicked men, has no power to change places with them. So to get a satisfactory meaning the LXX does three things: (1) It employs the first person of the verb, "I," referring to the Lord, instead of the Hebrew's third person. (2) It uses the preposition ἀντί, "instead of," twice, once for בְ, "in" (not usually "instead of"=תַּחַת), and once inserting it where the Hebrew has no preposition (before "his grave"). (3) It uses the causal conjunction ὅτι, "because," instead of the Hebrew's concessive conjunction עַל, "although."

The resulting LXX translation of Isaiah 53:9a differs significantly from the thought of the Hebrew texts: "And I (the Lord) will give [hand over] the wicked instead of his [the Servant's] grave and the rich instead of his [the Servant's] death, because he did no wrong." The LXX takes the innocence and righteousness of the Servant as the cause of the Lord's vindication of him. *The Lord, not the Servant,* renders justice apparently by *substituting the wicked and the rich* for the Servant at the point that he is about to die at their hands. The LXX, unlike the Hebrew, understands the Servant to have been *led to the verge of death but not subjected to it.* The softer expressions of the LXX in v. 8b — "led" to death, not "stricken," and "lifted up from the earth," not "cut off from the realm of the living" — prepare the reader for the more definitive language of v. 9 to the effect that the Servant did *not* die.

The LXX's alternative view of the Servant's fate continues. In **v. 10a** the Hebrew has: "And the Lord desires to bruise/crush him [דַּכְּאוֹ]; he will make (him) suffer" (MT הֶחֱלִי; 1QIsaᵃ ויחללהו, "and he will pierce/profane him").[12] But the LXX reads: "And the Lord desires to cleanse/purge him of the plague (of misfortune) [καθαρίσαι αὐτὸν τῆς

---

with" or "in close proximity to" the wicked. See Isaiah 53:12d, "He was numbered with [אֶת] the transgressors" (אֶת־פֹּשְׁעִים נִמְנָה, MT=Q). In both 9a and 12d, "with the wicked" and "with the transgressors" are in emphatic positions in the sentence, before the direct object in one and before the verb in the other.

12. On the translation of the *hiphil* of חלה as "make sick" or "cause to suffer" and efforts by scholars to emend it, see North, *Second Isaiah,* 231–32. The objections of G. R. Driver, "Isaiah 52.13–53.12," 96–97, cf. 98–101, that this rendering is "a solecism" and "inappropriate to the picture [of the Servant] and in any case cannot stand without an object" (i.e., the pronominal object "him") are more theologically than textually based. See BDB, 318: "*it pleased Yahweh to bruise him, making him sick*=to bruise him *sorely.*"

πληγῆς]."[13] The effect of the LXX's translation is to *avoid identifying the Servant's suffering with the Lord's will.* The Lord wants to save the Servant from his unjust suffering, not add to it by allowing him to die for some special cause.

The LXX's rendering of **vv. 10c–11a** accomplishes the same purpose:

MT:　　וְחֵפֶץ יְהוָה בְּיָדוֹ יִצְלָח: מֵעֲמַל נַפְשׁוֹ יִרְאֶה יִשְׂבַּע בְּדַעְתּוֹ

1QIsaᵃ:　מעמל נפשׁה יראה אור וישׂבע [11b] ובדעתו [11a] : ... [10c]

LXX:　　[10c] καὶ βούλεται κύριος ἀφελεῖν [11a] ἀπὸ τοῦ πόνου τῆς ψυχῆς αὐτοῦ, δεῖξαι αὐτῷ φῶς καὶ πλάσαι τῇ συνέσει, ...

The Hebrew reads: "[10c] And <u>the desire</u> of the Lord <u>will</u> <u>prosper</u> <u>in</u> his [the Servant's] hand. [11a] After the agony of his soul <u>he</u> <u>will</u> <u>see</u> (Q adds: <u>light and</u>) <u>he</u> <u>will</u> <u>be</u> <u>satisfied</u>.[14] [11b] By his knowledge..." The LXX, however, reads very differently: "[10c] And the Lord <u>desires</u>

---

13. The LXX rendering of דָּכָא, "crush/bruise" (fig., "be/make contrite," e.g., Isa. 57:15; Jer. 44:10), by καθαρίσαι, "to cleanse," may have been influenced by the Aramaic root דְכִי or דְכָא (=Heb. זָכָה), meaning "be pure, purify." See I. L. Seeligmann, *The Septuagint Version of Isaiah: A Discussion of Its Problems,* Mededelingen en Verhandelingen 9 (Leiden: Brill, 1948), 50. Elsewhere in Isaiah, however, the LXX has used words for דָּכָא that are closer to the Hebrew meaning: Isaiah 53:5, μαλακίζομαι ("become weak or sick, suffer" [=חלה]); 57:15, συντρίβω ("shatter, smash, crush"; of persons "mistreat, beat, bruise"); 3:15, ἀδικέω ("treat unjustly, harm, injure"). Since the MT uses דָּכָא in Isaiah 53:5 in its usual Hebrew meaning, it is very improbable that in 53:10 it is an Aramaism with a different meaning. See North, *Second Isaiah,* 231; against Driver, "Isaiah 52.13–53.12," 96, and Bernhard Duhm, *Das Buch Jesaia,* 5th ed. (Göttingen: Vandenhoeck & Ruprecht, 1968 [1st ed., 1892; 4th ed., 1922]), 403.

14. There are three possible senses of the MT of v. 11a. First, the two verbs "see" and "be satisfied" are independent of each other, and "see" means "see *the light of day*" following his death and would allude to his resurrection. The LXX's insertion of the word "light," however, does not imply resurrection. Second, the verb "see" is sometimes used absolutely for "receive revelation" (Isa. 30:10; Ezek. 13:3). Third, the verb "see" can be followed directly by a second verb which becomes its verbal object, e.g., Judg. 9:48, רְאִיתֶם עָשִׂיתִי, "you have seen me do" or "you have seen [that] I did." In Isaiah 53:11b the translation would be "*he will see himself satisfied*" or "*see with satisfaction*" the Lord's will prospering in his hand, suggesting the victorious outcome of the Servant's suffering and death. The absence of an intervening conjunction between the two verbs in the MT favors this interpretation. See Reicke, "The Knowledge of the Suffering Servant," 188–89; J. S. Skinner, ed., *The Book of the Prophet Isaiah, Chapters XL–LXVI* (Cambridge: Cambridge University Press, 1910), 147. But Qumran's inclusion of the word "light" and the conjunction "and" favors the first interpretation (the two verbs are independent). Both Hebrew versions make sense, although Qumran's "see light" might imply resurrection more readily to a Christian interpreter.

There is no need for proposals that conform the MT more to the LXX, such as that of D. Winton Thomas to regard רָאָה as a variation of רָוָה, "drink one's fill" or "be saturated, flooded." See Thomas, "Isaiah LIII," 80, 85, who does not supply "light" and translates "when he shall have drunk deep of his anguish"; and Driver, "Isaiah 52:13–53:12," 97–98, who supplies "light" and translates, "After his pains he shall be flooded with light, through his humiliation he shall win full justification" (104). See North, *Second Isaiah,* 65, 233–34, who argues against these proposals on other, but instructive, grounds.

to take away [11a] from the agony of his soul,[15] to show light to him[16] and to fill [him] with understanding. ... " In the LXX the Lord wants to *cut short the Servant's suffering,* not allowing it to finish its course and result in his execution. The vindication of the Servant begins before the Servant can die, not after he is dead.

This leaves **v. 10b** for consideration.

MT: אִם־תָּשִׂים אָשָׁם נַפְשׁוֹ יִרְאֶה זֶרַע יַאֲרִיךְ יָמִים

1QIsaᵃ: ‏...וַיַּאֲרִךְ...

LXX: ἐὰν δῶτε περὶ ἁμαρτίας, ἡ ψυχὴ ὑμῶν ὄψεται σπέρμα μακρόβιον

The Hebrew has: "If [=although][17] you (the Lord) make his soul[18]

---

15. Gelston, "Second Isaiah," 526–27; and John Day, *"DA'AT* 'Humiliation' in Isaiah LIII 11 in the Light of Isaiah LIII 3 and Daniel XII 4, and the Oldest Known Interpretation of the Suffering Servant," *VT* 30 (1980): 103 n. 19, argue on the basis of the LXX that the Hebrew text should be corrected by inserting the *hiphil* imperfect יַצִּיל, from נצל (*hiphil* "take away, deliver"=LXX ἀφαιρέω), at the beginning of v. 11 after בְּיָדוֹ יִצְלָח, which the LXX has dropped. The result is the following: "the desire of the Lord [is that] he will take away" (from the agony of his soul). This view, however, is improbable because it presupposes double haplography (the LXX overlooked or ignored the Hebrew "prosper in his hand," while the Hebrew texts ignored the verb presupposed by the LXX's translation "to take away"). A simpler explanation is that the LXX has ignored בְּיָדוֹ, "in his hand," as unintelligible and read יִצְלָח as יַצִּיל (altering ח to י and transposing the last two letters) in order to come up with the meaning it sees in the text. The LXX translators apparently had trouble making sense of the Hebrew text.

16. The LXX follows Qumran's insertion of "light and," but additionally has inserted an indirect object "to him" and changed the first verb "see" to the more active verb "reveal/show." These changes suggest one of two interpretations of the text by the LXX translators: First, the Lord reveals to the Servant a greater understanding of the Jewish law, since the LXX sometimes identifies the prescripts of the law with "light" or the "light of knowledge" (φῶς γνώσεως, Isa. 26:9; Hos. 10:12; cf. Ps. 35[36]:10; Jer. 10:13–14). Second, the translators understood the Hebrew "see light" as an idiom for "live," i.e., the Servant enjoys life again after his suffering ceases (see Ps. 49:19[20]; Job 3:16; 33:28). See Seeligmann, *Septuagint Version of Isaiah,* 108, 119.

17. According to Skinner, *Isaiah Chapters XL–LXVI,* 147, the chief difficulty of the sentence in the Hebrew is its hypothetical character, since it is introduced by אִם, "if." Elsewhere, however, the Hebrew text is clear about the Servant's death and its purpose. It already assumes that the Servant will die and that through his suffering and death he vicariously bears the sins of the many. The clauses that follow 53:10b describe the victorious outcome of the Servant's death. It is appropriate therefore to take "if" in the sense of "although" (cf. 53:9b which has עַל in the sense of "although"). G. R. Driver, "Linguistic and Textual Problems: Isaiah XL–LXVI," *JTS* 36 (1935): 403–4, advocates taking אִם with the preceding verb חלה, "be sick" (Aramaic "suffer;" cf. the Peshitta), and reading וְהֶחֱלִיאָם (וֹ). See Duhm, *Jesaia,* 402–3. Such efforts at emending the text arise from failing to find an appropriate meaning for the text as it stands.

18. The Hebrew תָּשִׂים, a *qal* imperfect form of שִׂים, "to put, place, set, make," serves as both the *third-person feminine* singular and the *second-person masculine* singular. Grammatically this verb may refer either to the feminine noun "soul" in "his soul" (נַפְשׁוֹ) or to someone besides the Servant, identified as "you," who will make an offering of the Servant's soul—most likely the Lord, who is the subject of the previous clause, which just described the Lord as desiring to crush or bruise the Servant and make him suffer.

The two translation possibilities based on this *grammatical* form are: *"his soul* [fem., i.e., the

an offering, he will see offspring; and (Q) he will prolong [his] days."
The LXX in contrast reads: "If you [plural, the wicked] give an offering,
your [plural] soul will see offspring long-lived." The LXX has altered the
singular forms of the verb and pronoun (you/his) to plurals (you/your).
This makes the action of offering a sacrifice (□שׁא= περὶ ἁμαρτίας) apply
not to the Lord who offers the Servant, but to *the wicked people* who have
caused the Servant to suffer (cf. "the wicked," 53:9a). They must offer
sacrifices for their sin of persecuting the Servant if they want to see their
families prosper in the future.

The translation on the facing page summarizes the preceding analysis, showing the major differences between the LXX and the Hebrew in
bold type.

The LXX has created a significantly different theology of the Servant in Isaiah 53:8–11 as compared to the Hebrew. In the Hebrew *the
righteous one, the Lord's Servant, gives righteousness to the many through
a divinely intended sacrificial death inflicted on him by wicked people.* The
LXX, in contrast, lacks the sacrificial overtones of the Hebrew text and
the divine sanction it places on the Servant's suffering.[19] But it does more
than this. It has a different view of the Servant's fate. In the LXX *the
Lord vindicates the righteous one who serves the many well by cutting short
his agony and saving him from death at the hands of wicked people.*

The above analysis raises the question, why did the LXX translators
undertake such a radical rewriting of the Hebrew text? R. R. Ottley
called the LXX version of Isaiah 53:10–12 a paraphrase of the Hebrew

---

Servant's soul="he himself"] will make an offering," or "*you* [masc., i.e., the Lord] will make his [the
Servant's] soul an offering." Some scholars think that the context requires the third person because
the Servant is the offering. See Delitzsch, *Isaiah,* 2:330–31; Skinner, *Isaiah XL–LXVI,* 147; R. B. Y.
Scott, "The Book of Isaiah," in *The Interpreter's Bible,* ed. George Buttrick (New York: Abingdon,
1956), 628. However, "his soul [=he] makes an offering" does not clearly mean "he makes *himself*
an offering" without the reflexive pronoun "himself" explicitly added.

Syntax favors the *second-person masculine.* The feminine would make the subject of the verb (in
that case, "his soul") come two words after the verb. The reader would have to wait until the second
word after the verb to learn the verb's subject after having been primed to understand the second-
person masculine "you" as the subject from the verb itself when another subject does not immediately
follow. "His soul" works better as a *second accusative object of the verb* □ישׂ, which takes a double
accusative with the meaning "make" (make something [into] something else), hence "*you make his
soul an offering.*" Similar syntax for ישׁפנ, "his soul," occurs in v. 12c, where it is the object, not
subject, of the verb and occurs two words after it: "he poured out to death his soul."

19. See Sam K. Williams, *Jesus' Death as Saving Event: The Background and Origin of a Concept,*
HDR 2 (Missoula, Mont.: Scholars Press, 1975), 112–15: "Thus the movement of the translation
[of the LXX] in v. 10 appears to be away from a concept of vicarious expiation" (114). This is true
of the LXX, but not the Hebrew.

Isaiah 53:4b, 8–11b

Hebrew	LXX

4b And we considered him
    stricken,
    and (Q) **smitten by God**
    and **afflicted**. . . .

And we considered him
    to be in distress
    and **under a blow of misfortune**
    and under **oppression**. . . .

8a By **coercion**
    and by judgment
    he was taken away. . . .

By **humiliation**
    his justice
    was taken away. . . .

b For he was **cut off**
    from the land
    of the living;
    by/for the transgression
    of my (MT) people
    the stroke (MT) **was upon him.**

For was **taken up**
    from the earth
    his life;
    by the lawless deeds
    of my people
    he was led to death.

9a And **he [the Servant]** (MT) makes
    with the wicked
    his grave
    and **with** the rich
    in his death (Q sg.),

And **I [the Lord]** will give/hand over
    the wicked
    instead of his grave,
    and the rich
    instead of his death,

b **although** he did no wrong,
    and (MT) no deceit was
    in his mouth.

because he did not do wrong,
    nor was found deceit
    in his mouth.

10a And the Lord desires
    to **bruise/crush** him;
    he will make [him] suffer (MT).

And the Lord desires
    to **cleanse** him
    of the plague.

b If/although you **[sg., the Lord]**
    make an offering,
    of **his** soul,
    he will see offspring; **and** (Q)
    he will prolong days.

If you **[pl., the wicked]**
    make an offering
    your [pl.] soul
    will see offspring
    long-lived.

c And **the desire** of the Lord
    in his hand will prosper.

And the Lord **desires**
    to take away
    from the agony
    of his soul,

11a **After** the suffering
    of his soul,
    he will see light (Q)
    and (Q) **he will be satisfied.**
    And (Q) **through his** knowledge

    to show to him light and
    to fill [him]

11b   with understanding,

b **will justify**
    the righteous one
    my servant
    the many.

to vindicate
    the righteous one
    who well serves
    the many.

and suggested that the many problems of the Greek text were due to imperfect knowledge of Hebrew and perhaps an illegible manuscript.[20] These problems may have occurred. But they do not explain the extent of the differences with the Hebrew text.

The LXX version of Isaiah 53:9–11 is more than a paraphrase. It represents a different view of the fate of the Servant. And the reason for that seems to be that the LXX translators had a theological bias against an unjust *death* of a righteous Servant of the Lord. This presupposition, combined with some perceived ambiguities in the Hebrew text, led them to see the extent and outcome of the Servant's suffering differently.

The Servant and the Sins of the Many

A second question raised by the above analysis is more troublesome. If the Servant does not die in the LXX, then what about the traditional Christian gospel? What is the relationship between the Servant and the sins of the many in the LXX, the primary biblical text used by the early church? In what sense can he be said to bear the sins of the many or to be delivered up because of them? Before suggesting an answer to this question, we must look briefly at the ten statements in Isaiah 53 that relate the Servant to the sins of others:

4a(1) This one bears our sins [Heb. bore our sufferings/sicknesses].

4a(2) He suffers pain for us [Heb. he carried our pains/sorrows].

5a(1) He was wounded [Heb. pierced] on account of our transgressions.

5a(2) He was made weak on account of our sins [Heb. crushed on account of our iniquities].

6b   The Lord delivered him over to our sins [Heb. laid on him the iniquity of us all].

8b   Because of the transgressions of my people he was lead to death [Heb. . . . the stroke was upon him].

---

20. R. R. Ottley, *The Book of Isaiah according to the Septuagint (Codex Alexandrinus)*, vol. 1, *Introduction and Translation* (London: C. J. Clay, 1904), 50–52, in a section entitled "Differences between the LXX and the Hebrew."

11c   He will bear their sins [Heb. iniquities].

12d   He was reckoned among the transgressors.

12e   He bore the sins [Heb. sin] of the many.

12f   He was delivered up on account of their sins [Heb. intercedes for the transgressors].

All of these statements, like the whole of v. 8 as noted earlier, can easily be read as proclaiming the Christian gospel. The early church certainly saw them this way in the light of the resurrection of Christ that many of them claim to have witnessed. But whether or not the translators of the LXX saw these statements this way is another question that depends on vv. 9–11. As we have seen, those verses in the LXX have nothing in them to support the death and resurrection of the messianic Servant of the Lord. Only the Hebrew text describes the death of the Messiah and alludes to his resurrection.

How, then, does the LXX view the sin-bearing work of the Servant in Isaiah 53? Verses 3–4 hold the clue:

Isaiah 53:3–4 (Hebrew)

[3] He was despised and rejected by men, and (Q) a man of sorrows (anguish, pain) and acquainted with weakness [חֳלִי]. Like one from whom men hid their faces, he was despised (Q and *we* despised him), and *we* did not esteem him. [4] Thus he bore our weaknesses [חֳלָיֵם = μαλακίαι], and he carried our sorrows [anguishes, pains]. And we considered him stricken, and (Q) smitten *by God,* and afflicted [נָגוּעַ מֻכֵּה אֱלֹהִים וּמְעֻנֶּה].

Isaiah 53:3–4 (LXX)

[3] Instead his appearance was despised, inferior to that of all men, a man under a blow [of misfortune] and knowing how to endure weakness [μαλακίαν], for his face was rejected and despised and not esteemed. [4] This one bears our sins [ἁμαρτίας = עֲוֹנֹת or חֲטָאִים] and suffers pain for our sakes, and we considered him to be in distress and under a blow [of misfortune] and under oppression [εἶναι ἐν πόνῳ καὶ ἐν πληγῇ καὶ ἐν κακώσει].

The LXX translation does two things. First, it understands the cause of the misfortunes, sufferings, and weaknesses of the Servant to be the people's *sins* (LXX translation of the Hebrew "weaknesses," v. 4), not their weaknesses as such or the Servant's own sins or weaknesses. Second, the LXX views the people as more sympathetic to the Servant. In the LXX the people don't consider the Servant stricken by God (it deletes the reference to divine intent in the Servant's sufferings in v. 3). They consider him to be under a blow of misfortune from oppressors. They don't fail to esteem him (the LXX drops the first-person plural "we" in v. 3). His oppressors do. The Servant's oppressors singled him out from among the people for punishment or persecution, and the people identify with him and feel his pain. His sufferings bring them back to their senses, for his sufferings convict them of their sins. The LXX, in contrast to the Hebrew, understands the Servant's bearing the sins of the many to have been accomplished not through a sacrificial death, but through humiliating sufferings and denial of justice with which the people identify and which stopped short of death.

This does not alter the fact that the LXX can be read from a Christian perspective to support Christ's sacrificial death for sins — *except in vv. 9a and 10–11b*. Philip does (Acts 8:32–35=Isa. 53:7–8). Peter does (1 Pet. 2:24=Isa. 53:5). And Paul does (Rom. 4:25a=Isa. 53:12f., cf. 5a). But they never quote from or allude to the LXX of vv. 9–11b, except v. 9b to describe the sinlessness of Christ or of his redeemed people (1 Pet. 2:22; 1 John 3:5b; Rev. 14:5). Why? Because vv. 9a and 10–11b in the LXX rewrite the outcome of the Servant's suffering, excising his sacrificial death and therefore his implied resurrection.

Implications

The Greek version of Isaiah 53 offers the Christian exegete considerably less support than the Hebrew versions for the doctrine of atonement from sin through Jesus' sacrificial death and resurrection. The LXX, like the Hebrew, contains numerous statements that the Servant bore the sins and weaknesses of the many and was reckoned without cause as one of them — a sinner. But taken in context, the LXX translators stopped short of seeing in the Servant's actions an atoning sacrificial death. Whether consciously or inadvertently, they chose grammar, syntax, and vocabulary at strategic points, especially in vv. 9a and 10–11b, that painted a different picture of the Servant.

We cannot, therefore, expect to find allusions to Isaiah 53:9a or 10–11b in the New Testament in support of the Christian gospel by looking to the LXX. Only the Hebrew texts preserve the language and theology that would make such allusions possible. We should expect that New Testament writers who knew one of these Hebrew texts or had access to knowledge of it would follow that Hebrew version of vv. 9a and 10–11b. The Christian doctrine of atonement rests upon an understanding of Isaiah 53 that is fully preserved only in the Hebrew versions. That Christians interpreted Isaiah 53 as we have it in the Hebrew is evidence that the early Christians knew and used one or more of these text traditions.

A number of New Testament passages need to be reexamined in the light of the Hebrew of Isaiah 53. This especially includes the eight texts that the Nestle-Aland *Greek New Testament* lists as containing allusions to Isaiah 53:10 or 11. These texts are Matthew 20:28; Mark 10:45; 14:24; Acts 3:13; Romans 5:15, 19; Philippians 2:7; and 1 John 3:5a. If allusions to Isaiah 53:10–11 exist, they would most likely be to the Hebrew, not the Greek.

Allusions to the Hebrew text of Isaiah 53:10–11 in the above New Testament passages would call into question the view that atonement theology about Jesus based on Isaiah 53 arose in a late stage of New Testament teaching represented by 1 Peter 2:24. The proposed allusions above in Paul's letters are unquestionably earlier than 1 Peter. In addition to these passages, Romans 4:25a already alludes to the Greek text of Isaiah 53:12f.[21] When Paul said that Christ was "delivered over for our transgressions" (LXX: "delivered over for their sins"), he did not mean, as implied by the LXX, that his sufferings stopped just short of death. He meant, as the Hebrew of Isaiah 53 states of the Servant, that Christ died sacrificially for sinners to provide atonement for their sins. It is not a big step from this to see in the next chapter of Romans (5:19b) an allusion to the Hebrew of the preceding verse in Isaiah 53 (v. 11b):

---

21. Romans 4:25a, παρεδόθη διὰ τὰ παραπτώματα ἡμῶν, exactly repeats Isaiah 53:12f. except for two minor changes: (1) altering the pronoun "their" (αὐτῶν) to "our" (ἡμῶν), which adapts Isaiah to Paul's context, and (2) changing "lawlessness" (ἀνομίας; some mss. ἁμαρτίας, "sin") to a synonym παραπτώματα, which connotes "transgression" of God's law.

> Romans 5:19b: through one man's obedience the many will be constituted righteous. (Greek)
>
> Isaiah 53:11b: through his knowledge the righteous one, my servant, will justify the many. (Hebrew)

We need to look more closely at this kind of evidence from Paul's letters and the Gospels in the light of the Hebrew versions.

It is difficult to say how much the early Christians might have noticed the differences between Isaiah 53 in the Greek and Isaiah 53 in the Hebrew or how much those differences would have bothered them. No doubt a man like the Apostle Paul, trained in the Hebrew Bible but writing with ease in Greek, would have noticed. But that was not a problem with which to bother his biblically illiterate, predominantly Gentile, Greek-speaking audience. It was a problem only for the theologians to discuss in private. Isaiah 53 (LXX), except for vv. 10–11b, still carried many statements implying atonement that could be used when explaining the Christian gospel. In the task of evangelizing the Greek-speaking world that didn't know Hebrew, the writers of the New Testament could use only their Greek Bibles. But the message they told out of Isaiah 53 was preserved more in the Hebrew texts than in the Greek translation. When the early Christians wanted to tell the message of Christ's sacrificial death using *vv. 10–11b,* they could not quote the Greek. They could only allude to the Hebrew.

A similar state of affairs exists in modern translations today. Most major English translations of Isaiah 53 follow the Hebrew more than the Greek text where they differ, especially in vv. 9a and 10–11b. But the average layperson doesn't know that and doesn't need to know it.

The LXX, after all, is a translation with all the strengths and weaknesses of a translation. A translation is sometimes influenced by theological bias, and that is the case with Isaiah 53 (LXX). The LXX translators manifest the kind of theological problem with the potential death of the righteous Servant of the Lord in Isaiah 53 that many Jews of Jesus' day had with Jesus' death on the cross. To them God would not allow a truly righteous man to die like a criminal at the hands of his persecutors and certainly would not attach atoning significance to such a death. But that is precisely what the Hebrew versions say. The "punch line" for the Christian gospel — the description of the Servant's divinely intended sacrificial death, his justification of the many, and allusions to his resurrection — occurs only in the Hebrew texts.

Appendix A:
The Qumran Variant Textual Readings
Compared to the MT and LXX in Isaiah 53

The Hebrew Old Testament critical edition *Biblia hebraica stuttgartensia* (*BHS*) lists nine textual variants from 1QIsa[ab] compared to the MT in Isaiah 53. Other textual variants exist and will be discussed after those in *BHS*. The nine Qumran variants in *BHS* are listed on the following page along with the parallel texts of the MT and LXX. At the end of each entry in bold type is a remark as to which of the Hebrew versions the LXX is closest and whether that difference is major or minor. The key things to note are (1) how many times the LXX agrees with the MT *or* Qumran, (2) how many times the LXX agrees with *neither* the MT *nor* Qumran, and (3) which of the disagreements if any represents a significant difference of meaning.

The LXX's comparison with these Hebrew variant readings breaks down as follows:

1. LXX ≠1QIsa[a] or MT, but the differences are minor (once, 53:3[b])

2. LXX = MT, and the difference with 1QIsa[a] is minor (once, 53:8[a])

3. LXX = 1QIsa[ab] (?), and the difference with the MT is minor (twice, 53:3[a], 12)

4. LXX = 1QIsa[ab], and the difference with the MT is minor (twice, 53:9[b], 11), *but* an accompanying word ≠1QIsa[ab] or MT, and this difference is *major*

5. LXX ≠1QIsa[a] or MT, and the differences are *major* (three times, 53:8[b], 9[a], 10)

This review of variant readings is mixed. The LXX does lean more toward the Qumran scrolls than to the MT where they disagree. It follows the MT once but Qumran four times (numbers 2–4 in the above list). But these four agreements between the LXX and Qumran, against the

53:3(a) 1QIsaᵃ ויודע *Qal* impf. act. part., "and knowing," or *niphal* impf. "he is known"(?)

1QIsaᵇ וידע *Qal* impf., "and he knows"

MT וִידוּעַ *Qal* impf. pass. part., "and being known [to or by]"

LXX καὶ εἰδὼς active participle, "and knowing"=**1QIsaᵃ (?), minor difference with MT**

53:3(b) 1QIsaᵃ ונבוזהו *Qal* (act.) impf.(?) 1pl. suffix, "and we despised him"

MT נִבְזֶה *Niphal* (pass.) part. masc. sg., "he being despised"

LXX ἠτιμάσθη aorist pass. masc. sg., "he was despised"≠**1QIsaᵃ or MT, but *minor* difference with both**

53:8(a) 1QIsaᵃ עמו "his [the Servant's] people"

MT עַמִּי "my [the prophet's or the Lord's] people"

LXX τοῦ λαοῦ μου "my people"=**MT, minor difference with 1QIsaᵃ**

53:8(b) 1QIsaᵃ נוגע למו verb: *pual* (pass.) perf. (ו = ֹ), "he was stricken upon himself"

MT נֶגַע לָמוֹ noun: "the stroke [was] upon him"

LXX ἤχθη εἰς θάνατον "he was *led to death*" ≠**1QIsaᵃ or MT, major difference with both**

53:9(a) 1QIsaᵃ ויתנו *Qal* impf. 3pl., "and they give/*make*" (his grave with the wicked)

MT וַיִּתֵּן *Qal* impf. 3sg., "and he gives/*makes*" (his grave with the wicked)

LXX καὶ δώσω Fut. 1sg., "I will give/*hand over*" (the wicked *instead of* his grave) ≠**1QIsaᵃ or MT, major difference with both (subject, verb nuance, object of verb, and preposition)**

53:9(b) 1QIsaᵃ בומתו "in his death"

MT בְּמֹתָיו "in his deaths"

LXX ἀντὶ τοῦ θανάτου αὐτοῦ "instead of his death," singular=**1QIsaᵃ, minor diff. with MT in noun, but major difference with both in preposition**

53:10 1QIsaᵃ ויחללהו "and he will pierce/profane him"

MT הֶחֱלִי "he will make [him] suffer"

LXX τῆς πληγῆς "[cleanse him] of the plague"≠**1QIsaᵃ or MT, major difference with both**

53:11 1QIsaᵃᵇ יראה אור "he will see *light*"

MT יִרְאֶה "he will see"

LXX δεῖξαι αὐτῷ φῶς "to show him *light*," extra word=**1QIsaᵃᵇ, but major difference with both in the LXX verb**

53:12 1QIsaᵃᵇ ולפשעיהמה "and for her/their[?] transgressions[?]"

MT וְלַפֹּשְׁעִים "and for the transgressors"

LXX καὶ διὰ τὰς ἀνομίας αὐτῶν "and for/on account of *their transgressions*" (some mss. ἁμαρτίας, "sins")=**1QIsaᵃᵇ (?), minor difference with MT**

MT, are not without some questions or mitigating factors. In two of the four readings, the LXX *probably or possibly* follows Qumran, because the meaning of the Qumran Hebrew is not certain (Isa. 53:3[a], 12). In the other two cases, the word in the LXX definitely follows Qumran, *but* an adjoining word differs significantly from both Qumran and the MT (Isa. 53:9[b], 11). Furthermore, all of the LXX's differences with the MT in the above variants are theologically or exegetically minor, *except* in three out of four cases where the LXX *also* differs with Qumran (Isa. 53:8[b], 9[a], 10, in number 5 above). The *major* differences between the four texts under consideration, one Greek and three Hebrew, are *in the Greek* where its translation runs counter to all three Hebrew versions. The significant differences are not between the Hebrew versions, but between the Hebrew and the LXX's Greek translation.

Isaiah 53 (Qumran) contains other variant readings that are listed below.[22] Most of these are either orthographic in nature (the addition of one of the consonants י, ו, or ה as a vowel indicator, or the addition of an א at the end or in the middle of a word) or have to do with the addition of the conjunction ו at the beginning of a word (eight times). These other variants follow the same trend of the more prominent variants noted by *BHS*.

53:2(a)	1QIsa^a	לו ונראנו	"...to him [2d לו], and we looked at *ourselves*[?]"
	MT	וְנִרְאֵהוּ	"and we looked at him"
	LXX	καὶ εἴδομεν αὐτὸν	"and we looked at him"=**MT, minor diff. with 1QIsa^a**
53:2(b)	1QIsa^a	ונחמדנו	"that we should desire [take pleasure in] *ourselves*(?)"
	MT	וְנֶחְמְדֵהוּ	"that we should desire [take pleasure in] him"
	LXX	οὐδὲ κάλλος	"nor beauty"≠**1QIsa^a or MT, minor difference with both**
53:12	1QIsa^a	חטאי רבים	"the sins of the many"
	MT	חֵטְא־רַבִּים	"the sin of the many"
	LXX	ἁμαρτίας (acc.pl.) πολλῶν	"the sins of the many"=**1QIsa^a, minor difference with MT**

53:3–11, *Waw* conjunctions (ו="and," etc.) at the beginning of words;

(1) *1QIsa^a includes* and MT lacks the conjunction (eight times):
  v. 3 (2x: ואיש, ונבוזהו) — LXX=MT 2x (no καὶ, no ו)
  v. 4 (1x: ומכה) — LXX=1QIsa^a (καὶ=ו)
  v. 5 (2x: ומדוכא, ומוסר) — LXX=1QIsa^a 1st time, MT 2d time
  v. 10 (1x: ויארך) — LXX=MT (no καὶ, no ו)
  v. 11 (2x: ובדעתו, וישבע)— LXX=1QIsa^a 1st time, MT 2d time

(2) *MT includes* and 1QIsa^a lacks the conjunction (one time):
  v. 7 (וּכְרָחֵל) — LXX=MT (καὶ=ו)

(3) **Summary: The LXX follows 1QIsa^a three times and the MT six times.**

---

22. See *Scrolls from Qumran Cave I: The Great Isaiah Scroll, the Order of the Community, the Pesher to Habakkuk*, photographs by John C. Trever (Jerusalem: Albright Institute of Archeological Research and the Shrine of the Book, 1972), XLIV.

The LXX's relation to these additional Hebrew textual variants is again mixed in character, and there is no theological or exegetical significance in them except in one instance. In 1QIsaᵃ 53:11a, the conjunction prior to "by his knowledge" (ובדעתו) shows that the thought of the Hebrew text connects this word with the one that immediately *follows* it rather than with what precedes it as in the LXX. In the translations below a comma indicates a break in thought before or after "by his knowledge."

53:11   1QIsaᵃ   ". . . , *and* by his knowledge he [the Servant] justifies [the many]"
         MT   "by his knowledge he [the Servant] justifies [the many]"
         LXX   "[the Lord desires . . . to fill the Servant] with knowledge, to vindicate [him] . . ."
                  ≠1QIsaᵃ **or MT, major difference with both**

As in the textual variants noted by *BHS,* major differences in these additional variants come only *in the LXX* where its translation differs significantly from both Qumran and the MT. The Hebrew versions differ very little from each other, and those differences are minor. A Greek translator looking at Isaiah 53 in both the MT and one of the Qumran texts would have very little reason to translate one differently from the other. The only differences that would be required by the Hebrew variants would be the addition of an insignificant word here and there ("and," "light"), the use of a plural instead of a singular or vice versa, the use of a different personal pronoun ("my" vs. "his"), or the use of a synonym or a different verbal tense.

12

The Heralds of Isaiah and the Mission of Paul

An Investigation of Paul's Use of Isaiah 51–55 in Romans

J. Ross Wagner

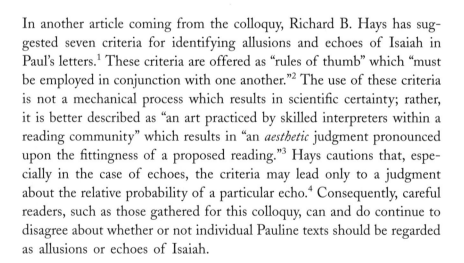

In another article coming from the colloquy, Richard B. Hays has suggested seven criteria for identifying allusions and echoes of Isaiah in Paul's letters.[1] These criteria are offered as "rules of thumb" which "must be employed in conjunction with one another."[2] The use of these criteria is not a mechanical process which results in scientific certainty; rather, it is better described as "an art practiced by skilled interpreters within a reading community" which results in "an *aesthetic* judgment pronounced upon the fittingness of a proposed reading."[3] Hays cautions that, especially in the case of echoes, the criteria may lead only to a judgment about the relative probability of a particular echo.[4] Consequently, careful readers, such as those gathered for this colloquy, can and do continue to disagree about whether or not individual Pauline texts should be regarded as allusions or echoes of Isaiah.

I am grateful to the members of the colloquy for their interaction with an earlier version of this article. In particular, I am indebted to Richard Hays and Chris Stanley for their detailed and helpful comments and criticisms.

1. Richard B. Hays, "Criteria for Identifying Allusions and Echoes of the Text of Isaiah in the Letters of Paul." See introduction, n. 1. A similar set of criteria is offered in idem, *Echoes of Scripture in the Letters of Paul* (New Haven: Yale University Press, 1989), 29–33.
2. Hays, "Criteria for Identifying Allusions and Echoes," 6.
3. "Criteria for Identifying Allusions and Echoes," 3 (emphasis his).
4. "Criteria for Identifying Allusions and Echoes," 6.

Throughout the discussions of the colloquy, it often appeared that the difference between a "yes" or "no" judgment about a particular allusion to Isaiah was the interpreter's sense of the thematic coherence, or lack thereof, between the alleged allusion, on the one hand, and Paul's argument and/or his use of Isaiah elsewhere, on the other. The present study is offered as a complement to Hays's paper and as an illustration of how his criteria, particularly the criterion of thematic coherence, may be applied to the question of Paul's use of Isaiah in Romans. It attempts to advance the discussion by exploring the thematic coherence that undergirds Paul's quotation of and allusion to Isaiah 52–53 in Romans. Rather than focusing on the alleged allusions to the fourth Servant Song (Isa. 52:13–53:12) in Romans, this study examines Paul's understanding of the larger context of this Song in Isaiah. We will argue that the larger "story" of Isaiah 51–55 has exercised a profound influence on the very foundations of Paul's theology as expressed in Romans. As a result, it is only with this larger story in mind that we can adequately address the narrower question of Paul's understanding of the Servant Song of Isaiah 53.

In Romans, Paul appeals explicitly to scripture to explain and justify to the Christians in Rome his missionary outreach "to the Jew first and also to the Greek" (Rom. 1:16). Throughout the argument of the letter, Paul enlists a multitude of witnesses from Torah, Prophets, and Psalms to attest to the fact that God's righteousness — his covenant faithfulness — is being revealed through the gospel Paul preaches. Particularly important for Paul's understanding of his own role in the outworking of God's redemptive purpose are three quotations from Isaiah 52–53: Isaiah 52:7 (Rom. 10:15); Isaiah 53:1 (Rom. 10:16); Isaiah 52:15 (Rom. 15:21). The manner in which Paul uses these quotations suggests that this section of Isaiah has exercised a profound and formative influence on his conception of his apostolic ministry. Paul finds in Isaiah a prefiguration or pre-announcement[5] of his own proclamation of the gospel of Christ to Jew and Gentile alike, wherever Christ is not yet known. This identification allows him, in turn, to maintain with utmost passion and sincerity that it is precisely in and through the gospel that God is displaying his fidelity to his promises to Israel.

---

5. Compare Paul's assertion that the gospel has been pre-announced by scripture, Romans 1:2: ὃ προεπηγγείλατο διὰ τῶν προφητῶν αὐτοῦ ἐν γραφαῖς ἁγίαις.

Our investigation of Paul's use of Isaiah 52–53 begins in the first section ("The Quotations") with an analysis of the three quotations noted above. We shall examine each quotation in its context in the argument of Romans, exploring the meaning of the words actually quoted as well as attending to the subtler echoes of Isaiah 52–53 that may be present in the context.[6] In the second section ("The Larger Story"), I will attempt a more wide-ranging account of the influence of the larger "story" of Isaiah 51–55 on the "story" underlying Paul's argument in Romans.[7] Finally, I hope to suggest some implications of this study that will prove valuable in generating further research on the interrelationship of Paul's theology and mission in Romans.

The Quotations

Isaiah 52:15 in Romans 15:21

Our study begins at the end of the letter, with Paul's quotation of Isaiah 52:15 in Romans 15:21. This passage provides a fitting point of embarkation both because it is at this point in Romans that Paul reflects most self-consciously on his own mission and because the relatively placid waters of Romans 15 are more easily navigable than the choppy seas of Romans 9–11.[8]

Romans 15:14–33 functions as an "apology" for the letter and as a specific request for help from the Roman churches.[9] The passage revisits

---

6. Because of the immense volume of secondary literature on Romans and because of the preliminary nature of this investigation, interaction with other interpreters of Romans will be kept to a minimum.

7. For the importance of recognizing the narrative substructure underlying Paul's specific arguments in a given letter, see among many recent treatments of the issue, R. B. Hays, *The Faith of Jesus Christ* (Chico, Calif.: Scholars Press, 1983); N. T. Wright, "Romans and the Theology of Paul," SBLSP (1992): 184–213, reprinted in *Pauline Theology III: Romans,* ed. D. M. Hay and E. E. Johnson (Minneapolis: Fortress, 1995), 30–67 (page references will be to this version); B. Witherington III, *Paul's Narrative Thought World* (Louisville: Westminster/John Knox Press, 1994).

8. For understanding Romans as a whole, however, chapter 15 is far more important than the backwater it would appear to be, based on the attention it is normally given by commentators.

9. The ongoing debate over the purpose of Romans cannot be pursued here. However, it appears that 15.14–33 provides crucial evidence for several of the purposes of the letter. I hope to develop the argument elsewhere in detail that Paul's desire to extend his mission to the western Mediterranean, with Rome as his base of operations, accounts for many of the features of the letter. See the suggestive hypothesis of Wright, "Romans," 34–36.

and extends many of the themes introduced by Paul in 1:8–15 concerning the scope and purpose of his ministry and his desire to establish a partnership in ministry with the churches in Rome. In seeking to introduce himself to churches with which he has had no prior relationship, Paul has the delicate task of offering to them his God-given gifts and calling to ministry among the Gentiles (15:15–21) while avoiding the implications that they are deficient in faith (15:14; cf. 16:19) or that he desires to take over in Rome (15:20). Paul makes it clear that he desires to come not only to minister to them, but also to receive encouragement from their faith (15:24, 32; cf. 1:12). In fact, Paul needs their support and assistance for mission in the western Mediterranean; he here makes a subtle plea for their backing in this new venture (15:24) and asks the Romans to begin supporting him by interceding for him as he takes the collection to Jerusalem.[10]

As part of his attempt to garner support for his venture to the west of Rome, Paul provides an account of the nature and purpose of his mission and a report of the fruit it has produced thus far. Although the churches in Rome show clear signs of God's working in their midst,[11] Paul has been bold enough to write to them in order to "remind" them (15:15) of the message and implications of the gospel (1:16–17). His rationale for doing this is the "grace given to [him] by God" (15:15; cf. 12:3), that is, his calling as an apostle (1:5: "through whom [Jesus Christ] we have received the grace of apostleship").[12] Paul understands the scope of his apostleship to encompass all the Gentiles (1:5; 15:16), among whom, he notes, are included the Roman Christians (1:6).

Paul figuratively places himself in the role of a priest, one whose ministry does not revolve around the altar but rather centers on the gospel (15:16; cf. 1:9). He describes his mandate as bringing about the obedience of faith (1:5; 16:26; cf. 15:18) or, employing metaphorical language

---

10. The *inclusio* formed by Paul's prayer for the Romans (1:9–10) and his appeal for their prayers on his behalf (15:30–32) illustrates his assertion that he expects their relationship to be one of mutual encouragement and support (1:12; 15:32).

11. In view of the many parallels between Romans 1 and 15, is it tempting to see in 15:14 a reversal of the language of 1:29 (μεστοὺς φθόνου, 1:29; μεστοί ἐστε ἀγαθωσύνης, 15:14; πεπληρωμένους πάσῃ ἀδικίᾳ, 1:29; πεπληρωμένοι πάσης [τῆς] γνώσεως, 15:14). These are the only two occurrences of μεστός and the only two occurrences of the perfect middle/passive participle of πληρόω in Romans. In these Christian communities, composed of Jew and Gentile glorifying God together (15:10), the effects of human rebellion (1:21) are being overturned.

12. Unless otherwise noted, translations of scripture texts are my own.

from the temple cult, as presenting the Gentiles to God as an acceptable and holy offering (15:16). Consequently, he is concerned not only
with the initial proclamation of the gospel, but also with the formation
of communities of believers who embody the truth of the gospel. In this
light, it is possible to recognize that one of Paul's central purposes in
writing Romans is to discharge his ministry of bringing about the obedience of faith among the churches in Rome.[13] Longing to visit in order to
strengthen them through the spiritual gifts he has been given (1:11), Paul
writes this letter in part as a substitute for his presence — and perhaps in
case he never reaches Rome (15:30–32).

Despite his foreboding about his upcoming trip to Jerusalem, Paul
continues to make plans for a visit to Rome on his way to proclaim
the gospel in Spain. He tactfully hints at his hope that Rome will serve
as a base of operations for his outreach to the western Mediterranean
(15:24).[14] His use of προπέμπω suggests that he hopes the Romans will
help outfit him for his journey, for NT usage of the word elsewhere
appears to refer to some kind of material assistance to travelers.[15]

In what appears to be the ancient equivalent of a modern missionary "prayer letter," Paul speaks of the success his mission has enjoyed to
this point in calling forth the obedience of the Gentiles (15:18). He is
swift to acknowledge, however, that his "boast" is in Christ Jesus, who
is working through him, and not in anything he has done on his own
(15:17–18).[16] His ministry is characterized by "the power of signs and
wonders" and "the power of the Holy Spirit," markers which attest to
the fact that Christ is working through his service of the gospel (15:19).[17]
Already in Romans 15:8–9 Paul has put Christ forward as the archetypal
missionary to Jew and Gentile, the one who not only became a servant
to the circumcised but who also is pictured as singing the praises of God

---

13. For this suggestion, see L. A. Jervis, *The Purpose of Romans*, JSNTSup 55 (Sheffield: JSOT
Press, 1991), 161.

14. In 2 Corinthians 10:15–16, Paul speaks of his strategy to use established churches as bases
from which further mission can be undertaken. Earlier in his missionary career, Antioch served as
such a home base.

15. See 1 Corinthians 16:6, 11; 2 Corinthians 1:16; Titus 3:13; Acts 15:3; 3 John 6. One wonders
if ἐμπίπλημι may here have similar connotations ("be filled, supplied by you" rather than simply
"enjoy your company").

16. Note the echo here of Jeremiah 9:22–23 (LXX)/1 Kingdoms 2:10.

17. See 2 Corinthians 12:12, "the signs of an apostle…signs and wonders and acts of power";
cf. Hebrews 2:4, "God testifying together with them through signs and wonders and various acts of
power and distributions of the Holy Spirit…"

in the midst of the Gentiles.[18] Paul's mission, then, is nothing less than the outworking of Christ's own mission.[19]

So powerful has been Christ's working through Paul's ministry that he is able to say that he has "fulfilled" (πεπληρωκέναι) the gospel of Christ from Jerusalem as far round in a circle as Illyricum (15:19), so that there is "no longer any room in these regions" for him to fulfill his apostolic calling (15:23). The precise meaning of Paul's claim has often been debated. John Knox is probably correct in suggesting that with the expression "in a circle" (κύκλῳ), Paul is envisioning the spread of the gospel around the Mediterranean and speaking of the portion of the circle that he has been involved in completing.[20] Paul asserts that as a result of Christ's working through him, he has "fulfilled" the gospel of Christ in these regions. In other words, he has faithfully discharged his vocation of bringing about the obedience of the Gentiles.[21] The surprising claim that his work is finished in the eastern Mediterranean is clarified by the explanation in 15:20: Paul has fulfilled his commission precisely by mak-

---

18. The "I" of Psalm 17:50 (LXX) appears to be Christ, as in Paul's use of Psalm 68:10 (LXX) in Romans 15:3. See J. R. Wagner, "The Christ, Servant of Jew and Gentile: A Fresh Approach to Romans 15:8–9," *JBL* 116 (1997): 473–85. See also A. T. Hanson, "The Interpretation of the Second Person Singular in Quotations from the Psalms in the New Testament," *Hermathena* 73 (1949): 69–72. On Christ as speaker of the Psalms see further R. B. Hays, "Christ Prays the Psalms: Paul's Use of an Early Christian Exegetical Convention," in *The Future of Christology*, ed. A. J. Malherbe and W. A. Meeks (Minneapolis: Fortress, 1993), 122–36; idem, "Israel's Royal Lament Psalms: Matrix for Early Christology?" (unpublished paper).

19. There appear to be important links between Paul's conception in Romans 15 of his mission as the outworking of Christ's mission and his statements elsewhere about "filling up what is lacking" in Christ's suffering ministry of redemption (see Col. 1:24ff.; Phil. 3:10; 2 Cor. 4:10–12). Paul's sense of participation in Christ lies at the root of his own understanding of his role as an apostle and missionary.

20. J. Knox, "Romans 15:14–33 and Paul's Conception of His Apostolic Mission," *JBL* 83 (1964): 11. Cf. J. C. Beker's comment, following Knox: "Paul is a world apostle with a specific strategy.... He does not haphazardly missionize the Roman Empire but conceives of his mission in terms of a 'circle'" (*Paul the Apostle* [Philadelphia: Fortress, 1980], 71). The problem remains whether Jerusalem and Illyricum represent boundaries within which Paul has worked, exclusive of these areas (see μέχρι in Phil. 2:30; Rom. 5:14), or locations in which Paul has actually preached (see μέχρι in Phil. 2:8; 2 Tim. 2:9). Paul describes two visits to Jerusalem in Galatians 1:18 and 2:1–10, but he does not explicitly mention a preaching ministry as part of these visits. Acts places Paul in Jerusalem four times before his last trip (anticipated in Rom. 15:25): Acts 9:26–30 (Paul preaches and is forced to leave); 11:29–30/12:25; 15:2; 18:22. It is probably futile to press Paul's language in Romans 15:19 too closely; the question of a Pauline ministry in Illyricum and in Jerusalem will not be decided from this text.

21. Knox ("Romans 15:14–33," 10) suggests that πληρόω has the sense of "filling" in the gaps left by other preachers. This interpretation seems strained in light of the common use of πληρόω to speak of the discharge of a commission (see Col. 4:17; Col. 1:25; Rom. 8:4; *koiné* examples in BAGD, s.v. πληρόω, 4b; MM, 520).

ing it his goal "to go where no one has gone before" with the gospel.[22] He has proclaimed the good news where Christ was not named[23] in order not to build on another missionary's foundation. Paul's ambition to go to unreached regions with the gospel arose not simply because of his own painful experience of outsiders thrusting themselves upon churches he had founded (as in Galatia and Corinth). Rather, his policy reflects his own understanding of his unique calling as an apostle.

Paul appeals to scripture in Romans 15:21 to justify his determination to preach the gospel to those who have not yet heard: "Those to whom it has not been announced concerning him will see, and those who have not heard will understand."

Romans 15:21	Isaiah 52:15 LXX	Isaiah 52:15 MT
ἀλλὰ καθὼς γέγραπται		
	οὕτως θαυμάσονται ἔθνη	כֵּן יַזֶּה גּוֹיִם רַבִּים
	πολλὰ ἐπ᾽ αὐτῷ καὶ	עָלָיו יִקְפְּצוּ מְלָכִים פִּיהֶם
	συνέξουσι βασιλεῖς	כִּי אֲשֶׁר לֹא־סֻפַּר לָהֶם רָאוּ
	τὸ στόμα αὐτῶν	וַאֲשֶׁר לֹא־שָׁמְעוּ הִתְבּוֹנָנוּ
οἷς οὐκ ἀνηγγέλη	ὅτι οἷς οὐκ ἀνηγγέλη	
περὶ αὐτοῦ ὄψονται,	περὶ αὐτοῦ ὄψονται,	
καὶ οἳ οὐκ ἀκηκόασιν	καὶ οἳ οὐκ ἀκηκόασι	
συνήσουσιν.	συνήσουσιν.	

At first glance, Paul's quotation from Isaiah 52:15b (LXX) appears to have few links to the context of Romans 15, not even a simple catchword connection. As will become evident through our investigation, however, this quotation is part of Paul's reading of Isaiah 52–53 as a prefiguration of the Christian mission and, in particular, of his own role of proclaiming the gospel to all the nations.

Paul links the quotation to his argument in Romans 15:17–20 by means of the phrase ἀλλὰ καθὼς γέγραπται.[24] The conjunction ἀλλά

---

22. It is important to recognize that φιλοτιμέομαι expresses an ambition or goal, not an inflexible rule. The contradiction some have found between Paul's statement of his purpose here and his desire expressed in 1:13–15 to proclaim the gospel in Rome is a false problem created by an overly wooden reading of Paul's language.

23. Paul refers to something more than name recognition or "nominal Christianity." Romans 10:13 (Joel 3:5) speaks of "calling on the name of the Lord"; in 1 Corinthians 1:2 Paul characterizes Christians as "those who call on the name of our Lord Jesus Christ." Compare 2 Timothy 2:19 (Isa. 26:13), where "naming the name of the Lord" means giving exclusive allegiance to him. Paul's emphasis on the importance of the Christian community as the body of Christ would lead one to assume that, for Paul, Christ is not "named" in a region (however he defined it) where a church does not exist.

24. This formula appears in Paul only in Romans and in 1 and 2 Corinthians: Romans 1:17; 2:24; 3:4, 10; 4:17; 8:36; 9:13, 33; 10:15; 11:8, 26; 15:3, 9, 21; 1 Corinthians 1:31; 2:9; 2 Corinthians

indicates that Paul's practice is quite the opposite of building on another's foundation. On the contrary, his strategy of pioneer church-planting accords with what scripture prophesied would happen.[25] Paul's quotation follows the LXX exactly;[26] he omits only the initial ὅτι to effect a smoother transition from his sentence to the quotation.[27]

The wording of the LXX is crucial to Paul's use of the quotation, for only the Greek has the phrase περὶ αὐτοῦ. Isaiah 52:15b (LXX) speaks not of any announcement in general, but one centered on a particular person, the Servant introduced in 52:13. This prepositional phrase περὶ αὐτοῦ, then, provides a critical link between Romans 15 and Isaiah 52:15b. In Romans 15, the αὐτοῦ of the quotation clearly refers to Christ (15:20).[28] Paul has been describing his activity as fulfilling τὸ εὐαγγέλιον τοῦ Χριστοῦ, the "gospel concerning Christ" (15:19). Compare Paul's expressions, "the gospel of his son" (1:9) and "the gospel of God, which was announced beforehand through the prophets in holy writings, concerning his son," (1:1–3, εὐαγγέλιον θεοῦ … περὶ τοῦ υἱοῦ αὐτοῦ).[29] Now in Isaiah 52:15b, Paul finds his own ministry "announced beforehand." He is one entrusted with the message about Christ, sent to those to whom the message has not yet come.

The immediately preceding half-verse of Isaiah 52:15 provides another important link between the quotation and Paul's exposition of

---

8:15; 9:9. See further J. A. Fitzmyer, "The Use of Explicit Old Testament Quotations in Qumran Literature and in the New Testament," in *Essays in the Semitic Background of the New Testament* (London: Geoffrey Chapman, 1971), 3–58. He notes that this formula is found in the LXX: e.g., 4 Kingdoms 14:6; Daniel 9:13 θ'. It corresponds to the formula כאשר כתוב found in the Dead Sea Scrolls (pp. 8–9).

25. In this instance, the καθώς of the quotation formula probably functions in a fully adverbial manner, modifying εὐαγγελίζομαι (v. 20).

26. For the purposes of this study, "LXX" will refer to the critical text of Isaiah by J. Ziegler, ed., *Isaias, Septuaginta: Vetus Testamentum Graecum*, 3d ed., vol. 14 (Göttingen: Vandenhoeck und Ruprecht, 1983).

27. A thorough treatment of Paul's citations of OT texts in Romans may be found in C. D. Stanley, *Paul and the Language of Scripture*, SNTSMS 69 (Cambridge: Cambridge University Press, 1992). Stanley explains the variant reading of B as an attempt to smooth out the grammar of the quotation by beginning with the verb instead of the relative pronoun (184, n. 344).

28. It is not accidental that in the context of Isaiah, the antecedent of αὐτοῦ in 52:15 is "my servant" (ὁ παῖς μου, 52:13). The implications of this for Paul's Christology in Romans will be discussed in Part Two below.

29. My interpretation of the syntax of Romans 1:1–3 takes the three prepositional phrases (beginning with διά, ἐν, περί) as modifying, in a parallel fashion, the verb προεπηγγείλατο. Following Hays's reading ("in holy writings concerning his son"; *Echoes*, 85 [see above, n. 1]), which has its attractions, does not eliminate the claim that the gospel is about God's son, but it does make the parallel with Romans 15:21 less exact.

his calling to serve Christ among the Gentiles (Rom. 15:16, 18). Isaiah 52:15a (LXX) reads, "thus many Gentiles will be amazed at him, and kings will shut their mouths" (οὕτως θαυμάσονται ἔθνη πολλὰ ἐπ' αὐτῷ, καὶ συνέξουσι βασιλεῖς τὸ στόμα αὐτῶν). In Isaiah, the antecedent of the pronoun οἷς (52:15b) is none other than these "many Gentiles" and "kings." Although Paul does not quote the first half of Isaiah 52:15, he clearly finds that the wider context of 52:15b harmonizes with his appropriation of the text as a prophecy of his own gentile mission.[30] The impression that Paul has carried out a sustained reading of this section of Isaiah as a whole is strengthened as we recall Paul's quotation of the verse which immediately follows 52:15, Isaiah 53:1 (Rom. 10:16), also adduced in reference to his ministry of proclamation.

Paul's citation of Isaiah 52:15 and the resultant echoes it evokes resonate with the wider theme explored previously in Romans 9–11: the paradox of Gentile inclusion and of Israel's hardening.[31] The negatively phrased descriptions of the Gentiles: "those to whom it had not been announced...those who have not heard" recall similar descriptions of the Gentiles earlier in the letter: "not my people...not loved" (Rom. 9:25–26; Hos. 2:23; 1:10 [LXX]), "those who were not pursuing righteousness" (Rom. 9:30), "those who are not a nation...a nation without understanding" (Rom. 10:19; Deut. 32:21), "those who were not seeking me...those who were not asking for me" (Rom. 10:20; Isa. 65:1). Just as Isaiah 52:15 speaks of a reversal of the negative condition of the Gentiles and of the inclusion of those formerly excluded, so also do these previous descriptions: "I will call them my people...beloved...children of the living God" (Rom. 9:25–26), "they attained righteousness, that is, the righteousness from faith" (Rom. 9:30), "I was found [by them]...I was revealed [to them]" (Rom. 10:20).

At the same time, the language of Isaiah 52:15 concerning "seeing" and "hearing" reminds the reader of the paradox of Israel's obduracy, over which Paul has agonized most poignantly in Romans 9–11. While the Gentiles, through Paul's preaching, are now seeing, hearing, and understanding, Israel has "heard," but has not believed the message

---

30. Again, the pronoun αὐτῷ finds its antecedent in "my servant" (Isa. 52:13).
31. Eighteen of twenty-eight occurrences of the term ἔθνη in Romans are found in Romans 9–11 (nine times) and Romans 15 (nine times), a measure of the importance of the theme of Gentile inclusion in these chapters.

(Rom. 10:16–18). God has given them "eyes that do not see and ears that do not hear, to this very day" (Rom. 11:8 [Isa. 29:10 and Deut. 29:3]; see 11:10). The resonance of Isaiah 52:15 with this larger theme of Romans suggests that Paul has found his own ministry inextricably linked with the paradoxical outworking of God's redemptive purpose. This hypothesis finds further confirmation through an examination of Paul's argument in Romans 9–11, particularly his use of Isaiah 52–53 in Romans 10.

Isaiah 52:7 and 53:1 in Romans 10:15–16

We encounter a formidable challenge as we turn to Paul's quotations of Isaiah 52:7 and 53:1 in Romans 10:15–16. The densely woven texture of the argument of Romans 9–11 makes it difficult to find seams at which to enter and leave the discussion without rending the fabric of Paul's case. The following discussion, then, will of necessity have a patchwork character, with important threads left dangling as being less relevant to the issues addressed in this study.

In Romans 9–11, Paul takes up the issue of God's faithfulness, which has been called into question by Israel's widespread refusal to believe the gospel. This question, introduced as early as 3:1–4, now at last receives sustained attention. Paul overflows with intense grief at his people's continuing resistance to the salvation which is their inheritance (9:1–5). The apostle turns to scripture to explain how it is that, despite Israel's obduracy, the word of God has not fallen to the ground. He makes the case that enjoyment of the blessings given to Israel has always been through promise and election rather than solely through physical descent (9:6–13). Scripture also undergirds Paul's claim that God is not unjust, for he is sovereignly free to bestow mercy on whomever he chooses. God brings glory to his name by bearing patiently with "vessels of wrath" and by dealing graciously with "vessels of mercy" he has called from among both Jews and Gentiles (9:14–29). Finally, Paul finds in scripture the assurance that a remnant of Israel *will* be saved, the true seed of Abraham (9:27–29; cf. 9:7).[32]

In 9:30–10:21, Paul begins to trace the etiology of Israel's failure

---

32. Hays, *Echoes*, 68.

to believe the gospel. This section of Romans is fraught with exegetical stumbling-stones, but we will plunge ahead and offer a reading that seems sufficiently complete to provide a context for understanding Paul's use of Isaiah 52–53 in Romans 10:15–16.

According to Paul, Israel pursued the Law[33] of righteousness as if it were attained by works rather than through faith, and so never "caught up" with the Law (9:30–32a). Instead, in the words of Isaiah 28:16 (conflated with Isa. 8:14), Israel stumbled over the stumbling-stone (9:32b–33). Paul's meaning remains somewhat ambiguous here. The stumbling-stone may be understood as God himself (favored by the context in Isaiah) or as the true nature of the Law (suggested by Paul's discussion of Israel's failure to pursue the Law rightly, but made more difficult by the expectation of a personal antecedent for αὐτῷ as the object of the verb πιστεύω, 9:33). The ambiguity may well be deliberate, with Paul intending to suggest both meanings.

Reiterating his intense desire and prayer that Israel experience salvation (10:1), Paul proceeds to a second diagnosis of Israel's plight. Zealous for God, but ignorant of God's righteousness, Israel sought to establish its own righteousness[34] and so did not submit to the righteousness of God which comes to focus in Christ (the *telos*, or goal, of the Law) and is available to everyone who believes (10:2–4). Paul frames his thesis in 10:4 in such a way as to weave together key terms from 9:30–33: Christ is the true goal of the *Law* for *righteousness* for everyone who *believes*. By the time his argument reaches Romans 10:4, the stumbling-stone has become a polyvalent metaphor with three interrelated referents — God, the Law, and Christ.[35] Paul next calls two witnesses, Moses and the personified "Righteousness from Faith," to support his thesis. Richard Hays rightly argues that Moses and "Righteousness from Faith" should not be

---

33. Following Dunn, I would argue that νόμος should be understood throughout Romans as a reference to "Torah," Israel's covenant document (J. D. G. Dunn, *Romans*, 2 vols., WBC 38A–B [Dallas: Word, 1988], lxiii–lxxii and *passim*).

34. At this point I am inclined to favor N. T. Wright's explanation of the phrase "their own righteousness" as a reference to Israel's trust in its national privilege and its maintenance of the markers of that privilege (*The Climax of the Covenant* [Minneapolis: Fortress, 1991], 243). This appears to be closer to the problem Paul addresses than the interpretation that sees here a caricature of Judaism as a religion of "legalism."

35. See Wright, *Climax*, 244. Also relevant is the discussion of H. Boers, "Polysemy in Paul's Use of Christological Expressions," in *The Future of Christology*, ed. A. J. Malherbe and W. A. Meeks (Minneapolis: Fortress, 1993), 91–108. Boers does not discuss this particular passage, however.

opposed to one another,[36] though they are given distinct voices.[37] Paul is not here contrasting "doing the Law" with "believing," but showing that, rightly understood, the Law points to Christ as its goal and fulfillment. The value of these witnesses for Paul depends on the fact that their testimony agrees. Moses (10:5 [Lev. 18:5]) avers that the Law was intended to lead to life (corresponding to "righteousness" in 10:4). As Paul interprets her statement, "Righteousness from Faith" (10:6–8 [Deut. 9:4; 30:12–14]) asserts that God has already done what is necessary for salvation in sending Christ and raising him from the dead and now calls for a response of faith to the "word of faith" that is at hand (corresponding to "for everyone who believes" in 10:4).

Paul's own ministry of proclamation "to the Jew first and also to the Greek" comes to the forefront in his bold claim that the "word [ῥῆμα]" of Deuteronomy 30:12–14 is (τοῦτ᾽ ἔστιν) the "word of faith [τὸ ῥῆμα τῆς πίστεως] which we preach" (10:8). It is just possible in this atmosphere so charged with metaphor that Paul intends his hearers to identify the "we" who preach the word of faith as Moses, "Righteousness from Faith," and Paul.[38] He certainly intends to stress the continuity between scripture and Christian proclamation, for he has argued in 10:4 that Christ is the true *telos* of the Law.[39] Although ῥῆμα is not a normal Pauline designation of the gospel message, he employs it here for the sake of identifying his message with the quotation of Deuteronomy 30:12–14 (cf. Ps. 18:5 [LXX] in Rom. 10:18).[40] In Romans 10:17 he will

---

36. *Echoes*, 76. See his detailed discussion of the entire passage, pp. 73–83.

37. Such a conceit is certainly possible for Paul, who already has fancifully personified "Righteousness." I wonder whether, in arguing forcefully against the normal reading of this passage that drives a wedge between 10:5 and 10:6, Hays has not overemphasized the continuity between Moses and "Righteousness from Faith" in this passage. His paraphrase of 10:6 obscures the distinction Paul makes between the two characters: "In another place, *as Moses writes*, this righteousness from faith . . . speaks like this . . ." (*Echoes*, 77; italics mine). In 10:6 Paul does not mention Moses explicitly at all; a distinct, though harmonious, voice is heard. Paul's refusal to collapse the two quotations from Moses' writings into one voice may be due to a desire to have two witnesses to substantiate his point.

38. This was brought to my attention by my colleague, Diana Swancutt. Cf. Hays's paraphrase, "which we also now preach" (*Echoes*, 77). This would not exclude, of course, a reference to other Christian preachers besides Paul. In his letters, Paul normally speaks of the work of proclamation (κηρύσσειν) in the plural (Rom. 10:14, 15; 1 Cor. 1:23; 15:11; 2 Cor. 1:19; 4:5; 11:4; 1 Thess. 2:9) except when emphasizing his personal role over against that of others (1 Cor. 9:27; Gal. 2:2; 5:11).

39. If 16:25–27 is indeed authentic (for which a reasonable case can be made), Paul here connects the revelation of the "mystery" of God's redemptive purpose both with "prophetic scriptures" and with "my gospel and the kerygma of Jesus Christ."

40. The term ῥῆμα appears with this sense in the undisputed Pauline letters only in Romans 10:8 (twice), 17, 18. Cf. Ephesians 5:26; 6:17.

speak of his message as ῥῆμα Χριστοῦ. The content of this "word of faith" or "word of Christ" is given in Romans 10:9, where Paul continues to play on the key terms "mouth" and "heart" from Deuteronomy 30:14. The "word of faith" calls a person to confess that Jesus is Lord and to believe that God raised him from the dead. Response to this message leads to "salvation," a term that here picks up the promise of "righteousness" in Romans 10:4.[41]

Paul draws two soteriological axioms in Romans 10:10: (1) with the *heart* one *believes*, leading to *righteousness;* (2) with the *mouth* one *confesses*, leading to *salvation*. He then proceeds to construct scriptural proofs for these two equations. First, scripture says, "Whoever *believes* in him will *not be ashamed*" (10:11).[42] Paul here revisits Isaiah 28:16, clarifying the force of the original by adding the word πᾶς, "everyone" (cf. 9:33). "Not being ashamed" corresponds to "righteousness" (10:10), being vindicated by or put in a right relationship to God. Paul draws out of the πᾶς in his quotation of Isaiah 28:16 the corollary that there is no distinction (οὐ γάρ ἐστιν διαστολή) between Jew and Greek (10:12). Employing the wording of Romans 3:22 verbatim, he substitutes for the indictment that all humans are sinful the good news that all humans have the same Lord (see 3:29–30), who deals generously with all who call on him.[43] This affirmation leads to the proof of Paul's second axiom. Joel 3:5 promises, "Whoever calls on the name of the Lord will be *saved*" (Rom. 10:13; cf. *salvation*, 10:10). The "call" of Joel 3:5 corresponds to "confess" in Romans 10:10. In addition, the citation from Joel is connected to Paul's quotation of Isaiah 28:16 through the repetition of πᾶς and through the verbal links with Paul's interpretive comment on Isaiah 28:16 that the "Lord" deals generously with all who "call on him" (Rom. 10:12).

---

41. Throughout this section (10:4–13), Paul seems to use "righteousness" language and "salvation" language virtually synonymously.

42. The antecedent of αὐτῷ remains polyvalent, as before. In the context it plausibly could refer to believing the "word of faith" concerning God's saving act in Christ (10:8–10; identified though not identical with the idea of the Law finding its goal in Christ, 10:4), or to trusting Christ as the focal point of God's saving action (compare 10:13, calling on the name of the "Lord" with the confession "Jesus is 'Lord,'" 10:9), or to trusting God as the one who raised Jesus from the dead (10:9) — or perhaps to all three.

43. The equal standing of Jew and Greek before God (though not without acknowledging the priority of Israel in both salvation and judgment: "to the Jew first and equally to the Greek") must be seen as one of Paul's major concerns in Romans; it finds expression in both the thematic statement of the letter (1:16–17) and in the grand finale of the peroration (15:8–9), as well as at key points within the argument of the letter (2:9–10; 3:9, 22, 29; 10:12).

In 10:8–13, Paul has outlined a progression from the "word of faith which we preach" to the response of a person who calls on the name of the Lord and so participates in righteousness and salvation. In 10:14–15, he then retraces this progression from the opposite direction through a rapid-fire burst of rhetorical questions. These questions build on one another in stair-step fashion, culminating in the necessity for preachers to be sent out with the message. Paul frames his questions in such a way that they connect with the scripture texts he cites in the immediate context. In particular, his language anticipates key terms from Isaiah 52:7 and 53:1: "call" (10:12–13; Joel 3:5), "believe" (10:9–11; Isa. 28:16/10:16; Isa. 53:1), "hear" (10:16; Isa. 53:1), "preach" (10:15; Isa. 52:7). In his use of Isaiah 52:7 to cap off the catena, we see the crucial role that Paul believes his own mission plays in the outworking of God's redemptive purpose.

In response to the last of his questions, "How will they preach unless they are sent?" Paul cites Isaiah 52:7 (LXX).

Romans 10:15	Isaiah 52:7 LXX ("Lucianic")	Isaiah 52:7 MT
καθὼς γέγραπται·		
ὡς ὡραῖοι	ὡς ὡραῖοι ἐπὶ τῶν	מַה־נָּאווּ עַל־הֶהָרִים
οἱ πόδες τῶν	ὀρέων [οἱ] πόδες	רַגְלֵי מְבַשֵּׂר
εὐαγγελιζομένων	εὐαγγελιζομένου ἀκοὴν	מַשְׁמִיעַ שָׁלוֹם מְבַשֵּׂר טוֹב מַשְׁמִיעַ יְשׁוּעָה
	εἰρήνης εὐαγγελιζομένου	אֹמֵר לְצִיּוֹן מָלַךְ אֱלֹהָיִךְ
[τὰ] ἀγαθά.	ἀγαθά ὅτι ἀκουστὴν	
	ποιήσω τὴν σωτηρίαν σου	
	λέγων [τῇ] Ζιων	
	Βασιλεύσει σου ὁ θεός	

Although the form of Paul's quotation resembles in some respects the "Lucianic" family of texts that preserves a revision of the LXX toward the Hebrew text represented by MT, Paul himself has made some important modifications to his source.[44] He omits the phrase "on the mountains," a specific reference to the area surrounding Jerusalem, in order to apply the quotation to the broader geographical scope of Christian proclamation. Furthermore, he does not cite the phrase, "announcing a message of peace" (εὐαγγελιζομένου ἀκοὴν εἰρήνης), either because

---

44. See the discussion of Stanley, *Paul and the Language of Scripture*, 134–41.

his *Vorlage* lacked the phrase[45] or because he wants to identify the "message" (ἀκοή) specifically with the "word of Christ" (see discussion below on 10:16–17). Most significant, Paul transforms the lone herald of the LXX (πόδες εὐαγγελιζομένου) into multiple preachers of the good news (οἱ πόδες τῶν εὐαγγελιζομένων). The modification is almost certainly Pauline, for there are no extant manuscripts, Hebrew or Greek, that read the plural here.[46] The effect of this change is to make explicit Paul's identification of the heralds of Isaiah 52:7 (οἱ εὐαγγελιζόμενοι) with the Christian preachers (κηρύσσοντες) mentioned in Romans 10:8, 14–15.[47]

That Paul sees his own ministry of proclamation prefigured in Isaiah 52:7 is further supported by the parallels between the message proclaimed by the heralds of Isaiah's oracle and the gospel preached by Paul. Drawing a connection between Isaiah's "evangelists" (οἱ εὐαγγελιζόμενοι) and Christian missionaries, Paul mentions the "evangel" (τὸ εὐαγγέλιον) in 10:16 for the first time since 2:16. This choice of words is deliberate, as seen by his reference everywhere else in Romans 10 to his message as "the word of faith/the word of Christ" (10:8, 17). A further correspondence between Paul and the heralds of Isaiah 52 is implicit, suggested by the echo in Romans of a portion of Isaiah 52:7 left unquoted by Paul. The message proclaimed by the one bringing good news is described in Isaiah 52:7b as a message of "salvation" (σωτηρία), an announcement to Zion that her God reigns. Likewise, Paul's proclamation is one of salvation (Rom. 10:9, 10, 13), yet one that has a specifically Christian character: it centers on God's decisive act of raising Jesus Christ from the dead. Paul's announcement corresponding to "Your God reigns," is the confession, "Jesus is Lord" (Rom. 10:9). This connection with Isaiah does not find explicit expression in the text of Romans, but nonetheless it makes its presence felt through the phenomenon of "intertextual space" created by Paul's juxtaposition of his world with that of Isaiah 52. That such a powerful link between these

---

45. Stanley, *Paul and the Language of Scripture*, 156.

46. The reading of the plural in Eusebius's citation of α′ and θ′ most likely was influenced by his familiarity with Romans 10:15. The variant cannot be explained through recourse to the parallel passage, Nahum 1:15 (2:1, LXX), for the Hebrew and Greek manuscript tradition uniformly reads the singular here as well.

47. Paul's use of the verb ἀποστέλλω in Romans 10:15 may be intended to remind his readers of his own call as an apostle (1:1, 5; 11:13).

texts depends on the word "salvation" (Isa. 52:7b), not quoted by Paul, evinces again the significance of the wider context of Paul's citations of scripture.

Closely linked in the argument of Romans 10 to Paul's quotation of Isaiah 52:7 is another citation from this section of Isaiah, this time from 53:1.

Romans 10:16	Isaiah 53:1 LXX	Isaiah 53:1 MT
Ἠσαΐας γὰρ λέγει·		
κύριε, τίς ἐπίστευσεν	κύριε, τίς ἐπίστευσεν	מִי הֶאֱמִין לִשְׁמֻעָתֵנוּ
τῇ ἀκοῇ ἡμῶν;	τῇ ἀκοῇ ἡμῶν;	וּזְרוֹעַ יְהוָה עַל־מִי נִגְלָתָה
	καὶ ὁ βραχίων κυρίου τίνι	
	ἀπεκαλύφθη;	

Although Paul and his associates have been sent to preach the good news, as Isaiah prophesied, they have met with resistance. Despite the fact that Christ is the *telos* of the Law for righteousness to all (πάντες) who believe (10:4), and that he is the one Lord over all (πάντες), Jew and Gentile alike, who offers salvation to all (πάντες) who believe/call on him (10:11–13), "Not all (οὐ πάντες) have obeyed the gospel" (10:16). Yet just as Paul has found in Isaiah a prefiguration of his ministry of proclamation, he finds there also a prophecy of the rejection of the message by some: "Lord, who has believed our message?"

Paul has not selected Isaiah 53:1 at random. A complex network of correspondences connects the wording of the citation (which agrees exactly with that of the LXX text tradition) to its context in Romans 10. The prophet calls out to the "Lord" concerning the unbelief of his hearers, who, ironically, ought to have been the ones calling on the name of the Lord for salvation (10:13). The lament, "who has believed?" evokes the promise of righteousness through Christ for all who believe (10:4), a promise announced both by Isaiah (Isa. 28:16; Rom. 10:11) and by Paul and his associates (10:9–10) who preach the "word of faith" (10:8). Isaiah's reference to the ἀκοή that meets with disbelief recalls Paul's statement that hearing (ἀκούειν) precedes believing and depends on preachers being sent (10:14–15). This ἀκοή also provides a link to the (metaleptically suppressed) ἀκοή of Isaiah 52:7, tightening the connection between the "message" of Isaiah 53:1 and the message of those who bring good news (Isa. 52:7), with whom Paul has identified himself and other Christian evangelists.[48]

The phrase *"our* message" clinches the argument that Paul finds a fundamental correspondence between his message and the message proclaimed by Isaiah. It is not simply that Isaiah long ago predicted something that is now fulfilled in Paul's ministry. Rather, Isaiah remains a living voice for Paul (λέγει, 10:16; cf. 10:20–21; 15:12). Paul is implying a relationship more complex than that of prophecy and fulfillment. His phraseology suggests something like a partnership between the ongoing witness of Isaiah in scripture and Paul's own proclamation of the gospel. By adducing Isaiah 53:1 as support for the claim that not all have believed "the gospel," Paul has identified the "message" of Isaiah 53:1 with Christian proclamation. He draws the same parallel in 10:17, concluding from Isaiah 53:1 that faith follows "hearing the message" (ἀκοή) and that this "hearing the message" comes from the "word/preaching about Christ" (ῥῆμα Χριστοῦ) which Paul has also termed the "word of faith which we preach" (10:8). The effect of Paul's claim that Isaiah's "message" concerns the "word of Christ" is to suggest that he understands the Servant Song of Isaiah 52:13–53:12 to refer to Christ, and, in some sense, to be Isaiah's preaching of the same "gospel" that Paul, now Isaiah's "coworker," also preaches. To this suggestion we shall return in the following section ("The Larger Story").

Paul's statement in Romans 10:17 that hearing the message should effect faith leads him to question in 10:18 whether it is possible that "they" (identified as "Israel" in the next verse) have not heard. "On the contrary" (μενοῦνγε), Paul answers, quoting Psalm 18:5 (LXX): "Their voice has gone out into all the earth and their words (ῥήματα) to the ends of the world." This passage fits well into Paul's argument for several reasons. The catchword ῥῆμα links this citation to Paul's use of ῥῆμα for the Christian gospel throughout Romans 10, beginning with his quotation of Deuteronomy 30:14 in 10:8. Moreover, in a context in which Paul has been speaking of Christian preachers in the plural (10:8, κηρύσσομεν; 10:15, κηρύξωσιν, τῶν εὐαγγελιζομένων; 10:16, ἡμῶν), the pronoun αὐτῶν would most naturally refer to Paul and his fellow missionaries.

---

48. Note also the occurrence of the key term ἀκούειν in Isaiah 52:15 (Rom. 15:21).

At first glance, it would appear that Paul has merely torn this citation from its context in Psalm 18 (LXX) and given it a quite different meaning.[49] To one familiar with the psalm, it would be obvious that the "voice" and "words" belong not to Christian missionaries, but to the "heavens." Yet the relationship that Paul's quotation sets up between Romans 10 and the rest of the psalm is more complex than that of text and proof text. The gravitational pull of the original context of the psalm makes itself felt in the intertextual space created by the conjunction of the two texts. This tension generates a suggestive correspondence between the message of the gospel and the witness of the heavens to the glory of God. The reverberations in Romans 10 of the original context of the psalm bring to mind Paul's opening argument that the truth of God's glory, clearly visible in the creation, has universally been suppressed by human beings (Rom. 1:18–21). Paul's quotation of Psalm 18:5 (LXX) to speak of Christian preaching implies that in the gospel message God's glory is once again made visible to humankind. Thus, just as people are without excuse for their refusal to acknowledge the glory of God revealed in creation, so Israel has no excuse for its continuing unbelief in the face of the gospel message it has heard. More scandalous yet, Israel's rejection of the gospel is analogous to humankind's refusal to worship God.

Echoes of the remainder of Psalm 18 (LXX) further suggest an even more damning proof that Israel has heard the message. Having shown that the heavens declare God's glory, the psalmist sings the praise of Torah as a revelation of God in harmony with, but far superior to, that found in creation. Torah brings joy to the heart and light to the eyes (18:9); through God's gift of Torah the psalmist can pray that the words of his mouth and the meditation of his heart will be acceptable in God's sight (18:15). These phrases resonate with Paul's argument that the Law itself points to Christ as its true *telos* (Rom. 10:4) and that the Law joins with Paul in proclaiming the "word of faith" that calls heart and mouth to acknowledge God's work of salvation through Christ (10:8–10). By means of intertextual echo, then, the phrases, "their voice . . . their words," take on multiple levels of meaning: the message "spoken" by creation, the message of Torah, and the message of Paul and his associates.

---

49. More sympathetically, Hays suggests that Paul has taken over the vocabulary of the psalm to give greater rhetorical weight to his assertion (*Echoes*, 175).

In light of its failure to heed these many witnesses, Israel's unbelief is tragic and inexcusable.[50]

As he wrestles in 10:19–21 with God's faithfulness in light of the paradox of Gentile acceptance of the gospel and Israel's disobedience (a theme which occupies his attention throughout Romans 11), Paul does not quote Isaiah 52–53 further. Consequently, we shall cut off our survey of Romans 9–11 here, leaving a good many threads dangling. It will appear from our investigation in the following section of the larger "story" of which Isaiah 52–53 is a part, however, that these texts do not lie far beneath the surface of Paul's argument in Romans 11.

Paul has marshaled an impressive array of scriptural texts to support his contention that the Christ whom he proclaims in the gospel is the true goal and completion of the Law. He enlists Moses, "Righteousness from Faith," Isaiah, and Joel as witnesses to the "word of faith" which he preaches. He appeals to the Psalms to show that creation and Torah proclaim the good news to Israel which he also announces. But Paul finds not only that the gospel is announced beforehand in the scriptures; he also uncovers in Isaiah 52–53 a prophecy of his own crucial role in God's redemptive plan. He is one of those spoken of in Isaiah 52:7, a herald sent to broadcast the good news that God reigns, that Jesus is Lord. Through his apostleship and preaching, people are able to hear, believe, and call upon the Lord. Tragically, he is also one who laments, "Lord, who has believed our report?" Confronted with the awful problem of Israel's resistance to the gospel, Paul finds in Isaiah 53:1 that facing the unbelief of his own people is also part of God's purpose for his ministry.

The Larger Story

We have seen that the individual quotations of Isaiah 52–53 in Romans 10:15, 16, and 15:21 have been carefully chosen by Paul and that not only the words quoted, but also the wider echoes of these passages, con-

---

50. Johannes Munck asks how it is that Paul can consider all of Israel to have heard the gospel and argues that Paul's statement here is analogous to his claim that he has "fulfilled" the gospel in the East (15:19, 23): "Although [the apostles sent to the Jews] have not been everywhere or preached the gospel to every single Jew, yet they have finished the work as far as Israel as a whole is concerned. The parts to which they have preached may be taken as the whole, the Jewish people; and Paul may therefore assert, as he does in what follows, that Israel is unbelieving and hardened" (*Paul and the Salvation of Mankind* [Richmond: John Knox, 1959], 277).

tribute to the rich texture of Paul's argument in Romans. It remains to be explored whether there is evidence that Paul is influenced by the "story" of Isaiah 52–53 (which really belongs to a larger unit consisting of 51–55) and whether this story as a whole may provide insight into the theological "story" that undergirds Paul's particular argument in Romans. Specifically, we want to note where Paul locates himself within this story.

The overarching theme that binds together Isaiah 51–55 is the announcement of God's deliverance of his people from their bondage in exile. The difficulty of delineating precisely the structure of these chapters is well known;[51] this present synopsis is offered only for the purpose of grasping the flow and content of the passage as a whole. Three major units compose Isaiah 51–55: The first division announces God's promise of deliverance for his captive people (51:1–52:12). The central section speaks of the role of the "Servant" in effecting this deliverance (52:13–53:12). The final unit (54:1–55:13) gives further assurances of deliverance and calls on God's people to return to him. We shall devote most of our attention to the first of these units, showing how the themes sounded here are echoed throughout the latter two.

Within the first division, 51:1–52:12, a series of imperatives delimits smaller units of thought. The first three units begin with the call, "Hear me" (51:1, 4, 7). Isaiah 51:1–3 reminds Israel of God's promises to Abraham and Sarah (51:2) and promises that Zion will be made like Eden (51:3). The call to "hear" is addressed to "those who pursue righteousness and seek the Lord" (οἱ διώκοντες τὸ δίκαιον [MT: צדק] καὶ ζητοῦντες τὸν κύριον). Paul appears to develop from this portrait of God's people a "negative" which he then uses to portray the Gentiles in Romans. In the paradox of the divine plan of redemption, the Gentiles are the ones "who did not pursue righteousness" (ἔθνη τὰ μὴ διώκοντα δικαιοσύνην) but who grasped it (Rom. 9:30), those who were not seeking the Lord (τοῖς ἐμὲ μὴ ζητοῦσιν) but who found him (Rom. 10:20, quoting Isa. 65:1). The Gentiles occupy the role that according to Isaiah should belong to Israel. Paul's explicit citation of Isaiah 52:15 (Rom. 15:21) will intimate that the inclusion of the Gentiles, while a shocking

---

51. On the structure of Isaiah 40–55 see H. C. Spykerboer, *The Structure and Composition of Deutero-Isaiah* (Meppel: Krips Repro B.V., 1976); C. Westermann, *Isaiah 40–66: A Commentary* (Philadelphia: Westminster, 1969); J. A. Motyer, *The Prophecy of Isaiah* (Downer's Grove, Ill.: IVP, 1993).

inversion of the expected denouement of the story of redemption, had been foreseen by Isaiah all along. Moreover, having made the negative, Paul does not destroy the original picture, for in Romans 9–11 he argues strenuously that, despite its present hardening, Israel has not been excluded from the people of God.

The next unit, 51:4–6, announces that God's salvation will encompass the entire world. His law and his judgment will go out for a light to the Gentiles (51:4). The terms "my righteousness" (ἡ δικαιοσύνη μου) and "my salvation" (τὸ σωτήριόν μου) appear twice in parallel with one another (51:5, 6). They will appear again in similar fashion in 51:8. These words also appear linked together in Romans 10:10 (cf. 5:9; 10:1–3). It may be that Paul's use here of the terms as virtual synonyms stems from Isaiah's use of the terms in just this way. The "arm of the Lord," introduced in the prologue to Second Isaiah (Isa. 40:10–11), figures prominently in this oracle (twice in 51:5). The LXX reads, "and in my arm the Gentiles will hope" (καὶ εἰς τὸν βραχίονά μου ἔθνη ἐλπιοῦσιν).[52] There is here a close verbal correspondence with the citation of Isaiah 11:10 in Romans 15:12, where Paul clinches the case he has been making in the letter that through Christ's ministry Jew and Gentile are brought to glorify God together: "In him [the root of Jesse] the Gentiles will hope" (ἐπ' αὐτῷ ἔθνη ἐλπιοῦσιν).

In the third unit, 51:7–8, God calls his people not to fear their enemies, for he is about to accomplish everlasting deliverance. God addresses Israel as "you who know judgment[53] ... my people, in whose heart is my law." This description, with its echoes of Jeremiah's new covenant passage (Jer. 31:33), may also be evoked by Paul's description of certain Gentiles[54] who "show the work of the Law written in their hearts" (Rom. 2:15; cf. 2:29) and so are accounted righteous before God (Rom. 2:13). If so, it would suggest that Paul would have read 51:7 in light of the preceding three verses and found Gentiles included in God's people.

Four of the last five units of 51:1–52:12 begin with a double imperative: "Awake! awake!" (51:9; 51:17; 52:1), "Depart! Depart!" (52:11). The remaining unit opens with a double affirmation, "I am, I am the one

---

52. The MT reads, "and my arm shall rule the peoples" (וּזְרֹעַי עַמִּים יִשְׁפֹּטוּ).
53. While the MT reads צֶדֶק here, the LXX has κρίσις rather than δικαιοσύνη.
54. Probably Paul is envisioning gentile Christians. So C. E. B. Cranfield, *Romans*, 2 vols. (Edinburgh: T. & T. Clark, 1975), 1:156.

who comforts you!" (51:12). The effect of these doubled expressions is
to heighten the sense of urgency and expectation aroused by the advent
of God's deeds of redemption. The unit 51:9–11 calls on the arm of the
Lord (cf. 51:5)[55] to awake and perform mighty deeds of deliverance, as
at the Exodus long ago (51:9–10). The pericope closes with the promise that the Lord's ransomed shall return to Zion with joy and singing,
evoking images of a new exodus (51:11).

In the following section, 51:12–16, God emphatically avows that he
(alone) is Israel's comforter, rebuking Israel for fearing human oppressors
and forgetting its Creator, the one who made heaven and earth. God
promises the speedy release of those who are oppressed (51:14). He reaf-
firms to Zion, "You are my people" (51:16). This text recalls the oracle
of Hosea 1:10; 2:23 (LXX), a prophecy quoted by Paul in Romans 9:25–
26. If, as we are hypothesizing, Isaiah 51–55 has exercised an important
influence on Paul's thought in Romans, this passage (Isa. 51:16) further
contributes to the bold irony of Paul's use of the words "my people" to
refer to Gentiles. At the same time, these words from Isaiah lend support
to Paul's emphatic denial of the insinuation that God has abandoned "his
people" (Rom. 11:1–2).

The unit 51:17–23 is introduced by a call to Jerusalem to awake and
rise up, for the God who has punished her (51:17–20) now assumes the
role of his people's advocate (51:22) who announces the end of her punishment (see 40:2) and takes vengeance on Israel's enemies (51:21–23).
The following pericope, 52:1–10, also opens with a call to Zion to awake
and take off her bonds (52:1–3). God recounts his people's captivity at
the hands of Egypt and Assyria and the scorn this has brought on God's
name "among the Gentiles" (52:4–5). Therefore, God vows that he will
act to vindicate his name (52:6).

Recognizing both the context of 52:5 in the story of Isaiah and Paul's
deep engagement with this story is essential to understanding his quotation of this verse in Romans 2:24. On the surface, Paul appears harsh
and vindictive, totally oblivious to the wider context of Isaiah 52:5 as
a word of comfort and assurance to Israel.[56] Yet such an impression is

---

55. The LXX reading here, "Awake! awake, O Jerusalem, and put on the strength of your arm,"
appears to have arisen under the influence of the similar phrases in 51:17 and 52:1.

56. Fitzmyer comments on Paul's use of scripture in Romans 2:24: "Paul, writing frequently
in the rhetorical style of a preacher, often fails to take into consideration the original context of

mistaken. Within 52:1–10, 52:5 functions as a word of judgment. This verse does put the blame for her exile squarely on Israel's shoulders; God is dishonored among the Gentiles because of Israel. The LXX, which Paul quotes here, specifies that it is "among the Gentiles" that God is blasphemed.[57] The LXX further intensifies the sense of blame and accusation in 52:5, addressing Israel directly ("Now why are you here?"), introducing a complaint by Israel against the Lord ("Because my people were taken away for nothing, *you marvel and you cry aloud*"), and reading a phrase absent from MT: "on account of you" (δι' ὑμᾶς).[58] Paul actually appears to soften the blow a bit by eliminating "continually." He also draws attention to the primary issue at hand, the reputation of God, by advancing the phrase "the name of God" (LXX, "my name") to the beginning of the quotation.

Paul does not quote the next verse, 52:6, in which God says that he will now vindicate his name by redeeming his people from exile. Yet he appears to intend that his quotation of 52:5 be understood as a prelude to the announcement of redemption for Israel in the gospel. In the structure of the argument of Romans, this verse is part of Paul's case that all people, Jew and Greek alike, are under sin (3:9). Paul's quotation of Isaiah 52:5 is appropriate precisely because he believes that without the gospel, Israel still is in exile, still in bondage to the power of sin.[59] Romans 2:24 precedes the exposition of the gospel (the righteousness of God *for the Jew first* and also for the Greek [1:16]) in Romans 3:21ff., just as the word of judgment in Isaiah 52:5 precedes the announcement of the return from exile.[60] Following hard on Isaiah 52:5, vv. 7–10 depict a herald coming to Zion with the good news, the message of "salvation" — "Your God reigns!" (52:7).[61] Paul quotes this verse (Rom. 10:15)

---

the Old Testament and twists the quotation which he uses to his own purpose" ("Use of Explicit Quotations," 44; see n. 24 above).

57. This is implied but not stated in MT.

58. See Stanley, *Paul and the Language of Scripture*, 84–86, for a full discussion of the reading of the LXX at Isaiah 52:5 and of Paul's modifications to that text.

59. Wright has argued that the belief that Israel still was in exile was widespread in first-century Judaism. His discussion and further references may be found in *The New Testament and the People of God* (Minneapolis: Fortress, 1992), 268–72. Wright's reference to *m.Yad* (p. 270, n. 108) should read 4.4 rather than 4.7. See more recently J. M. Scott, ed., *Exile: Old Testament, Jewish, and Christian Conceptions*, Supplements to the Journal for the Study of Judaism 56 (Leiden: Brill, 1997).

60. See the discussion of this passage in Hays, *Echoes*, 44–46.

61. The LXX ties 52:6 and 7 together syntactically, so that God himself is the one who brings the good news. It is noteworthy that Paul's quotation of 52:7 more nearly approximates the reading of

in connection with his own proclamation of the gospel, providing further evidence that he is aware of the larger connection between 52:5 and 52:7 within the text of Isaiah and that he employs each of these passages with this context in mind. If Paul sharply criticizes his fellow Jews, it is not as an outsider hurling insults, but as a prophet, wounding that he may heal.

The themes of "hearing" and "seeing" are woven into the oracle of 52:1–10 at several points. In 52:7, the herald announces a "message" (ἀκοή) of peace, and God promises to cause salvation to be "heard" (ἀκουστή). These words take up the call to "hear" repeated previously at key junctures in Isaiah (51:1, 4 [2x], 7, 21). The language of "hearing" appears again in 52:15, "those who have not heard," and in 53:1, "who has believed our message [ἀκοή]?" The call to hear is repeated at the end of Second Isaiah, in 55:2 (ἀκούσατέ μου) and 55:3 (προσέχετε τοῖς ὠτίοις ὑμῶν…ἐπακούσατέ μου).

The urgency that in Isaiah 51–55 is repeatedly attached to hearing God's proclamation helps to account for Paul's emphasis in Romans 10 that faith comes from hearing the message. It further illuminates the significance of the Gentiles "who have not heard" (Rom. 15:21; Isa. 52:15) now hearing and understanding the gospel that Paul preaches. When heard in the background of Romans, the earnest appeal to "hear" in Isaiah 51–55 also heightens Israel's culpability for having "heard" the good news of redemption and yet failed to respond in faith (Rom. 10:16–18).

"Seeing" plays a similar role in Isaiah's prophecy. Not only do the watchmen see the Lord's mercy on Zion — "For eyes to eyes [i.e., "face to face"][62] they shall see" (ὅτι ὀφθαλμοὶ πρὸς ὀφθαλμοὺς ὄψονται, 52:8) — but "all the ends of the earth shall see the salvation from God" (52:10b; note 52:10a, "the Lord will reveal his holy arm before all the Gentiles"). This latter promise is echoed in 52:15, where "those to whom it has not been announced concerning him," the Gentiles, "shall see." When Paul quotes Isaiah 52:15 in Romans 15:21, then, what he understands them to "see" through his ministry is "the salvation from God."

---

the "Lucianic" recension, whose syntax is closer to that of the MT (Stanley, *Paul and the Language of Scripture*, 135–37). For Paul, the heralds are not to be identified with God, but with preachers such as himself.

62. C. F. Keil and F. Delitzsch, *Commentary on the Old Testament*, vol. 7: *Isaiah* (Peabody, Mass.: Hendrickson, 1989), 300.

Another important term within Isaiah 51–55 that first appears in the section 52:1–10 is "mercy." In 52:8, the LXX states that the watchmen will see "when the Lord has mercy on Zion" (ἡνίκα ἂν ἐλεήσῃ κύριος τὴν Σιων).[63] The thought is repeated in the call to rejoice taken up in the next verse: "the Lord has had mercy [ἠλέησε] on [Jerusalem]." The last major section of Isaiah 51–55 reprises this theme of God's mercy: "For a short time I abandoned you, but with great mercy I will be merciful to you [μετὰ ἐλέους μεγάλου ἐλεήσω σε]... with everlasting mercy I have been merciful to you [ἐν ἐλέει αἰωνίῳ ἠλέησά σε], said the one who delivers you, the Lord" (54:7–8, LXX). Similarly, 54:10 states, "my mercy toward you will not depart," and 55:7 promises that the Lord will have mercy on the one who returns to him. Isaiah's linking of the message of the herald (52:7) with God's having mercy on Zion helps to explain how Paul connects God's "mercy" with the gospel (Rom. 11:30–32; 15:8). God's mercy is extended to the Gentiles, who inherit what God has promised to his own people Israel, but Israel is not thereby abandoned: God's promise to bestow "everlasting mercy" (54:8) that "will not forsake" his people (54:10) undergirds Paul's insistence that Israel too will be shown mercy (11:31).

Isaiah 52:10 functions both as a summary of the first major section of Isaiah 51–55 (51:1–52:12) and as a pivotal link with the following section (52:13–53:12). The LXX reads, "And the Lord will reveal (ἀποκαλύπτω) his holy arm before all the Gentiles, and all the ends of the earth will see the salvation from God." The "arm of the Lord" has been an important term for God's saving activity (51:5 [2x], 9 [MT]; see 40:10–11). The wording of 52:10 is taken up in the question of 53:1, "to whom has the arm of the Lord been revealed?" The verbal correspondence suggests that the answer is, "to the Gentiles" (see 52:15, "many Gentiles shall marvel at him"). Moreover, Isaiah 53:1 links the "arm of the Lord" with the "Servant." It is precisely in this message about the Servant that God's saving activity is revealed.[64] In view of Paul's evident reading of Isaiah 51–55 (and especially 52–53), it is reasonable to hear in Paul's claim that in the gospel God's righteousness is revealed

---

63. The LXX diverges from the MT here, which reads, "they see the return of the Lord to Zion." But see 1QIsaᵃ, which ends the verse with ברחמים.

64. In this light, it is not hard to see how the Gentiles hoping in the arm of the Lord (51:5) could be equated with the Gentiles hoping in the "root of Jesse" (Isa. 11:10, quoted in Rom. 15:12; see the discussion of Isa. 51:5 above).

(ἀποκαλύπτω, Rom. 1:17; cf. 16:25) an echo of Isa. 52:10, an echo whose reverberations whisper of the concentration of that revelation in the Servant.

The revelation of God's saving work to the Gentiles and to the "ends of the earth" in 52:10 restates the important theme of 51:4–5 that the Gentiles and "the islands" will hope in the arm of the Lord. The reference to Gentiles also points back to the previous mention of Gentiles in 52:5, "because of you my name continually is blasphemed among the Gentiles." In 52:10, the Gentiles now see God's vindication of his name as he saves his people. It also points ahead to the statement that "many Gentiles" will marvel at the Lord's Servant (52:15) and that "proselytes" will be included among the people of God (54:15, LXX: "Behold, proselytes will come to you [προσήλυτοι προσελεύσονταί σοι, a beautiful play on words!] through me and will take refuge with you").[65] Interestingly, 52:10 also anticipates the role of David in 55:3–5, whom God has given as a witness "among the Gentiles," as a "ruler and governor for the Gentiles." The statement that the ends of the earth will "see" God's salvation links 52:10 with the references to "seeing" in 52:8 and 52:15 and with the message of "salvation" in 52:7. Within Isaiah 51–55, then, 52:10 functions as a major hub in a complex network of relationships; it connects verses throughout this section of Isaiah, including those cited by Paul: 52:5, 7, 15, and 53:1.[66] The presence of these relationships within the text of Isaiah makes Paul's use of these verses appear less akin to arbitrary proof-texting and more like close reading of this portion of Isaiah as a whole.

The final section of Isaiah 51:1–52:12 is the brief call in 52:11–12 to "go out." This reference to a second exodus forms an artistic *inclusio* with the announcement of the new exodus in 51:9–11. Isaiah 52:12 consciously echoes the language of Exodus 12:11, 33–34, 39 (which de-

---

65. MT reads quite differently here.

66. It is possible to see in 52:10 the basis for a further link between Paul's quotations of Isaiah 52:7 and 53:1 and his citation of Psalm 18:5 (LXX) in Romans 10:15–18. As we have seen, Isaiah 52:10 connects 52:7 and 53:1 within the text of Isaiah. Paul similarly has connected these two texts in Romans 10:15–16, suggesting that he is aware of the role 52:10 plays in the argument of Isaiah. There is a significant parallel, if not exact verbal correspondence, between Isaiah 52:10, which says that "all the ends [τὰ ἄκρα] of the earth [ἡ γῆ] will see the salvation from God" and Psalm 18:5 (LXX), which says "their voice has gone out into all the earth [ἡ γῆ] and their words to the ends [εἰς τὰ πέρατα] of the world [ἡ οἰκουμένη]." The parallel is strengthened by Paul's identification of the "salvation" of God (Isa. 52:10=message of "salvation," Isa. 52:7) with the gospel message and by his claim that the phrase "their words" likewise refers to Christian proclamation.

scribe the hasty departure of Israel from Egypt) even as it transforms the tradition: "For you shall not go out in haste, and you shall not go in flight" (RSV). Isaiah 52:11–12 provides a fitting conclusion to the larger section 51:1–52:12 by emphasizing the main theme of this passage, the return from exile.

We have already suggested the multiple ways in which the latter two sections of Isaiah 51–55 are interrelated with the first. It remains only to indicate the basic structure of these sections and to point out one or two more important connections. The second main section of Isaiah 51–55 is the Servant Song (52:13–53:12). It falls into two main sections, a prologue (52:13–15) and the Song itself (53:1–12).[67] Paul quotes from the verses on either side of the seam joining these two parts (52:15; 53:1). His choice of words in Romans 4:25 may allude to Isaiah 53:5, 12, while his phraseology in Romans 5:15 and 19 may echo Isaiah 53:11–12. Yet, surprisingly, nowhere in Romans does Paul quote explicitly from the heart of the Song. A possible explanation for this is that Paul did not read the Servant Song christologically. Another solution suggests itself, however, in view of Paul's use of Isaiah 52:7, 15, and 53:1 to speak of his own proclamation as a Christian missionary.

Paul's quotations of Isaiah in reference to his ministry carry with them clear christological implications. In the context of Romans, the "him" of whom they have not heard or been told, but whom they shall see and understand (52:15), is Christ (15:20)! The "good things" announced by the messengers of 52:7 and the content of the "message" of 53:1, according to Paul, consist of the ῥῆμα Χριστοῦ (10:17; cf. τὸ εὐαγγέλιον τοῦ Χριστοῦ [15:19]).[68] Paul completes two stages of the equation: (1) heralds of Isaiah 52–53=Paul and other Christian preachers; (2) message concerning the return from exile and the Servant of the Lord=gospel of Christ. The last step of the equation, Servant=Christ, remains metaleptically suppressed, lingering behind the text as an unspoken implication

---

67. Although the fourth Servant Song is commonly analyzed as consisting of a central "we" section (53:1–11a) framed by the Lord's statements about the Servant (52:13–15; 53:11b–12), the LXX recognizes no clear shift in speaker between 53:11a and 53:11b. Thus the two-part analysis suggested here seems appropriate.

68. For a similar suggestion, see the paper prepared by Martin Hengel for the colloquy, "Some Considerations about Isaiah 53 and Earliest Christianity." He notes that Romans 10:16 (quoting Isa. 53:1) and Romans 15:21 (quoting Isa. 52.15) "are related to the missionary *Gospel* of Paul, whose content is the crucified messiah, nothing else: 1 Cor 2:2, Gal 3:1, etc." (p. 2, point number 8; emphasis his).

which, for those who have ears to hear, carries far greater rhetorical power than an explicit argument.[69]

The last main section of Isaiah 51–55 (54:1–55:13) in many ways functions as an epilogue to the Servant Song and to 40–55 as a whole. Isaiah 54 may be divided into two discourses in which the Lord addresses his people: "O barren one" (54:1–10) and "O afflicted one" (54:11–17). The first discourse contains a renewal of God's "marriage covenant" with Israel and concludes with the promise, "my mercy toward you will not depart, and your covenant of peace will surely not leave" (54:10, LXX). Paul's emphasis on God's covenant with Israel (Rom. 9:4; 11:27, quoting Isa. 27:9) and on his set purpose to have mercy on "all" (11:32) resonates with these strong affirmations of God's faithfulness to his people. The second discourse speaks of the security of redeemed Israel and the permanence of their vindication by God (54:17). As we have seen, the LXX explicitly includes gentile proselytes among those who will take refuge with Israel (54:15).

Isaiah 55 extends an open invitation to come and enjoy the blessings of the salvation God has wrought (55:1, "come"; 55:6, "seek," "call," etc.). Integral to this invitation is the promise of God's making with his people an "eternal covenant" that centers on David. Isaiah 55:5 reports God's promise to David (note the use of the second-person singular pronoun throughout v. 5): "Gentiles, who did not know you, shall call on you, and peoples, who did not know you, shall take refuge with you (καταφεύξομαι) on account of your God, the holy one of Israel, for he glorified you" (LXX). This pledge recalls the statement in 54:15 that "proselytes shall take refuge (καταφεύξομαι) with you" and implies the fulfillment of the promise of 52:13: "my Servant will be glorified." The plausibility of this last suggestion is increased by the fact that both David (55:4) and the Servant function as witnesses to the Gentiles (52:15 and 53:1 portray the Servant as revealing "the arm of the Lord" to

---

69. "He hints and whispers all around Isaiah 53 but never mentions the prophetic typology that would supremely integrate his interpretation of Christ and Israel. The result is a compelling example of metalepsis: Paul's transumptive silence cries out for the reader to complete the trope" (Hays, *Echoes,* 63). One explanation of Paul's failure to capitalize on the opportunity to exploit the Servant Song christologically recognizes that he is not concerned explicitly with Christology in the letter, but with the relationship of Jew and Gentile in God's redemptive purpose. In Romans, Paul gives surprisingly little attention to Christology *per se,* although the "story" of Christ is never far from the surface of his argument.

"many Gentiles"). These correspondences suggest an identification of the Servant with Davidic imagery within the context of Isaiah.

Paul's development of the theme of "calling on (ἐπικαλέω) the name of the Lord" from Joel 3:5 and his identification of "the Lord" with Jesus (Rom. 10:9), the descendant of David (Rom. 1:3; cf. 15:12 [Isa. 11:10]), raises the question of whether Isaiah 55:5 ("Gentiles . . . shall call on [ἐπικαλέω] you") played a role in his choice of Joel 3:5 as a call to respond to the preaching of Christ. Although Paul never explicitly cites Isaiah 55:5,[70] it is unlikely that he was unfamiliar with this text and its connections to other parts of Isaiah 51–55. In the absence of solid evidence, however, we will have to conclude that the question of the role of Isaiah 55:5 in Paul's theology remains unanswerable.

Concluding Reflections: The Story of Isaiah in Romans

We have seen that Isaiah 51–55 presents a fairly coherent "story" of God's redemption of his people out of bondage in exile and the proclamation of a new exodus. We have also observed many points of contact between Paul's thought and this story that go beyond the explicit quotations of these texts in Romans. Paul's citations are not plunder from random raids on Isaiah, but the fruit of careful reading of the text in light of his own situation as an apostle to the Gentiles. Moreover, the interrelationships among the texts Paul does cite, both within Isaiah 51–55 and within the argument of Romans, strongly suggest that Paul has integrated the story of Isaiah 51–55 into the particular theological story which lies beneath the argument of Romans. A clear example of this is the way in which Paul's use of Isaiah 52:5 (Rom. 2:24) becomes intelligible in light of the overarching story of Isaiah 51–55 (above, pp. 214–216). Our investigation supports Tom Wright's hypothesis that in Romans Paul has engaged in "a deep meditation on the whole passage [Isaiah 52f.] as a major clue to the divine covenant purposes for Israel."[71]

The evidence suggests that this portion of Isaiah functions at a foundational level of Paul's understanding of his own role as an apostle and missionary. Paul finds in Isaiah a prefiguration of the part he now plays

---

70. He does appeal to Isaiah 55:10 in 2 Corinthians 9:10.
71. Wright, "Romans," 58; see n. 7 above.

in the drama of redemption. His appropriation of these texts could be said to reveal a "missiological" hermeneutic.[72] In Romans, Paul does not exploit the christological potential of the Servant Song; rather, he appeals to Isaiah to explain to the Romans his own ministry "to the Jew first and also to the Greek." Contrary to the argument of Paul Dinter, the apostle does not conceive of himself as the *Servant* of Isaiah 52:13–53:12.[73] Rather, he finds himself playing the crucial part of a *herald* who announces the good news, the word of Christ, to Israel (52:7) and to those who have not heard, the Gentiles (52:15). He also finds that he shares the pain caused by the unbelief of his people in the gospel (53:1). Yet Paul's theology is grounded in the bedrock of Isaiah's affirmation that God is faithful to his people and is working salvation for them. The promises in Isaiah 51–55 of redemption for Israel give him a confidence in his proclamation and a sense of trust that as he carries out his ministry "all Israel will be saved" (Rom. 11:26).[74]

To return to Hays's criteria (above, pp. 193–194), there appears to be a strong thematic coherence among the citations of and allusions to Isaiah 52–53 which we have examined. In Romans, Paul's reading of this portion of Isaiah centers on the theme of the eschatological mission to the Gentiles. Paul's primary use of Isaiah 52–53 in Romans is not christological, but "missiological." This observation is not meant to prejudge the question, raised by others in this colloquy, of whether or not texts such as Romans 4:25 or 5:15–19 are allusions to Isaiah 53, evincing Paul's christological reflections on that text. It is to insist, however, that the discussion of further alleged allusions to the Servant Song of Isaiah 52:13–53:12 in Romans must be carried out within the context of Paul's reading of the larger story of Isaiah 51–55.

---

72. This description would fall under Hays's more general characterization of Paul's reading of scripture as "ecclesiocentric."

73. P. Dinter, "Paul and the Prophet Isaiah," *Biblical Theology Bulletin* 13 (1983): 48–52.

74. On this difficult verse see Wright, *Climax*, 249–50; see n. 34 above. I agree with Wright that Paul sees the salvation of "all Israel" (polemically redefined as the Christian communities in which Jew and Gentile are united) occurring through the mission to Jew and Gentile that he is carrying out. Yet I would not want to downplay the eschatological edge to his argument. There seems to be in Paul's agonizing over the Jews' obduracy a hope that the outcome of his continued outreach to the Gentiles will be a massive turning of the Jews to Christ (11:13–15). Paul's mission is thus an essential means to that end. He is caught in the "already-not yet" situation in which some Jews have responded to Christ but the redemption of Israel (Jew and Gentile) prophesied in Isaiah has not yet been realized fully.

13

Concepts of *Stellvertretung* in the Interpretation of Isaiah 53

Daniel P. Bailey

Introduction

The term *Stellvertretung* does not occur in any major German translation of Isaiah 53, but it does occur almost of necessity in German-language theological exegesis concerned with the relationship of the "one" and the "many" — certainly one of the central questions of Isaiah 52:13–53:12 on any reckoning.[1] Different languages have different terms for this relationship, but German excels, both because of the theologians who make the language and because of the theologians who are made by the language, in focusing attention not only upon the role of the Servant and upon the role of the many, but upon the thing that now exists between them because of their related destinies.

This "thing" has been given a name: *Stellvertretung* — in English: "place-taking"; perhaps even more abstractly, "in-our-place-ness." The main idea is that one person takes another's place, though this process or event can be conceived in different ways; and the main question is what we should call this when it happens, assuming that we wish to give it a name. In English, however, there can certainly be no objection to saying that the Servant has *taken the place* of the "many" or the "we," because qualifications are always possible. Perhaps the Servant has taken up

I would like to thank the trustees of the two Cambridge-based foundations that supported my participation in the Baylor colloquy: the Research Fund of Jesus College and the Bethune-Baker Fund of the Faculty of Divinity.

1. The "one" is easy enough to identify in this passage; for the "many," see the interpretive framing sections in Isaiah 52:14 (cf. v. 15) and 53:11–12. This group is generally thought identical with the "we" who speak in 53:1–6.

or entered only the "place" or situation of suffering in which the people already found themselves in the exile.[2] The Servant does not then experience, in principle, any punishment or suffering that the people are not already experiencing in exile; except for his innocence and the intensity of his sufferings, the Servant's sufferings are not *qualitatively* different from those suffered by the rest of the exiles. We might say, then, that the Servant has *taken up* the position of suffering or punishment without *taking it over* from the people; his "place-taking" does not exclude others from being in the same place.[3]

On the other hand, perhaps the Servant has taken the place of the people in such a way that he was left there alone — standing in the place of divine condemnation where only the people belonged, and where they need never stand again (thanks to the Servant), although initially they did not realize it and only despised the Servant for it. On this understanding there was a moment in the story when the Servant and the people where *not* in the same "place," as it were.

I may perhaps be accused of overdrawing the distinctions at the outset, and my English may sound strange since it is arguably a kind of broken-down German (the language I am imitating: not my native lan-

---

2. As claimed for example by R. N. Whybray, *Thanksgiving for a Liberated Prophet: An Interpretation of Isaiah 53,* JSOTSup 4 (Sheffield: JSOT Press, 1978; repr., 1985), 30, 58–61, 74–76 (cf. 48). See also Whybray, *The Second Isaiah,* Old Testament Guides (Sheffield: Sheffield Academic Press, 1983), 77. The former work is cited elsewhere in this volume, e.g., by M. D. Hooker (see p. 95, n. 4). For a critical review of Whybray's *Thanksgiving,* see H.-J. Hermisson in *TLZ* 106 (1981): 802–4.

3. Whybray supports the understanding above, yet with a different use of terminology. The notion of "place-taking" or "vicariousness" that Whybray judges *inappropriate* to the thought of Isaiah 53 is clearly *not* the somewhat unusual *inclusive* notion presented above. He uses "in place of" in its normal, exclusive sense. Hence Whybray says: "[T]he Servant cannot be said to be suffering, or to have suffered, *in place* of the exiles in such a way that they escape the consequences of their sins, since . . . it cannot be said that these have escaped punishment: they are actually suffering the consequences of defeat and banishment. The Servant . . . [as] one of them, shares their suffering. . . . [H]e has suffered more intensely than they, and the 'we' who speak here confess that, at any rate compared with themselves, he is innocent; nevertheless this is shared and not vicarious suffering" (*Thanksgiving for a Liberated Prophet,* 30, italics original). M. D. Hooker in her essay in this volume (see her nn. 7 and 8 in their context) understandably relates Whybray's idea of shared suffering to the German expression *inkludierende Stellvertretung.* Nevertheless, this idea of solidarity in suffering only *approximates* what O. Hofius means by the German expression (see below, "Christ in Our Place: The Incarnation," p. 240). Even if Hofius held Whybray's view, he would probably not describe Isaiah 53 as *inkludierende Stellvertretung* so long as the Servant was seen merely to have suffered *alongside* the exiles, *sharing* sufferings similar to theirs. For this still falls short of Hofius's idea of a divine Savior who can fully enter our place or situation "wo kein anderer Mensch an unsere Stelle treten kann" (Hofius, "Gottesknechtslied" [below n. 5], 115 with n. 40, quoting H. J. Iwand, *Gesetz und Evangelium* [1964], 101).

guage). Nevertheless, talking about Isaiah 53, or about Christianity for that matter, entirely without the use of terms such as "place," "position," or "situation" and without the question of who is in this place and who is out of it — and who actually *deserves* to be in or out of it — would be very difficult indeed.

The term or concept *Stellvertretung*, together with its English etymological equivalent "place-taking," is more useful and potentially clearer than the usual Latinate English terms "representation" and "substitution." Unlike "place-taking," neither of these more usual English terms forms a precise equivalent to the German (though they are regularly used as translation equivalents), since German already has both terms *Repräsentation* and *Substitution* as distinct from *Stellvertretung* (there is overlap between all three terms but no perfect synonymity). The concept of "place-taking," along with its associated wordplays — displacing, replacing, taking one's own place, taking up another's place, taking over another's place, entering another's place, etc. — is actually a useful kind of interpretive language, because it makes it possible to record important exegetical observations.

At Baylor we studied the use of the concept of *Stellvertretung* by three German biblical scholars, none of whom could be present at the conference: the Old Testament specialists Bernd Janowski (Tübingen) and Hermann Spieckermann (Hamburg) and the New Testament specialist Otfried Hofius (Tübingen). I prepared draft translations of essays by each of these authors, which were distributed to panel members in advance. The shortest of the three essays, by Spieckermann, was read at the colloquy by William Bellinger.[4] However, the two longer studies by Janowski and Hofius (see below) could only be summarized as the basis for what turned out to be a lively discussion. This part of the program, which I led, was introduced by a brief oral presentation illustrating some of the problems of translating *Stellvertretung* and relating it to the English-language discussion of the atonement. The two focal essays in the present study are therefore these:

---

4. H. Spieckermann, "Konzeption und Vorgeschichte des Stellvertretungsgedankens im Alten Testament," main paper read at the Fifteenth Congress of the IOSOT, Cambridge, England, 20 July 1995. For a summary, see pp. 253–54 in my other contribution to this volume, "The Suffering Servant: Recent Tübingen Scholarship on Isaiah 53."

O. Hofius, "Das vierte Gottesknechtslied in den Briefen des Neuen Testamentes" ("The Fourth Servant Song in the Letters of the New Testament")[5]

B. Janowski, "Er trug unsere Sünden: Jesaja 53 und die Dramatik der Stellvertretung" ("He Bore Our Sins: Isaiah 53 and the Drama of Taking Another's Place")[6]

If this essay were a full-blown exercise in "comparative hermeneutics,"[7] it would have to focus on something broader than *Stellvertretung* in recent *German* exegesis, since the essential concepts are also at work, sometimes in decisive ways, in the studies of non-German writers. For example, we saw during Morna Hooker's lecture (included in this volume) how an English-speaking and particularly a British scholar might approach the subject in terms roughly parallel to those used in German.

Unfortunately, however, comparative hermeneutics — in this case the question as to the deeper reasons why British and German biblical scholars might come to different interpretations of Isaiah 53 or its New Testament reception (which could have a lot to do with *Stellvertretung,* etc.) — is still too young a field to be treated properly in a brief essay like this one. A long history of the development of theological terminology and methods would have to come first. Therefore the important task of comparing British Old and New Testament scholars with their German counterparts — whether Whybray with Janowski, or Hooker with Hofius — must be considered a goal of ongoing research.

The aim of this essay is therefore to explore the process of biblical interpretation which is at work in the major essays by Hofius and Janowski (see pp. 236, 245 below), with some reflection on the Baylor colloquy's discussion of the theme of *Stellvertretung* as it relates to Jesus and the

---

5. Short title: "Gottesknechtslied," by O. Hofius, *NTS* 39 (1993): 414–37; repr. in *Der leidende Gottesknecht: Jesaja 53 und seine Wirkungsgeschichte, mit einer Bibliographie zu Jes 53,* FAT 14, ed. Bernd Janowski and Peter Stuhlmacher (Tübingen: Mohr-Siebeck, 1996), 107–27. References throughout are to the Tübingen reprint. Summaries of this essay and the one by Janowski (see n. 6) are available in chapter 14 of the present volume.

6. Short title: "Er trug unsere Sünden," by B. Janowski, *ZTK* 90 (1993): 1–24, cited here according to the pagination of the reprint in Janowski and Stuhlmacher, eds., *Der leidende Gottesknecht* (above n. 5), 27–48. The essay is reprinted in two other places. See Janowski, *Gottes Gegenwart in Israel* (Neukirchen-Vluyn: Neukirchener Verlag, 1993), 303–26, and with revised subtitle and additional material, "Er trug unsere Sünden — Stellvertretung nach Jes 52,13–53,12," in B. Janowski, *Stellvertretung: Alttestamentliche Studien zu einem theologischen Grundbegriff,* SBS 165 (Stuttgart: Katholisches Bibelwerk, 1997), 67–96.

7. This term was introduced by R. Morgan in a review of *Romans Interpreted,* by C. Grenholm, in *JTS,* n.s., 42 (1991): 470–71.

Servant. I have been asked to pay particular attention to the problems of formulation and method that may hinder international communication.

The Theme of *Stellvertretung* at Baylor

In contrast to well-known German technical terms such as *Rechtfertigung, Heilsgeschichte,* or *Vorlage,* which appear regularly in English-language biblical studies, *Stellvertretung* is not the sort of German word that one expects to see regularly in *JBL,*[8] even though it is the "πίστις Χριστοῦ" of recent German biblical and theological scholarship (at least in terms of its popularity).[9] Nevertheless, literature on this theme did form a significant part of conference preparation and discussions, and this has left a few traces elsewhere in this volume. These deserve comment, in the first instance briefly, and in the second more fully.

Morna Hooker

The most obvious example of the use of the concept of *Stellvertretung* elsewhere in this volume is the essay by Morna Hooker. She refers several times to the distinction made in recent German exegesis, particularly by O. Hofius, between *inkludierende* and *exkludierende Stellvertretung.* These concepts, along with their English counterparts (not equivalents!) "representation" and "substitution," are tightly woven into Hooker's own argument about potential soteriological uses of Isaiah 53 in the New Testament.

Yet one item remains in Hooker's essay that I myself ought to explain somewhat further, and that is her translations of *inkludierende* and

---

8. I have seen *Stellvertretung* written out only twice in the literature of English-language *biblical* scholarship (systematic theology is different), tellingly both times by scholars who have studied or worked in Tübingen. See Richard Bell, review of *Romans and the Apologetic Tradition,* by A. J. Guerra, *JTS,* n.s., 47 (1996): 229 (referring to H. Gese and O. Hofius); Seyoon Kim, *The "Son of Man" as the Son of God,* WUNT 30 (Tübingen: Mohr-Siebeck, 1983), 55 n. 69. Kim rightly complains of John Bowden's mistranslation of Martin Hengel's use of *Stellvertretung* by "representation" instead of "substitution."

9. The potential breadth of the topic of *Stellvertretung* can bee seen in the major systematic-theological *Habilitationsschrift* by Karl Heinz Menke, *Stellvertretung. Schlüsselbegriff christlichen Lebens und theologische Grundkategorie,* Sammlung Horizonte, n.s., 29 (Einsiedeln: Johannes, 1991). For those aspects of the *Stellvertretung* debate that apply to biblical (particularly OT) scholarship, see Janowski, *Stellvertretung* (above n. 6).

exkludierende Stellvertretung in terms of "inclusive" and "exclusive" *place-taking*. The notion of "place-taking" may sound a bit odd, since it is not an established English technical term and is certainly not the standard translation of *Stellvertretung*.[10] Hooker has taken the term rather from my draft translation of Hofius's study, with which she interacts. For the moment, then, any oddity about the terminology of "place-taking" must be attributed not to Professor Hooker but to me. Fortunately, the problem should sort itself out in the discussion of Hofius's terminology (pp. 236–245).

N. T. Wright

A second essay that takes up the theme of *Stellvertretung* is the essay by N. T. Wright. At the conference and in his subsequent book on *Jesus and the Victory of God*,[11] Wright has been concerned that those who work as historians not get caught up in what he refers to as text-based, abstract atonement theology, worked out scholastically through the definition and distinction of terms like "representation," "substitution," and *Stellvertretung*. His own alternative, a more broadly based, consistently historical, not exclusively text-oriented approach, is available in this volume. Near the end of his presentation, he says:

> I suggest, then, that the categories of the sixth or fifth or fourth centuries B.C.E., and those of the sixteenth and subsequent centuries C.E., are not necessarily good guides for our understanding of Jesus. Listening to the debate between substitution and representation [or *Stellvertretung*] in however a sophisticated and nuanced fashion it may be carried on, leaves me as a historian with the same feeling I have when I meet people — as I don't, fortunately, very often — for whom the key question in the New Testament is whether the Rapture comes before or after the Tribulation.

Stellvertretung was not in Wright's manuscript but was a verbal aside; given his point, he was certainly right to mention it in this context.

---

10. Since coming independently upon "place-taking" as a workable translation of *Stellvertretung*, I have seen the same English expression used in this connection only once. See Colin Greene, "Is the Message of the Cross Good News for the Twentieth Century?" in *Atonement Today: A Symposium at St John's College, Nottingham*, ed. John Goldingay (London: SPCK, 1995), 232.

11. Vol. 2 in Wright's series, Christian Origins and the Question of God (London: SPCK, 1996).

(The "sophisticated and nuanced" discussion he refers to may well be that which occurred concerning Janowski and especially Hofius — the discussion of Spieckermann was less highly charged — and then also in connection with Hooker.)

One could quibble about Wright's implication that representation, substitution, *Stellvertretung* and the like are categories of the sixteenth and subsequent centuries C.E. (his B.C.E. categories, relating to the understanding of Isaiah 53 in its original setting, do not concern us here). For certainly Wright, as a historian, knows that the interpretation of New Testament patterns of salvation in terms not taken from the Greek New Testament (although they are related to NT words, e.g., ἀντάλλαγμα) began almost immediately, for example with the sweet "exchange" or ἀνταλλαγή that is praised as the grounds of salvation in Christ as early as the *Epistle to Diognetus* (9:5), or again with the ἀντίψυχον or idea of "ransom" used in the writings of Ignatius.[12]

These terms and concepts are hardly so late as the sixteenth century; yet in attempting to point to a subject matter central to Christian faith, the Greek terms — or rather the authors who use them — are doing exactly the same thing, in principle if not always in content, as is done by later, generally Latinate terms such as "representation," "substitution," or "vicariousness," or by the non-Latinate *Stellvertretung* ("place-taking"). Indeed there is even a material overlap between the Greek and English terminology, since ἀνταλλαγή as used in *Diognetus* is not very different from what Hooker means by "interchange in Christ," though she usually traces the idea historically not to Diognetus but to Irenaeus.[13]

What Wright vigorously disputes, however, is the claim that this notion of "vicariousness" (or whatever we decide to call it) constitutes what we should primarily be trying to understand when we read passages like Isaiah 53 or its Pauline reception in Romans 4:25. Wright's main objection to the essays of Janowski and Hofius, voiced clearly during our discussions but implicit also in his own essay, is that these German authors treat as the real subject matter of exegesis the pattern or event

---

12. For references see BAGD, 76, s.v. ἀντίψυχον.

13. See the index under Irenaeus (four entries) in Morna D. Hooker, *From Adam to Christ: Essays on Paul* (Cambridge: Cambridge University Press, 1990). In addition to the clear citations of Irenaeus on pp. 4–5, 22, 42, and 59 (as noted in the index), there is also an unindexed but nevertheless unmistakable allusion to his thought in the phrase on p. 182: "Christ became what we are in order that we might become what he is."

of *Stellvertretung*, while Wright does not consider this the proper subject matter of a historical reconstruction of Israel's developing Servant
traditions.

Wright would agree, I think, that we are bound to come up with abstract nouns for our subject just because we need nouns. This does not
necessarily mean that the discussion or interpretation will be abstract or
even far removed from the thought-world of the biblical writers. But it is
interesting to ask just how closely our terms relate *etymologically* to whatever it is we consider our subject matter at the narrow level of exegesis.
Take for example the Latin term *aseitas*, English "aseity."[14] This is literally God's *a-se*-ness, his "from-himself-ness" or self-existence, and it
points to its subject matter rather directly. Unfortunately we do not have
a parallel term for the atonement: Christ's *pro-nobi-tas* does not exist as
a noun-label for the soteriological use of *pro nobis* or ὑπὲρ ἡμῶν in the
New Testament. And not even the German exegetes have tried to come
up with a direct abstraction of this: there is no such term as "for-us-ness"
or *Hyperizität*.[15]

Of course I did not say that there is no such *thing* as "for-us-ness"; we
could probably think of many things about Dietrich Bonhoeffer's "man
for others" that could come under such a heading, not all of them directly related to the interpretation of ὑπέρ. My point rather is that if we
had a term formed from a preposition such as "for-us-ness," it could presumably be used simply to label its subject matter objectively. To take a
term such as "for-us-ness" upon one's lips would not then commit one to
a particular atonement theology; it would simply mean that we wish to
discuss the subject matter associated with ὑπὲρ ἡμῶν in the New Testament.[16] The problem in the Greek text of Isaiah 53 concerns prepositions

---

14. See Richard A. Muller, *A Dictionary of Latin and Greek Theological Terms Drawn Princi-
pally from Protestant Scholastic Theology* (Grand Rapids: Baker, 1985), 47, s.v. "aseitas"; F. Hauck
and G. Schwinge, *Theologisches Fach- und Fremdwörterbuch*, 7th ed. (Göttingen: Vandenhoeck &
Ruprecht, 1992), 25, s.v. "Ase'ität."

15. This requires qualification. In German biblical scholarship it is generally the term *Stellvertretung* itself that does duty for what we might think of as "for-us-ness." Janowski in particular
suggests that *Stellvertretung* expresses the essential idea of the soteriological ὑπέρ in the NT ("Er
trug unsere Sünden" [above n. 6], 30). German systematic theology, by contrast, makes use of several
noun phrases very much like Christ's "for-us-ness" or "for-others-ness," e.g., "Für-die-anderen-Sein,"
"Für-einander" (see Menke, *Stellvertretung* [above n. 9], 132, 283).

16. A term such as "for-us-ness" would remain theologically neutral only so long as it was understood to point to the subject matter expressed by ὑπέρ in the NT without suggesting a particular
interpretation of that preposition. Something less neutral would be expressed by noun phrases such
as "instead-of-us-ness" or "because-of-us-ness."

other than ὑπέρ, such as διά plus the accusative (Isa. 53:5, 12). But the point remains the same: we could devise an objective term for this subject matter if we wished.

However, objectivity of this sort is precisely what we do not have with our English terms "representation" and "substitution." These terms do not simply name a subject matter, such as the *relationship* of the Servant to the many. Rather, they immediately suggest a particular position on it. One cannot affirm that representation has occurred and yet deny that vicarious or penal-substitutionary suffering has occurred in the relationship between the one and the many without saying something very important and specific.[17]

I have said enough to affirm Wright's main point with regard to "representation" and "substitution," which is that they are theologically loaded terms that, as soon as they are used, immediately require such definition and attention that they could easily shift the focus away from wider historical issues.

Historical Criticism or Doctrinal Criticism?

Looking at the outward agenda of the Baylor conference, it could easily seem that twenty or so mainly Christian biblical scholars[18] had gathered because there are pressing *historical* questions about the original social setting of Isaiah 53, or about whether Jesus thought of himself as a figure very much like the original Servant who bore the sins of the many, combined perhaps with worries that New Testament Christianity seems to understand Isaiah 53 in ways out of keeping with pre-Christian Jewish understandings.

Yet while this historical agenda is not in any sense a pretense, it can only in a very short-term view of the history of Christian thought be considered as the ultimate reason why Christian biblical scholars would

---

17. It is clear that something very important from the perspective of the authors is said when writers discussing the atonement affirm the formulation of "representation" but disapprove of the use of "substitution." Nevertheless, we have no full-scale critical history of the representation-substitution debate that covers the terminology of both biblical scholars and systematic theologians, and therefore the sensitive issue of what various scholars mean by their terms — whether using different terms, or the same terms in different ways — cannot be settled here.

18. I remember meeting only one Jewish scholar, Ronald Hendel, who responded to Paul Hanson's paper.

gather for such a conference. In terms of cause and effect, Christian scholars would not now be debating the issue of Jesus and the Servant, either in agreement with or in reaction against nineteenth-century critical historical methods, were it not for the eighteenth-century criticism that Christianity would be irrational if it laid a passage like Isaiah 53 at its heart. It was philosophical and doctrinal criticism that in part gave rise to historical criticism, and this is an emphasis that the essays of Janowski and Hofius can help us to keep in mind.

The question of the essential *truth* of the *message* of Isaiah 53 is not a historical one (the passage involves at least as much poetry as history or biography) but an exegetical and theological one — a problem of what Hofius refers to as "theological reflection about truth claims."[19] Admittedly, most members of the Baylor colloquy did not seem to be asking questions like this one or to be posing the question in this way, as the vigorous discussion of Hofius showed. Nevertheless, I would suggest that in the longer view of the history of interpretation, doubts about whether Isaiah 53 is true, and whether *God* would actually strike down his Servant and "load" him with alien guilt in order to make many righteous (this resembles the picture of God that Hofius finds in the OT text),[20] preceded everything else we know about the current task of interpreting this text. This includes the relatively recent device of saying that the Servant was originally never viewed as having borne sins substitutionarily for others, but was only thought at the time of the exile to have suffered, as a (relatively) innocent one, a greater share than others of the consequences of the nation's sins.[21]

Immanuel Kant

It is neither possible nor necessary to discuss in detail the origins of different kinds of historical or truth-related questions about the message of Isaiah 53. What is clear in any case is that many German *biblical* scholars have noticed that traditional penal-substitutionary readings

---

19. Hofius, "Gottesknechtslied" (above n. 5), 107: "die theologische, an der Wahrheitsfrage orientierte Reflexion."

20. See, e.g., Hofius, "Gottesknechtslied," 111 (italics original): "Ist es ... theologisch denkbar, daß *Gott* die Schuld bestimmter Menschen auf einen anderen Menschen oder auf andere Menschen überträgt?"

21. So, e.g., Whybray (above nn. 2–3).

of Isaiah 53 present a *philosophical* problem, a question of theological truth. The chapter's apparent message, the punishment of the innocent instead of the guilty, raises the same problem of the transference of guilt between persons that is discussed by the Enlightenment philosopher Immanuel Kant.

German biblical scholars working on Isaiah 53 or on the atonement refer to Kant with surprising regularity, and they all seem to quote the same passage. When we read works representative of what I might call British participation theology, we may expect to encounter over and over again a certain quotation from Irenaeus to the effect that "Christ became what we are in order that we might become what he is."[22] With the same regularity there appears in German exegetical and theological literature a somewhat longer quotation from Kant.[23] But whereas the British reception of Irenaeus is universally positive, German ways of responding to the legacy of Kant are complex and anything but uniform. The passage that German biblical scholars always seem to come back to is this:

> Moreover, so far as we can judge by our reason's standards of right, this original debt, or at any rate the debt that precedes whatever good a human being may ever do (this, and no more, is what we understood by *radical* evil; see the first section), cannot be erased by somebody else. For it is not a *transmissible* liability which can be made over to somebody else, in the manner of a financial debt (where it is all the same to the creditor whether the debtor himself pays up, or somebody else for him), but the *most personal* of all liabilities, namely, a debt of sins which only the culprit [*der Strafbare*], not the innocent, can bear, however magnanimous the

---

22. Irenaeus *Adv. Haer.* V, preface (ed. W. W. Harvey, Cambridge, 1857), 2:314. This is a favorite quotation of British Pauline scholars writing on the atonement. See, e.g., D. E. H. Whiteley, *The Theology of St. Paul* (Oxford: Blackwell, 1st ed., 1964, or 2d ed., 1974), 133; Morna D. Hooker (above n. 13); James D. G. Dunn, "Paul's Understanding of the Death of Jesus as Sacrifice," in *Sacrifice and Redemption: Durham Essays in Theology,* ed. S. W. Sykes (Cambridge: Cambridge University Press, 1991), 36; C. M. Tuckett, "Atonement in the NT," *Anchor Bible Dictionary* (1992), 1:519.

23. For quotations of this passage from Kant (see the next note) see, e.g., Gerhard Friedrich, *Die Verkündigung des Todes Jesu im Neuen Testament,* Biblisch-Theologische Studien 6 (Neukirchen-Vluyn: Neukirchener Verlag, 1982), 151 with n. 22; and Hans-Richard Reuter, "Stellvertretung: Erwägungen zu einer dogmatischen Kategorie im Gespräch mit René Girard und Raymund Schwager," in *Dramatische Erlösungslehre: Ein Symposion,* ed. Jósef Niewiadomski and Wolfgang Palaver, Innsbrucker theologische Studien 38 (Innsbruck and Vienna: Tyrolia, 1992), 180 with n. 4. Cf. Gerhard Barth, *Der Tod Jesu Christi im Verständnis des Neuen Testaments* (Neukirchen-Vluyn: Neukirchener Verlag, 1992), 3, 68.

innocent might be in wanting to take the debt upon himself for the other.[24]

Although the Baylor colloquy represented a gathering of mainly historically minded scholars, it is interesting to reconsider the conference and to ask to what extent some of its subcurrents may still revolve around questions like the ones Kant has raised. Kant seems alive and well in that at least four authors associated with this volume say things that can be compared with or related to his challenge about *Stellvertretung*,[25] two indirectly, and two directly.

Morna Hooker and N. T. Wright

Morna Hooker in her contribution to this volume formulates the problem of "vicarious" suffering (for which she offers various definitions) in such a way that it does not line up exactly with the concerns or definitions of Kant, whom she does not in any case have in mind in this context. In Hooker's view of verses like Isaiah 53:5 (see her section on Isaiah 53), the Servant suffers *because of* or *as a result of* the sins of others; their sins were the cause or occasion not only of their own sufferings (which they do not escape), but also of the Servant's sufferings which, unlike theirs, were undeserved. The Servant therefore suffered *alongside* the rest of Israel; the pattern is one of *shared* rather than substitutionary suffering. Since in this understanding *both* the culprits and the innocent bear

---

24. Immanuel Kant, "Religion within the Boundaries of Mere Reason," in Kant, *Religion and Rational Theology*, trans. and ed. Allen W. Wood and George Di Giovanni (Cambridge: Cambridge University Press, 1996), 113 (at 6:72). Original German: "Die Religion innerhalb der Grenzen der bloßen Vernunft" (1st ed., 1793; 2d ed., 1794), *Kant's gesammelte Schriften*, ed. Königlich Preußischen Akademie der Wissenschaften (Berlin: Reimer, 1907), 6:72: "Diese ursprüngliche, oder überhaupt vor jedem Guten, was er immer thun mag, vorhergehende Schuld, die auch dasjenige ist, was, und nichts mehr, wir unter dem *radicalen* Bösen verstanden (S. das erste Stück), kann aber auch, so viel wir nach unserem Vernunftrecht einsehen, nicht von einem andern getilgt werden; denn sie ist keine *transmissible* Verbindlichkeit, die etwa wie eine Geldschuld (bei der es dem Gläubiger einerlei ist, ob der Schuldner selbst oder ein anderer für ihn bezahlt) auf einen andern übertragen werden kann, sondern die *allerpersönlichste*, nämlich eine Sündenschuld, die nur der Strafbare, nicht der Unschuldige, er mag auch noch so großmüthig sein, sie für jenen übernehmen zu wollen, tragen kann."

25. Kant did not actually use the term *Stellvertretung* because it was apparently coined by Georg Friedrich Seiler as late as 1778–79 (see Menke, *Stellvertretung* [above n. 9], 83), little more than a decade before Kant's "Die Religion" of 1793. However, it is customary to apply the term *Stellvertretung* anachronistically to writings treating the same theme even before the invention of the term. Thus both Janowski and Hofius consider Kant's statement to be a statement of the essential problem of *Stellvertretung* (Janowski explicitly: see "Er trug unsere Sünden," 29 n. 6), independent of the precise terms Kant used.

the consequences of sins, Hooker envisages a situation different from, although not precisely opposite to, the one declared irrational and immoral by Kant (cf. the suffering of the innocent in both views), in which the guilty escape their personal moral liabilities by means of a one-for-one *transfer* of liabilities between guilty and innocent parties.

A similar but less developed statement that can be compared with concerns of the Enlightenment is found at the end of N. T. Wright's essay in this volume. He rightly suggests that the idea of *representation* or shared suffering, understood as distinct from and as exclusive of substitution or transferred punishment, was developed in the history of theology "in order to protect God from talking or acting nonsensically or immorally." However, whether the language of representation actually succeeds in "protecting God" is another question, since even in participatory or representative understandings of Isaiah 53 and of Christology, the innocent one still ends up suffering *as a result of, because of,* or *on behalf of* the guilty, and God still stands behind this event.[26]

Otfried Hofius and Bernd Janowski

Explicit reactions to Kant are found only with the two German authors under review, O. Hofius and B. Janowski. Unlike our two British authors, these writers feel directly obligated to declare Kant either right (at least as far as he goes) or wrong, or irrelevant. In the following analysis of Hofius and Janowski, we shall see how an essentially Kantian criticism about the nonrepresentability of subjects in matters of guilt has played a role in their different approaches to Isaiah 53 and the problem of *Stellvertretung*.

The main focus of attention below is upon Hofius because he was perhaps regarded as the most controversial German interpreter whose ideas were discussed at the conference. However, the briefer treatment of Janowski which follows is no less important, for he offers a significant alternative to Hofius's approach to the Old Testament text.

---

26. Apparently the only "nonsense" or "immorality" against which God is here protected is a quasi-financial or judicial transfer of debts from one party or account to another. But if there are philosophical or theological problems with a God who arranges and accepts the suffering of the innocent as a *representative* of the guilty, it is not clear that they are solved by the current formulations about "representation" — not in any case if people are, with respect to their sin and guilt, nonrepresentable *(unvertretbar),* as Hofius for example claims (see "Gottesknechtslied" [n. 5], 114). It makes very little difference to the idealistic criticism of vicarious atonement whether the innocent one is said to *represent* others in their guilt, to *substitute* for them, or both.

On *Stellvertretung* and the Making of a "New Text": The Hermeneutics of O. Hofius

One of the most challenging hermeneutical suggestions discussed at the conference was O. Hofius's idea that the reception of Isaiah 53 in the New Testament letters places it within a framework theologically so different from its original setting that the text as we know it in the New Testament must be considered in some respects a "new text" (p. 127).[27] This conclusion represents one example of Hofius's mature thinking on the question of how a biblical theology of the two testaments might be approached (although some of his other studies find more continuity between the testaments than the one under review). Hofius's essay on Isaiah 53 and its reception in New Testament letters may therefore be explored here as a case study in recent German interpretation, with the qualification that this essay shows Hofius at his most independent (and therefore only loosely represents recent German trends): his main point of dependence in this essay is upon Hartmut Gese's theory of the cult.

Isaiah 53 as an OT Text: "Exclusive Place-Taking"

Hofius comes closer than Janowski does to agreeing with Kant, citing exactly the portion of Kant reprinted above (see Hofius, 11 n. 27). He finds Isaiah 53 to be unique within the Old Testament for its message that one person has "carried," in a manner that is substitutionary or *stellvertretend*, the guilt of *others*. The Servant thus suffers "the penal consequences of *alien* guilt" (109).[28] That which according to the so-called deed-consequences connection or *Tun-Ergehen-Zusammenhang* ought to have struck back only upon the doers of the sinful actions has now struck

---

27. I.e., p. 127 in O. Hofius, "Gottesknechtslied" (above n. 5). Running page numbers inserted in the text refer to this work.

28. German: "die Straffolgen *fremder* Schuld" (Hofius, "Gottesknechtslied," 109, italics original). The combination of the term *Straffolgen* or "penal consequences" with the immediately following *Tun-Ergehen-Zusammenhang* (see Hofius's next sentence) seems somewhat unusual because the latter concept was originally developed by Klaus Koch in order to suggest that the consequences of sin in this world do not necessarily spring from a *Vergeltungsdogma* or "doctrine of divine retribution." See K. Koch, "Gibt es ein Vergeltungsdogma im Alten Testament?" *ZTK* 52 (1955): 1–42; ET: "Is There a Doctrine of Retribution in the Old Testament?" in *Theodicy in the Old Testament,* ed. James L. Crenshaw (Philadelphia: Fortress; London: SPCK, 1983), 57–87. For literature critical of Koch's conception, see Janowski, "Er trug unsere Sünden" (above n. 6), 28 n. 4.

the innocent and righteous Servant instead (see Isa. 53:9b, 11b). Nor does it simplify matters that Yahweh himself is behind this plan. For he has "laid on him the iniquity of us all" (53:6b); it was Yahweh's plan or "will" to "crush him" (53:10a).

Based on these and other observations on the Old Testament text, Hofius concludes that its pattern of *Stellvertretung* or place-taking has to be described as inclusive only of the Servant and *exclusive* of the guilty. Only one party is in the place or position of punishment. The text's mode of operation could therefore be termed one of *exkludierende Stellvertretung* or "exclusive place-taking" (112). Hofius realizes that *Stellvertretung* in everyday German usage is normally understood as a transaction that excludes one party and includes another, much like English "substitution," but he adds the potentially redundant adjective *exkludierend* for the sake of a theological wordplay later in his essay.

Beyond this, however, Hofius's introduction of the unusual term *exkludierende Stellvertretung* may seem abrupt. He is in fact presupposing more than a decade of collegial work in the Tübingen Protestant theological faculty, beginning with H. Gese's seminal essay on Old Testament atonement,[29] which B. S. Childs regards as still the best resource available.[30] Hofius's own essay on Pauline atonement and its Old Testament roots, presupposed here, draws heavily upon Gese.[31] These earlier essays must be read and digested in order fully to understand the use of the term *Stellvertretung* in recent German exegesis.[32]

Nevertheless, we can catch up with Hofius's German by means of a few simple observations. The easiest way to understand *exkludierende Stellvertretung* is to think of it as a noun phrase that contains a whole

---

29. Hartmut Gese, "Die Sühne," in Gese, *Zur biblischen Theologie: Alttestamentliche Vorträge,* BEvT 78 (Munich: Kaiser, 1977; repr., Tübingen: Mohr-Siebeck, 3d ed., 1989), 85–106. ET: "The Atonement," in *Essays on Biblical Theology,* trans. K. Crim (Minneapolis: Augsburg, 1981), 93–116.

30. See Brevard S. Childs, *Biblical Theology of the Old and New Testaments* (London: SCM; Minneapolis: Fortress, 1992), 503–8, esp. 503.

31. Otfried Hofius, "Sühne und Versöhnung: Zum paulinischen Verständnis des Kreuzestodes Jesu" (1983), reprinted in Hofius, *Paulusstudien,* WUNT 51 (Tübingen: Mohr-Siebeck, 1989), 33–49.

32. A more wide-ranging work such as Janowski's recent (since the Baylor conference) introduction to and appendix of secondary sources on *Stellvertretung* will help those interested in German scholarship as a whole to relate the efforts of the biblical scholars to those of the German philosophers, systematic theologians, political and social theorists, etc. See Janowski, *Stellvertretung* (above n. 6), 13–39, 97–134.

sentence within itself, for *Stellvertretung* is a verbal noun.[33] The kernel sentence underlying the verbal noun is contained in the latter half of the following definition: "Stellvertretung besagt, daß einer *an* die *Stelle* des anderen *tritt*."[34] This example shows that the crucial components of the meaning of *Stellvertretung* are *Stelle* + *treten* + (an implied) *an* (accusative) — the morpheme *-ver-* contributes little to its meaning.[35]

Explaining *Stellvertretung* then becomes almost a matter of linguistic tautology. Just as in English the expression "place-taking," if we had such a term, would presumably denote simply "one person taking another's place," so in German *Stellvertretung* means "eine Person tritt an die Stelle einer anderen." In normal usage this has the effect of *excluding* the person who was originally "in this place" *(an dieser Stelle)*, but this exclusive understanding can also be made explicit:

Eine Person tritt an die Stelle einer anderen so, daß diese *ersetzt* oder *ausgeschlossen* wird.[36]

One person takes the place of another in such a way that the other is *replaced* or *shut out (excluded)*.

---

33. On the history and word formation of *Stellvertretung* see Janowski, "Er trug unsere Sünden," 30: "The German abstract noun 'place-taking' first came into being rather late, in the course of the eighteenth century and in the context of Socinian criticism of the doctrine of satisfaction within Old Protestant orthodoxy. Luther did not yet use the noun; but he did use verbal paraphrases for the idea it reflects, for example: 'Jesus Christ, God's Son, came *in our stead*' ('an unserer Statt,' WA 35: 443 line 21). We may therefore suspect that when the word 'place-taking' came into use, its task was to bring a concept previously formulated with *verbs* to expression as a technical *term*. The German abstract term must therefore actually be read as a *noun of action*, fully in accordance with the biblical traditions that have preserved the originally verbal structure of place-taking."

34. Walther von Loewenich, "Christi Stellvertretung: Eine theologische Meditation zu Luthers Auslegung von Gal. 3,13," in von Loewenich, *Von Augustin zu Luther: Beiträge zur Kirchengeschichte* (Witten: Luther-Verlag, 1959), 150 (italics added).

35. The noun *Stellvertretung* probably derived historically from the adjective *stellvertretend* in the collocation *stellvertretende Genugtuung,* "vicarious satisfaction" (so Menke, *Stellvertretung* [n. 9], 82–83). An etymological argument along the lines that *Stellvertretung* comes from *Stelle* and *Vertretung* ("representation") cannot be used to argue that *Stellvertretung* means "representation" — a common assumption in English translations of German biblical studies that is wrong more often than it is right (see, e.g., above n. 8). The proper place to look for the concept of "representation" (*Vertretung* as distinct from *Stellvertretung*) in the German Bible is not necessarily to theologies of the atonement or suffering but to the theology of prayer. According to the original as well as the modern Lutheran translation, the Holy Spirit *"vertritt* die Heiligen, wie es Gott gefällt" (Rom. 8:27) — he *represents* the saints, *intercedes for* them, according to the will of God.

36. This is something of an inversion (in the direction of *exkludierende Stellvertretung*) of the definition by Menke, *Stellvertretung* (n. 9), 17. According to this definition, *Stellvertretung* designates all those procedures "in denen eine Person so an die Stelle einer anderen tritt, daß diese nicht ersetzt, sondern im Gegenteil zur Einnahme ihrer [eigenen] Stelle befähigt wird."

This is the understanding behind Hofius's expression *exkludierende Stell-vertretung*, except that Hofius uses the verb *exkludieren* rather than *ausschließen* (used earlier by Gese)[37] or *ersetzen*.

Radical Sin in Kant and the Bible

By describing the drama of Isaiah 53 as a pattern of *exkludierende Stell-vertretung*, Hofius takes a clear position on the problem posed by Kant. If the innocent Servant takes the place of the guilty in such a way that he experiences the full weight of the divine punishment of their sins and yet also somehow blocks them from experiencing it, we have precisely the bearing of alien guilt that Kant said is out of keeping with our reason's standards of right.

Hofius agrees with Kant, but not only for rationalistic reasons. Arguing in part from Psalm 51:5 (MT v. 7: "I was born with iniquity") that sin is not just something accidental and potentially removable about a person but something central and essential, Hofius suggests that only new creation (see Psalm 51:10 [MT v. 12]) — something that would not be done for sinners simply by their being represented by another in matters of guilt (even if this were possible) — can set sinners free from the sin that conditions their very *being (Sein)*. The following is Hofius's conclusion about the meaning of Isaiah 53 as an *Old Testament* text (114):

> Sin is no more removable or transferable than death is. In the sit-uation of sin, as in the situation of death, people are in principle unrepresentable [*unvertretbar*]. Just as it is impossible for people to die the death of others, so it is impossible for them, being sinners *themselves*, to make the sins of the others their own. When this is acknowledged it also forces a conclusion about the fourth Ser-vant Song. What this Song says about the Servant's substitutionary death [*stellvertretendes Sterben*] is theologically incomprehensible as it stands and as it is meant. This holds independently of the answer to the heavily contested question, *Who* is meant by "the Servant" according to the Old Testament text? Whether it deals with the prophet Second Isaiah himself, or collectively with faithful Israel, or with a future messianic figure, in any case we must conclude: being

37. See Gese, "Sühne" (above n. 29), 97: "ausschließende Stellvertretung."

freed up from sin and guilt through *human* substitution [*menschliche Stellvertretung*] is theologically simply unthinkable!

By "unthinkable" Hofius apparently means not only unimaginable but *unworkable* (unfortunately he does not pause for very long to ask what the text will have meant to its first readers: did they realize its theological limitations?). The text in Isaiah, as an Old Testament text, does not set out an operative pattern that would effectively deal with humanity's *ontological* problem of sin as Hofius understands it, based on his reading of selected Old Testament and widely gathered New Testament texts. For him, Paul, John, the authors of Colossians and Ephesians, Mark and the author of Hebrews, all know of sin only in one form: *Person-Sünde*, sin as it is bound up with persons, all of whom partake of the *total* and *radical* fallenness of all humanity (113–14). Even a future Messiah could not make Isaiah 53 into a saving text or a saving message, for Hofius believes that the historical Jewish messianic expectation does not involve a divine, incarnated figure.[38]

The direction of Hofius's thought is clear: *What is wrong with Servant theology is that it is not (incarnational) Christology.* The conception of sin in Isaiah 53 is inadequate to humanity's true situation, and the solution offered is inadequate because the Servant, at best an agent of merely human substitution, cannot serve as a representative dying figure in any ontological sense. In short, the Servant, by dying, cannot effect in others the typically Pauline kind of death to sin and subsequent new creation that in Hofius's view will alone suffice to free sinners from their sin. What sinners need is to die and rise with Christ; they cannot die and rise with the Servant, not as a historical figure and not in the terms in which the text describes the relationship between the one and the many.

Christ in Our Place: The Incarnation

This, however, does not mean that Hofius finds no New Testament soteriological use of Isaiah 53 or even that he finds his own exegesis running aground on the shores of Kant's rationality. Hofius agrees with Kant as

---

38. Hofius therefore says in a later study that Jesus is not the Jewish Messiah in any sense in which that term could have been understood in the first century. See O. Hofius, "Ist Jesus der Messias? Thesen," in *Der Messias*, ed. Ingo Baldermann et al., *Jahrbuch für Biblische Theologie* 8 (1993): 103–29.

far as he goes; but Kant, in denying that sins can be *transferred*, like financial debts, from one account to another, does not put any limit on what might be possible when not only sins as discrete acts, but the existence of all human persons as sinners, are taken up in a single representative figure through the *incarnation*. The limitation by which the Servant could take upon himself the punishment of others but not their old existence as persons dominated by sin — the limitation of a merely human substitution — is therefore dealt with by Hofius under the heading of *inkludierende Stellvertretung* or *inclusive* "place-taking," the essence of an incarnational Christology.

The expression *inkludierende Stellvertretung* involves a German wordplay that can also be reflected in English. Place-taking is normally *exclusive* in both English and German. If I take your place it usually means that you are no longer in that place: I have become your replacement or substitute. "The player was injured, so a fresh teammate *took his place* (became his *substitute*)." Or: "I have a ticket to the performance but cannot go. Would you like to *take my place*?" In Christology, however, because of Christ's preexistence and divine status, he can enter our human place in a way that does not displace us but incorporates us (115). This is why Hofius qualifies inclusive place-taking as the only *divine* type of place-taking (116). Both Christ and the rest of humanity are still "there" when Christ takes or enters humanity's place: *er trat an ihre Stelle und starb an ihrer Stelle* ("he stepped *into* their place [in the incarnation?] and died *in* their place"). This sounds like substitution, but it need not be. Christ died "in their stead (=place)," but not necessarily *instead of* them: they died, too, "with" him. *Christ did not die in place of humanity; he died while he was in the place of humanity.* These two English expressions are formally almost identical, but they can carry very different meanings in theology.

Is the Jewish Sacrificial System Participatory?

Despite the initial appearances of an exclusively dogmatic method, Hofius is able to claim a *biblical-theological* precedent for this understanding of inclusive place-taking. Hofius believes that the incorporative idea cannot be found in the historical person of the Servant or in the fourth Servant Song as an Old Testament text; but it can be found in the symbolism of the levitical sin-offering (116).

The levitical sin-offering, according to H. Gese and his followers (including both Hofius and Janowski), was a *representative, participatory, incorporative* event.[39] Through the gesture of the hand leaning on the head of the animal, the people, through their priestly representative, become *identified* with it, although they do not transfer their sins to it. The cultic ritual itself is one of dedicatory atonement, in which the people experience more than just a negative procedure of the removal of sin. Cultic, dedicatory atonement is for tabernacle or temple worshipers "*a coming to God that consists in passing all the way through the sentence of death.*"[40]

This passage is crucial to Gese, and Hofius has cited it many times. The citation in his essay on Isaiah 53 (126) comes in an explanation of what "bringing you to God" (see ἵνα ὑμᾶς προσαγάγῃ τῷ θεῷ) means in 1 Peter 3:18, where Isaianic language about suffering for sins is reflected in the expression περὶ ἁμαρτιῶν ἔπαθεν (126). Since Hofius believes that an *inclusive* event of cultic dedication, *representative* of the people's life before God, is effected when sacrificial blood, the life substance (see Lev. 17:11), comes into contact with the holy objects (particularly the mercy seat), blood can be regarded as the symbolic medium that "brings people to God." Although blood is not mentioned in 1 Peter 3:18 (but see 1:2, 19), a cultic *thought* of "being brought to God" is still there, and therefore Hofius feels justified in calling it an "event of atonement" *(Sühnegeschehen)*, even in the absence of an explicit mention of blood.

The people of Israel cannot be conceived as having symbolically died and risen again with the fortunes of the original Isaianic Servant.

---

39. Verbs like *repräsentieren* or *partizipieren* are not often used by Gese ("Sühne," above n. 29) because he does not like Latinate *Fremdwörter*. However, these words, whose English equivalents play an enormous role in current Anglo-American discussions of Paul, are also sometimes used in German discussions of the cult. Thus Gese's former student B. Janowski (*Sühne als Heilsgeschehen: Studien zur Sühnetheologie der Priesterschrift und zur Wurzel KPR im Alten Orient und im Alten Testament*, WMANT 55 [Neukirchen-Vluyn: Neukirchener Verlag, 1982]) speaks of a situation in which "der Opfernde durch das Aufstemmen seiner Hand auf das Opfertier *an dessen Tod realiter partizipiert*, indem er sich durch diesen symbolischen Gestus mit dem sterbenden Tier *identifiziert…*" (220, italics original; see the further context; cf. p. 59). Similarly, "so *repräsentiert* der stellvertretende Tod des Opfertieres die Lebenshingabe des sündigen Menschen" (221, italics added).

40. Gese, "Sühne" (n. 29), 104: "ein Zu-Gott-Kommen durch das Todesgericht hindurch." See the ET (n. 29), 114 (modified above).

Nevertheless, Hofius would say that *cultic* worshipers in ancient Israel experienced something akin to death and resurrection (or new creation) in the death of the animal with whom they had identified their destinies. This happened as the animal was killed and its blood brought into the Most Holy Place up to the mercy seat (at least in the priestly conception), symbolizing life-giving contact with God.

Unfortunately for most outsiders to the recent German scene, Hofius spells out very little of this cultic background in his essay on Isaiah 53 (beyond giving two bibliographic references)[41] because it has long been considered an assured result in Tübingen. Nevertheless, Hofius does make clear what *truth* is expressed by cultically patterned thinking about Jesus. The key terms in the citation below — the idea that sacrifice does not merely take away an external pollution or sin, the idea of a sacrifice that becomes identical with the sinner, the idea that the sacrifice effects the sinner's symbolic death and resurrection, the idea of sacrifice as a "coming to God," the idea of sacrifice as "inclusive place-taking" — all were first worked out in Gese's theory of the cult. But Hofius applies them, more extensively than Gese ever did, to salvation in Christ (116):

> Christ has not simply come alongside the sinner in order to take away something — namely, guilt and sin; he has rather become identical with the sinner (see 2 Cor. 5:21; Gal. 3:13) in order through the surrender of his life to lead sinners into union with God and thus to open to them fellowship with God for the first time. Christ thus dies not only "in the place of" [*anstelle*] the sinner; he dies "for" him in such a way that his death is as such the sinner's death and his resurrection is as such the sinner's "coming to God" (see 2 Cor. 5:14b).... What is at issue in "inclusive place-taking" is the fundamental recognition that only God the creator is able to free sinners from their sin; he does this by making sin and indeed sinful people themselves his own problem in all seriousness. "Inclusive place-taking" is not human but *divine* place-taking. The letter to Diognetus expresses this well when it declares in view of

---

41. See Hofius, "Gottesknechtslied," 116 n. 43, with reference to Gese, "Sühne" (n. 29), and Hofius, "Sühne und Versöhnung" (n. 31).

Christ's death (9:2): "God took our sins upon himself" (αὐτὸς τὰς ἡμετέρας ἁμαρτίας ἀνεδέξατο).[42]

These, then, are the presuppositions of Hofius's view. Isaiah 53, wherever it is integrated into the New Testament letters, is integrated into a pattern of Christology that derives not so much from Isaiah itself as from the *levitical cult* (although it is the cultic *idea* more than the *tradition history* as such that Hofius is after, p. 116). Since Hofius does not think that the Hebrew term *asham* in Isaiah 53:10 has a cultic background or that Isaiah 52:13–53:12 is a cultic passage, it goes without saying that the cultically conditioned reception of Isaiah 53 in the New Testament letters will yield a different result from the chapter's meaning in its original setting. The original levitical cult evidences an *inclusive* or *representative* understanding of atonement. Even though the original Servant idea does not evidence this pattern, its language is adaptable to the New Testament's cultic, incorporative understanding of atonement.[43]

Hofius's Hermeneutic

Hofius concludes his essay with a hermeneutical reflection. His main point all along has been to insist that an existential inclusion in the Christ event — an event of *divine* place-taking — is the New Testament's pattern of salvation, and not only in Paul. But the meaning of Servant language in its original setting is different. The human limitations of the Servant mean that the text of Isaiah 53 could never mean the same thing when applied to him as it means when applied to Christ. It follows that the text when applied to Christ becomes in effect a new text (127):

> Through its christological reception in the New Testament, the fourth Servant Song acquires a sense that was *not* originally its own, one that changes it in content and meaning so that we must talk in certain respects about a *new* text. Once the name of the Son of

---

42. Hofius, "Gottesknechtslied," 116 n. 47, refers to the entire context of *Diognetus* 9:2–5.

43. In order to indicate the essential difference in the NT reception of this OT passage, Hofius will often label the new framework simply as *sühnend,* "atoning," without saying explicitly that it is incorporative or inclusive, but he means the same thing. He therefore finds cultic or *sühnetheologische* patterning in virtually every instance where soteriological language from Isaiah 53 has been taken up in the New Testament letters, e.g., in 1 Corinthians 15:3 (p. 120); Romans 4:25 (122); 2 Corinthians 5:21 (123); Hebrews 9:28 (124); 1 Peter 2:21–25 (125–26); and 1 Peter 3:18 (126).

God, Jesus Christ, is entered for the words "my servant" — which point to a mere human — the coordinates of the fourth Servant Song as a whole are changed. For now Christ's death and resurrection determine the meaning of *sin, being a sinner,* and *existential place-taking for sinners.* That the Old Testament text was open for such a christological reception is amazing [*erstaunlich*] enough. Yet at the same time it needs to be said: only through the christological reception does this text become theologically affirmable and therefore a text for which we can take responsibility in the preaching of the church.

If by a "new text" is meant a text in which all the terms and concepts have been deepened and invested with new insight, given a meaning that they could not have had in their original, pre-Christian setting, then Hofius's conclusion is unavoidable: "Jesus Christ, in his person and in his work, is not merely and not primarily explained by Isaiah 53: Isaiah 53 is rather explained *by him*" (127).

B. Janowski: Isaiah 53 as a Drama of Recognition

We could not do justice to Janowski's essay "Er trug unsere Sünden: Jesaja 53 und die Dramatik der Stellvertretung"[44] at the Baylor colloquy, nor will it be possible to do so here, partly because Janowski carries on a running conversation with systematic and historical theology and even modern sociology along with his biblical exegesis. Nevertheless, since we have already studied Hofius in depth, some details of Janowski's approach will emerge by way of comparison.

First, by contrast to Hofius, Janowski does not modify the normal idea of *Stellvertretung* as an event whereby one person takes the place of others in punishment in such a way that the others are *excluded* from it. As Gese's student and the author of the world's most detailed book on cultic atonement,[45] Janowski is perfectly familiar with the concept of *inkludierende Stellvertretung* that Hofius derived from the cult and used to describe the New Testament's reception of Isaiah 53. However,

---

44. See Janowski, above n. 6: running page references in the text refer to this work.
45. Janowski, *Sühne* (above n. 39).

Janowski does not here expound the cult or Isaiah 53 in the New Testament, and therefore he uses *Stellvertretung* on its own in the same sense as Hofius's *exkludierende Stellvertretung*.

Although Janowski agrees with Hofius that the place-taking in Isaiah 53 is exclusive, amounting to one person substituting for others in matters of guilt, he does not seem so influenced by, or perhaps we should rather say, so much in agreement with Kant as Hofius. Janowski cites the same passage from Kant (28) as Hofius cites, but he also includes criticisms of Kant (28–29 nn. 6, 8), concluding that the idealistic criticism of *Stellvertretung* does not need to be answered in this context because the Bible formulates the problem differently (45).[46]

In Janowski's essay we have something approaching the traditional concept of substitution. This is not, then, Whybray's idea that the Old Testament passage is partly about the sufferings all exiles share in Babylon,[47] nor is it the same as Hofius's attempt to suggest that Isaiah 53 as an Old Testament text is inadequate to human need because it does not live up to the ideal of divine, *inkludierende Stellvertretung*. However, neither is Janowski's view primarily one of how God can justly transfer both guilt and its penal consequences from one party to another. The concern that Janowski highlights in the text focuses not so much on theodicy or atonement theology as on problems of religious epistemology, how Israel comes to recognize both her guilt and its cancellation so as to be changed and ultimately saved. This process of recognition or rethinking occurs in several stages in a single text that Janowski understands as follows.

Isaiah 52:13–53:12 revolves around the perspective of the "we" before and after the Servant's death and the subsequent oracle from God about the Servant's exaltation and future success (the Servant here is taken to be identical with the prophet Second Isaiah). Janowski mentions two factors that were operating simultaneously before the Servant's death, but he does not try to work them into a system. Using a form-critical argu-

---

46. Indeed, as an apparent direct counterpoint to Kant's notions of rationality, Janowski concludes his introduction to the concept of *Stellvertretung* by quoting the social ethicist H.-R. Reuter to the effect that *Stellvertretung* presents an "idea of an intercession of one person for all others as a reality that is *already a given to reason*" (31, italics added).

47. Given Whybray's somewhat unusual and unduly restrictive definition of "vicarious suffering" as the opposite of "shared suffering" (what is shared cannot be vicarious), it seems almost as though the Servant would have to suffer outside Babylon to do anything vicarious, i.e., that which is not *shared* with other Babylonian exiles. For criticism of Whybray's definition of vicariousness or *Stellvertretung*, see the review by Hermisson (above n. 2).

ment from the psalms of complaint (e.g., Psalms 3; 31; 41; pp. 37–39), Janowski concludes that since the "we" are described in language reminiscent of the enemies of the righteous in the Psalms, the historical "we" within Israel during the exile must actually have behaved as the Servant's enemies, persecuting him and excluding him; ultimately a semijudicial case was brought against him that led to his death and his burial among the wicked (the details of vv. 7–10a are therefore taken fairly literally, p. 40). Part of the Servant's suffering therefore appears due to the actions of the other exiles, although they do not recognize this at first.

The other element of the Servant's sufferings is due to God himself, (see vv. 6b and 10a), though once again, God's hand in this suffering is not recognized by the "we" until after the Servant's death. In keeping with God's plan, the Servant voluntarily makes the surrender of his life an *asham*, not a cultic sacrifice as such but a more general "means of wiping out guilt" that is normally provided only when the guilty realize their guilt and take responsibility for it. Since this is precisely what the exiles as a community are in no position to do, the Servant does it for them. "Israel, which is in no position to take over the obligation arising from its guilt, must be released from it in order to have any future" (43).

Although all this can be said to be going on in the events leading up to the Servant's death, the "we" will initially have taken a much more simplistic view of the Servant's situation. So long as the "we" were relying on the traditional framework of the *Tun-Ergehen-Zusammenhang*,[48] the ancient worldview of a virtually automatic "action-consequences connection" in which actions carry their own consequences and people basically get what they deserve, it was logical prior to the Servant's death and Yahweh's word of his exaltation for them to think that it was his own sin and not theirs that he was bearing. Their treatment of him as a God-forsaken sinner only made his sufferings worse: "[W]e accounted him stricken, struck down by God, and afflicted" (Isa. 53:4).

The change in perspective is possible for the "we" only after Yahweh's two oracles (especially the first: 52:13–15; cf. 53:11b–12) to the effect that the prophet was not a justly punished sinner but a righteous Servant who will yet have success in his mission. Only with this in-breaking

---

48. See Janowski, "Er trug unsere Sünden," 27–28, n. 4 (and above on Koch, n. 28), for secondary literature on this theme.

of God's perspective are the "we" able to see that the standard deed-consequences connection cannot have been at work in the Servant's case (e.g., pp. 38–39). The Servant has instead taken up an "alien" fate in a "role reversal" of the guilty and the innocent that allows consequences alien to the Servant's own behavior to strike him alone. He thus releases others from the same fate so as to fulfill his mission of "bringing Israel back" (see Isa. 49:5–6) from the catastrophe of exile in 587 B.C.E. (41).

For Janowski, then, the drama of *Stellvertretung* lies precisely in that it is not reducible to a single abstract pattern of either representation or substitution. At the time when the crucial events are happening, the sufferings undergone by the Servant seem neither representative nor substitutionary, for they appear to have nothing to do with anyone else. But after God makes it clear that the one has taken the place of the many, there are elements that might be regarded as both representative and substitutionary. The sufferings are substitutionary because something is done for the "we" that they could not do for themselves (and now no longer need to do for themselves), and representative because what the Servant suffered represented their fate and not his. It is because of this after-the-fact realization that another has already taken their place, *representing* them in their guilt, that the "we" cry out (36–37):

> Nevertheless, our sicknesses — he bore them,
> and our pains — he took them upon himself;
> yet we (previously) accounted him as one afflicted,
> as one stricken by God and bowed down.
>
> (Isaiah 53:4)

In adapting Janowski's ideas for a wider audience, we would do well to remember some common human experiences of place-taking.[49] Experience suggests that the recognition that someone else has suffered because of us and for us, even instead of us, can be all the more painful when it comes long after the fact — too long after the fact for us to do anything to change it other than to change ourselves in response. The community's confession of guilt above is therefore as far from the cheap notion of their "going scot-free" (a common criticism of notions of substitution

---

49. The following examples are in line with Janowski's thoughts on "The Reality of *Stellvertretung*" (44–47) but have been developed independently.

that do not involve representation)[50] as the penetrating meditation on the idea of substitution by Paul Gerhardt is far removed from the outlook of the modern prosperity gospel (an approach that is often wrongly seen as the necessary corollary of substitutionary views):

> Nun, was du, Herr, erduldet, ist alles meine Last;
> ich hab es selbst verschuldet, was du getragen hast.
> Schau her, hier steh ich Armer, der Zorn verdienet hat;
> gib mir, o mein Erbarmer, den Anblick deiner Gnad![51]

Perhaps in conclusion we may expand upon what Janowski seems to regard as an important noetic or *erkenntnistheoretische* dimension of the Servant text.[52] Israel was unprepared for the Servant's exaltation and in no position to recognize the representation of its own fate in his sufferings at the time when they were actually occurring, needing instead God's word to break in and provide this recognition only later. By analogy we may consider it likely that the disciples, whether or not Jesus had prepared them to think of his mission in terms of Isaiah 53, were not able to recognize fully the extent to which it was their own sins that were being borne up to the cross (see, e.g., 1 Pet. 2:24) until later, after the granting of the Holy Spirit.

If this statement applies to the original disciples it certainly applies to Paul. As the "we" speakers in the drama of Isaiah 53 recognized their own sin only in looking back on the Servant's fate from God's perspective, so Paul seems to regard Christ's death on the cross not only as an event of redemption but also as an event that, in hindsight, reveals the nature of sin (providing perhaps even a different perspective on it than the law does; see Rom. 3:20). Without Christ's death and Paul's reflection on it, partly helped along by Isaiah 53 (as in the first two instances below and perhaps the third), we would know less about "our sins" (1 Cor. 15:3), "our trespasses" (Rom. 4:25), "the many" who

---

50. E.g., Whiteley, *Theology* (n. 22 above), 131; Tuckett, "Atonement" (n. 22 above), 519. See Whybray, *The Second Isaiah* (n. 2 above), 77, and also above, n. 3, for the idea that the exiles in Babylon had *not* gone "scot-free."

51. Paul Gerhardt (1607–1706), "O Haupt voll Blut und Wunden," in *Evangelisches Kirchengesangbuch* (Stuttgart: Verlag des Ev. Gesangbuchs, 1953; repr., 1986), no. 63.4.

52. See Janowski, "Er trug unsere Sünden," 38: "ein tiefgreifender Prozeß der Erkenntnis"; 44: "ein *durch Erkenntnis verwandeltes Israel*" (italics original). See in conclusion 46–47 (46: "Niemand ist aber aus sich allein zu solcher Erkenntnis fähig") and the literature on the *Erkenntnisproblem* (esp. by J. Fischer) in Janowski, 46–47 n. 62.

were made sinners (Rom. 5:19), "this present evil age" (Gal. 1:3), the "curse" (Gal. 3:13), the "old creation" (2 Cor. 5:17), the "reign of sin" (Rom. 5:21), the "old man" (Rom. 6:6), the "body of sin" (Rom. 6:6), and the "overlooking of previous sins" (Rom. 3:25). Paul says that "while we were still sinners Christ died for us" (Rom. 5:8), but this also works in reverse: only when we realize that the Son of God had to die for us do we understand what it means to be sinners.

Through first seeing their guilt borne by another and only later confessing it as their own (see Isa. 53:4–6), the people of Israel are granted a life-changing knowledge that could be had no other way. There may be structural analogies with Paul and other New Testament writers beyond the proven verbal parallels with the Servant texts. This new perspective may also provide a different angle on traditional debates about the atonement. The Servant's story carries a message for the story's "we" figures as well as for modern readers, whether his sufferings are conceived as representative or substitutionary or both.

14

The Suffering Servant

Recent Tübingen Scholarship on Isaiah 53

Daniel P. Bailey

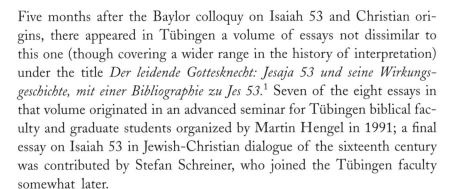

Five months after the Baylor colloquy on Isaiah 53 and Christian origins, there appeared in Tübingen a volume of essays not dissimilar to this one (though covering a wider range in the history of interpretation) under the title *Der leidende Gottesknecht: Jesaja 53 und seine Wirkungsgeschichte, mit einer Bibliographie zu Jes 53.*[1] Seven of the eight essays in that volume originated in an advanced seminar for Tübingen biblical faculty and graduate students organized by Martin Hengel in 1991; a final essay on Isaiah 53 in Jewish-Christian dialogue of the sixteenth century was contributed by Stefan Schreiner, who joined the Tübingen faculty somewhat later.

James Carleton Paget and I had the privilege of attending the original lectures on which the Tübingen volume is based. Therefore when a working group in Cambridge led by William Farmer and Morna Hooker in the spring of 1995 was looking for a means of preparing for the Baylor colloquy, Dr. Carleton Paget suggested that we might want to try to get hold of the unpublished manuscripts of the Tübingen volume. This being granted by kind permission of the authors and editors, we proceeded to summarize and discuss most of the essays.

The following abstracts of individual essays can therefore be considered an informal result of our discussions (though I alone am responsible for the wording). These summaries were part of the material distributed to Baylor panel members in advance, although at the colloquy itself

---

1. Ed. Bernd Janowski and Peter Stuhlmacher, Forschungen zum Alten Testament 14 (Tübingen: Mohr-Siebeck, 1996).

we discussed only the studies by Spieckermann (not itself part of the Tübingen volume but planned for the English version), Janowski, and Hofius, based on translations which likewise had been distributed in advance. Since there is as yet no major review of the Tübingen volume in English (Joachim Schaper's review is due to appear in the *Journal of Theological Studies* in October 1998), and since a planned English translation will probably not appear until a year or two after the present volume,[2] it may be useful for a wider audience to have an overview of recent Tübingen work.

While my own analysis of the two essays by Otfried Hofius and Bernd Janowski appears in the previous chapter, this is perhaps an appropriate place to mention that our preparations for the Baylor colloquy did not include the translation or distribution of Martin Hengel's substantial forty-two page contribution, "Zur Wirkungsgeschichte von Jes 53 in vorchristlicher Zeit."[3] Given the predominantly historical-critical interests of the conference, this is undoubtedly the essay from the Tübingen volume (besides those already mentioned) that could have made the greatest difference in our deliberations.

In particular, if Hengel's then-unpublished perspectives on the reception of Isaiah 53 in pre-Christian or non-Christian Jewish sources had been more widely available to members of the panel, we might have come more quickly to texts that we touched upon only briefly in the open discussion near the end of the conference (e.g., Daniel 11–12) or indeed hardly at all (e.g., the two Qumran manuscripts of Isaiah as well as the Aramaic *Testament of Levi*, 4Q540/541=4QAhA). This approach might in turn have modified slightly the direction of some statements elsewhere in this volume: maybe Isaiah 53 had a greater pre-Christian influence than some of these articles suggest.[4] Nevertheless, the historical points

---

2. Provisional title: *The Suffering Servant: Isaiah 53 in Jewish and Christian Sources*, ed. B. Janowski and P. Stuhlmacher, trans. D. P. Bailey (Grand Rapids: Eerdmans, forthcoming).

3. Hengel, "Zur Wirkungsgeschichte," in Janowski and Stuhlmacher, eds., *Der leidende Gottesknecht* (above n. 1), 49–91.

4. Compare, for example, Morna Hooker's statement (n. 8 of her essay, with the accompanying text) to the effect that there were almost no pre-Christian Jewish traditions deriving from Isaiah 53 that might convey the idea that one person's suffering can have atoning power for others. Hengel, by contrast, believes that there might have been *a few* such traditions, including Daniel 11–12, the LXX of Isaiah 53 (which has its own interpretive tendencies), and 4QAhA=4Q540/541 ("Zur Wirkungsgeschichte" [above n. 3], 91; cf. 69–75). However, Hengel qualifies with the word "perhaps" most of his potential evidence about salvation through the substitutionary suffering or death of an individual for the sins of others. Even if Hengel's texts support his interpretation, it would call for only a slight

not covered at Baylor should perhaps not be overemphasized. Some of the issues have now been addressed by N. T. Wright, who in his recent book makes Hengel the mainstay of his footnotes on the pre-Christian Servant idea,[5] coming to conclusions that combine perspectives of both Hengel and M. D. Hooker.[6]

Following are abstracts (not critical reviews!) of the eight essays in the Tübingen volume, with the addition of an abstract of a related paper by Hermann Spieckermann delivered in Cambridge in 1995.

"The Conception and Pre-history of the Idea of Vicariousness in the Old Testament," by Hermann Spieckermann

The concept of substitution or "vicariousness" (*Stellvertretung*) in the Old Testament is very closely bound up with Isaiah 53.[7] However, the vicarious activity there depicted of the suffering Servant is unique. It is therefore necessary to clarify the main characteristics of the idea of vicariousness as well as its possible traditio-historical antecedents. Although the intercession of the one for the sins of the many and the thought of divine initiative are clearly characteristic of the chapter, subordinate themes like the sinlessness of the Servant and his acceptance of his fate remain more difficult to explain. These characteristics, both primary and secondary, must guide research into the Old Testament roots of the no-

---

modification of a minor point in Hooker's essay; Hengel's evidence does not necessarily challenge Hooker's overall argument, which lays the emphasis elsewhere.

5. See N. T. Wright, *Jesus and the Victory of God,* Christian Origins and the Question of God 2 (London: SPCK, 1996), 588–91 nn. 187–89, 191, 192, 198, with reference to Hengel, "Zur Wirkungsgeschichte."

6. See Wright's conclusion (*Jesus and the Victory of God,* 590), with footnotes to both Hooker and Hengel (here in parentheses): "Indeed, the use of Isaiah 40–55 as a whole, and in its parts, seldom if ever in pre-Christian Judaism includes *all* those elements which later Christian theology brought together (as, for instance, in 1 Peter 2:21–25): servant, Messiah, suffering, *and* vicarious sin-bearing (cf. Hooker, *Jesus and the Servant,* 53–54, 56–58). It is conceivable that we find the idea of sin-bearing, with reference to Isaiah, in some Jewish texts, but this is far harder to prove than messianic meanings (Hengel, 'Zur Wirkungsgeschichte,' conclusion: he cites 4Q540/541 [=4QAhA] as a possibility [i.e., for the idea of sin-bearing]. This is not exactly a firm or wide base upon which to build.)."

7. See H. Spieckermann, "Konzeption und Vorgeschichte des Stellvertretungsgedankens im Alten Testament," main paper read at the Fifteenth Congress of the International Organization for the Study of the Old Testament, Cambridge, England, July 20, 1995, forthcoming in the congress volume, ed. J. A. Emerton, VTSup (Leiden: Brill). Discussion of this paper at the Baylor colloquy was led by William Bellinger.

tion of vicariousness. It is usual and appropriate to seek these roots in the priestly atonement procedures and in the prophets' intercession for the people. Studies of exemplary texts from Amos, Jeremiah, and Ezekiel show that the decisive preliminary theological work for the concept of vicariousness was accomplished in the seventh and sixth centuries, with the cult providing the theological framework. Despite these clarifications, it is still not possible to reconstruct a self-contained pre-history for the idea of vicariousness in Isaiah 53. The pre-history sheds some light, but not enough to remove the mystery or uniqueness from chapter 53. This lack of predictability provides the best evidence that Isaiah 53 is trying to say something new.

"The Fourth Servant Song in the Context of Second Isaiah," by Hans-Jürgen Hermisson

The office of the Servant in the four Servant Songs (Isa. 42:1–4; 49:1–6; 50:4–9; 52:13–53:12) is essentially a prophetic one, summing up past conceptions and experiences of the prophetic office (not simply biographical details of the Servant) and incorporating some royal features. Nevertheless, the universal message of salvation given to this prophetic Servant transcends previous conceptions. The primary reference in *all four texts* is to the prophet Second Isaiah himself (perhaps even in 49:3), who is also spoken of outside the Songs as God's Servant (e.g., 43:10; 44:26; 44:21–22). However, the individual prophetic Servant Second Isaiah cannot fulfill his worldwide mission as a light to the nations without God's servant Israel, whom he calls back to God and prepares to be the prime exhibit before the world of God's saving power (see 49:5–6). Only through the *cooperation* of God's two servants — the prophet who preaches God's word and Israel who receives it — is the Servant role fulfilled. One-sided designations of the Servant as "individual" or "corporate" are therefore too simple, and the supraindividual or bigger-than-life dimensions show that there is a future element to the Servant idea not exhausted by the individual prophet. (Although the Songs are not prophecies of Christ, no violence is done to them when read in this light.) While the first two Songs do not include suffering as part of the Servant's office and while the third includes it only as the natural consequence of prophetic activity, the fourth Song, composed by the prophet's pupils, makes suffering the essential means to the accomplishment of the Servant's task. The Servant bore substitutionarily the sins of the "many" in Israel, particularly the sin of *unbelief*. Therefore while the Servant's faith may be seen as *representative* of the faith that Israel may develop in the future, in the past the individual Servant has been a *substitute — not a representative —* for the servant Israel in matters of both faith and suffering (p. 18). The reward and success of the Servant in his mission becomes a theme linking all four texts (cf. 42:4; 49:4; 50:7–9 with 52:13).

"He Bore Our Sins: Isaiah 53 and the Drama of Taking Another's Place," by Bernd Janowski

According to Immanuel Kant, individual responsibility means that no person or party can represent another in matters involving personal guilt. Isaiah 53 provides an alternative to this narrow and dismissive understanding of the concept of representation or "taking another's place." Bernd Janowski sees the heart of the passage's drama in the recognition or the change of perspective that God brings to the speakers in the "we" sections, who stand for all Israel (53:1–11a). The "we" figures come *unexpectedly* to see themselves and their guilt *represented* in the fate of another — the Servant whom they formerly despised and who had already *substituted* for them in bearing their sins, making his life an *asham*, a means of wiping out guilt. However, this recognition occurs only after the (innocent) death of the Servant, here identical with the prophet Second Isaiah himself. Prior to the Servant's death, Israel simply assumed that his sufferings were the result of *his own* guilt. They kept their distance from this "man of sorrows" (v. 3), accounting him "stricken, struck down by God, and afflicted" (v. 4). But Yahweh's oracle at the start of the passage (52:13–15) breaks through this human aloofness and self-confidence. Yahweh's Servant will not fail in his mission; guilt there is indeed, but it is not the Servant's own (see 53:11b–12). Once the "we" figures see this, they acknowledge their own guilt as well as its cancellation, becoming changed in the process.

"The Influence of Isaiah 53 in the Pre-Christian Period,"
by Martin Hengel

Does the fourth Servant Song possess any history of pre-Christian influence worthy of the name? Or does this simply rest upon the wishes of a few conservative exegetes? Martin Hengel takes a middle position. The reception and further development of Isaiah 53 is probably to be detected in a wide variety of pre-Christian Jewish writings — including Hebrew and Aramaic texts as well as original Greek texts and translations: even the LXX of Isaiah 53 shows interpretive tendencies. The view that Isaiah 53 was without much influence therefore needs modification. The passage was not only read and interpreted; it was apparently also interpreted *messianically*. Nevertheless, the passage's influence in early Judaism is not all of the same type, nor all of the type that would necessarily support the preaching of early Christianity regarding a *suffering, atoning figure* who bears the sins of others *vicariously*. Outside the Hebrew and Greek texts of Isaiah 53, and *perhaps* Daniel 11–12 and one text from Qumran (an Aramaic *Testament of Levi*, 4Q540/541=4QAhA), the motif of vicarious suffering tends to disappear in the Jewish tradition, especially where the motif of the coming Judge is prominent. Hengel nevertheless believes that Jewish traditions of eschatological messianic figures who suffer and make atonement may very well have circulated in pre-Christian times. Jesus and the earliest church therefore *could* have known them and appealed to them. This would explain how first Jesus and then his disciples could suppose that their message of the Messiah's vicarious atoning death would be understood among their Jewish contemporaries.

"Isaiah 53 in the Gospels and Acts," by Peter Stuhlmacher

The New Testament's christological interpretation of Isaiah 53 goes back to Jesus' own understanding of his mission and death, here explored by a traditio-historical argument. Jesus' understanding, in turn, depends upon a demonstrable early Jewish Messianic interpretation of Isaiah 53. Messianic interpretations of the chapter, both ancient Jewish and early

Christian, are commonly attributed to an "individualistic" understanding of the Servant, as opposed to the "corporate" understanding favored in much recent scholarship. The dichotomy is, however, a false one. In Judaism the individual figure of the Servant-Messiah is the prince appointed by God, who rules over the people of God and simultaneously *represents* them before God. So also with Jesus. He is the Son of God who leads the people of God; yet that people also constitutes his body. One can call this understanding "individual" only so long as one also remembers the collective aspect and refuses to oppose the two conceptions.

"The Fourth Servant Song in the Letters of the New Testament," by Otfried Hofius

Otfried Hofius believes that a nuanced and critical view of the various ways in which one person may be said to *take another's place* is essential to understanding the reception of Isaiah 53 in the New Testament. In the original passage the Servant has taken the place of the speakers or onlookers in the "we" sections. They are in effect outside or *excluded from* the Servant's fate: "*he* has borne our infirmities and carried our diseases" (v. 4); "*he* shall bear their iniquities" (v. 11); "*he* bore the sin of many" (v. 12). Substitution and transference of guilt have therefore occurred — a taking of another's place that exempts or *excludes* the other party (hence "exclusive place-taking" or *exkludierende Stellvertretung* in the recent German parlance). However, while such notions from Isaiah 53 may have been applied to Jesus without much reflection by those responsible for some of Christianity's earliest formulaic sayings, the writers of the New Testament letters, who preserve these sayings, are more conscious of the need to interpret them. Christ always takes the place of others in a way that still *includes* them as persons, thus affecting their very being. Sins are not here viewed as detached or detachable from persons. This "inclusive" understanding of *place-taking* in the New Testament (which has analogies in the OT cult) provides the pattern into which the authors integrate Isaiah 53, thereby making it in effect a "new text."

"The Servant of Isaiah 53 as Triumphant and Interceding Messiah: The Reception of Isaiah 52:13–53:12 in the *Targum Jonathan* with Special Attention to the Concept of the Messiah," by Jostein Ådna

The departures of the Aramaic translation of Isaiah 52:13–53:12 from the wording of the Hebrew text — beginning with the Aramaic, "Behold, my servant, *the Messiah,* shall prosper" in 52:13 — are well known. What they reveal of the translator's procedure and theology is, however, a debated matter. In contrast to some earlier investigators, Jostein Ådna does not believe that the translator's changes in favor of a triumphant rather than a suffering Messiah can be traced to any conscious anti-Christian motive. Neither can the translator's procedure fairly be labeled as arbitrary reinterpretation or atomistic exegesis. Rather, the Targumist provides a unified and consistent interpretation of Isaiah 53 that does not differ substantially from his treatment of other parts of the book. Working probably between the destruction of the temple in 70 C.E. and the Bar Kochba revolt in 135, the translator confirms and develops a typical Jewish view of the Messiah as the one who would rebuild the temple, instruct the people in the law, and intercede for Israel. In thus uniting a multiplicity of eschatological roles in a single mediator figure, the Targumist proceeds by a way that has analogies in the New Testament, even though there the authors conceive the messianic office very differently.

"The Man Jesus Christ in the Sight of God: Two Models of the Understanding of Isaiah 52:13–53:12 in the Patristic Literature and Their Development," by Christoph Markschies

Isaiah 52:13–53:12 is not a central text in the church fathers, but it is an important text. Christoph Markschies traces two ways in which the fathers understood it — by an "exemplary" model and by a "christological" model. In the former the Servant is viewed as an example of the true Christian, and the text is taken as ethical instruction. In the latter model Isaiah 53 speaks of a unique event of salvation in Christ that cannot be imitated, only believed. Although the boundaries between these two interpretive models are fluid, generally the christological model comes to predominate. The exemplary model thrives only in the early period, for example in *1 Clement* (c. 96 C.E.) and in the second-century acts of the martyrs. Here Isaiah 53 has already become Hellenized along the lines of a hero cult. Hellenization of a different kind takes place with the christological model. Initially a genuinely Jewish framework is maintained, especially in literature of Jewish-Christian debate, e.g., Justin Martyr, Aphrahat the Persian, and later *Adversus Iudaeos* literature. In the later phases, however, distinctively Greek resistance to the idea that the divine nature in Christ could have suffered affects the great Isaiah commentaries and doctrinal works of Origen, Eusebius, and Hilary. Patristic exegesis of Isaiah 53 thus diverges gradually not only from the original Old Testament sense of the passage, but also from its original Christian sense. Today we can interpret the text properly only by having both Jewish and patristic exegesis as conversation partners, without repeating their errors.

"Isaiah 52:13–53:12 in the Exposition of the 'Book for the Consolidation of Faith' (*Sepher Ḥizzuk Emunah*) of Rabbi Isaac ben Abraham of Troki," by Stefan Schreiner

The city of Troki, in present-day Lithuania, represents in microcosm the Polish-Lithuanian commonwealth of the sixteenth century. Here representatives of various religious traditions — Protestants, Roman Catholics, Russian Orthodox, Unitarians, and Jews of the Rabbanite and Karaite traditions — had the opportunity for serious religious dialogue. Rabbi Isaac ben Abraham (c. 1525–c. 1586), leader of the Karaite community in Troki, participated in these discussions and wrote his influential anti-Christian polemical work, the *Sepher Ḥizzuk Emunah*, as a result. While previous studies have praised this work's masterful summary of fifteen hundred years of Jewish-Christian debate, little attention has been devoted to its refutation of Christian proofs from Isaiah 53, which forms one of its longest chapters. As Stefan Schreiner shows, Rabbi Isaac's treatment is valuable because it goes beyond brief polemical theses to serious exegetical engagement with the text. The problems that Jews and Christians discussed four hundred years ago were much the same as those that occupy the Jewish-Christian dialogue today.

15

Reflections on Isaiah 53 and Christian Origins

William R. Farmer

◆

He was wounded for our transgressions,
    tortured for our iniquities;
  upon him was the chastisement that made us whole,
    and by his blood drawn by the whip we are healed.
All we, like sheep, have gone astray;
    each of us has gone his own way;
  and the Lord has laid on him
    the guilt of us all.
He was oppressed, he submitted to being struck down,
    and he did not open his mouth;
  like a lamb that is led to the slaughter,
    and like a ewe that is dumb before its shearers,
  so he did not open his mouth.
After arrest and judgments he was taken away;
    and as for his fate, who gave a thought,
  how he was cut off from family and friends,
    stricken to death for the transgression of my people?
He was buried with the transgressors,
    given a grave among the refuse of mankind;
  although he had done no violence,
    and there was no word of treachery in his mouth.
Yet the Lord took thought for his tortured servant,
    and healed him who had offered himself a sacrifice for sin;

so shall he prolong his life, and see his children's children,
    and in his hand the Lord's cause shall prosper.
After all his travail he shall be bathed in light;
    after his disgrace he shall be fully vindicated;
so shall my servant vindicate many,
    himself bearing the penalty of their guilt.
Therefore, I will allot him a portion with the great,
    and he shall share the spoils of victory with the triumphant,
because he poured out his soul to death
    and was counted among the transgressors;
yet he bore the sin of many,
    and made intercession for the transgressors.

—Isaiah 53:5–12

Introduction

The following reflections have not taken place within a vacuum. They have their historical, sociological, and theological context. Properly speaking, this context is the world of theological scholarship. This world is not to be confused with the world of biblical scholarship, which, in the United States at least, is a more highly secularized enterprise. Since the world of theological scholarship must embrace and relate meaningfully to the world of biblical scholarship, the context within which these reflections take place is correspondingly complex.

At issue in these reflections is the question whether the use of the suffering Servant (Isaiah 53) to interpret the mission of Jesus began with Jesus or only with the postresurrection church. I am aware that within the world of biblical scholarship a strong case can be made for each of these opposing positions. I also realize that there is little prospect of breaking this impasse without reconceiving the problem. In this regard, rather than focus on certain sayings of Jesus preserved in the Gospels, as has been done in the past, I have attempted to approach the problem within the wider context of the nature of Christian faith, as reflected in Christian literature up to Justin Martyr. Within that context, without neglecting the Gospels, I tend to focus attention on certain texts found in the letters of Paul.

Governing all of these reflections is my long-held conviction that the backbone of church history is preserved for us in Galatians chapters 1–2. I place great importance on the historical information that Paul spent fifteen days visiting Peter in Jerusalem three years and some months after his conversion (Gal. 1:18) and that he returned to Jerusalem fourteen years later for an important apostolic conference. At this conference his way of presenting the gospel to the Gentiles was accepted by the pillars of the church and he was given the right hand of fellowship by these church leaders, who agreed further that he was to be in charge of the mission to the Gentiles as Peter was to be in charge of the mission to the Jews (Gal. 2:1–16). In my mind there is a rich network of historical information preserved in Galatians and in other letters of Paul that serves historians well as a promising beginning point for the sort of reflections which follow.

The heart of the text in question is Isaiah 53:5–12, given above. I propose to begin these reflections with a survey of some of the quotations, allusions to, and echoes of this remarkable text in normative writings of the early church and then to proceed to look at the bearing of this survey on the question of Jesus and the problem of Christian origins.

If one thinks in terms of quotations of this text, one's attention is immediately focused on certain citations by Paul,[1] the author of the Acts of the Apostles,[2] the author of 1 Clement,[3] and Justin Martyr.[4]

If one restricts oneself to clear allusions in the New Testament to this text, one's attention is immediately focused on the allusions found in 1 Peter.[5]

If one thinks in terms of clear New Testament echoes of this text, one's attention immediately focuses on the echoes in Romans;[6] 1 Corinthians;[7] Galatians;[8] Philippians;[9] and Hebrews.[10]

---

1. Romans 10:16 citing Isaiah 53:1, and 15:21 citing Isaiah 52:15.
2. Acts 8:32–33 citing Isaiah 53:7–8.
3. *Letter to the Corinthians* 16 citing Isaiah 53:1–12.
4. *First Apology* 50–51 citing Isaiah 52:13–53:12.
5. 1 Peter 2:22–25 alluding, among other sources, to Isaiah 53:4, 5, 6, 7 and 9.
6. Romans 4:25 echoing Isaiah 53:4–5, and Romans 5:19 echoing Isaiah 53:11 (see also 5:15b).
7. 1 Corinthians 15:3 echoing Isaiah 53:4–9.
8. Galatians 1:4 echoing Isaiah 53:8–9, Galatians 2:20 echoing Isaiah 53:8–9 (see also 1 Tim. 2:6 and Titus 2:14).
9. Philippians 2:7–8 echoing Isaiah 53:10–12, and Philippians 2:9 echoing Isaiah 53:13.
10. Hebrews 9:28 echoing Isaiah 53:12.

1 Corinthians 15:3

There is a widespread consensus among exegetes that the text in 1 Corinthians 15:3 is crucial for making a case that Isaiah 53 was important not only for Paul, but for the pre-Pauline church from which Paul received the tradition which he subsequently passed on to the churches that he founded. The text reads as follows:

> For I passed on to you as of first importance what I also received, that Christ died in behalf of our sins according to the scriptures.

The reference to Christ dying in behalf of the sins of others exhibits a certain verbal kinship with the text of Isaiah 53:4–9, and many would conclude that there is indeed an echo of Isaiah 53 in this passage.[11] However, this verbal kinship is not by itself compelling evidence of a clear connection between 1 Corinthians 15:3 and Isaiah 53:4–9. What serves to make this connection compelling is a conceptual similarity. Nowhere else in the scriptures that were available to Paul is there a text which speaks so explicitly of a savior figure who dies in behalf of the sins of others.[12] It is this conceptual kinship more than any particular verbal kinship which leads scholars to identify Isaiah 53 as the most important scripture being referred to in this traditional formulation.

In addition to the above-mentioned explicit quotations and allusions to, or echoes of, Isaiah 53 in Acts and the letters of the New Testament, there are passages in the Gospels of Matthew, Mark, and Luke which call for our attention.

Matthew 20:20–28||Mark 10:35–45

In Matthew 20:20–28 there is a story concerning the request made to Jesus by the mother of James and John that her sons have the privilege of sitting on Jesus' right and on his left, in seats of privilege and authority.

---

11. The following passages from the LXX text of Isaiah 53 offer linguistic parallels to the text of 1 Corinthians: "Surely he has borne our sins" in Isaiah 53:4, "He was wounded for our sins, and bruised for our iniquities" in Isaiah 53:6. Isaiah 53:6 is also paralleled in 1 Corinthians 11:23, where the text refers to the night when Jesus was "handed over."

12. Psalms 22 and 69, which refer to the suffering of the righteous, do not bring this suffering into any relationship with the sins of others.

Jesus ends his negative response to this request by disclosing that he had not come to be served but to serve and "to give his life as a ransom for many." Thus those who would be first among his disciples should follow his example of being ready to serve others and, as the context makes clear, they need to be prepared to suffer and give their lives if necessary, in which case they would appear to be participating with Jesus in the redemptive role of the Servant of the Lord, whose redemptive life and death is expounded in Isaiah.

Of course one cannot establish this connection by appealing alone to the criterion of verbal similarity between the text of Isaiah 53 and this saying of Jesus. Verbal agreement is indeed present in the reference to the redemptive act in behalf of "the many." But to establish this connection requires recognition of an additional criterion, namely, that of conceptual similarity. Nowhere else in the life and faith of Israel outside of Isaiah 53 do we find a reference to a savior figure who gives his life in a redemptive act that benefits "the many." The conceptual similarity, if not essential identity, would appear to be clear. Taken together, the conceptual similarity and the verbal agreement indicate a connection of some kind.

Galatians 1:3–4 and 2:20

It is also possible to point out that in the case of the echo of Isaiah 53 in Galatians 1:3–4, "Grace and peace from God our Father and the Lord Jesus Christ, who gave himself in behalf of our sins...," the connection with Isaiah 53 is strengthened when one recognizes the "conceptual" similarity involved. Nowhere in the life and faith of Israel outside of Isaiah 53 do we have the concept of a savior figure who *voluntarily* gives up his life in behalf of the *sins* of others. In Galatians 2:20 Paul develops this concept of a savior figure who voluntarily acts sacrificially in behalf of others by identifying this act as one motivated by ἀγάπη.[13] Paul does not explicitly state that the sacrificial act of love in which the Son of God was involved was in behalf of Paul's *sins*. But that is clearly

---

13. "The life I now live in the flesh, I live by faith in the Son of God who loved [ἀγαπήσαντός] me and gave himself over in my behalf."

understood.[14] Once again, the best conceptual origin known for this soteriological statement is Isaiah 53. The key concept of voluntarily giving up one's life "in behalf of" the other finds its most adequate scriptural antecedent in Isaiah 53. All such soteriological statements in the New Testament appear to find their ideal conceptual origin in Isaiah 53.[15]

Matthew 26:26–30||Mark 14:22–26

We turn now to another passage in Matthew which appears to echo Isaiah 53. In Matthew 26:26–30 we have an account of the institution of the Lord's Supper.

> While they were eating, Jesus after taking bread and after blessing it, broke it, and after giving it to his disciples he said: "Take, eat, this is my body." And after taking a cup and after giving thanks he gave it to them saying, "Drink of it all of you. For this is my blood of the covenant which is being poured out for many for the forgiveness of sins. I say to you that I will not drink again from the fruit of the vine until that day when I will drink it new with you in the kingdom of my Father." And after singing a hymn they went out to the Mount of Olives.

The part of this text to which our attention is drawn are the words, "for this is my blood of the covenant which is being poured out for many for the forgiveness of sins." These words appear to reflect a conscious allusion to the words in Isaiah 53 where the Servant of the Lord "pours out his life"[16] for "many" as a "place-taking" act of atonement that comports with God's forgiveness of the sins of the "many." The expression "pours out" is a clear echo of, if not a conscious allusion to, the language and concept of Isaiah 53. Jesus' blood that is being poured out for "many"[17] opens the way for the forgiveness of sins.

---

14. See Galatians 1:4. Paul understands that the love that Jesus Christ has for the sinner is grounded in God's love for the sinner. He makes this quite explicit when he writes, "God showed his love for us in that while we were yet sinners Christ died for us" (Rom. 5:8). Here again we have a text from the Apostle which is conceptually related to Isaiah 53.

15. See 1 Timothy 2:6 and Titus 2:14.

16. "Pours out his *nefesh.*" *Nefesh* resides in the blood. So as one pours out his blood he is pouring out his *nefesh,* his life.

17. Note again the reference to the "many" that we find in Matthew 20:28||Mark 10:45.

The linguistic connections between Matthew 26:28 and Isaiah 53 appear to be strong. But how are we to understand their origin? Did Jesus actually take a cup on the night he was offered up, i.e., the night he freely allowed himself to be handed over to the authorities without either fleeing into the wilderness or offering effective resistance to the arresting authorities, and did he associate his life-blood that was going to be "poured out" with the cup from which he asked his disciples to drink? If we had only the text of Matthew 26:26–30[18] we would need to contend with the possibility that this story is no more than a "cult legend," i.e., a story that grew up out of the cultic practice of the early Christian church. After all, it seems intrinsically unlikely that Jesus would go so far as to behave in the way he is pictured as behaving in this text. As unlikely as such behavior appears, however, the historical evidence indicates that (1) he did interpretively and prophetically identify his blood with the cup he held in his hands, and that (2) he did instruct his disciples to drink of it. The evidence also indicates that (3) he conveyed to his disciples by what he did and said that his death was vicarious or sacrificial, that it was being voluntarily undertaken in behalf of others. Specifically, the evidence indicates that (4) all this symbolic action was meant to be understood in relationship to "the covenant." The historian will find multiple attestation for all four of these points, even though the exact language Jesus used cannot always be so fixed.[19]

A Summary Statement

In order to appreciate the weight of the historical evidence that supports this conclusion it is necessary to step back and take a comprehensive look at the evidence we have reviewed thus far. Except for two additional quotations of Isaiah 53, one in the Gospel of Matthew[20] and another in the Gospel of Luke,[21] and references in Luke to the necessity that the

---

18. Which is partially, but not entirely supported by Mark 14:22–26. Mark omits the words, "for the forgiveness of sins."

19. The words in Matthew 26:28, "poured out for many for the forgiveness of sins," are only partially confirmed in Mark and not at all in 1 Corinthians. In 1 Corinthians the reference is to the "new covenant."

20. Matthew 8:17 quoting Isaiah 53:4.

21. Luke 22:37 quoting Isaiah 53:12.

Christ must *suffer*[22] and possibly the reference to the expectation that Jesus would *redeem* Israel (Luke 24:21), we have surveyed all of the most frequently mentioned passages in the New Testament that bear on the topic of Isaiah 53 and Christian faith. This survey indicates that the interest in Isaiah 53 that clearly appears in *1 Clement* and Justin Martyr was already present in some of the books of the New Testament.[23] These books include the Gospels of Matthew, Mark, and Luke, the Acts of the Apostles, Paul's letters to the Romans, 1 Corinthians, Galatians, Philippians, and the pastoral epistles 1 Timothy and Titus, as well as 1 Peter and Hebrews. This evidence indicates that there is an Isaianic soteriology deeply embedded in the New Testament which finds its normative form and substance in Isaiah 53.

Jesus and the Problem of Christian Origins

Before we consider more evidence of the normative role of Isaiah 53 in the birth and development of Christian faith, it is important to address the question of Jesus and Christian origins. To what extent did Isaiah 53 become increasingly important to the early church as it sought to make sense out of the tragic death of Jesus, and as it sought to defend its faith in Jesus as the Messiah against the charges that the crucifixion of Jesus placed him under the curse of Deuteronomy (21:22–23) and thus disqualified him for a messianic role in the life and faith of God's people? And to what extent was Isaiah 53 normative for Jesus' own understanding of God's purposes for his people, and therefore for himself and for his disciples? At stake for Christian faith is the nature of Jesus' freely pouring out his life for God's people as an atoning sacrifice that comports or is congruent with the forgiveness of their sins, and thus their restoration as God's redeemed and faithful children. This would in turn govern what is normative for the life and faith of every member of the Body of Christ.

For a traditional theology or for any neo-orthodox version of Christianity which can bypass or relativize this kind of historical question by a confused appeal to the solution that it is the risen Christ, rather than Jesus of Nazareth, who is normative for Christian faith, this question of

---

22. E.g., Luke 24:26, 46.
23. Though these writings had not at that time been formed into a New Testament canon.

Christian origins will be of no great concern. But for those who respect the discipline of the history of Christian doctrine, this question is of crucial importance. Put in doctrinal terms, does the atoning effect of Jesus' sacrifice require that he freely accepted this death? Or can this requirement be sacrificed? Can it be theologically finessed in some way? For example, can it be argued that the church can survive with a Christology in which Jesus is believed to have been dragged to his death against his will? Must we believe, as the church teaches us in the Eucharist, that the cruel and painful death Jesus experienced at the hands of the authorities was "a death that he freely accepted"?

How can contemporary theologians of the church responsibly proceed in this matter? It matters whether Christians can give reasons for the faith that is in them. How theologians of the church answer the question of Christian origins is decisive for anyone who believes that Christian theology coheres with truth responsibly established. This is particularly the case with regard to truth concerning Christian origins.

Under these circumstances we ask: Where do we find the most promising point to begin our inquiry concerning Christian origins? First we acknowledge that, while this is a question fraught with theological significance, it is strictly speaking a matter that must be settled on historical grounds. Paul himself makes historical claims and draws upon his own experience as well as scripture in his effort to effectuate theological norms for his churches. The recognized rules of evidence that apply in settling the probabilities as to the historical origins of any institution or movement apply in our case as well.

We begin with the question of the trustworthiness of the evidence as we have it. Many would like to begin with the two relevant sayings of Jesus preserved in the Gospels of Matthew and Mark. But how has the evidence concerning the two Gospel sayings mentioned above come to us? The verbatim agreement between the parallel texts is exceedingly high. So high, indeed, that copying of some kind is indicated in both cases. Thus we appear not to have two independent witnesses to either of these sayings.

As for the Gospel of Mark, the church has always taught that the author of the Second Gospel was not a disciple of Jesus. The church has always referred to him as an "apostolic man," one who was close to one or more of the twelve (Peter in particular) who had known Jesus on a firsthand basis, but who himself was not a disciple of Jesus and presumably not an eyewitness of what Jesus did or taught. As for the Gospel of Matthew, traditionally, until the eighteenth century, this Gospel was believed to have come from the hand of the Apostle Matthew, and thus from a close eyewitness to what Jesus did and said during his ministry. In this case we could receive in relative confidence these two sayings of Jesus as evidence ultimately going back to the eyewitness testimony of the Apostle Matthew. However, the way Gospel studies have developed during the past two hundred years makes this approach to our problem difficult. There is no consensus among New Testament historians today as to the authorship of either Matthew or Mark. To claim authenticity for either of these sayings on the basis of the eyewitness testimony of either evangelist would be difficult if not impossible to sustain in any open discussion of the question by any responsible group of historians. This does not mean that historians could not agree that these two sayings are probably authentic. It only means that the historical argumentation would need to proceed from some other basis than confidence that historians know beyond a reasonable doubt the identity of the authors of these two Gospels, and that either of them was in a position to give evidence as to what Jesus did or said on the basis of eyewitness testimony.

Should it be said, therefore, that the historian is at a total loss in finding any evidence concerning Jesus that rests on eyewitness testimony? No, this is not the case. While confidence in the traditional attribution concerning authorship of New Testament books has eroded almost across the board, there is one major exception to this rule. There is one traditional attribution of authorship which after two hundred years of relentless historical inquiry remains intact. The Apostle Paul stands out among all the historical figures to whom the authorship of New Testament books has been attributed as almost certainly the author of a minimal set of New Testament writings. This includes Romans, 1 and 2 Corinthians, Galatians, and Philemon. He probably is the author of an additional one or more of the books traditionally attributed to him. Philippians would fall into this category. Thus, of the books we have cited as containing passages important for understanding the role of Isaiah 53 for Christian faith, four were probably written by an author who can be identified. These four books are Romans, 1 Corinthians, Galatians, and Philippians.

All of these books contain important autobiographical information concerning Paul. One in particular, Galatians, preserves an extended autobiographical account which reveals important data concerning Paul's relationships with those who were apostles before him, in particular Peter and John (Gal. 1:1–2:21). The Acts of the Apostles provides important information about Paul and confirms that he indeed did meet certain of those who were apostles before him, including Peter and John. But do any of Paul's authentic letters preserve tradition concerning Jesus which would throw light on the particular question of Christian origins with which we are concerned in these reflections? The answer is yes. And would Paul have had opportunity to discuss this tradition with some of those who were apostles before him, including Peter and John? Again the answer is yes. And would either Peter or John have been in a position to give eyewitness testimony as to the reliability of this Jesus tradition? Again the answer is yes. Both Peter and John are presumed to have been eyewitnesses to the tradition in question. In which authentic letter of Paul is this tradition to be found? It is to be found in Paul's first letter to the Corinthians.

1 Corinthians 11:23–26

In the eleventh chapter of his first letter to the Corinthians, vv. 23–26, Paul gives an account of the institution of the Lord's Supper which parallels in significant respects the account given in Matthew and Mark, though the differences between the two accounts suggest that they are quite independent of one another, or at least that they have had separate histories of transmission.

Paul writes:

> For I received from the Lord [i.e., as originating from Jesus] what I also handed on to you, that the Lord Jesus in the night in which he was handed over took bread and after giving thanks he broke it and said: "This is my body which [is given up] in behalf of you. Do this in memory of me." Likewise, after supper he also [took the cup], saying: "This is the cup of the New Covenant in my blood. Do this whenever [or as often as] you drink [it], in memory of me."

There follows a rubric to the effect that as often as the disciples of Jesus eat this bread and drink this cup they give witness to his death until he returns. There is a question whether this rubric originated with something that Jesus said about continuing to observe this ceremonial meal until his return after his forthcoming death, or whether it was added in the cultic development of the tradition. But otherwise, the tradition that Paul says that he had received is remarkably congruent with the essential features of the nearly identical accounts preserved in the Gospels of Matthew and Mark. Both the account in 1 Corinthians and the account in Matthew and Mark represent Jesus, on the same occasion, as taking bread and after breaking it identifying it with his body. This is followed by Jesus taking the cup and identifying it with his blood. In both cases Jesus' blood is associated with the covenant (διαθήκη). In Paul's account this covenant is explicitly identified as the "New Covenant."

It seems likely that if Jesus referred only to "the covenant," as in Matthew and Mark, rather than to the "New Covenant" as in 1 Corinthians, this more restricted expression would nonetheless have been used in the light of what Jeremiah had written about that covenant which God in the latter days was going to write upon people's hearts, a covenant which was going to bring God to his people and his people unto him so that both the house of Israel and the house of Judah would become God's people. This covenant would create a new people of God who would not say "you should know the Lord." For these people of God would all know the Lord because he would forgive them their iniquity and their sins he would remember no more (Jer. 31:33–34).

This reference to a New Covenant which would be based on the forgiveness of sins is coherent with the forgiveness of sins that comports with the Servant's pouring out his soul unto death in behalf of the many in Isaiah 53. However, there is no reference to sacrifice, let alone blood, in Jeremiah's New Covenant. It follows that someone has seen Jeremiah's New Covenant in relationship to the atoning death of the Servant of the Lord in Isaiah 53, and has recognized the essential role of the suffering Servant of Isaiah in effectuating the covenant that God had promised to write upon his people's hearts. If Jesus saw this, as I think probable, we may have identified a cardinal point for a credible answer to the question of Christian origins. For in this case Jesus himself would stand at the originating point of Christian life, and Isaiah 53 would be significantly constitutive of what was scripturally normative for Jesus.[24]

Paul's Fifteen-Day Visit with Peter in Jerusalem

Paul presumably received the tradition that he passed on to the church in Corinth from the church which he had once persecuted. He himself has written concerning what the churches of Christ in Judea knew about him at the time he spent fifteen days with Peter in Jerusalem only three years, or a little more, following his conversion. What these churches knew about Paul at that time was based upon reports that they had received, namely, "He who formerly persecuted the church, now proclaims the faith that he once ravished" (Gal. 1:18–22). As a sign that these churches received this news with approval, Paul adds: "And they glorified God because of me" (Gal. 1:22–24).

Paul had the opportunity to inquire from Peter, prior to undertaking his missionary work in Asia Minor and Achaia, about the tradition he was later to pass on to the Corinthians concerning what Jesus did and said at supper on the night that he was handed over. Assuming Peter was present that night, the historian can regard the tradition that Paul has passed on in this instance as going back to the eyewitness testimony of apostles before him. This tradition was passed on to Paul within the first decade of the life of the church. We may presume that the Greek form of the tradition passed on by Paul was authorized under the supervision of earlier apostles, including those like Peter and John who were eyewitnesses of the event and responsible for the original formulation of the text in Hebrew or Aramaic. We may presume this, even if, as seems unlikely, Paul did not himself review the matter of its trustworthiness with Peter or other earlier apostles.

We must bear in mind that the commonly spoken language of Jesus and his disciples was not Greek. Yet this was the language used by Paul in handing on to his Greek-speaking churches the tradition that he received. The tradition Paul received concerning the Lord's Supper was

---

24. This does not exclude the possibility that Jesus also had Exodus 24:4–8 in mind when he identified his blood with the "covenant." But the text does not seem to me to require this conclusion.

probably originally formulated orally in Aramaic or Hebrew. In any case, what Jesus actually did or said that night would have been observed and heard by disciples whose first language was not Greek. It is always necessary when rendering the account of an important matter from one language to another to be sure that the true meaning of the original account is conveyed in the new account. This concern gave Paul a practical reason for valuing the opportunity to talk directly with Peter. Had there been any reason to question the reliability of the traditions he was passing on to his churches concerning what happened on that night and on other significant occasions, we can be morally certain that Paul would have discussed these with those who had direct knowledge of them.[25]

Such considerations help remove reasonable doubt in the mind of the historian as to whether Jesus did speak and behave as represented in the account of the Lord's Supper preserved in Matthew. At the points that create the greatest doubt for historians, that Jesus would have identified his body with the bread to be eaten, or his blood with the cup to be drunk, the account in 1 Corinthians accords with and confirms the account given in Matthew and Mark. The historian thus has little alternative but to acknowledge what the evidence appears to indicate: Jesus seems to have behaved and spoken in a most remarkable way and in a most definitive manner on this occasion.

The very early evidence passed on to Paul by the church he had been persecuting and which was implicitly validated by Paul's fifteen-day visit with Peter, suggests that the basic account of the institution of the Lord's Supper in the Gospel of Matthew was probably not formulated as a cult legend as has been proposed.[26] It appears more likely that Jesus behaved and spoke as remembered on the night he was handed over. We prob-

---

25. In this regard it is important to know that the usual translation of ἱστορῆσαι as "to visit," in the phrase "to visit Peter," is inadequate to Paul's intended meaning, i.e., "to visit for the purpose of making inquiry." The ἵστωρ in ancient Greece was the one who interrogated witnesses. See "Peter and Paul and the Tradition Concerning 'The Lord's Supper' in 1 Cor 11:23–26" in *One Loaf, One Cup: Ecumenical Studies of 1 Cor 11 and Other Eucharistic Texts*, The Cambridge Conference on the Eucharist, August 1988, edited with an introduction by Ben F. Meyer (Macon, Ga.: Mercer University Press, 1993), 38–43.

26. E.g., by Rudolf Bultmann, *History of the Synoptic Tradition*, trans. John Marsh (Oxford: Basil Blackwell, 1963), from *Die Geschichte der synoptischen Tradition*, 3d ed. (Göttingen: Vandenhoeck & Ruprecht, 1958). Bultmann makes no reference to the Eucharistic texts in Paul's letters. A post-Bultmannian shift in the direction of beginning such study with Paul's letters, the methodology followed in these reflections, may be seen clearly in *One Loaf, One Cup.*

ably shall never be able to reconstruct the exact words Jesus used on that occasion; subsequent memories would have reflected the mind-set of those relating the story. What is consistent in the accounts preserved in 1 Corinthians and in the Gospels of Matthew and Mark reflect the stabilizing effect of Jesus' memorable actions. That he took bread and broke it and gave it to his disciples would be memorable. Whether he "blessed" it or "gave thanks" over it could be expected to vary in the telling. That he took the cup and identified it with his blood while making reference to the covenant is also memorable. But exactly when he did this could have varied with the telling. As it is we have two extremely valuable accounts of the institution of the Lord's Supper, each supporting the other at the most telling points. When taken together, not with the purpose of emphasizing the discrepancies, and thus increasing doubt concerning the reliability of the tradition, but with the purpose of seeking to penetrate to the meaning of the event, we find the two accounts mutually supportive, each supplementing and complementing the other. It is especially noteworthy that both accounts recognize Jesus' sacrificial death as having been made in behalf of others, whether in connection with the breaking of his body (1 Cor. 11:24) or the pouring out of his blood.[27] Looking at the two accounts in this way we can understand why the church has observed the command of Jesus that the faithful repeat his action in remembrance of his sacrificial death on behalf of sinners. There is no more central act in the life of the church, and it is Isaiah 53 which grounds this action in Israel's faith in God's redeeming love for the sinner.

The Absence of the Expression "Poured Out for Many" in 1 Corinthians 11:25

We come now to a consideration of the fact that the important words attributed to Jesus in Matthew 26:28||Mark 14:24, "poured out for many," do not occur in the account of the Lord's Supper in 1 Corinthians 11:25. If the text of the tradition Paul was handing on to the Corinthians read, "This cup is the new covenant in my blood *poured out for many*," the task

---

27. Matthew 26:28||Mark 14:24.

of the historian would be less difficult. For then it would be possible to appeal to the criterion of multiple attestation. If these words, so reminiscent of Isaiah 53, appeared in 1 Corinthians 11:25, as well as in the text of Matthew 26:28||Mark 14:24, the historian could point to this as sufficient evidence that Jesus spoke these words. How else would one explain their presence in two accounts which appear to have had separate histories of transmission? The absence of these words in the tradition being passed on by Paul provides reasonable doubt that they were used by Jesus. Because of this reasonable doubt I have been led to develop the comprehensive argument laid out in these reflections.

This reasonable doubt can be especially acute for the historian who thinks in terms of a doctrinal development based on the priority of Mark. For in this case one would note (1) that there is no linguistic evidence linking our earliest text concerning the Lord's Supper, in 1 Corinthians 11:23–26, to Isaiah 53; (2) that only a text later preserved in Mark contains the words "poured out for many" from Isaiah 53; and (3) that it is only in the text preserved in the still-later Gospel of Matthew that the additional words "for the remission of sins" come into the doctrinal history of the Christian church.

This example illustrates how the theory of Markan priority can lead the historian to conclusions that call into question cardinal doctrines of Christian faith. No doctrine is more central to Christian faith than the teaching that "Christ died for our sins." Some exegetes appear to have little idea how their work affects Christian doctrine. Perhaps they think of Christian doctrine as having come into being largely through church councils later in the history of the church. The truth is that Christian doctrine begins with biblical texts and with the earliest interpretations of those texts, which we find in the New Testament itself. To think that whether or not Mark is our earliest Gospel is a question of little or no doctrinal consequence is naive.[28]

---

28. Rigorous scientific reliance upon Markan priority will in the long run certainly serve to undermine confidence in the church, if it is allowed to work its way into the minds and hearts of the faithful. We see this in the work of the "Jesus Seminar." The good intentions of these scholars notwithstanding, the effect of their historical conclusions leads to skepticism, not faith. It is a mistake to attack these scholars as incompetent. It is admissible, however, to call attention to the ways in which their questionable research paradigm is leading them to conclusions that call into question basic doctrines of the church.

The Question of the Full Range of the Role of
Isaiah 53 in Christian Faith

We turn now to the larger question of the full range of the role of Isaiah 53 in Christian faith. Thus far we have focused on the single feature of the redemptive role of the sacrificial death of the Servant. In fact, this aspect is only one part of the story of the Servant with relevance for Christian faith. Taken by itself it tends to be a contentious thorn in the flesh of that ecumenical community of exegetes seeking to understand what provides norms for Christian faith and enables a repentant church to engage in renewal and self-correction.

The full story of the Servant which has shaped Christian faith from the beginning includes his birth and development, his suffering ministry as preparatory for his redemptive death, his burial, and finally his vindication and exaltation. This vindication and exaltation we take to be essential to the Christian doctrine of the resurrection. When Jesus reflected on the meaning of the resurrection for himself and for the life and faith of God's people, did he think in terms of a certain kind of story found at the close of the Gospels of Luke and John (Luke 24:36–43; John 20:26–29), or did he think in terms of the vindication and exaltation of the righteous as set forth in Isaiah and reflected in Paul and Matthew?[29] To ask the question is to answer it. So, what does this approach mean? It strongly suggests that Isaiah 53 is important not only for understanding the soteriology of Christian faith, but also for understanding its eschatology. But if Isaiah 53 is important not only for understanding the cross but also the resurrection of Christ, then Isaiah 53 is basic for understanding the essence of Christian faith. At the same time, the fuller gospel accounts found in Matthew and Luke, including the birth and development of the Servant-Messiah, his suffering, death, burial, and resurrection, all summarized in the creedal statements about the second person of the Trinity, find their normative scriptural prefigurement in the Book of Isaiah, and primarily in Isaiah 53. No doubt the early church continued to make use of Isaiah 53 in interpreting Christian faith. But what was the role of Jesus in this matter? Was he likely to have been disinterested in this text as far as his understanding of

---

29. 1 Corinthians 15:1–58; Philippians 2:1–12; Matthew 28:1–10, 16–20.

God's will for himself and for Israel was concerned, or did he recognize, perhaps more fully than anyone else, the importance of Isaiah 53 for an understanding of true faith in the God of the covenant? Did he see the redemptive death of the suffering Servant of the Lord as an atoning path Israel would have to travel in order to become a light unto the nations and to lead them to salvation?

According to the Scriptures

The word κατά followed by a noun in the accusative case is frequently used in Greek to introduce the norm which governs something. In this case the statement that "Christ has died for our sins" is said to be in accord with some norm. What is that norm? Where in the scriptures is one man's death represented as a life given up for the sins of others? Only in Isaiah 53. This text, long before the time of Jesus, had been accepted as scripture in Israel, where it could function as a norm for the life of the faithful. We can tell from Paul's letters that this is how Isaiah 53 functioned for the Apostle's life. We know that Isaiah 53 functioned this way in the life of Dr. Martin Luther King, Jr. And it certainly functioned this way in the life of Archbishop Oscar Romero. For all these Christians, Isaiah 53 had a pre-history in the life of the church.

At what point in the life of the Body of Christ did Isaiah 53 begin to function as a norm? We can see the text beginning to function this way no later than on the night that Jesus was handed over, with the intentional act of Jesus in taking the cup and saying to his disciples: "This is my blood of the New Covenant. Do this in remembrance of me." What was Jesus expecting his disciples to do? Was he not asking his disciples to identify themselves in a most profound manner with his decision to offer up his life as a ransom for many? What is the alternative? Where else can we go, but to Isaiah 53, in order to make sense of what Jesus did that night?

Isaiah 53 and the Rule of Faith

"Rule" (κανών) in this context is only another word for "norm." The rule of faith was normative for the church fathers before the New Testament canon was fixed by church councils. My conjectural conviction is that the rule of faith began with Jesus' reading of "the Law and the Prophets" and his resolve to live and die in accordance with that reading. When Clement of Alexandria defined the rule of faith for the church as "the concord and harmony of the Law and the Prophets with the covenant delivered at the coming of the Lord,"[30] he no doubt had in mind Isaiah 53 and Paul's statement reporting the tradition he had received that (1) "Christ died for our sins according to the scriptures, and (2) he was buried, and (3) on the third day was resurrected according to the scriptures" (1 Cor. 15:1–4). Here, better than at any other point in the history of the church, we are put in touch with what is meant when we speak of the rule of faith. The harmony and concord of the Law and the Prophets with the covenant brought into effect by Jesus Christ comes to expression nowhere more clearly than in the concord and harmony between the story of the Servant in Isaiah 53 and the pre-Pauline tradition concerning Jesus, passed on to the church in Corinth. This harmony and concord is spelled out more fully in the Gospel accounts, where it is specified that prior to his death, burial, and resurrection, Jesus *suffered* under Pontius Pilate. Those "gospel" accounts which neglected or obviated one or more of these essential correspondences between the story of the Servant and the story of Jesus, (1) suffering, (2) death, (3) burial, and (4) resurrection, were never fully accepted by the church. Gospels which raised questions as to whether Jesus really suffered,[31] or neglected his death and resurrection,[32] were not received as canonical.

Paul's Canon as Based on Isaiah 53

But, one may ask, can this concern for a canon (i.e., rule) of faith, affirmed by Irenaeus, Tertullian, Clement of Alexandria, and Origen, be traced back to the New Testament itself? Is there evidence that any of the apostles had a concern for appealing to a norm for the faith of the church? The answer is yes. We find this concern as early as Paul. Near

---

30. *Stromata* VI.15.125.3.
31. I.e., in the *Gospel of Peter* Jesus felt no pain as he hung on the cross.
32. The *Gospel of Thomas*, et al.

the end of his letter to the Galatians,[33] Paul summarizes the case he has been making against those who are perverting the gospel of Christ by preaching a different gospel, which is not really a gospel at all (Gal. 1:6–9). Paul writes:

> It is those who want to make a good showing in the flesh that would compel you to be circumcised, and only in order that they may not be persecuted for the cross of Christ.... But far be it from me to glory except in the cross of our Lord Jesus Christ, by which the world has been crucified to me, and I to the world. For neither circumcision counts for anything, nor uncircumcision, but a new creation. And whoever walks by this canon (κανών)...[34]

The previous referent for "this" in the phrase "walks by *this* canon"[35] is "the cross of our Lord Jesus Christ" in v. 14. "The cross of our Lord Jesus Christ" is what is most normative for the Apostle Paul. It is the only thing about which he is willing to boast. "The cross of our Lord Jesus Christ" stands for "Christ's sacrificial death for our sins" mentioned in Galatians 1:4. The Lord "gave himself for our sins." Paul placed this programmatic statement at the very beginning of his letter and makes it basic to his whole case. This is made clear in the conclusion of his famous address to Peter: "I have been crucified with Christ; it is no longer I who live, but Christ who lives in me; and the life I now live in the flesh I live by faith in the Son of God, who loved me *and gave himself for me*" (Gal. 2:20). Paul's whole case against those perverting the gospel presupposes and is based upon Isaiah 53:10–12.

Conclusions

From the standpoint of these reflections, the essential canonical-doctrinal development appears to have come in four successive stages, beginning with (1) Jesus' reading of the Book of Isaiah as an important part of the "Law and the Prophets"; leading (2) to Jesus' transmission of this reading

---

33. Galatians 6:11–15. For a developed discussion of the relationship of this text to that of the *regula* see "Galatians and the Second Century Development of the *Regula Fidei*," *The Second Century: A Journal of Early Christian Studies* 4, no. 3 (Fall 1984): 143–70.

34. Galatians 6:12–16.

35. Or "rule" or "norm."

to his disciples through his teaching and by its enfleshment in his own life, death, and resurrection; followed (3) by his disciples' postresurrection transmission of this scriptural norm to Paul; culminating (4) in Paul's own apostolic defense of this norm against those who were seeking to pervert it and against those pillars of the church who were not walking in a straightforward manner with reference to its truth.

16

The Servant and Jesus

The Relevance of the Colloquy
for the Current Quest for Jesus

N. T. WRIGHT

Introduction

I am enormously grateful for the chance to take part in this colloquy. I have caught up with some old friends and made some new ones. I have greatly enjoyed listening, in particular, to scholars in a field that fascinates me but that I don't normally have time to attend to, namely, the study of Isaiah in its original setting(s). But I am particularly grateful because my own work has brought me back again in recent weeks, for the ninety-ninth time, to the great question of Jesus' attitude to his own death; and I suspect that, in the providence of God, I am here to learn and think, first and foremost, rather than to teach or admonish.

I am in fact in a strange position in terms of my personal history of interaction with issues of this seminar. I read Morna Hooker's book *Jesus and the Servant* before I read anything of Jeremias; from the beginning of my theological research, the question she so sharply raised has been with me as part of my own mental furniture, challenging the sloppy thinking that so often characterized the would-be biblical background in which I grew up. Morna's own view of the book's reception is, I know, rather less optimistic; all I can say is that when I began reading theology at Wycliffe Hall, Oxford, in 1971 her work was regarded as the thing with which one had to come to terms. Some would have said, no doubt, that we all knew it was wrong but we couldn't quite say why. All I know is that when I came to do my final examinations in June 1973, and discovered that

Dr. M. D. Hooker was to be one of the examiners, I resolved that, unless I were really stuck for a question to answer, there was one topic that I would be wiser to steer away from. (I have to say, however, that my Old Testament examiners gave me a treat: the first question I answered in the first exam was a discussion of the sentence, "The Servant Songs can only be understood in the light of Second Isaiah as a whole." What a gift.)

At the same time (though this has been a subtext of this colloquy, rather than an explicit theme for discussion), it may be of interest that I read Bill Farmer's book on *The Synoptic Problem* before I read B. H. Streeter's massive book *The Four Gospels,* and was thus inoculated in advance against swallowing its conclusions whole. As a result, I have never completely caught the disease called Q, though from time to time I have experienced that shivery feeling, and the concomitant double vision, that those who have a chronic case of the Q disease reveal as their normal state. I have experienced, though, an interesting phenomenon: my inability to make up my mind on the synoptic problem has not, I think, in any way impaired my ability to read Matthew, Mark, and Luke *as* Matthew, Mark, and Luke, nor indeed my ability — though some would no doubt question this — to think and write about this historical Jesus. But more of this anon.

Our discussion in these three days has, of course, ranged much wider than the question of Jesus; and to that extent my official subject for this article is somewhat narrower than any attempt to draw together the threads of the colloquy as a whole. Nevertheless, as we have looked at wider questions — notably those of Pauline theology and echoes of scripture, and those in particular of the original meaning of Isaiah itself — we have been looking at issues which do in fact relate quite closely to the question of Jesus. Studying Paul, despite what you might think from some recent work, is in fact closely related to studying Jesus. Paul, after all, is our earliest Christian writing, and to ignore him in favor of other purely hypothetical sources is sheer folly. The original meaning of Isaiah, and its re-use in subsequent Old Testament writing such as Zechariah, does tell us something about the range of available options for subsequent readers; though it is clear to me that if there is a lacuna in this conference it is at the point of discussing how Isaiah might have been read by Jesus' own contemporaries. This is not at all to deny that Jesus and his first followers were great innovators; we cannot study Jesus simply as the product of blind *religionsgeschichtlich* forces and influences. It is simply to say that if we are to understand Richard Hays's criterion of "availability" there is a lot more to be said than merely discussing what Isaiah 53 meant four hundred years earlier, fascinating and important though that is.

Studying Jesus Today: Introduction

The current state of play in the study of Jesus is notoriously difficult to describe. The roll call of recent writers in the United States alone shows the range of different options available: from Sanders to Borg, from Charlesworth to Crossan, from Meier to Mack, from Johnson to the Jesus Seminar. My own reading of this confused state of play is that we have reached again, by a circuitous route, the question that was posed by Schweitzer a century ago, as being reflected in the clash between his own work and that of William Wrede. Skepticism faces eschatology. Either you say, with Wrede and the Jesus Seminar, that Jesus was a teacher of timeless truths, into whose pure early teaching his first followers injected a quite unwarranted note of eschatology, resulting in Mark and his successors being theologically motivated fictions. Or you say, with Schweitzer and Sanders, that Jesus does indeed belong with the Jewish eschatology of his day; and that, though of course the evangelists have their own reasons for arranging things the way they have, and though of course the tradition has been shaped by the interests of the early church, the Gospels' portrait of Jesus as the eschatological prophet of the Kingdom of God is substantially on target.

This is a gross oversimplification, of course, and there are numerous important variations on either side. I said to Dominic Crossan last year that we needed to revise Norman Perrin's dictum of thirty years ago, that the *Wredestrasse* had become the *Hauptstrasse;* and he replied that it wasn't a *Strasse* any longer, but an autobahn, with lots of intersections and a good deal of traffic going in various directions. I agree; but I think, in fact, that there has been so much heavy traffic on the *Wredebahn* in recent years that it is time to rebuild properly the old *Schweitzerbahn,* which always offered a quicker route and a better view. But, again, more of this anon.

On both routes, however, there is a railway crossing that cannot be

avoided. Did Jesus believe that he would die a violent death, and, if so, did he give that death any meaning, not least in relation to the aims which had governed his life and work up to that point? Schweitzer, of course, said that Jesus did come to believe it was part of the divine plan that he should die violently, and offered as a hypothesis a way of construing that belief which fitted Jesus closely to what Schweitzer had reconstructed as a first-century eschatological worldview. Wrede and his followers, of course, deny all this. Within the current state of scholarship there is, as on everything else, a wide range of opinion.

What I shall do, therefore, in order to be as faithful as I can to the brief I was given, is to set up some Jesus-questions as they appear to me in current study, with an eye to our present debate; and then to ask what contribution our own discussions might have to make to them. And I begin with some important questions of method.

Studying Jesus: Method

To begin with, we must beware of false antitheses. It really does not help to play off history against theology, as though history could be done without presuppositions and without an overarching worldview, or as though Christian theology had only a loose connection with history. Nor does it help to play off the Jesus Seminar against other writings as though the Seminar represents history, or scholarship, and the other writings theology, or orthodoxy. Life just ain't that simple. Nor will it do to invoke giants of the past either as heroes or as villains, such that to label something Bultmannian becomes a way of condemning it before we start, or such that to link something with the Reformation becomes a way of endorsing it before we start.

Rather, we must embrace wholeheartedly the historical task as a matter of hypothesis and verification. Methodological skepticism, as practiced by Wrede, the Jesus Seminar, and thousands in between, is not the same thing as serious historiography. Serious historiography proceeds by the disciplined and controlled use of historical imagination, the reconstrual of a world other than our own, and the testing of that, as a hypothesis, by a fresh and further reading of all the evidence. It does not proceed by examining little bits of evidence piecemeal and forcing them, one by one, to justify their existence. That is in fact a combination of positivism and phenomenalism, two somewhat discredited epistemologies. The positivist insists that we need proof, copper-bottomed, cast-iron proof for every-thing: we only know what we can prove. The phenomenalist insists that seeing things tells you about your own eyes and sense-data, not about the things you are seeing; historically applied, this means that Mark's account of something tells us about Mark, not about the event. In combination, the positivist insists that we must have proof, and the phenomenalist in-sists that it isn't available. Nobody would conduct their real life like that for half a day; yet this pseudoscientific combination has been power-ful enough to make whole generations of scholars and students think things about Jesus and the Gospels that no serious, hard-nosed historian of other subjects and periods would allow for a moment. John Roberts, one of the best-known English historians at the moment, says in his monumental history of the world that historians of other peoples and periods are often happy to make do with far more fragmentary and puz-zling texts than the Gospels, and that the serious historian has no need to be unduly skeptical of them.

We may note one spin-off of this problem. Gospel scholars often operate a heads-I-win-tails-you-lose policy with regard to biblical quo-tations in the Gospels. If Jesus is not portrayed as referring to a biblical idea or theme, well, that proves he wasn't interested in it, perhaps that he didn't even know it. If he is portrayed as referring to a biblical idea or theme, well, that only proves that Mark or Matthew, or whoever, wanted to saddle Jesus with it. If there is a reference to prophecy, that is the cunning work of later historicizers; if there isn't, that proves that Jesus was a nonprophetic sage. Frankly, if life was like that, all gamblers would be millionaires.

In particular, history cannot be reduced to the history of ideas. We have done so much of our scholarship under the shadow of the Enlight-enment that we have reduced historiography to the tracing of lines of ideas, of who *thought* what, who *was influenced by* what, who *read* which texts in what way. That is, of course, very important, but it is only part of the whole. By itself, it reduces human beings to brains attached to eyes, tongues, and hands that hold pens. Human beings, in fact, live in a much richer world than that: a world where what is done not only matters as much but often speaks more powerfully than what is said or thought; a world where the symbolic ordering of life carries meanings that may be hard to articulate, for those involved and for the historian, but are nonetheless vital and nonnegotiable as part of the whole package. We live in a world in which stories are far more powerful than abstract thought, creating worlds and subverting them, changing the course of lives and communities. This is the real world that historians ought to study. Until we lift our eyes beyond the horizons of questions and answers and examine praxis, symbol, and story we will be condemned, if I may borrow the language of American cultural symbols, praxis, and story, never to get beyond first base.

Within historiography in general, and the study of Jesus as one example of it, it is also important to insist that we can in principle study human intentionality. Of course, there is often not much material available, and we thus often have to admit defeat. But serious historians have never confined themselves to asking "what happened"; they also regularly ask "why did so-and-so, or such-and-such a community, behave in the way they did?" Human motivation, including that vital but elusive category, human awareness of vocation, is a proper subject of historical study. This is not a matter of psychology. We can say, beyond reasonable historical doubt, that Saul of Tarsus, later known as Paul, believed he had a vocation from the God of Abraham, Isaac, and Jacob to announce to the pagan world that this God was now offering salvation to the whole world in and through Jesus Christ; in other words, we know as historians that Paul believed he was called to be the apostle to the Gentiles. We know, likewise, that John the Baptist believed he was called by this same God to prepare people for the great coming day in which this God would act to judge and save his people. If we can say that sort of thing about the two figures who stand closest to Jesus on either side, what is to stop us in principle from asking the question: what did Jesus think he was supposed to be doing? What was motivating him? We who think we don't live out of a metanarrative — though that merely reveals our own self-induced blindness — may find it odd to think of somebody, not obviously megalomaniac, seriously pondering the unique role that he or she might be called upon to play. In our world, people talk like that when they are founding a new cult, or perhaps a new seminar. First-century Jews would not have found it odd at all.

One final note about method. Here I am between Scylla and Charybdis. If I talk about source criticism, I risk offending Morna Hooker, who is convinced it isn't relevant to the issue of Jesus and Isaiah; if I fail to mention it, I risk offending Bill Farmer, who is convinced that it is. I fear I shall end up being smashed by the rock and drowned by the whirlpool, because I do want to say something about it, but not exactly what Bill would like to hear. I understand that if we use the Two Source Hypothesis the apparent references to Isaiah in the Gospels may seem as though they are endangered; Q does not encourage us to think that Isaiah was important for Jesus. If, however, we use the Two Gospel Hypothesis, we appear to get Isaiah thrown into more prominence. I have to say that I think this is more of a chicken-and-egg question than synoptic puzzlers usually admit. There is no such thing as a neutral, objective source theory. Streeter and his forbears advocated Mark and Q not least in order to shore up a somewhat truncated orthodoxy against the ravages of D. F. Strauss and the rest. The current Q school, at least in America, has a very different agenda: to subvert orthodoxy by playing off an isolated Q against Mark and the others — though this can only be done, as we see taken to absurd lengths in Koester and Mack, by arbitrary and fanciful subdividing of Q into layers and strata. In fact, as even the Jesus Seminar and Crossan bear tacit witness, and as the whole of what I have called the Third Quest takes for granted, source theories are not in fact the way to do historical-Jesus research. They are a fascinating and vital part of the study of the early church, which is of course integrated with historical-Jesus research in all sorts of ways. But they do not offer us a high road back to Jesus. Life, again, just ain't that simple. You cannot first work out the synoptic puzzle and then assume that the earliest sources give the most direst access to Jesus. That's not how history works; nor is it how those I regard as the most serious recent writers on Jesus actually operate. And now, as Herodotus would say, so much for source criticism; and so much, too, for method.

Studying Jesus: The Basic Persona

Well, what then about Jesus? The question that is currently posed as between those on the *Wredebahn* and those on the *Schweitzerbahn* has to do with the basic persona of Jesus: was he a sage, a teacher of wisdom, a cynic wordsmith, or was he a prophet, the announcer of the long-awaited Kingdom of God? Does Jesus stand in the wisdom tradition or the apocalyptic tradition? Is Jesus the teacher of an atomized and ahistorical wisdom, or is he conscious of being part of the great ongoing Jewish story and drama? Here I have to say that the dominant voices in the Jesus Seminar have skewed the issue radically. They have insisted that apocalyptic is of necessity bombastic, dark, and threatening, a bullying and dualistic worldview — which happens to have been held by Jesus' Jewish contemporaries, by John the Baptist, by Paul, by all the early church except the noble Q people and the Thomas Christians, but not by Jesus himself. (That's a great piece of nineteenth-century liberalism, isn't it?) They have rescued Jesus from apocalyptic by rescuing him, more or less lock, stock, and barrel, from Judaism itself. In particular, they have insisted, astonishingly, that Jesus did not make use of the Hebrew scriptures in his teaching. From this point of view, the question of Jesus and Isaiah is stillborn; Paul, once more, is the inventor of Christianity. This is sometimes reinforced, as in Crossan, by the suggestion that Jesus may not even have known or used the Hebrew scriptures at all; that he was either illiterate or at least not interested in texts, which were a later scribal preoccupation. At this point, most of us round this table, whatever our other differences, seem clearly to believe that Jesus did know the Jewish scriptures, and did regard them as important for himself and his followers; the only question is, which ones did he make central and thematic?

I regard it, in fact, as historically certain that Jesus regarded himself, and was regarded by his contemporaries, as a prophet, like John the Baptist only more so. Moreover, I regard it as overwhelmingly historically probable that Jesus regarded himself as, intended to act as, and was perceived to be acting as, an *eschatological* prophet, announcing the Kingdom of God. The stories he told, the praxis in which he engaged, and the symbols of his work all combine to say: the Kingdom of God is happening here and now. It is a false antithesis, for all its frequent repetition, that Jesus preached about God and the church preached about Jesus. The whole point of Jesus' work was that he believed that the God of Israel was acting uniquely in the events he was initiating. (That doesn't make Jesus odd; it puts him firmly on the first-century map, where dozens of groups believed the same thing, ending up anathematizing and often murdering each other as the terrible story of the Jewish War wound to its close.)

But what, then, does this eschatological Kingdom of God mean? Forget the caricatures of Kingdom theology perpetrated by a good deal of scholarship, not least but not only in the Jesus Seminar. A good many of them are simply retrojections of a shabby pseudoapocalyptic which characterizes some fundamentalist preaching. Grasp instead the story, the praxis, and the symbols of first-century Judaism, within which there was a sustained longing for Yahweh, Israel's God, to act within history to save Israel from the pagans, and to restore her kingdom, her temple, her law, and her land as they had been in the great days of the past. They were living in a story in search of an ending, and the differences between Jewish groups can be plotted in terms of how they thought the story would end, what role they would take in that ending, and what variations within the symbolic world of Judaism would flag up both that ending and their role within it. But the overall belief may be described as follows. They believed that Yahweh would become King; in other words, they believed that the exile would end at last (or, if you like, the New Exodus would occur); that evil, by which they would mean paganism and the debased forms of Judaism, would be defeated; and that Yahweh himself would return to Zion.

Central to this whole expression of Jewish hope, not as a set of isolated texts but as part of the controlling element of the story, is of course the whole prophetic corpus. Even the Torah itself could be read, and indeed seems to have been read, as story and as prophecy, the story which includes the promise to Abraham, the Exodus, and the approach to the promised land, and the prophecy that the scepter shall not depart from Judah and that a star shall arise from Jacob — Genesis 49 and Numbers 24, as we now know, being quite important at least for Qumran. Within the whole prophetic corpus stand several passages which seem to have been important for Jesus' self-understanding. Zechariah is clearly of great significance; Malachi, arguably so too. Daniel, controversially but I think crucially, was central to the expectation of the first-century Jews, particularly the revolutionaries; Jesus made it central in his own understanding of his own vocation. But when we ask where, in scripture, we find the clearest statements of a coming time when messengers would announce the Kingdom of God, we turn to Isaiah, and to chapters 40–55 in particular.

I think, in fact, that we have been too shortsighted in focusing on the fourth Servant Song and on the precise meaning of various phrases within it. We have reminded ourselves tirelessly that first-century readers were ignorant of Duhm's analysis and all that has followed it, and yet we have failed to take seriously, I believe, the very passage that sums up the whole of Jesus' public ministry, Isaiah 52:7–12. "How lovely upon the mountains are the feet of the *mebasser,* the herald of good tidings, the one who publishes salvation, who says to Zion, Your God reigns!" Astonishingly, the concordance worship that has characterized so much New Testament scholarship has sometimes meant that this passage hasn't been considered relevant, because it doesn't use the *phrase* "Kingdom of God"; but that is obviously what it means. And when Zion's God becomes king, three things will happen, according to this short and pregnant passage. The exile will end at last, with a purified people returning home; evil will be defeated, as Babylon falls at last; and, most important, Yahweh himself will return to Zion. Again, I find it astonishing that the theme of Yahweh's return to Zion has been so largely ignored in New Testament scholarship, though it is assuredly one of the two great themes of Second Isaiah as a whole, announced in chapter 40 as the main message of good news, and reinforced here in particular.

The other great theme is, of course, forgiveness of sins. Here I want to stress a point which seems to me vital, and regularly overlooked. From the exile to Bar Kochba, and arguably beyond, exile itself was seen as the punishment for sins; so forgiveness of sins was another way of saying "end of exile." We who live in the shadow of the medieval church, of Martin Luther, of soul-searching pietism, and now of navel-gazing self-help spiritualities, have to make a huge historical effort of the imagination to get this right. Read Daniel 9, Ezekiel 34–37, Jeremiah 31, and above all Isaiah 40–55, and you will see that if exile is the result of sin, return from exile simply *is* the forgiveness of sins. Forgiveness, in other words, in this period isn't first and foremost a matter of private piety, of the individual wrestling with a troubled conscience. If you're in prison, being granted an amnesty doesn't mean you can feel good inside yourself. It means you are free to go home. This is all summed up in a little verse in Lamentations, 4:22: "The punishment of your iniquity, O daughter Zion, is accomplished; he will keep you in exile no longer."

Jesus' announcement of the Kingdom, therefore, and his regular offer of forgiveness of sins, mean, in effect: this is how exile is ending! This is how God is becoming King! This is how evil is defeated! This is how Yahweh is returning to Zion! This, I submit, is thoroughly historically grounded and believable within Jesus' world. Lots of other first-century Jews thought they knew how God was becoming King, and thought they themselves would be key instruments of that kingship. Jesus belongs on that map.

But, just as Israel's story as a whole was, from the first-century point of view, a story in search of an ending, so Jesus' own story of the wandering Galilean prophet announcing the Kingdom of God was a story in search of an ending. What did Jesus think would happen next? Would he be content to heal a few more people, teach some more how to pray the Lord's Prayer, tease a few more with parables and aphorisms, hope that his timeless message of the love of God would spread to a wider audience? If that were really so, as Sanders argued a decade ago, it is very hard to see how Jesus could have been an important historical figure. Rather, I believe, and have argued in detail elsewhere, that Jesus understood his vocation in terms of establishing a following of sorts in Galilee, and then going to Jerusalem to force a showdown with the authorities. His claim could never be that he had access to a secret wisdom which could make individuals feel better about themselves, and order their lives more satisfactorily. His eschatological message, his way of peace and salvation, had to be announced to Zion.

Studying Jesus: Reasons for the Cross

What then did Jesus think would happen when he got there? Let us stress once again: this is not a matter of isolated proof texts or allusions to particular passages. It is a matter of the whole story of what Jesus was deliberately doing, of the whole complex praxis in which he had been engaged, and at last of the whole symbolic universe which he both invoked and subverted. His actions spoke louder than his words (footnotes, if you want, to Austin, Searle, Thiselton, and other philosophers of language who have struggled to say in the post-Enlightenment world what was blindingly obvious to everyone in Jesus' world). His action in the temple functioned like burning a flag, or like tearing up a contract. His action in the upper room functioned like running up a new flag, like writing a new contract; or, in his language, like establishing a new covenant. This was how the exile would end. This was how evil would be defeated. This was how Yahweh would return to Zion. This was how the Kingdom of God would come. This was how sins would be forgiven. If we look, as the post-Reformation and post-Enlightenment world has taught us, for biblical texts that will give us an intellectual grid on which we can plot and perhaps domesticate these actions, we are looking for the wrong thing and will get into great problems, as our debates have borne witness. If we look at Jesus' acted parables, his symbolic praxis, his encoded meta-narratives, we will find his understanding of his own death looming up out of the mist like a great and ugly mountain where we were expecting a small and climbable hill.

It is not, perhaps, surprising that scholarship has tried to make the mountain less daunting by reducing it to terms of this or that theory, this or that text. But it isn't a matter so much of text as of texture; and history demands that we take seriously the richly textured symbolic universe in which Jesus lived. He believed that the great crisis of Israel's history was fast approaching, the crisis through which Yahweh would become King, the crisis as a result of which exile would end, sins would be forgiven, the Gentiles would be judged and saved, evil would be defeated at last. And, as Schweitzer saw so clearly a century ago, he believed that this would come about through the messianic woes bursting upon Israel — or rather, upon Israel's representative, the human figure who stands in for the people of the saints of the Most High. He would suffer at the hands (or should it be the paws?) of the beast, and be vindicated. In his vindication Israel would receive the Kingdom; Yahweh would become King at last, and evil would be defeated once and for all.

I believe, therefore, that Jesus did not consider his own death in terms of an abstract or ahistorical atonement theology. He did not think of himself going to his death in order to set in motion a piece of celestial mechanics whereby a timeless system of purely spiritual salvation would be set up. He saw himself as possessed of the awesome vocation to bring Israel's history to its climax; to be the means of ending exile at last, of defeating paganism as a good Messiah should do, and of overturning the renegade and faithless Judaism that was still occupying center stage. He saw himself as being called upon not merely to announce, but more importantly to enact, the end of exile, the return of Yahweh to Zion, *in other words,* the forgiveness of sins. This was a wager, a terrifying Pascalian wager. He knew he might be wrong. Others made great claims and were shown to be charlatans. And the irony was, of course, that the sign of their mistake, of their being self-deceived, was that they ended up on crosses. The problem with a crucified Messiah is *not* that there happens to be one text in Deuteronomy which says a hanged man is accursed. That could only be imagined when we have left history behind and entered into a world of pure abstract ideas. The problem with a crucified Messiah is that the true Messiah was supposed to defeat the pagans, not to be executed by them.

It is within this world, I suggest and propose, that we must ask the question of Jesus' relation to Isaiah 53. Of course, if we are looking for a bit of detached teaching with an Old Testament background in which Jesus will say "look, I am the Servant of Isaiah 53," we will look in vain. Of course it will always be open to the historian to try to reduce the matter to things that can be proved by a complex web of allusion and echo. But in the middle of the picture is a hypothesis that can be stated as follows: Jesus made Isaiah 52:7–12 thematic for his Kingdom announcement. He lived within the controlling story according to which Israel's long and tangled relationship with her God, and with the gentile world, would reach a great climax through which exile would be undone, so that Israel's sins would be forgiven at last, and the whole world would see the glory of God. He spoke of this in terms of Daniel, Zechariah, and other passages. But if we ask how the message of Isaiah 52:7–12 is put into effect, the prophecy as Jesus read it had a clear answer. The arm of Yahweh, which will be unveiled to redeem Israel from exile and to put evil to flight, is revealed, according to Isaiah 53:1, in and through the work of the Servant of Yahweh.

Now let us be clear. Jesus did not speak of this when faced with Caiaphas: the trial setting called for the judgment scene of Daniel 7, and the question about the temple called for a statement of messianic enthronement (because of the nexus between king and temple). He did not speak of it directly when instructing his puzzled disciples; if they had understood it, they would not have followed him to Jerusalem. He spoke of it in his actions, in the temple and in the upper room, and in his readiness to go to the eye of the storm, the place where the messianic woes would reach their height, where the *peirasmos* would become most acute, and in bearing the weight of Israel's exile, dying as her Messiah outside the walls of the capital city. We catch echoes of this, rather than direct statements, as Jesus' words cluster around his actions. To give his life as a ransom for many; my blood of the new covenant, shed for you and for the many for the forgiveness of sins, in other words, for the end of exile. In terms of the controlling metaphor we have used during the time of the colloquy, Jesus was not pussyfooting around Isaiah 53, refusing to put his head in the bowl and drink the cream. He was himself, if I may put it like this, both cat and cream: the cup that my father has given me, shall I drink it? Only, as we study the history of his last actions, and let those actions resonate within the symbolic universe which he inhabited, we discover here something greater than a cat, and in the cup something stronger than cream.

Conclusion

It is time to stand back from the picture I have been painting, which I offer as a historical hypothesis, not of course as a complete argument. I have been trying to suggest that we can, as historians, discover a portrait of Jesus in which praxis, story, and symbol are even more important than the history of ideas and texts, but within which ideas and texts settle down and make themselves at home. Within this hypothesis, I have suggested that Isaiah 40–55 as a whole was thematic for Jesus' ministry and Kingdom announcement, which is to be understood not in terms of the teaching of an abstract and timeless system of theology, not even of atonement theology, but as the historical and concrete acting-out of the return of Yahweh to Zion to defeat evil and to rescue his people from exile, that is, to forgive their sins at last. Within this notion, in turn, I have suggested that the allusions to Isaiah 53 are not, in fact, the basis of a theory about Jesus' self-understanding in relation to his death; they may be, rather, the telltale signs of a vocation which he could hardly put into words, that the *mebasser* of Isaiah 52:7 (and Isaiah 40:9) would turn out to be himself, the Servant, representing the Israel that was called to be the light of the world but had failed so signally in this vocation. The only way that such a vocation could be articulated without distortion was in story, symbol, and praxis: and all three came together in the temple, and in the upper room, and ultimately on the large and ugly mountain just outside the city gates. This is not so much an argument from silence, though I recognize that it may be castigated as such. The silence only pertains to words and texts, and even then it is not in fact complete. When we examine story, symbol, and praxis, there is no silence.

Another objection which is sure to be raised in several minds, around this table and farther afield, is whether this remarkable construct is predicable as having been in Jesus' mind and worldview, or rather only in the evangelists and their sources. With this question, we are back to the heads-I-win-tails-you-lose situation. For my part, I believe it was a great gain in the 1950s and 1960s that Matthew, Mark, and Luke were recognized as theologians, not mere chroniclers. Perhaps the 1990s should become the decade in which we realize something that was after all staring us in the face, that Jesus too was a theologian — but one whose theology was expressed not as another movement in the history of ideas, or as a collection of texts finely exegeted, but as one who believed that in and through his own work, life, and death, the very subject matter of theology, of Israel's prophetic, apocalyptic, eschatological, and redemptive theology, was coming to birth.

I suggest, then, that the categories of the sixth or fifth or fourth centuries B.C.E., and those of the sixteenth or subsequent centuries C.E., are not necessarily good guides for our understanding of Jesus. Listening to the debate between substitution and representation, in however a sophisticated and nuanced fashion it may be carried on, leaves me as a historian with the same feeling I have when I meet people — as I don't, fortunately, very often — for whom the key question in the New Testament is whether the Rapture comes before or after the Tribulation. The critical nest of meaning in the second-temple Jewish world did not focus on substitution and representation, but on exile and how it would be undone; on a social and political liberation with an inescapable theological and spiritual dimension; on the temple, its destruction, cleansing, and rebuilding; on the fulfillment of the whole of Torah, prophets, and writings, not simply on isolated bits and pieces of text.

When we reach him, as we have happily done during this weekend, we find Paul firmly convinced that this whole complex of meanings and events has in fact come to pass, and, in coming to pass, has been radically redefined, so that he as a zealous Jew now finds himself as the one who welcomes the pagans to equal membership in God's people. We have no evidence whatever, outside the baseless speculations of a few scholars, that there were any Christians in the earliest church who didn't think the climactic event in God's purpose for Israel had occurred in Jesus Christ. Their perceptions of this climactic event, and the large-scale redefinition of exile and restoration it occasioned, were in the process of formation, and were in any case much larger and richer than simply the tracing of a few lines of thought and ideas from a few texts, however beloved. We therefore find them expressing their understanding of the death and resurrection of Jesus in a multiplicity of ways, not least, like Jesus himself, in story, symbol, and praxis as much as in articulated and text-based abstract theology. Paul himself uses dozens of different ways to say all this, depending on the context and his particular argument. It is clear, however, that when he did use Isaiah 53, such as in Romans 4:25, this application was not a new idea or a throwaway line; its quasi-formulaic nature, and its careful location at the end of a great section of argument, tell heavily against that. But he is not constructing, there or in Galatians 3 or in 2 Corinthians 5, an abstract theology of how sinners in general find salvation in general. He is arguing about how, within history, the one God of all the world has revealed his righteousness and salvation in dealing with the Babylons of this world, the principalities and powers, and has thrown open the Davidic promises for everyone to share. In other words, he is articulating on a grand scale the message of Second Isaiah. And when, in the middle of his theology, we find him saying things like Romans 4:25, I have no problem in saying that he, like Jesus, regarded Isaiah 53 as one central piece of a picture that was far wider and richer than any single text. It is not the only, or even the controlling, element in his thought. Genesis and Deuteronomy and the Psalms must be given their due. Nor is the death of Jesus, whether as representative, substitute, or whatever, the only meaning he finds in Second Isaiah. As we have seen, his own apostleship, his own suffering, are part of the picture as well. He, like Jesus, exegeted the text not just as a matter of theory but as a matter of symbolic vocation.

Why did Paul, our earliest witness by far, come to this view? Because of the resurrection, certainly. But the resurrection only vindicates what was in question before. Nils Dahl argued a generation ago that Jesus must have been known as Messiah before his death if the resurrection were to have the effect of installing him in that position. I think we can and must go further. Jesus lived, taught, and acted as though Israel were summed up in him. He would be the Israel who would go into exile on behalf of the Israel in exile. He would suffer the fate which summed up perfectly the present exilic condition of God's people. And he would do so in the belief that God would raise him from the dead, inaugurating the real "return from exile" which would be the sign that sins had indeed been forgiven, not only for Israel but also for the world.

The relevance of our colloquy discussion for the wider debate about Jesus, therefore, focuses of course on the meaning of Jesus' death. But we cannot remain content with an atonement theology that simply chops away at its own logic, anxious on the one hand to maintain a traditional formula which has meant so much to so many, anxious on the other hand to protect God from talking or acting nonsensically or immorally. Atonement is something bigger than that altogether. According to Paul, it is about how the creator is revealing his righteousness in order to re-new the whole cosmos. According to Jesus, it is about the destruction of the temple that has come to symbolize rebellion against the true God, and about the construction of a returned-from-exile community, a community of prodigals who have come back from the far country to find an astonishing welcome laid on for them, a community of the renewed covenant whose sins have been forgiven. This community is constituted, not by a set of ideas, but by a person; not by a dogma, no matter how true and valid, but around a set of symbols and praxis; not by a bowl of exegetical cream, but by a broken loaf and a cup of wine.

If we put the central things in the center, it is surprising how easily the other things settle down and make themselves at home. If our debate, not least its puzzles and unresolved tensions, serves to remind us that Christian theology is not about words and ideas but about a person, it will have had a relevance for the study of Jesus far beyond the dotting of a few *i*'s and the crossing of a few *t*'s. As the old saying goes, when you have dotted your *i*'s, it may be time at last to open them.

Contributors

EDITORS

W. H. Bellinger, Jr., is Professor of Old Testament at Baylor University.

William R. Farmer is Professor Emeritus of New Testament at Southern Methodist University and Research Scholar at the University of Dallas.

CONTRIBUTORS

Daniel P. Bailey is a graduate student in New Testament Studies at Jesus College, Cambridge University.

Otto Betz is Professor Emeritus of New Testament at Tübingen University.

R. E. Clements is Professor Emeritus of Old Testament at Kings College, University of London.

Paul D. Hanson is Professor of Old Testament at Harvard University Divinity School.

Morna D. Hooker is Professor of New Testament at Cambridge University.

Adrian M. Leske is Professor of New Testament at Concordia University College of Alberta.

Roy F. Melugin is Professor of Old Testament at Austin College.

Mikeal C. Parsons is Professor of New Testament at Baylor University.

Henning Graf Reventlow is Professor Emeritus of Old Testament at the University of Ruhr.

David A. Sapp is a graduate of the doctoral program at Southwestern Baptist Theological Seminary.

J. Ross Wagner is Visiting Instructor at Duke University Divinity School.

Rikki E. Watts is Professor of New Testament at Regent College.

N. T. Wright is the Dean of Lichfield Cathedral.

Index of Ancient Sources

APOCRYPHA

SECOND TEMPLE
AND RABBINIC TEXTS

Index of Names

◆

Index of Subjects

---◆---